4×8 Ridge
2"×6" Rafter
6"×6" Hip Rafter.
Purlin
8"×8" Post
Joist
Plaster Cornice
W.I. Grating
2"×6"
Plaster Cornice
2"×6" Studs 16" C to C.
Wood.
9'-9"
Ribbon 1"×6"
Hanger
2"×6" Joists 16" C to C.
Plaster Cornice
Wood
Matched Sheathing.
Continuous Studs
Plaster Cornice
Plaster Bracket.
Turned balusters
2"×8" 16" C.
hanger

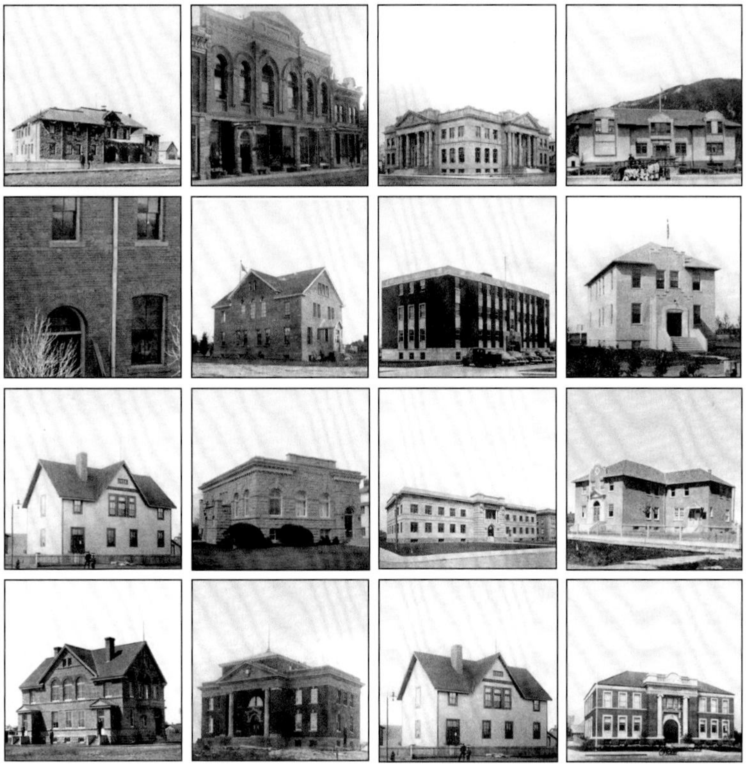

# FOUNDATIONS OF JUSTICE

DAVID
MITTELSTADT

# FOUNDATIONS OF JUSTICE

ALBERTA'S HISTORIC COURTHOUSES

UNIVERSITY OF CALGARY PRESS

The Legal Archives Society of Alberta

Published by the University of Calgary Press
2500 University Drive NW Calgary, Alberta,
Canada T2N 1N4 www.uofcpress.com

Library and Archives Canada Cataloguing in Publication

Mittelstadt, David, 1966-
Foundations of justice : Alberta's historic courthouses / David
Mittelstadt.

Includes bibliographical references and index.
ISBN 1-55238-123-4

1. Courthouses—Alberta—History. 2. Historic buildings—Alberta.
3. Alberta—History,Local. I. Title.

FC3662.M57 2005 971.23 C2004-906829-6



We acknowledge the support of the Canada Council for the Arts for our publishing program. We acknowledge the financial support of the Government of Canada through the Book Publishing Industry Development Program (BPIDP) for our publishing activities. We acknowledge the support of the Alberta Foundation for the Arts for this published work. We thank the Alberta Historical Resources Foundation for its support of this project. The publisher would also like to thank the following donors for their generosity: Bennett Jones LLP Calgary, Macleod Dixon LLP Calgary, McCarthy Tetrault LLP Calgary, McLennan Ross LLP Calgary, Miller Thomson LLP Calgary, Justice Frans Slatter, Justice Allen Sulatycky, Judge Frank Maloney

This book has been published with the help of a grant from the Canadian Federation for the Humanities and Social Sciences, through the Aid to Scholarly Publications Programme, using funds provided by the Social Sciences and Humanities Research Council of Canada.

Design by Mieka West.
Printed in Canada by Friesens Corporation, Altona, MB.

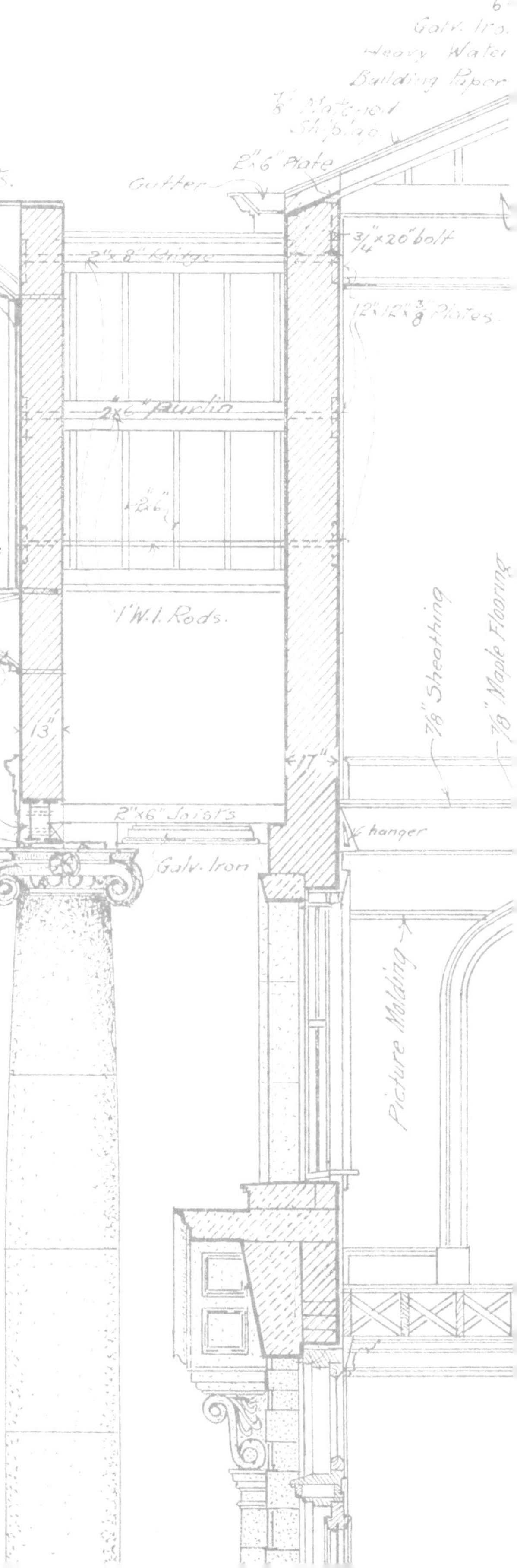

Skylight
4"x8" Ridge
scuttle
2"x6" Rafter
10"x10"
8"x8" Post
2x6
7/8" Shiplap
2"x2" Herring Bone Bridging
W.I. Strap 1/2"x3"
8x8
2"x4" Studs
2"x6" Studs
14'-0"
7/8 boards
3" Concrete
1" Tile
Continuous studs
2"x2" Herring Bone Bridging
2"x12" Joist 16" C to C
1"x6" Ribbon
Wood
Wood
Plaster bead
Wood Casing
11'-10"
Gl.
2"x12" Joist
Plaster Cornice
Plaster Bracket
Plaster Cornice
Plaster Bracket
Gl.

# TABLE OF CONTENTS

# LIST OF ABBREVIATIONS USED IN PHOTO CREDITS

| | |
|---|---|
| *AI* | *Alberta Infrastructure* |
| *GMA* | *Sir Alexander Galt Museum and Archives* |
| *GPRM* | *Grande Praire Regional Museum* |
| *HDM* | *Hanna District Museum* |
| *LASA* | *Legal Archives Society of Alberta* |
| *LPL* | *Lethbridge Public Library* |
| *MHA* | *Medicine Hat Archives* |
| *NA* | *National Archives* |
| *PAA* | *Provincial Archives of Alberta* |
| *RDDA* | *Red Deer and District Archives* |
| *WCA* | *City of Wetaskiwin Archives* |

# FOREWORD

About 1936, as a young Boy Scout, I accompanied my Scout Leader on a trip to Calgary from High River, where we lived. My Scout Leader was the eminent country lawyer, Mr. C.F. Heseltine, K.C. He had an errand at the courthouse in Calgary and I waited outside in the car, gazing at a building I considered magnificent. On his return, I asked. "What is the Court House like inside?" He immediately took me on a tour of the building. I was not merely impressed; I was awe-struck at the entryway, at the two marble staircases that surround the foyer, both leading to a marble-clad entry to the second floor, at the decorative wooden panels, at the marble floors and the elaborate plaster moulding topping the walls. In Foundations of Justice David Mittelstadt describes the 1914 Calgary courthouse as "excessively austere" and its architectural style as "austere classicism." But coming at twelve years of age from High River (a region not noted, perhaps, for perfection in architectural style) I was open-mouthed.

During our tour, Mr. Heseltine introduced me to Mr. Justice Ives, who happened to be passing by. Then and there, I resolved to be a lawyer one day though, in the Great Depression of that era, five years at University then seemed a remote possibility. Later, with that problem solved by the educational grants to war veterans, I came to know the 1914 Calgary courthouse well as a lawyer and judge.

In this book, David Mittelstadt has described each of the courthouses in Alberta built before World War II. He has done so after massive research, examining architecture and even stuctural engineering. His work is, however, much more than an examination of structural detail. He has captured the flavour of life in the early communities of Alberta. He describes the efforts of Albertans to lobby politicians to move court proceedings from schoolhouses, opera houses and from hotels where trials competed with noise from the local barroom. Citizens saw the courthouse as the tangible demonstration that their community was going to be a permanent habitation in western Canada. Incidents of local history and political lore spring from these pages to bring alive the early days of Alberta's past.

An important part of Alberta history is reflected in the cases heard in Alberta courthouses. Mr. Mittelstadt describes many of these trials, such as the Fisk murder trial in Calgary in 1889. He describes the efforts of Judge Travis, a teetotaler and leader of the temperance movement, to subdue the "whiskey ring" in Calgary, in the process sentencing to jail a leading hotel owner and the editor of the Calgary Herald. He recounts the trial of a member of a lynch mob in Edmonton, in which the jury returned to Mr. Justice Rouleau "after hardly a minute" with a verdict of Not Guilty. The trial of Emilio Picariello and Florence Lassandro brings to life the bootlegger era of southern Alberta. The McPherson case in Edmonton at a later period virtually ended one section of Alberta's political history.

At times, Mr. Mittelstadt brings an engagingly different perspective to some aspects of courtroom events. That a judge's entry into the courtroom from a restricted area behind the dias is "a clever piece of judicial theatre" hadn't previously occurred to me, though it may, indeed, achieve that function. However, on one occasion when the judge's retiring area behind a courtroom was under renovation, I had occasion to follow a court orderly to a courtroom where I was to preside over the arraignments for the criminal trials to be held in Calgary over the next three months. I wore a judge's robe with scarlet facing as we threaded our way through a corridor crowded with the friends and colleagues of the persons to be arraigned. The hair stood up on the back of my neck. I confess to a preference for the route to the dias that is judicial theatre.

This is a superbly researched and readable book of interest to lawyers and lay people alike. It will fill a gap in the previously recorded history of Alberta.

The Honourable James H. Laycraft, O.C.; LLD (Hon)
Chief Justice of Alberta (Retired)

# PREFACE & ACKNOWLEDGMENTS

There is no shortage of books on North American courthouses. Most of them, however, are American and not Canadian. Many states have a volume or even two dedicated to their halls of justice. These works embrace a wide range of approaches to the topic. A few are learned treatises on architectural history. Some provide a comprehensive narrative on the development of courthouses in a particular state. Others are catalogues, which to greater and lesser degrees inform us about the circumstances and particulars of each courthouse. And a number hardly talk about the courthouses at all, but instead chronicle the trials, events, and personalities associated with each building. Each approach has its strengths, its weaknesses, and its own audience. Tackling a history of Alberta's early historic courthouses started with the question: how best to go about it.

My approach has encompassed a bit of all of the above. This book was not written only for architectural historians, although they will find things of value in it. Nor is it written primarily for the legal historians, though there is some wonderful material for them. I have tried to write a book that will appeal to the people who worked in the courthouses, for the people who walked by them every day and were curious, for the people who live in each of the towns and cities that has an old hall of justice, and for anyone who is fascinated by old buildings, an increasingly scarce commodity in forward-looking Alberta. What struck me most when I started this book were not the architectural wonders of our old courthouses in Alberta – many of them were small and utilitarian structures – but the rich and fascinating social and political history surrounding them.

This is a popular history of Alberta's early courthouses. First and foremost, the story of each hall of justice is presented from its genesis to its eventual fate of demolition, rehabilitation, or continued use for the courts. I felt this would appeal to many readers, who will first and foremost want to know the story of *their* courthouse. It will also make the book a valuable reference work. Within the narratives of the buildings, especially in the similarities in the circumstances around their construction, I also try to paint a larger picture of the whys and wherefores of courthouse building in Alberta before World War II. The book touches on general architectural history and places these buildings within that history, as much as my humble understanding of architecture allows. It is an ambitious book, discussing how society at large perceived and valued courthouses, as well as the nitty-gritty of how they were planned and built.

No history is ever the product of one person. It reflects the interest and hard work of a whole raft of individuals, from archivists to local historians, from those who find the money and to those who read the endless drafts and manuscripts. I am particularly indebted to G. Edward Mills, a historian who produced a report on Alberta's courthouses for Parks Canada in 1978. He blazed the trail. Another scholar who has made an important contribution was Dr. Terry Chapman, a legal historian who wrote a very useful article, "Courts and Courthouses of Southern Alberta." This project was the brainchild of the Legal Archives of Alberta an organization dedicated to preserving and exploring Alberta's legal history, and its president, Graham Price, and Executive Director, Kirsten Olson. This is really their book; I was just the hired help.

For all their help with research, I would like thank to Wendy McGee, Michelle Purcell, Liana Hayes, and the rest of the staff at the Provincial Archives of Alberta, Diane Johnston and Alberta Infrastructure, Lindsay Moir, Jennifer Hamblin, Pat Molesky, Jim Bowman, and Doug Cass at the Glenbow Museum Archives and Library, Carolyn Hill and the Wetaskiwin City Archives, Michael Dawe and the Red Deer and District Archives, Greg Ellis and the Sir Alexander Galt Museum Archives, Barbara Morrow and the Grande Prairie Public Library, Mary Matting and the Grande Prairie Museum, Lorraine Giebelhaus and the Vegreville Regional Museum, George Panzer of the Hanna and District Museum, Kathy Wolansky and the City Clerk's Department of the City of Lethbridge, and Leslie Orleni and the Municipality of Crowsnest Pass. I would like to acknowledge the Cardston Museum and Archives, the Town of Cardston, the Town of Hanna, the Town of Vegreville, the National Archives, the City of Edmonton Archives, the City of Calgary Archives, and the Medicine Hat Museum and Archives.

I am forever indebted to Dorothy Field, the Honourable J. Herbert Laycraft, the Honourable John W. McClung, the Honourable Ernest Marshall, Lindsay Moir, Graham Price, Lorne Simpson, and Janet Wright for reading versions of the manuscript, and Peter Enman for his sensitive editing. I also owe a great deal to Carmen and Rob Pratt, Dustin Hittel, and Allana Philon for their hospitality.

This book was made possible thanks to the generous support of the Alberta Law Foundation, the Alberta Historical Resources Foundation, and Legal Archives Society of Alberta.

# THE LEGAL ARCHIVES SOCIETY OF ALBERTA

The Legal Archives Society of Alberta (LASA) is dedicated to preserving, promoting, and understanding the evolution of law and society in Alberta by establishing and preserving the archival record of the province's legal community. LASA was established as an independent Society in 1990 but has its roots in the Heritage Committee of the Law Society of Alberta. Members of the Heritage Committee realized that the history of the legal profession in Alberta was poorly documented and that, consequently, a crucial part of the province's history remained undeveloped. The Society was launched with the support of the Law Society of Alberta and a major grant from the Alberta Law Foundation.

To date, LASA's collection includes 500 linear metres of archival records and graphic materials from lawyers, judges, and legal organizations throughout the province dating from the late nineteenth century. Programs have expanded in recent years to include historical-research services, a legal history library, an exhibits and interpretation program, and oral history projects. LASA has also established an historical publication program, and this book is our fourth offering. Thirty per cent of LASA's budget is now supported by donations from over three hundred members in the legal community. The Law Society of Alberta continues to provide core-grant funding. LASA remains one of only a few independent legal archive programs operating in North America.

Work on this book began in 1999 when LASA received research grants from the Alberta Law Foundation and the Alberta Historical Resources Foundation. We commissioned David Mittelstadt to begin the research. We soon realized the stories behind Alberta's courthouses were more complex than initially thought, incorporating the social, legal, and architectural histories of the towns in which they were built. The Alberta Law Foundation graciously granted us further funding and we were able to produce a manuscript suitable to present to a publisher by early 2002. The Honourable James H. Laycraft, Q.C., LLD, retired Chief Justice of Alberta, and the Honourable J. W. McClung, Justice of the Court of Appeal, acted as our editorial board and offered assistance, suggestions, encouragement, and wise counsel.

Courthouses are significant landmarks for many Alberta towns and cities. They are symbols in stone and brick of permanence, strength, and justice. Many early Alberta courthouses no longer exist, but we are proud to bring many of their stories back to life.

Kirsten Olson
Executive Director

Graham Price, Q.C.
President

---

*For further information about the Legal Archives Society of Alberta please contact us at 510, 919 – 11 Ave. S.W., Calgary, Alberta T2R 1P3, tel: (403) 244-5510, fax: (403) 541-9102 or www.legalarchivessociety.ab.ca.*

# INTRODUCTION

For a period of fifty years in Alberta prior to World War II, courthouses were contentious and controversial buildings. As people came first to a district of the Northwest Territories and then a new province named Alberta, they expected to see, among other signs of coming civilization, commodious halls of justice. The courthouse was not just a domicile for the courts, but satisfied a much more complex set of expectations, involving civic pride and fundamental concerns about maintaining a proper respect for the law among the new citizens of a new land.

The courthouse, as a specific form of architecture, is not much more than three hundred years old.[1] Courts of law are ancient, but until relatively recently, they did not have separate and identifiable structures to house them. Instead, whether Greek, Roman, royal or ecclesiastical, the court of law performed its function in a location that was a civic or ceremonial space not restricted to the administration of justice alone. The growing power and independence of courts from government, and the increasing complexity of the law, eventually created a need for a separate domicile. Permanent officials and offices, with ever more staff, ever more records to store and ever busier courts, required a special building. As the nineteenth century drew to a close, the functional requirements of the courthouse created monumental edifices throughout North America. They joined hundreds of smaller buildings across the continent dedicated to the rule of law.

Symbolism as well as pragmatism influenced the evolution of the courthouse into a distinct form of public architecture. In the United States, the idea of a judiciary as a third part of government, separate from the executive and legislative and acting as a check on both, and before which all citizens were equal, bestowed on the courthouse a certain sanctity. In Canada, the institutions for the administration of justice came directly from British tradition, which was presented as a model of impartiality and equitableness that not only descended from the Crown but also partook of the dignity and majesty of the royal writ. The law was itself an entity that could be embodied in robes, wigs, gavels – and courthouses. The courthouse became a hall of justice, and even the smallest building for the courts was expected to have a special quality in its demeanour.

Alberta was a relative latecomer to this architectural tradition. The rule of law did not appear on the prairies until 1874, when a long line of dusty officers and men of the North West Mounted Police made its way west to confront American whisky traders. Settlers soon followed and within ten years there was a railroad across the prairie and numerous settlements, while within thirty years Alberta was on the verge of becoming a proud new province of the Dominion of Canada. The people who wrought this change came from all corners of the world, but most were from eastern Canada, Great Britain, and the United States. They brought with them preconceptions of the institutions needed for civilizing the frontier. One of the public buildings they valued most was a courthouse. Governments, meanwhile, wrestled with the problem of bringing the timely and efficient administration of justice to its citizens, including domiciles for the courts. The first attempts were makeshift and temporary, but soon after, courthouses appeared that were simple but permanent and more substantial. Their later replacements were more imposing and impressive, built in current architectural styles and making full use of the construction technology of the day. They were buildings that not only sought to express the time-honoured values that enshrouded the law, but were also an announcement of the vigour and prosperity of a new society.

This book is concerned with the courthouses of Alberta built before World War II, the province's early halls of justice. It tells the story of each of these courthouses, some of which remain, others of which have disappeared forever.

Less than two dozen buildings were constructed or converted before 1950 to house the courts in Alberta. Of these, eighteen were built primarily to house the courts and can be called courthouses. Before Alberta was declared a province and still part of the North-West Territories, it was administered in part by the federal government of Canada, and courthouses were built by the Dominion Department of Public Works. This first group of courthouses included edifices in Calgary (1890), Lethbridge (1894), Medicine Hat (1900), Fort Macleod (1904) and Red Deer (1906), as well as a planned facility for Edmonton that was never built. Through two different administrations of opposing political camps, the policy of the Dominion government was to only supply courthouses as absolutely necessary and at a low cost, a policy that conflicted with the aspirations of the residents of the Territories.

The Province of Alberta took over the construction of courthouses in 1905. During the reign of the Liberal Party from 1905 to 1921, a second group of courthouses was built, including buildings at Cardston (1909), Wetaskiwin (1910), Fort Saskatchewan (1910), Lethbridge (1911), Edmonton (1912), Calgary (1914), Taber (1918), and Medicine Hat (1920). In a spirit of optimism, the province built monumental halls of justice to accommodate a rapidly expanding judicial system and the high expectations of the voting public. The Liberals had hoped to build even more courthouses, but a difficult recession after World War I plunged the province into financial difficulties and cost the Liberals their hold on power.

The third group of courthouses was built under the administration of the United Farmers of Alberta, which lasted from 1921 to 1935. The UFA government constructed buildings at Blairmore (1923), Grande Prairie (1928), Hanna (1929), Red Deer (1931), and Vegreville (1931). All but one of these courthouses were utilitarian, built to service areas on the margins of the province. As with the Territorial courthouses, they stressed low cost at the expense of monumentality, and did not participate in the mainstream of architectural fashion. Like their predecessors, the UFA planned more buildings, but the Great Depression intervened. Courthouse construction was not again undertaken until the beginning of the 1950s, when yet a third political dynasty, Ernest Manning's Social Credit, ushered in the age of modernism in courthouse design for Alberta.

These are the halls of justice that will be discussed individually and in some detail in the following chapters. The early courthouses of Alberta will be chronicled in three sections: the Territorial period, the early provincial period, and the later provincial period. Each section is preceded by its own introduction that explains further the policies of the governments involved in courthouse building, the process of design and construction, and some of the particular circumstances that influenced how courthouses were built.

Alberta's courthouses did not set precedents in architecture. Many were small, undistinguished buildings and generally were derivative of prevailing trends, and as time went on, fell almost entirely behind architectural fashion. The real story of Alberta's halls of justice lies in the complex interplay between the communities and government, symbolism and pragmatism, and the obsession of a frontier society with growth. New settlements invested the courthouse with a great deal of significance, as a necessary public work, as a symbol of civic progress, and also as a physical embodiment of the rule of law. Governments felt the same desire to maintain the symbolic elements of the courthouse, but generally within the solidly pragmatic parameters of providing facilities while keeping costs down. The tensions between the two provide a fascinating window into an aspect of Alberta's history generally unexplored.

## The Courthouse
### General Themes and History

Certain common themes emerge from the stories of the individual Alberta courthouses, which themselves are characteristic of the history of the courthouse in North America. As people came to Alberta, they brought with them certain preconceptions about courthouses. Although the specialized courthouse did not become common until the early nineteenth century, over the next hundred years courthouses would become larger and more complex. Expanding legal systems required buildings to house the courts, judiciary and related administration, and these edifices quickly became landmark public buildings. At the time settlement started in the Canadian west, while the courthouse was still a relatively new type of building, it was also well established.

In North America, courts were first held in makeshift or temporary quarters: taverns, halls or sometimes in the open air. These circumstances were repeated over and over on the frontiers of British North America, including Alberta. Courthouses were few and far between in the Territorial period, and even into the 1950s courts were at times held in everything from churches to movie theatres in the province. If the courts often had to turn to community halls to perform their work, early courthouses themselves were sometimes used for more than just dispensing justice. Until well into the twentieth century, especially in frontier areas, the courthouse also often functioned as a meeting place for the local community. It might be used for theatrical events, dances, or political meetings, and created a certain tradition of the courthouse as a public institution and gathering place.

Courthouses participated fully in the prevailing notions in the nineteenth and early twentieth centuries that public buildings should be imposing in character and therefore architecturally distinguished, and were generally designed in the architectural styles popular at the time. In the eastern United States, for example, a distinctive form of architecture was used for the majority of courthouses built in the mid-nineteenth century – Classical or Greek Revival, usually featuring a white, temple-form portico on a stone or red brick building, surmounted with a cupola or bell tower. The sheer number of this type of building has made it an archetype of the county courthouse. In Canada, the earliest courthouses were built in simple vernacular styles, but became ever more sophisticated buildings done in the prevailing mode of the day: Classical Revival, Italianate, Second Empire, Romanesque Revival, and Beaux-Arts classical. Until the middle of the twentieth century, like other public buildings, courthouses were generally built in styles that used historically derived architectural forms.

If styles came and went, by the late nineteenth century, the special demands of the courthouse had been codified into some standard design precepts. The most important requirement was a commodious courtroom or courtrooms. It was frequently the centrepiece of the building. The courtroom had to be a space large enough to hold a substantial number of people. Trials could attract sizeable crowds, and it was of the highest importance to allow spectators access to the proceedings. Witnessing trials was considered both edifying and part of the due process of the law, although crowds attending sensational prosecutions treated it more as an entertainment. Courtrooms were expected to be dignified spaces, and the decor was usually appropriate to the proceedings. It could be quite elaborate, sometimes with full-blown classical schemes executed in plaster and wood. Fine oak or maple for wainscoting and door and window trims were especially favoured.

The courtroom itself was divided spatially by a balustrade, the "bar," separating spectators from judge, jury, prisoners and opposing counsel, while the jury was isolated in its box. The judge's bench was raised and often had an elaborate backing, elevating him from the rest of the room and emphasizing his authority. The witnesses were also provided with a raised box for their testimony, making them one of the focal points in the room. It was also considered very important to allow the various actors in the judicial drama access to the stage away from spectators. For reasons of security, but also in the interests of better theatre, judges, jurors, witnesses and the accused did not enter the courtroom through the same portal as the public. Ideally, separate rooms were placed adjacent to the court for them. In more sophisticated designs, a private corridor and stairwell allowed the judge and others to enter their chambers unseen and unmolested by the public prior to being called into the courtroom. The better courtrooms allowed the judge to enter directly behind his bench, emphasizing his remoteness from the crowd of spectators.

A secure holding area for prisoners was another unique demand courthouses put on builders and architects. Early courthouses were often also the local jail, but it became less and less common to combine the two functions in one building. Prisons and jails became larger and themselves more specialized, and there was often resistance to placing the courthouse near the business district of town if it included a large jail. It was still necessary to have cells in the courthouse to hold those facing criminal charges, so that they were not transferred back and forth from the courthouse during trials. Often in the basement storey there would be a few cells and a guardroom; sometimes the holding area was on the top floor of the building for security. The cells usually required a separate outside entrance, and many ingenious plans provided a stairwell that went straight from the cells to the courtroom without entering other areas.

The courthouse was also often the meeting place for the local bar. In Alberta, a law library was placed in courthouses from before the turn of the century,[2] and this was a common feature of halls of justice everywhere. The barristers usually had a room where they could retire and robe and prepare for trials. In the days when students articled rather than taking university degrees, the courthouse might often be used for classes in law as well, sometimes in another room of the building, but frequently in the library.

Certain conventions had become standard in courthouse design by the time the first examples appeared in Alberta. The courtroom – or courtrooms – and its antechambers for witnesses, judges, and juries were located on the second floor, providing better security and more insulation from noise within the building. The offices of the court and other government bodies such as the county administration were usually on the first floor. Other chambers, such as a law library, the judges' offices, an overnight suite for judges who travelled on circuit, a caretaker's office and suite, and offices for the police, might be located variously on the first or second floor, in the basement or in an attic storey. For a courthouse of any size, the main entrance was an impressive affair, both externally and internally, usually with a well-appointed foyer. Often a wide hall would lead to a grand staircase, taking the visitor to the courtroom. Public and ceremonial spaces were well-finished and decorated, often with expensive stone or wood finishes, while office space was plain. Until well after World War I, courthouses, even very large ones, were rarely more than three storeys high, and tended to be large rectangular or square structures, often surmounted by high domes or clock towers that made them prominent landmarks. By the end of the nineteenth century, most jurisdictions in North America could boast a courthouse, many of them substantial, even monumental, buildings of brick and stone.

Albertans therefore had strong expectations about what a courthouse should look like inside and out. The majority of residents in Alberta, both in the Territorial period and after the province was established, were immigrants, many from Ontario, the Maritime provinces, or the United States. They brought their memories of county and urban courthouses west with them and wanted the courthouse in their new home to be similar – perhaps not necessarily as large or as well appointed, but certainly along the same lines. In the Territories, for instance, everyone wanted a stone courthouse, especially after one was built in Calgary in 1890. Thus, places like Macleod and Red Deer energetically drew attention to their supplies of good sandstone. Wooden buildings were impermanent – fine for the frontier, but not what a town wanted to impress newcomers. People had strong beliefs about what a courthouse should be like, and by the late nineteenth century, this meant an imposing building of stone or brick construction

The new residents of Alberta also brought with them strong beliefs about why courthouses were important, beliefs that had a fundamental influence on their procurement and construction. In North America, the courthouse symbolized not just the law but government. Local rule by means of the county was ubiquitous in British North America, whether in the United States or the crown colonies of Canada. Based on ancient English forms of the shire, the exact organization and powers of county government, as well as its lasting vigour, varied from region to region. The county might be elected and democratic, as in New England, or appointed and aristocratic, as in the Virginias or the Maritimes.[3] One of the earliest and most important functions of the county was to provide local courts of civil and criminal jurisdiction. The county seat also became the logical place for higher circuit courts to sit for assizes. Thus the county was often mandated to choose a location for its government and provide for a courthouse there. In both Canada and the United States, counties also became responsible for other administrative duties, starting with the registration of land titles, but also collecting taxes and tolls, road construction, succour of the poor and so on. The courthouse became the natural location of other administrative functions, centred on the county clerk's office. By the middle of the nineteenth century, in American and Canadian jurisdictions, the county courthouse combined judicial and administrative functions and played a central role in people's lives.

Contemporaries were alive to the advantages to their community of being the county seat.[4] There were commercial benefits to having sittings of the court and housing the county offices. It ensured a steady stream of traffic to the town, especially on court days. The prestige and economic benefits of being the county seat meant towns competed aggressively, igniting "county wars" that sometimes involved the courts themselves due to electoral frauds, riots, arson and other civil disorders.[5] To accompany intensive lobbying of state legislatures or colonial assemblies, a town might build a courthouse in hopes of becoming the seat, or offer a site for such a building and financing. When courthouses became outmoded, other towns sometimes used the need of a replacement as a pretext for moving the county seat to their town, where a handsome new building would be promised. The presence of a courthouse was quickly taken as a sign that a community was important, prosperous and more importantly, permanent. In most areas of North America, the actual construction of a courthouse became and remained a local responsibility and quickly became a focus of local pride.

In Alberta, concern with civic progress, known as boosterism, immediately emerged as one of the forces involved in courthouse construction. Boosterism, the constant promotion of a town or district by its residents, was endemic in prairie towns and cities of the late nineteenth and early twentieth centuries.[6] Growth was paramount, and as the settlement of the prairies progressed, towns and villages competed ferociously for rail lines, businesses, industries, and government offices, – anything to ensure the future prosperity of their community. As had been true on earlier frontiers, the courthouse could be a symbol of stability and importance for a growing centre, something not lost on civic boosters on the prairies.[7]

As elsewhere, there was an element of simple economic self-interest in this lobbying. Courthouses in Alberta were generally used only for the judiciary and were never the seat of local government, but they still conferred economic benefits. The real prize for towns was to be named the headquarters of a judicial district, which meant permanent offices of the clerk of court and sheriff for the district, and up to 1934, a resident judge. Both in the Territorial period and after the province was established, every town desperately wanted to be the headquarters of a judicial district as it was a tremendous advantage for local lawyers and the business community. Towns also protested loudly if existing districts were modified in any way that seemed to diminish their importance as the headquarters. Better access to the courts expedited local legal matters, especially civil affairs, generated business for the local advocates and also brought people into town to conduct their legal affairs. The editor of the Stettler Independent summed up the advantages of being the town with the courthouse:

> Anyone who has lived in Ontario or the United States, for example will know that a Judicial Centre is the most prosperous town in a county, and while other towns may go back such a centre never does.[8]

A permanent courthouse was seen as the best way to ensure district offices remained in a town once they were established. Court offices also made it a necessary facility. There was the risk of fire, an ever-present hazard in frontier towns with their preponderance of wooden buildings. As long as court offices were in temporary quarters, the records of the court were very vulnerable, a danger that remained well into the 1930s in Alberta. No courthouse meant inconvenience dealing with the clerk of court or the sheriff: their respective offices might be separated and an unlucky litigant might have to tramp about a town's business district. For the officials themselves, it meant carrying papers and ledgers from office to trial venue or judge's chambers, and putting up with insufficient office space: sometimes court officials worked out of their houses.

The judge, meanwhile, might have no office in which to do his work or to keep a law library, and no convenient place to hold chambers. The rented or borrowed spaces used throughout Alberta for trials, which included taverns, theatres, churches, and schools, were not very suitable. Improvised courtrooms were often too small, too noisy and too draughty, with no place to sequester witnesses or juries. There was also the uncertainty – a venue might not be available, forcing officials to scramble about to find a spot to hold court. These difficulties faced the judiciary right into the 1950s in Alberta.

The courthouse had a symbolic role just as important as its pragmatic function, which was expressed through its external appearance and architecture. As stated above, as prominent public buildings, courthouses were expected to show architectural distinction and a substantial quality. The site of the courthouse was important and intended to showcase these qualities: in many states, in county seats large and small, the courthouse was part of an open public space. Usually it was a large, central parcel, quite often adjacent to the business section of town or on the highest point.[9] Often it was combined with a town or city hall to form vast civic piles, such as can still be seen in Canadian centres like Toronto. In the late nineteenth and early twentieth centuries, populous counties found it necessary to build large, monumental and specialized courthouses. In most jurisdictions in North America, building courthouses was a local responsibility. This meant the buildings were quickly appropriated as symbols of civic pride.

Beyond adding to the architectural merit of a town, the appearance of a courthouse also fulfilled an even more basic symbolic function. It was expected to be the physical embodiment of the law, a way of manifesting in concrete terms abstract notions of justice. Albertans, whether citizens of the Territories or the province, appreciated that there was a powerful symbolic function to the courthouse. One aspect of makeshift facilities that offended people was the lack of dignity. The public felt strongly that borrowed and rented rooms simply did not give the court the proper atmosphere and could contribute to contempt for the law. The judge lacked the remoteness necessary to create the right impression of impartiality – the fact he might have to fight his way through a crowded room to his improvised bench was seen as harmful to his authority.[10]

There was also strong desire in Alberta to avoid the lawlessness and vigilante justice that characterized the American frontier. There was a significant degree of unease when the immigration boom of the early twentieth century brought settlers who were not from good Anglo-Scottish stock. A proper courthouse was seen as an important bulwark of the law. Thus a petition from Red Deer in 1903 stated:

> The only available place for holding court here is in the Sample Room of the Alberta Hotel, a place not calculated to impress any one with that solemnity and dignity which characterized Her Majesty's Courts of Justice, especially in a new country like this where so many different nationalities are represented....[11]

Such sentiments were not restricted to the Territorial period, but remained a concern of Albertans up to World War II.

To this end, many towns in Alberta vigorously pursued government to construct a courthouse. Unlike other areas of North America, courthouse construction in Alberta was never the responsibility of local jurisdictions, but higher levels of government. Different civic bodies, including town councils, the boards of trade, and local political associations joined in the lobbying. The degree to which the campaigns, involving letters, petitions and delegations by the score, influenced government policy is a central question. To contemporaries, both the Dominion and provincial governments seemed quite deaf to their demands, but at the same time it is clear that the calls of constituents for a hall of justice could be influential, even to the extent that unnecessary buildings were sometimes erected.

Both the Territorial and provincial governments felt many of the same concerns as their citizens. For the Dominion, however, underlying all of its decisions about courthouses was the understanding that its responsibility for public buildings was temporary until the Territories had enough people to graduate to provincial status. There was also the nagging uncertainty surrounding the possible direction of development in the Territories, especially which centres would grow into major cities. It was easiest just to build the bare minimum for facilities. With only limited political representation for the area, it was possible for the government to hold to a parsimonious policy. Economy was more important than symbolism and civic pride.

For the provincial government, realities were more complex. Provincial politicians were far more invested in Alberta and, belonging to the climate of incessant promotion, wanted to have magnificent public buildings. Authorities also had to contend with a rapidly expanding judicial system and create facilities adequate for the administration of justice that also met with public approval. The temptation existed to use public works like courthouses for electioneering. Local supporters of the administration generally felt that extensive public works in their constituency were a proper reward, and governments were not afraid to take advantage of the political benefits that building courthouses could bring. At the same time, demands for courthouses were so incessant that many had to be ignored. Provincial administrations also quickly learned Alberta could only financially support so much in the way of public works. Eventually, the province turned toward a pragmatic policy much like that of the Dominion before it.

Albertans took an enduring interest in their halls of justice. They had strong beliefs about the role of courthouses, above and beyond their pragmatic function as facilities for the judiciary. Courthouses were seen as an expression of a fundamental value of society, the rule of law. Fuelled by expectations created elsewhere, people wished to see substantial buildings they would automatically recognize as courthouses and that would also be an advertisement for the prosperity and permanence of their towns and cities. It was considered important enough that a great deal of time and energy was used to convince government that these buildings were necessary. But the expectations of civic boosters did not necessarily have the sympathy of government, and the clash between residents and bureaucracy, whether in far-off Ottawa or Edmonton, is a major part of the story of Alberta's historic courthouses. These are some of the issues that will surface in the narratives of the courthouses.

# PART ONE
# THE TERRITORIAL COURTHOUSES

The first courthouses in Alberta were designed and built by the Dominion Department of Public Works, which had little experience in constructing buildings for the courts. In the older provinces, courthouse construction was either a local or provincial responsibility. Domiciles for the court were generally designed by private architects on commission, and thus showed a great range of styles, some of them quite idiosyncratic. The Territorial buildings all came from the same architectural staff and thus tended to bear a strong resemblance to each other. The Territories also presented a particular challenge to the department, in providing facilities for a frontier society that would be sure to grow and change in ways impossible to predict, while keeping costs down.

The transfer of Rupert's Land from the Hudson's Bay Company to the Dominion of Canada in 1869 presented an enormous challenge to a fledgling nation. The newly christened North-West Territories were almost entirely devoid of settlement outside of the area around the Red River. To ward off American encroachment and establish Canadian sovereignty over the area, in 1873 the Conservative government of John A. Macdonald passed legislation to create a special police force for the Territories, the North West Mounted Police. The Act made the new mounted police force both enforcers and adjudicators of the law in the Territories. The superintendents and inspectors were ex officio justices of the peace, and an 1874 amendment gave the Commissioner of the force the judicial powers of a magistrate.[1] Thus the police could try the same offenders they arrested.

The NWMP was a creation unprecedented in the English-speaking world, a quasi-military police with added judicial powers.[2] But despite the potential for abuse, it was a perfect solution for the Territories. The vast distances and lack of settlement made a properly constituted court premature. Minor offences could be dealt with expeditiously, which was especially important when dealing with the highly mobile whisky traders. It would take a year before the police were ready to head out to the Territories, but once there, they quickly established the rule of law. When the Mounties first came, there were almost no permanent settlements in what is now Alberta outside of fur-trading posts like Fort Edmonton and Roman Catholic missions such as St. Albert. The building of the Canadian Pacific Railway gave the first boost to the Territories. By the time the railroad was completed in 1886, there were hamlets scattered throughout the region, including the first incorporated towns, Calgary and Regina. Cattle ranching had become the predominant industry, especially in the south, and there was great expectation that the land would soon be flooded with settlers, turning it into the breadbasket of Canada.

Initially, the North-West Territories were administered by a Lieutenant Governor and an appointed council. The administration of justice was a shared affair between Governor and Council and the federal Department of Justice. As the population grew, there was agitation for representative government. The Territories were given parliamentary representation with four members in 1886, divided among the districts of Alberta, Assiniboia, and Saskatchewan.[3] An elected Territorial Assembly was set up in 1888, although it had no real legislating powers until 1897.

By the turn of the century, new prospects for growth and prosperity fuelled a movement for provincial autonomy. Residents wanted control over their own affairs, and increasingly resented what was seen as insensitive and inefficient government from Ottawa. A Territorial bureaucracy was created in 1897 to accompany the new powers of the Assembly and included a Department of Public Works and an Attorney General.[4] Without much revenue, however, the power of the Territorial government was still limited. In matters of public works, the Dominion was still responsible for a great deal, including courthouses.

*A living symbol of the law: Colonel James Macleod, Territorial Justice, c. 1890. Glenbow Archives, NA-2258-1.*

## The Territorial Courts

Before the appearance of the North West Mounted Police, the administration of justice in Rupert's Land had been haphazard when it existed at all. The original 1670 charter of the Hudson's Bay Company had allowed for it to establish courts, but the fur traders were more interested in commerce than governance. The company finally established a court for the Red River colony in the mid-nineteenth century, but its scope and powers were limited, and although the courts of Upper

Canada theoretically had jurisdiction in the Territories, there was no machinery to allow the courts to act there. To rectify this, the 1873 Act authorizing the creation of the North West Mounted Police allowed for the appointment of stipendiary magistrates – salaried judges with limited powers – to hold courts for offences where trial by a jury was not necessary. The Act also allowed for the appointment of justices of the peace and established the Court of Queen's Bench of Manitoba as the superior and the appeal court for the Territories.[5]

In late 1875, the Liberals under Alexander Mackenzie, Canada's second prime minister, finally named Matthew Ryan, a Liberal lawyer from Montreal, and Colonel James F. Macleod, assistant commissioner of the NWMP, as magistrates. The appointments were to take effect from January 1, 1876. Earlier that year, parliament also amended the earlier acts, deciding there would be three magistrates and making them part of the Territorial Council, and also clarifying the powers of the Lieutenant Governor for the administration of justice. The governor and council could appoint justices of the peace, create judicial districts and provide for civil and criminal courts within each district.[6]

Initially the magistrates only had jurisdiction over minor offences. Amendments to the Act in 1877 and 1880 gave them much greater powers.[7] Alone the magistrate could try offences with maximum sentences of seven years; more serious charges, including capital crimes, required the aid of one or two justices of the peace and a jury of six. The stipendiaries were also given civil jurisdiction but had to empanel a jury for major trials. The magistrate's court became a court of record, styled the District Court, and provisions for appointing clerks were made.[19] To reflect their greater power, the stipendiaries now had to be advocates of at least five years' standing. Magistrates were also assigned to districts and expected to reside there, although they had the same powers throughout the Territories. The three judicial districts first formed were Bow River, Saskatchewan, and Qu'Appelle, headquartered in Fort Macleod, Battleford, and Regina respectively. Ryan proved unsatisfactory and was replaced by Charles Borromee Rouleau, a Quebec lawyer, and a third magistrate added, Colonel Hugh Richardson. The appointment of judges remained in the hands of the Dominion government.

With only a handful of settlers in the Territories – less than two thousand in the whole provisional District of Alberta[9] – the court dockets the magistrates faced were not large. The vast distances they had to travel, and in all seasons, was much more of a hardship. Conditions were deplorable. Colonel Macleod, in letters to his wife, recorded travelling by dog sled in the winter and horseback in the summer, being caught in sudden thundershowers, and often sleeping outside.[10] Courts were held in whatever buildings were available, usually the barracks of the mounted police, but sometimes in the open air.[11] The judges were responsible for court documents, such as they were, and when the magistrate's court was made a court of record in 1877, they had to act as their own clerks and court recorder until the new officials could be appointed. The magistrates travelled constantly, including spells in Regina as Members of the Territorial Council. As settlers rapidly multiplied in the early 1880s, the workload for the judges grew by leaps and bounds. Complaints were heard from all quarters about the lack of sufficient courts and magistrates, complaints which quickly swelled into a chorus.

## The Territorial Supreme Court

In response to the demands from the Territories for better courts and in anticipation of an influx of settlers after the completion of the Canadian Pacific Railway, an amending Act was assented to on February 18, 1887, establishing the Supreme Court of the North-West Territories, with all the general powers of a superior court and recognizing the laws of the Territories as laws of England as of 1870, with subsequent changes and additions.[12] It was able to try all cases, civil and criminal, and also deal with appeals. A bench of five judges was created, each with the powers granted the superior court judges of England and Canada, and which would sit en banc at the Territorial Capital in Regina to hear appeals. The judges, now styled justices, had to be lawyers of ten years' good standing or judges from another superior court. Macleod, Richardson and Rouleau were all appointed to the new court, joined by two new faces, Edward L. Wetmore and Thomas H. McGuire, the former from New Brunswick and the latter from Ontario.[13]

The new Act also allowed for other improvements in the administration of justice. There was provision for clerks of court and a sheriff for each judicial district and for these officers to appoint deputies as directed by the Territorial Council.[14] These officials did not have to be lawyers, and were usually prominent local citizens. The Lieutenant Governor and council remained in charge of the administration of the courts and scheduled sittings, but the Dominion now took control of creating judicial districts.[15] Five districts were set up, with each justice assigned to a district. The Northern Alberta district was headquartered in Calgary and covered the region north to Edmonton, while Southern Alberta was based at Fort Macleod and included everything west to the British Columbia border, south to the American border, and east to Maple Creek. In addition, there was the district of Saskatchewan, centred in Prince Albert and covering the northern part of that future province; the district of Eastern Assiniboia with headquarters in Moosomin, near the present Manitoba border, and finally the district of Western Assiniboia, based in Regina. Macleod remained in Southern Alberta, while Rouleau took over Northern Alberta.

The Territorial Supreme Court was still a circuit court. Within each district, criminal and civil sittings were held regularly at certain designated spots, usually where there was a substantial NWMP post. For towns like Macleod, Lethbridge or Medicine Hat, court might be held from two to four times per year. Sheriff and clerk usually travelled with the justice on circuit to act in their official capacity. Sittings were proclaimed by the Lieutenant Governor and council, but were generally scheduled by the justice himself.[16] Although there were now more judges, constant travel remained the lot of the Supreme Court justice.

*Supreme Court in session: Justice David Lynch Scott (seated centre) and officers of the court, 1897. NA, C19008.*

The new court did not diminish complaints about the administration of justice. The long intervals between courts in towns outside the major centres remained a major irritant, as were the long court dockets and lack of sufficient judges for the work in Calgary and Edmonton. Towns throughout the Territories lobbied hard for more sittings of the court, for more judicial districts and the appointment of more judges, and for a resident judge for their community, and were not above trying to steal a justice from other towns. Calgary, Macleod, and Lethbridge had a rather prolonged fight over Justice Macleod which ended with Calgary victorious in 1894.

The 1887 Act saw the court established as it would remain up to 1907, two years after the formation of the provinces of Alberta and Saskatchewan, when it was finally replaced by provincial courts. In 1902, the government decided that one of the five justices would be the chief justice to head the bench and appointed McGuire.[17] The bench's personnel in Alberta changed: Justice Macleod died in 1894, and was replaced by David Lynch Scott.[18] He was moved north to Edmonton in 1902 as the resident judge, although the town was not made a separate judicial district.[19] After Rouleau's death in 1901, McGuire was moved to Calgary to replace him. In 1903, Arthur L. Sifton was appointed Chief Justice when McGuire retired.[20] Horace Harvey was made the sixth justice in 1904 and based in Macleod.

*Lawyer, booster, judge and politician: A.L. Sifton, Chief Justice and second Premier of Alberta. LASA*

## Courthouse Policy – The Conservatives

From 1878 to 1896, under the leadership of John A. Macdonald, the Conservative Party ruled Canada. Macdonald and his government were great nation builders, and along with the CPR and the National Policy, the Conservatives also undertook a massive program of public buildings through the 1880s. Under the direction of Sir Hector Langevin, Minister of Public Works, the government provided sundry public buildings that not only housed services like post and customs offices but also were symbolic of the dynamism and prosperity of the new Dominion.

Superficially it looked like the Conservatives planned an impressive program of courthouse construction in the Territories, with buildings in a number of towns, including Calgary, Regina, Maple Creek, Wolseley, Moosomin, and Prince Albert. Appearances were deceiving: outside Calgary and Regina, the proposed buildings were generally small and utilitarian. Calgary's position on the rail line and as the clear commercial centre of the Territories made the investment in a substantial building there worthwhile. Elsewhere, the government tried to practise strict economy and aimed to build small and simple courthouses.

The Conservative government did not have an explicit policy for deciding on the placement of courthouses; apparently it depended on which locality yelled loudest. Aside from lobbying efforts on the part of different towns, the main factor behind the decisions of the Department of Justice was the opinion of the Territorial

*Canada's builder: Sir Hector Langevin, Minister of Public Works.*
*NA, C23373*

justices about the need for courthouse accommodation.[21] Some halls of justice, like Calgary's and the Moosomin courthouse in Saskatchewan, were built in the judicial headquarters of a district, while others, such as Wolseley's in Saskatchewan, were not. Thus the placement of courthouses did not correspond directly to the organization of the Territorial courts. The lack of a coherent policy was a source of confusion and irritation to residents in the west.

The Dominion government was never comfortable with building in the Territories. Compared to the work being produced in the rest of Canada, even the more substantial edifices designed for the prairies were utilitarian and for the most part devoid of the rich architectural decoration used on buildings in the east.[22] Part of the problem was uncertainty about the future of the Territories. With the exceptions of Calgary, and Regina as the Territorial capital, it was almost impossible to predict what settlements would become important towns and which might stay small villages, or disappear altogether.

In the early years of the 1890s, the pace of building by the Department of Public Works slowed. Worsening economic conditions reduced spending and made the department even more cost-conscious, as did the scandal that enveloped Langevin in 1891.[23] The small size and plain appearance of the Conservative's Territorial courthouses was partially a result of this new atmosphere. The severe depression that took hold shortly after Langevin's resignation quickly brought to an end any further construction plans on the part of the Conservatives.

## Courthouse Policy – The Liberals

In 1896, the Liberals under Sir Wilfrid Laurier swept into power, ending twenty years in the political wilderness. The Conservative era had ended rather dismally, and the new Liberal government found itself dealing with an economy still in a depression. Once the recession of the 1890s began to wane, however, the Liberals showed themselves to be even keener builders than the Conservatives. The tremendous growth that Canada underwent at the beginning of the twentieth century required a dramatic expansion of public facilities.[24] Laurier's government adopted very much the same attitude as its predecessors toward public buildings as an expression of the vitality of the Dominion.

*The Honourable David Mills, Liberal Minister of Justice. NA, PA-25912.*

After a tour of the North-West in 1898, Senator David Mills, the Minister of Justice, came back to Ottawa more sympathetic to the demands for courthouses. Late in 1899, Mills announced that the government would erect a number of new courthouses in the North-West.[25] The Liberals built five courthouses, Medicine Hat (1900), Macleod (1904), Red Deer (1906) as well as Carnduff and Yorkton in Saskatchewan. A sixth building for Edmonton did not get past the planning stage.

None of the structures was very large or expensive. Three of the five were simple wood frame buildings. The Liberals retained the same attitude as the Conservatives toward public buildings in the Territories: build cheap and only when necessary. Even at the end of the century, a great deal of uncertainty remained about how the Territories would develop. Matters were complicated further by the growing movement toward provincial autonomy in the Territories. It was a significant disincentive to erecting monumental public buildings.

As with the Conservatives, the Liberals did not have an explicit policy governing where courthouses were built. Vocal demands for a building likely influenced the government's decisions; the town of Red Deer, for example, was not a judicial centre but had a well-mobilized lobby, including the local Liberal Association, and got itself a courthouse. The MP for Alberta from 1896 to 1905, Edmonton Bulletin publisher Frank Oliver, was an indefatigable campaigner on behalf of his constituents and generally backed most demands for courthouses, even in towns that were strong supporters of the Conservatives. The Liberals appeared to follow an opportunistic policy, placing courthouses at strategic points but also attempting to placate residents of the Territories.

Keeping costs down remained a preoccupation for both the Departments of Justice and Public Works. David Mills, the Minister of Justice, perhaps thinking of the courthouses of Ontario, initially promised substantial stone buildings for the Territories. After seeing plans for simple wooden buildings produced by the Department of Public Works and fielding complaints from local residents, his department asked for stone edifices, and at least one such set of plans was created, for Macleod. The Chief Architect of Public Works, who thought the cost would be exorbitant, soon dissuaded the justice ministry from this folly. The appearance of the buildings remained a concern, but the desire for economy overrode the instinct to provide the courts with a properly imposing domicile.

## Architecture and Design

The Territorial courthouses were the bailiwick of the Dominion Department of Public Works, and two men were responsible for them: Thomas Fuller and David Ewart. The two served consecutively as the Chief Architects of the department through almost twenty years of federal courthouse construction.

Fuller, the architect who had achieved national fame by designing Ottawa's Parliament Buildings, was Canada's second Chief Architect, appointed in 1881. Originally from England, Fuller had apprenticed in the office of James Wilson of Bath, where he became a partner before emigrating to Canada in 1857.[26] He quickly established a reputation for himself that culminated in his successful entry, along with partner Chilton Jones, in the competition for the new legislative buildings in Ottawa. He was widely acknowledged as one of the nation's most talented architects.

That talent was not expended on the two Alberta courthouses built under Fuller's direction, at Calgary and Lethbridge. Although the Chief Architect was credited with the designs produced by his office, he did not draw up every building. All of his Territorial courthouses likely only received cursory attention from

*Canada's designer: Thomas Fuller, Dominion Chief Architect. NA, PA-116162*

Fuller. The Calgary courthouse, although a large and expensive building, was relatively simple and unadorned. It did not require a master's touch for planning and drafting. For the Lethbridge courthouse, a smaller and cheaper building, Fuller's involvement was probably limited to giving it final approval. Minor buildings such as Lethbridge were likely handed over to younger staff members as a form of their training.[27] Interestingly, Fuller's son, Thomas, drafted the plans for the Lethbridge building. He had joined the Chief Architect's office as a very young man at the behest of his father, and would later become the Chief Architect himself.

David Ewart succeeded Thomas Fuller as Chief Architect of the Dominion in 1897.[28] Born in Scotland in 1841, Ewart had attended the Edinburgh School of Art and before coming to Canada in 1871.[29] He went straight to work for the Chief

*A worthy successor: David Ewart, Dominion Chief Architect. NA, PA-129119*

Architect's branch and quickly rose to a position of responsibility. He was acting Chief Architect briefly before Fuller was hired in 1881, and stayed on as Fuller's assistant. Ewart took over the branch at a time when the government, freed from the constraints of a major depression, was drastically expanding its public works projects. Ewart never had the reputation in architectural circles of his former superior, and did not leave the same individual stamp on federal buildings.[30] He was an able bureaucrat who, confronted with much greater demands in terms of design output, encouraged more standardization in design. This can be seen in the Territorial courthouses produced under his tenure: the 1899 Medicine Hat structure was intended to be a template for others in the North-West. Like Fuller, Ewart likely had a relatively minor role in their design. According to his correspondence, Ewart usually provided a beginning sketch, but left it to other architects and draftsmen in the department to turn it into a fully realized design, although he would keep in close touch with their progress.

None of the Territorial courthouses in Alberta had any pretensions to high architecture. Ewart's staff produced courthouses with a distinctly residential appearance. The more substantial brick Red Deer and Macleod courthouses, with their cross gable roofs and slightly picturesque appearance, seemed to take cues from the Queen Anne Revival style popular for homes at the turn of the century. It sometimes found its way into public buildings like town halls and fire halls in the late nineteenth and early twentieth centuries. The Macleod courthouse, with its gables combined with arcades of arched windows on the front and side elevations, also bore some resemblance to the post offices built by the department, and the Red Deer courthouse did indeed become a post office. The smaller Territorial courthouses may well have been designed with such conversions in mind, on the assumption they would be superseded in the near future.[31]

The Department of Public Works and the Chief Architect designed the courthouses to the specifications of the Department of Justice. That department, at least with the later courthouses, in turn relied on the advice of the Territorial justices.[32] It was not an efficient arrangement. When the Chief Architect's Branch produced plans, they were sent to Justice for approval and suggestions, and that ministry also forwarded them to the judges for their approval. As will become apparent, it led to long delays for most of the buildings. Another factor that led to long waits was indecision in the Department of Justice about just how expensive the courthouses should be. During the Liberal's tenure, the ministry decided on fairly cheap buildings and that was what they got, in most cases some years after Mills' 1899 announcement of new courthouses.

Throughout the Territorial period, contracts were awarded on tender, going to the lowest bidder. All but one of the contracts for the courthouses in Alberta went to local builders, although bids were received from companies as far away as Ottawa. The courthouses were simple enough that local contractors could build them, and they likely had a major advantage in procuring materials and labour at more competitive rates. There was always pressure to use local suppliers. The Chief Architect's branch, which was responsible for supervising construction as well as design, did not have any explicit policy as to where builders got their building supplies, as long as the specifications in the contract were met. Civic leaders did not have to be worried: the high cost of shipping construction supplies in the Territories meant that local material, especially brick and stone, was usually used.

Both Fuller and Ewart faced much the same difficulties in monitoring the progress of construction and making sure contractors followed the specifications given to them. There were officers appointed in Winnipeg and later Regina to act as regional supervisors, but to look after building projects, a local man would be appointed clerk of works, following the policy adopted years before in the rest of Canada. The clerk was there to supervise the contractor, approve his accounts, deal with minor problems and report more significant difficulties to Ottawa for attention.

The position had also become by tradition an important part of the patronage process.[33] Patronage left open the possibility that the clerk would not necessarily be experienced in building, and as far as the department was concerned, an incompetent clerk could spell disaster for a project. Consequently, the clerk of works had little authority.

The Chief Architect's Branch also kept an eye on their projects by sending its junior architects out to check on progress and handle major problems. Departmental correspondence shows that a senior member of the Chief Architect's office frequently visited major undertakings, and the west was no exception. In 1890, Ewart himself did a tour of inspection of the branch's projects through the North-West and British Columbia.[34] His travels took him from Moosomin to Victoria, and he returned to Calgary the following year to choose a site for the new post office. Ewart's tour demonstrates that the department took projects in the west seriously, and also that the architect's office had some familiarity with the area.

Once courthouses were built, they remained the responsibility of the department and the Chief Architect. Public Works looked after their maintenance and upkeep, appointing caretakers who took their direction directly from the Chief Architect's office. Courthouse caretakers were expected to keep the buildings secure as well as in good repair. Perhaps more so than in other public buildings, there was a great deal of tension between the officers of the court, such as the sheriff (and by extension the Department of Justice), the users of the edifices, and the caretakers as officers of Public Works, over who controlled the buildings. This was ultimately worked out in favour of the sheriffs, but it did not prevent more conflicts. Both caretakers and sheriffs also had to rebuff attempts by groups in the community to use the courthouses for things other than the administration of justice. The Department of Justice followed a policy from the outset of exclusion, reserving the courthouse for the operation of the courts. Plenty of exceptions were made, but in general it cut ties to a tradition where the courthouse was to some extent a building of the community, a tradition that was still very much alive in other parts of North America.

The Territorial courthouses were by and large economical buildings intended foremost to provide facilities for the administration of justice. They were built for the moment, not for the future. Calgary's courthouse, larger and more substantial, was to some extent the product of a more grand idea of public structures. But by and large, the Dominion sacrificed the symbolism of the courthouse in the interests of economy. This did not sit well with the residents of the Territories. As will be shown more explicitly in the following stories of the Calgary, Edmonton, Lethbridge, Medicine Hat, Macleod, and Red Deer courthouses, not only did the buildings not live up to expectations, the citizens of the North-West had to wait years and engage in endless lobbying to get them built. Courthouses became contentious structures, a product of the clash between civic aspirations and the dictates of public policy.

# CALGARY

Frontier justice in Calgary ended on Wednesday, August 13, 1890, when court facilities for the Judicial District of Northern Alberta moved from a wooden immigration shed on what is now 10th Avenue to the first proper courthouse built in the North-West Territories. The Territorial courthouse was the first of three domiciles built over seven decades for the superior courts in Calgary. The 1890 edifice was the first substantial courthouse in the North-West Territories and inaugurated a round of courthouse construction in the region by the Dominion government. The imposing stone bulk of Calgary's hall of justice became the standard to which towns in the Territories aspired. It was an example of the importance of good political connections in obtaining valuable public buildings, as Calgary was one of few centres in the Territories that did not have to mount a massive lobbying campaign to get a courthouse. The construction of the edifice also demonstrates the manner in which the Dominion Department of Public Works carried out large commissions in the Territories, especially the difficulties in managing projects so far from the Chief Architect's offices in Ottawa. Ironically, although the Calgary hall of justice was one of the first built in the North-West, it would remain the largest and most impressive of the Territorial courthouses.

## Calgary – The Early Days

The story of Calgary begins with the appearance of "F" Troop of the North West Mounted Police, under the command of Inspector Ephrem Brisebois, at the confluence of Bow and Elbow Rivers in August 1875. They were the first agents of the law in the immediate area, and the post was christened "Calgary" the following year by Colonels Macleod and Irvine of the NWMP. The small fort quickly attracted settlers and a few businesses, and a small hamlet appeared.

The settlement occupied a strategic location on the Bow River, and it was destined for great things. The Dominion government's range leasing laws of 1881, intended to encourage cattle ranching in the arid west, gave the town its first boost, but it was the Canadian Pacific Railway that changed Calgary's fortunes dramatically for the better. When the company decided on a more southern crossing through the Rocky Mountains, Calgary was right on the new route. The rails began marching across the prairie from Winnipeg in 1881, and by August 1883 they had reached the police post. The decision to make Calgary a divisional point on the railroad transformed it almost overnight into the largest settlement in Alberta and the undisputed commercial centre. Incorporation as a town followed in 1884, and in 1894 Calgary became the first city in the North-West Territories, with a population of just over four thousand.

## The Courts in Calgary

For ten years after its founding, the administration of justice for Calgary came from Fort Macleod, further south. There resided one of the legendary figures of the Canadian West, Colonel James Farquarson Macleod. His bailiwick as stipendiary magistrate, the Bow River Judicial District, stretched across the southern part of the Territories and as far north as Calgary. Until 1885, Macleod was Calgary's judge, but lived at Pincher Creek and had his judicial headquarters in Fort Macleod.

As Calgary grew, resentment brewed over the fact there was no judge resident at the town. With the judicial headquarters at Macleod, applications to the court had to be sent south to the clerk of court. It led to big backlogs and long waits in getting matters dealt with in the courts, or the considerable expense of sending one's lawyer to Macleod.

Given that many cases in the courts related to business and commerce, any delays often disrupted the local economy, a situation that was intolerable in a commercial centre like Calgary. The solution was simple: Calgary would take a judge away from someone else, in this case, Fort Macleod.

In March 1885, the Minister of Justice in Ottawa forwarded petitions from Calgary and Fort Macleod to Colonel Macleod for his comments. Town councillor S.J. Hogg and "eighty four" other residents and settlers had requested the appointment of a resident Stipendiary Magistrate for Calgary. In their petition, the supplicants argued that Colonel Macleod looked after an enormous area, and that the Calgary division of the judicial district was itself large enough to be a separate district. The sittings of the Judicial Court held in Calgary "on an average of four times a year at irregular periods," and their inability to communicate directly with Judge Macleod more than once a week when the stagecoach delivered the mail, were judged completely inadequate.[35]

Fort Macleod countered with their own petition signed by 147 residents. They reminded the government that the interests of the Macleod Division were "of equal if not greater importance than those of the Calgary Division" and that their location close to the International Boundary Line meant that there was a "greater necessity for prompt judicial action, especially in extradition matters."[36] In the end the government listened to the concerns of both parties and solved the problem by increasing the number of Stipendiary Magistrates in the North-West Territories from three to four, appointing Judge Jeremiah Travis to Calgary on July 30, 1885. If the Calgary petitioners had known what awaited them under Travis, they might have withdrawn their request.

## A Temporary Solution

With the arrival of the railroad, the North-West had anticipated a flood of immigration. Some of the first substantial public works undertaken in the Territories by the Dominion government were immigration "sheds" to provide quarters to newly arrived settlers while they arranged for jobs, lodging or homesteads. Despite the name, the structures were hardly sheds, but substantial two-storey frame buildings, with kitchens and dormitory style sleeping accommodations. In the Estimates for 1885, $7,000 was allocated for a shed in Calgary.[37] Designed by the Dominion Department of Public Works for the Department of Agriculture, the structure was fifty-one by twenty-nine feet with a one-storey annex for the kitchen. The contract was let to M.P. Zindford on November 24, 1884, and the building was finished early in the new year at a cost of $4,884.[38] Located on the south side of the railroad tracks, it was the first substantial government edifice erected in Calgary since the NWMP fort, and one of the largest buildings in town.

The Department of Justice soon commandeered the immigration shed at the request of Judge Jeremiah Travis. Unhappy with the lack of facilities in his judicial headquarters, Travis sent a request to the Minister of Justice for proper accommodations.[39] Action was swift; by September 1885, hardly more than a month after Travis had arrived, the immigration shed was fitted up for a courtroom and an office for the judge at a cost of just over $800.[40] Travis wrote with pleasure to George Burbridge, the Deputy Minister of Justice, to tell him the new courtroom had been well received by both the local bar and the public.[41] At the first session of court, the members of the bar gave a speech thanking their new magistrate.

The quick response of the Department of Justice was unusual in the Territories. Calgary benefited from the favour of the Conservative administration of John A. Macdonald, due to the fact it was, from the beginning, a party stronghold in the Territories. A Conservative Association was formed in the spring of 1885, to which the local paper, the Calgary Herald, looked for aid in winning more attention from the Dominion government.[42] Travis would turn out to be a disaster, and replaced within a year. But this would actually help cement bonds between the town and government, when Charles Borromee Rouleau became the judge in Calgary.

---

### JUDGE TRAVIS AND THE WHISKY RING

Judge Travis made a good start in Calgary, but it did not last.[43] Travis was a teetotaler and supporter of the temperance movement, then gathering force in eastern Canada. He was appalled by the open traffic in liquor in his jurisdiction. Despite legal prohibition in the Northwest Territories, Calgary was a wide-open town, with gambling, prostitutes, and booze freely available. More than a little self-righteous, Travis made it his crusade to enforce prohibition. He did so notwithstanding the fact that it was a very unpopular statute both with the public and the police, and that as the magistrate he was supposed to be an arbitrator, not enforcer, of the law. Members of the more respectable element in town told the magistrate of a "whisky ring" that controlled the liquor trade. The Mayor, George Murdoch, and the town solicitor,

Henry Bleeker, were alleged to be members of the sinister cabal. Rumours were rampant that Murdoch and the town police chief, James Ingram, were taking kickbacks from brothels and saloon keepers. This was especially awkward for Travis, as Murdoch was the local Justice of the Peace and would sit with the magistrate on the bench for some trials.

Matters quickly came to a head when two plainclothes mounted policemen arrested hotelman, former mountie and town councillor Simon John Clarke. He had bodily prevented the detectives from searching his establishment, and was hauled off and charged with obstruction and resisting arrest. When the case came to trial in November 1885, Travis fired his first salvo in the war against the Whisky Ring. Clarke was found guilty and given a sentence of six months of hard labour. Many Calgarians were outraged. A town meeting, dominated by the pro-Clarke sympathizers, was held to protest the verdict. The angry mob in Boynton Hall resolved to send a deputation to Ottawa to overturn the Travis decision. Physical threats against the judge were heard that night. Predictably, Travis was not cowed, but rather the opposite. The war became more heated when the judge fired Hugh Cayley, his Clerk of Court, for allegedly showing up at court drunk. Cayley, however, was also editor of the *Calgary Herald* and a friend of the rowdy element. His paper joined in the attacks on the judge wholeheartedly.

Travis responded by charging Cayley with contempt of court and then giving him a jail sentence. It was an imprudent move. A parade of drunken supporters accompanied Cayley to the NWMP lockup. In the midst of the rising uproar, a civic election was held in Calgary. Shortly before the election, G.E. Marsh brought a charge of corruption before Travis's court against the incumbent mayor and council over irregularities in the voters' list. Travis now had a weapon to use against Mayor Murdoch and several of the town councillors. He found that they had been guilty of corruption in rigging the voters' list, disqualified them from running and barred them from elected office for two years. The election, however, went forward as planned on January 6, 1886, with the improper list and Murdoch and disputed councillors Dr. N.J. Lindsay and I.S. Freeze still on the ballot. They were returned with a healthy majority. Travis disallowed the result; he then installed another mayor and council.

The new mayor, James Reilly, represented the somewhat more respectable Calgarians who supported the judge. His government, however, was paralyzed when the town's books and seal disappeared. While chaos reigned in Calgary, the fight between Travis and the Whisky Ring took on national importance. The Liberal press seized upon it to embarrass the Conservative government of John A. Macdonald. Travis was ordered to set Cayley free: unfortunately for the magistrate, Cayley's uncle was a prominent Conservative. On March 22, 1886, the government appointed Judge Thomas Taylor of Winnipeg to investigate the situation. Although Travis could marshal a great deal of evidence to support his actions, Taylor found that the magistrate had exceeded his authority. Taylor's report sat in Ottawa for a year before finally being released in June 1887. In the meantime, the government sidestepped the controversy when it reorganized the courts of the North-West Territories. Travis did not join the other magistrates on the new Territorial Supreme Court. Given a pension, he was sacrificed to political expediency. The Territorial Council called a new municipal election for Calgary. George Clift King was elected mayor and the power of the Whisky Ring was broken.

The arrival of Rouleau, a meticulous legal authority, devout Roman Catholic and community leader, changed the whole tone, demeanour and behaviour of the Calgary bench after Travis's disastrous tenure. Rouleau was no stranger to the Territories. His appointment as the Stipendiary Magistrate at Battleford had predated Travis by three years. The judge had been forced to flee with his family during the Riel Rebellion. With Calgary in near insurrection over Travis, it was expedient to send Rouleau there in the spring of 1886 rather than back to Battleford. When the Supreme Court of Northwest Territories was established, Calgary became the headquarters of the judicial district of Northern Alberta, with Rouleau as the resident justice. Calgary gained not only an excellent judge but also a valuable connection to the Conservative government in Ottawa. Rouleau had run for Parliament as a Conservative in Quebec in 1875, and had ties with the Macdonald government and the lieutenant of the Quebec Conservatives, lawyer and Minister of Public Works Sir Hector Langevin.

## The Courthouse of 1890

Through the turmoil of the Travis affair, Calgary continued to grow, not as rapidly as the townspeople might have hoped, but rapidly enough that the Immigration Hall quickly became outmoded as a courtroom. It was a story repeated many times in the towns and cities of Alberta: the hall had no room for permanent offices of the Sheriff or the Clerk of Court, facilities for the barristers, or separate chambers for witnesses, juries, and holding prisoners. While the court lists were small and proceedings relatively informal, these shortcomings could be ignored. As the end of the decade approached, this was no longer the case.

The inadequacy of the Hall was clear during the infamous Fisk murder trial in 1889. William "Jumbo" Fisk was charged with the brutal murder of a young Cree woman. It was a quite a spectacle and turned attention toward the town's dismal court facilities. A Calgary Herald reporter described the scene.

> When the Hon. Mr. Justice Rouleau took his seat on the extemporized bench in the make shift [sic] court room at the dingy immigration shed across the track this morning ... he gazed down from his eminence upon a motley crowd consisting of all sorts and conditions of men blocking the dingy little room to the doors. Within the precepts of the railing which defines the arena wherein the members

> of the bar are wont to exercise their ingenuity and air their eloquence, was gathered most of the legal talent of the town.... As the judge takes his seat the crown prosecutor gathers his gown about him, gives a final look at the bundle of official documents, arranges a pile of formidable law books in front of him and casts an enquiring gaze over in the direction of a table beside the little wooden box like a packing crate on end, which does duty as a prisoners dock.[44]

The Department of Agriculture wanted also wanted their hall back. The local immigration agent, J.R. Miquelon, had never been happy with the way Judge Travis and the court had moved into his building.[45] When Rouleau came to Calgary, it was worse: Travis used the kitchen for his office before being relieved of his post, while Rouleau took over the rest of the main floor, leaving Miquelon with only the upper floor. In the summer of 1886, Miquelon requested that Travis be ordered out and that the kitchen be restored to his use. Far from relinquishing the building, the following year the Department of Justice asked for the whole structure as a courthouse.[46] At the beginning of 1888, although Travis was gone, the arrangements had not changed. Miquelon was desperate: he faced withering criticism from the local press when he was forced to house recently arrived immigrants in tents rather than the building constructed for that purpose.[47]

---

JUMBO FISK

Life on the frontier had a dark and squalid side. Nowhere was this more clear than the 1889 trial of William "Jumbo" Fisk for the murder of Rosalie New Grass. Fisk had come into Calgary and picked up the fifteen-year-old Cree girl off a street corner. Like altogether too many young native girls living around Calgary, she was a prostitute. They retired to the Turf Club, a saloon, where bartender George Kelsay let him use a room. Witnesses later reported hearing moans and thumping from upstairs. Fisk came down and took Kelsay up to the room to look at an unconscious Rosalie. She was bleeding heavily. After conferring, the two men decided that Fisk should go to the police and report the incident himself – but first, they would have some dinner. Accordingly, at around 8 p.m., Fisk approached Chief Constable Dillabaugh, saying he was in a "bad fix."

By the time Dillabaugh saw Rosalie, she was dead, lying in a bloodstained bed. He called in the coroner, Dr. Lafferty. A thorough investigation was made. Fisk freely admitted having sexual relations with the young girl. In his post-mortem, Lafferty found that she had died from internal injuries somehow inflicted during sex. An examination of Fisk was made, and Dillabough discovered a bloody handprint on a wall, which matched that of Jumbo. The chief arrested Fisk. On March 2, 1889, a preliminary hearing began, and three days later Justice of the Peace George Murdoch remanded Fisk to the next sitting of the Supreme Court on a charge of murder.

"A life at Stake," the *Calgary Herald* announced a month later as Fisk came to trial in front of Justice Charles Rouleau. From the outset it was a difficult trial. Fisk was not an upstanding citizen, but despite the horrible nature of the crime, the sympathies of many townsfolk lay with him and it was difficult to empanel a jury. The crown had a strong case. Witnesses saw Fisk and Rosalie go to the room where she died, heard yells and moans of pain, the medical evidence was damning, and the bartender's testimony painted Fisk in a most unsympathetic light. The courtroom was stunned when the jury returned from its deliberations to announce a verdict of not guilty. Rouleau was outraged. According to reports, he pounded the table and shouted, "I am not prepared to hear that verdict, gentlemen. You will be taken back to reconsider it." In the end the jury was unable to agree on a verdict.

It seems scarcely credible that the jury was prepared to acquit Fisk on the testimony available. There were insinuations in the *Calgary Tribune* of bribery, but nothing was ever proven. In refusing to accept the verdict, Rouleau had the support of the better elements of the community. The *Tribune* roundly condemned the original jury. Comparing Fisk to Jack the Ripper, the paper commented: "The idea which seems to possess the minds of some people, that because a crime or offence is committed against an Indian, therefore the crime is lessened, is inhuman in the extreme." [48] At a new trial in July, Fisk still cheated the hangman. He was found guilty of manslaughter and sentenced to fourteen years in the penitentiary.

Fortunately for the beleaguered agent, by 1888 the Chief Architect's office of the Department of Public Works was at work designing a permanent court facility in Calgary. Calgary's new domicile for the courts would be one of the least controversial of all the Territorial buildings. In contrast to the other towns in the North-West, the citizens of Calgary hardly had to fight at all for their new courthouse. Admittedly, there were many good reasons for constructing a good courthouse in Calgary. The town was a judicial seat, it was positioned right on the railroad, it was the most populous centre in the North-West and would almost certainly become a major city, it had a busy court, and perhaps most importantly, it was a Conservative Party stronghold. Already promised a building, perhaps when John A. McDonald and Hector Langevin visited Calgary in 1886, the town council and local board of trade sent petitions to Ottawa in early 1888 as a reminder.[49]

The decision to build a courthouse came in time for a request for funds in the government's supplementary estimates for 1888–89.[50] The department asked for an initial grant of $10,000 with a projected final cost of $38,150 for the structure.[51] Chief Architect Thomas Fuller and his staff began design work sometime in the spring of 1888. In May, Fuller requested information about the local stone and brick from B.C. Kenway, the clerk of works for the NWMP barracks under construction in Calgary.[52] Plans and specifications for the courthouse were sent to Calgary in September 1888 for the perusal of the public, and tenders called for soon after. In November, the contract was given to John Gillies McCallum, a former town councillor and builder in Calgary.[53]

McCallum was an experienced builder who had his own supply of award-winning sandstone from his Sunnyside quarry: in 1896, McCallum shipped a giant carved bassinet to the World's Fair in Chicago, where it was given a ribbon.[54] McCallum lost no time starting after signing the contract on November 9, 1888.[55] Over the winter he intended to dig out the foundation and cut the stone for the walls in time for the spring building season. There was a small delay of several days while McCallum waited for Henry Peters, the Territorial Clerk of Works for the Department of Public Works, to come from Regina to position the building on the government's site in section 16, west of downtown. The entire block between what would become 4th Street and 5th Street and 6th and 7th Avenues Southwest was reserved for the Dominion. The courthouse was placed facing east along 4th Street. McCallum was to have the building completed for September 1, 1890.

Fuller did not have an easy time finding a man in Calgary he could rely on as Clerk of Works to oversee the project. After several unsuccessful appointees – one dismissed within weeks for drunkenness – less than two weeks before the courthouse contract was signed, a new man, Herbert D. Johnson from Calgary, was hired at the salary of $100 a month.[56] Johnson replaced Kenway on the barracks project, and was site supervisor for the courthouse. The new appointee lasted much longer than his predecessors, and duly became responsible for projects throughout Alberta.[57] Johnson had some architectural training and had designed at least two small commercial blocks on Stephen Avenue in Calgary. As the local representative of Public Works, the community held Johnson in some esteem, and local papers would later refer to him as the "Government Architect." In his first job, Johnson had little power – he was there to make sure the contractor followed the specifications to the letter, and report problems immediately to the Chief Architect. At first Johnson was not trusted even with this; Peters from Regina was still coming out to inspect the work when McCallum began excavating the foundation in December.[58] He continued to visit the site over the next year. When problems were encountered with the placing of doorways and the main stairs in the building, Johnson immediately wired the department for instructions. [59]

The edifice that Johnson was responsible for was both impressive and quite simple in appearance. The building measured ninety-one by fifty-seven feet, with a long facade facing east onto 4th Street.[60] It took advantage of the area's abundant local sandstone, and was one of the first substantial buildings in the town built of the material.[61] The exterior used rough, unfinished stone arranged in random courses. The two-storey building, for all its rustic quality, had a complex design. The shallow-pitched mansard roof proclaimed it to be a federal government building – for a period of nearly twenty years, this roof style was emblematic of Dominion edifices.[62] The facade was irregular, with two projecting pavilions, both lower than the rest of the building, and the one on the right much smaller and suggestive of a tower. It had the main staircase to the second floor and the courtroom. The main entrance was a recessed porch with a Romanesque arcade of three arches. The roof over the courtroom on the second floor was higher than the rest of the second storey to allow for a fifteen-foot ceiling. The courtroom's large windows looked out

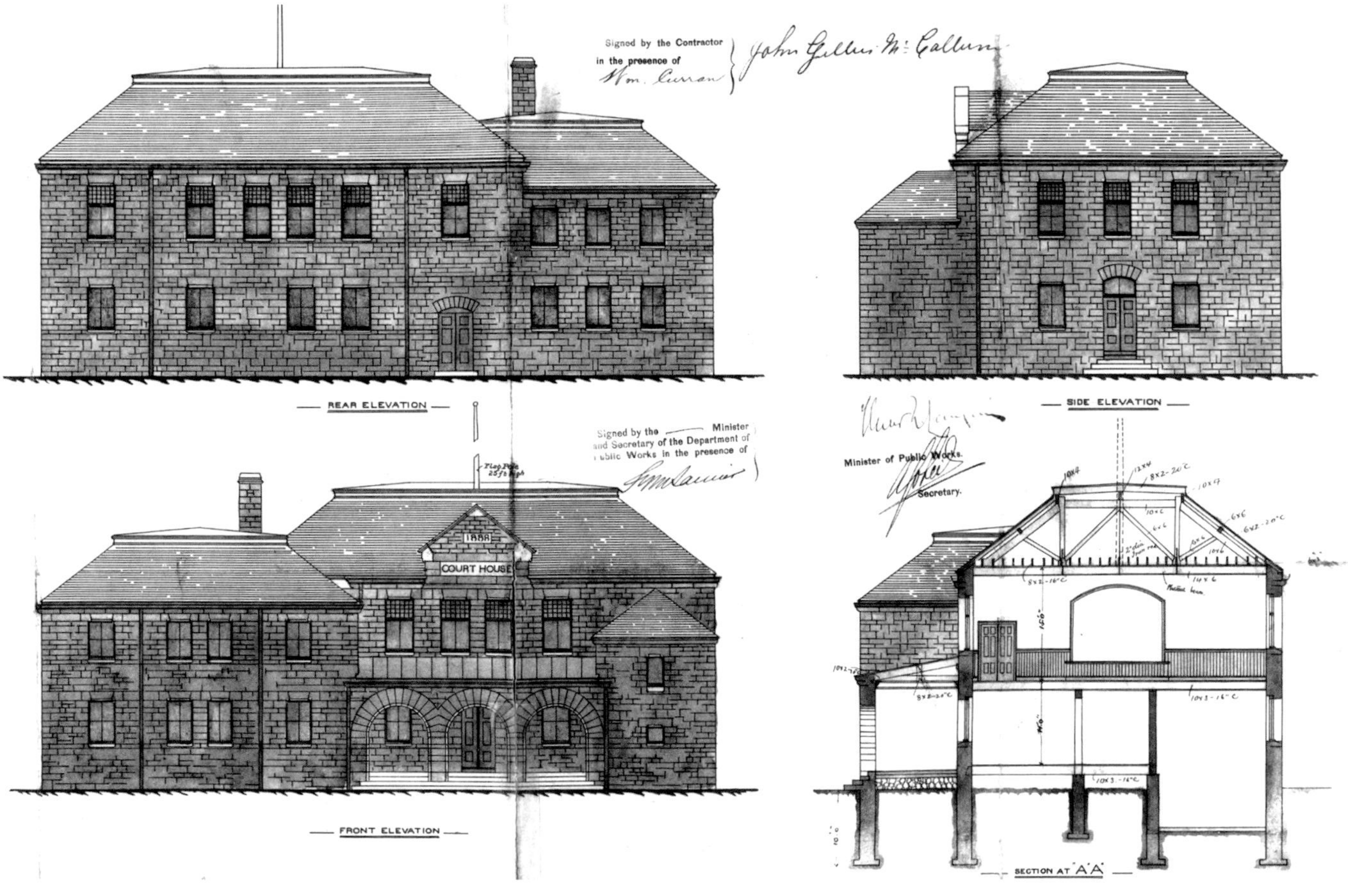


Elevations, Calgary Territorial Courthouse, 1890. NA, NMC86382.

over the porch, while above a carved plaque on the gabled parapet announced the building's dour purpose and the year it was conceived, 1888.

Internally, the design followed the standard pattern for courthouses, with a large courtroom on the second floor. A high, curved ceiling and large windows made for a bright space, finished throughout with cedar.[63] Along with the courtroom and judge's chamber, there was a robing room for the barristers and two rooms for jury deliberations on the second floor. The main floor had an office for the sheriff and clerk as well as the vault, a fireproof brick room for holding the court records. There were chambers for witnesses, lawyers, and a grand jury room – an oddity that demonstrates a lack of familiarity with the Territorial judicial system, which had never implemented a grand jury system. The building also had facilities for holding prisoners for trial, and the cells and jailer's office were accessed from a door on the north side of the building. There was originally no basement, simply a rubble foundation with crawl spaces, but this was changed at the beginning of construction into a full cellar.[64] The architect made sure there was a second stairwell that allowed court officials, jury and witnesses access to the courtroom out of sight of the public. Behind the judge's bench there was a large arched entry, an attractive feature that allowed him to leave his private chambers and appear immediately behind his dais, a clever bit of judicial theatre.[65]

Floor plan, Calgary Territorial Courthouse, 1890. NA, NMC86381.

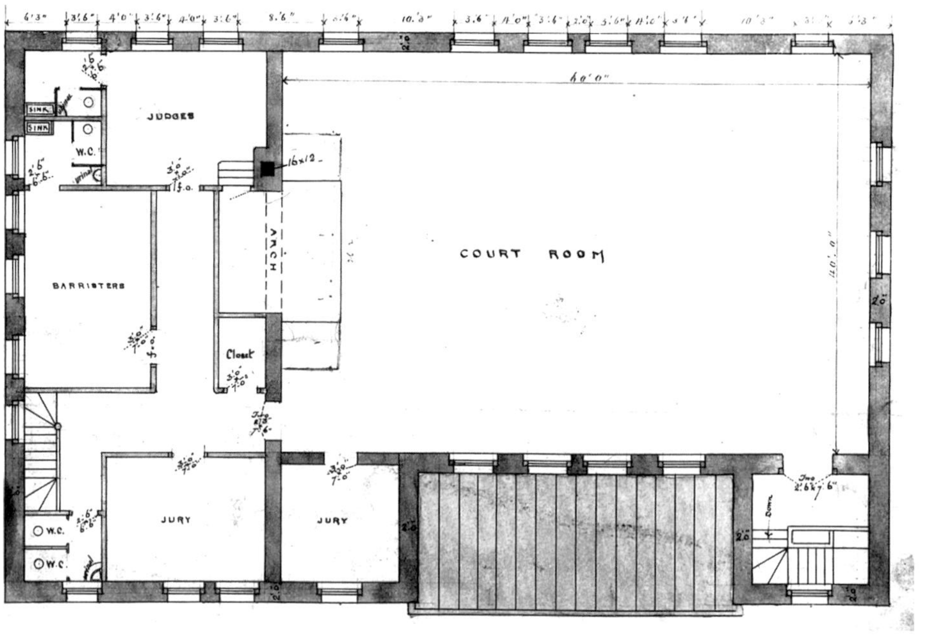


Fuller's courthouse was influenced by the Richardson Romanesque style then in vogue. Based on the early medieval architecture of France and Spain, Richardson Romanesque was characterized by rough faced stone, often in contrasting colours, arched openings for windows and doors executed with thick columns and heavy arches, and rich carved decoration. The irregular massing of the Calgary courthouse gave the building a picturesque quality in keeping with the style. A writer for the *Calgary Tribune* who suggested a tower for the structure must have been familiar with Romanesque buildings, as this was indeed common. The appearance of the courthouse would have benefited from such a feature. The use of unfinished stone was likely both practical and aesthetic, a mix of pragmatism and art dictated by the shortage of skilled workmen, especially stonemasons, in the area but also effectively giving the building a massive rugged quality. There was little architectural decoration. Window surrounds were basic and there were only stilted stone voussoirs – stone arches – over the secondary entrances. The Calgary courthouse resembled some contemporaneous court buildings in Texas and elsewhere, inviting speculation that the Chief Architect's office drew inspiration from architectural journals to tackle an unfamiliar type of building.[66]

The Calgary courthouse was built in a time of increasing restraint in the Department of Public Works. The designs produced by the Chief Architect had gone from ornate to economical, and from symbolic to pragmatic, by the end of the 1880s.[67] This was especially true of buildings in the North-West Territories. The lack of ornamentation kept costs down, as well as being more practical and easier to build. But while Calgary's building did not compare to the edifices constructed by the department in the populous east, for a small prairie town of less than four thousand it granted some necessary dignity and presence to the Supreme Court of the North-West.

Work on the courthouse proceeded apace through the fall. It was closed in by October, much to the excitement of the Calgary Tribune. Somewhat prematurely, it announced to its readers that the building would soon be open, alluding in a romantic fashion to Calgary's image as a wide-open cow town: "The court house will be ready in a short time to transact business with neatness and dispatch. It is a fine large building and has several comfortable slumber rooms in the basement, and also a few on the upper floors, for which no extra charge will be made. Visitors during business hours will be requested to leave their guns, etc, in the keeping of the boss man."[68] The building was actually many months from completion. The Daily Herald complained of the delay in July 1890: "The new courthouse, which, it was supposed, would be ready for occupation in the spring, is still not complete ... there is a well founded impression that the building will not be ready even when the supreme court sits in September."[69]

McCallum had finished his contract ahead of schedule; the delay was due to the plumbing and finishing. In the end the local papers were surprisingly uninterested in the completion of the new building. Not that it was unimportant to the town; the Herald was quite put out when the Dominion Illustrated News did not print a photograph of the courthouse in its special Calgary edition.[70] There was no official opening, however, and the press merely noted that the courts had moved after they left the immigration shed for the new building on August 13, 1890. The Herald wrote, "... this afternoon we learn that the records of the court have been removed to the new building and the old furniture of the officials sent over; and after today the Judge's, Clerk's and Sheriff's offices will be in the new court house."[71]

The only near-ceremonial moment came in early September when Justice Rouleau accompanied Sir Hector Langevin on a tour of the courthouse. Returning to Ottawa from a visit to the west coast, Langevin stopped in Calgary for a day and met with local party supporters and officials. Rouleau accompanied Langevin in the police rig on a tour of the town and a visit to the police barracks. There was a private dinner at the Alberta Hotel, chaired by Rouleau and attended by thirty local dignitaries, including Senator James Lougheed and Mayor Lafferty.

Langevin's legacy to Calgary was a vast improvement over the cramped makeshift court facilities in the immigration shed. When finished, the sandstone hall of justice was easily the finest facility of its type west of Winnipeg and east of Vancouver, and rivalled the law courts that would be shortly built in Regina, the Territorial capital. It also marked a coming of age for Calgary. Although the town would grow little through the depressed years of the next decade, it was poised for great things. It became the first incorporated city in the Territories in 1894. Town solicitor A.L. Sifton drew up the new charter; he would sit in Calgary's courthouse as Chief Justice of the North-West Territories and become the second premier of Alberta.

*Civic monument: Calgary Territorial Courthouse, c. 1890s. Glenbow Archives, NA-1497-13*

## The First Decade – Some Modifications

Calgary was fortunate that the Dominion built a courthouse when it did. Shortly after its completion, government spending on public works plummeted. Consequently, only minor changes were made to the courthouse over the next twenty years. Much to the frustration of the local legal community, even relatively inexpensive but important renovations were difficult to procure from cost-conscious government departments. In 1898, the court en banc, or appeal court, for the Territories began sitting in Calgary, and Rouleau pestered the Department of Public Works to make changes to the bench to allow all the justices to sit before the court.[72] It is noteworthy mostly for the amount of effort the learned judge exerted to get a minor but still important alteration done. Much to his annoyance, Rouleau had to write the Deputy Minister of Justice, E.L. Newcombe, after already making application to the Department of Public Works, as the latter ignored his request. This was still not the end of it – despite Newcombe's intervention, just two weeks before the first session of the appeal court, Rouleau sent a terse telegraph to the deputy minister demanding the alterations be completed. The work was finally done, just in time.

The most significant alteration in the courthouse was the addition of a library. The Law Society of the North-West Territories, after its formation in 1898, established law libraries at all the major points in the region. Following old custom, the society asked that they be placed in the local courthouse – if one existed. Later in 1899, the local bar in Calgary, led by Peter McCarthy, agitated for a room to be set aside and furnished properly for the library, and a room for Judge David Lynch Scott to use for chambers.[73] They too ran up against indifference and inertia on the part of the Departments of Justice and Public Works. McCarthy and his compatriots got Herbert Johnson, still the local agent of Public Works, to make an

*Rustic but effective: Calgary Territorial Courthouse, c. 1890s. Glenbow Archives, NA-1378-1*

estimate for the proposed changes. They then enlisted Frank Oliver, the Liberal MP for Alberta, as their man in Ottawa. Oliver was always helpful with such requests, and sent on the material to the Department of Justice.

It was not until late in the fall that the Chief Architect's office finally drew up plans for the alterations. The floors in the basement were to be lowered, a window and stairs added, the existing cells for prisoners moved and the two new rooms enclosed, which also required alterations to the heating system.[74] Despite the completion of plans, no work was ordered, until finally McCarthy asked for the aid of Clifford Sifton, the Minister of the Interior. "I have no doubt if you would kindly look into this matter, tenders will be called for for [sic] the alteration" McCarthy wrote Sifton in August.[75] Sifton was obliging, sending on the letter to William Mulock, Postmaster General and acting Minister of Public Works. He referred the matter to David Ewart, now Chief Architect, who called for tenders in September. The contract was awarded to local builder J.C. McNeill, who had the lowest bid at $1,245.

Along with the changes for the library, Ewart also decided to upgrade the heating system for the building, duly giving the contract to William Head of Calgary in December 1900. While under Ewart's control, other amenities were added to the building – electric lighting, telephones, and perhaps most importantly, it was eventually hooked up to the city's water and sewer system. The building had originally used its own well and septic field.

As the new century got underway, the now decade-old courthouse seemed to be holding up well. That would quickly change. Calgary's population had remained unchanged for ten years; now in only a decade it would grow tenfold. While no one expected the courthouse to last forever, by 1904 there would be demands for its replacement, and only twenty years after it was built, it would be desperately overcrowded when a new era dawned on the prairies.

The Territorial courthouse was finally replaced in 1914 but continued to serve a useful existence. The Calgary Herald had suggested a good use for it ten years before: "The present courthouse, it is urged, would make an excellent jail, its outside appearance being eminently suggestive of such an institution."[76] The Department of Public Works did just that, converting the interior to office and cells for the Royal North West Mounted Police in the spring of 1914, at a cost of $3,670.[77] When the Alberta Provincial Police took over the building in 1918, the local commander was delighted with the building, commenting that: "The quarters occupied at Headquarters, Calgary are all that can be desired, and centrally located. The Guardroom is large and airy, there being 18 cells for the male prisoners, and two separate for females."[78] Later the province transformed the old courthouse into provincial offices.[79] In 1956, it again took on a judicial function, housing Calgary's family and juvenile courts.

The construction of the Territorial courthouse had been relatively uncontroversial, but its destruction was an important watershed that helped make people aware of the threat to heritage buildings. Unfortunately, the old building sat on a prime block of land. When it was apparent in the 1950s that a new modern courthouse was necessary for Calgary, the site of the Territorial building was a logical choice. The 1914 courthouse could continue to function normally while a new structure was erected, and the government would not have to buy more land. Although a sound strategy, it did not reckon with the emotional connection many Calgarians had with the building.

The impending demolition of the Territorial Courthouse galvanized the public in Calgary, and there was determined opposition to the government's plans. City of Calgary Alderman Mary Dover had a special link to the old Territorial courthouse: she was the granddaughter of Colonel James Farquarson Macleod. She decided to fight to save the old courthouse. Dover was not the only concerned alderman. Grant MacEwan, later to become Lieutenant Governor of Alberta, was a fellow traveller, as was Ernie Starr.[80] Calgary City Council early in 1957 passed a resolution requesting that the province retain the Territorial Courthouse as a historic site and convert it into a provincial museum and archives.[81] Two thirds of city council supported the idea, but not every alderman was so enthusiastic. Mayor Don Mackay, the epitome of latter-day boosterism for Calgary, was not pleased. He did not want to see the proposed three-million-dollar courthouse, with its attendant benefits for the city's economy, derailed by romantic whimsy. The city commissioners, the all-powerful administrators of the civic corporation, sided with the mayor, as did the Calgary Bar Association, which took the position that the old building "has no particular historic value."[82] The province was not interested in the museum proposal and stood its ground.

Dover was not yet defeated. She approached the Historic Sites and Monument Board in April, backed by the Association of Alberta Architects, which had passed unanimously a resolution to preserve the building.[83] Dover also went to the citizens of Calgary, personally circulating a petition. She found a great deal of public support. "I am having no trouble getting signers, from a zoo attendant to a judge's wife.... Comment here is generally that this is the last old original building here not being torn down.... People want it kept."[84] While Dover had public opinion and hundreds of signatures on her side, the provincial cabinet remained unmoved. The Monuments Board was not much help. A proposal for saving the building was deferred several times; finally the board decided to write Clifford Wilson of the Glenbow Museum for an opinion, only to find the courthouse had been demolished![85]

The end came in the middle of March 1958.[86] All the appeals having been exhausted, the execution began. There were no demonstrators blocking bulldozers or waving placards, and the old building came down in only a few days. One of Calgary's links with its pioneer past was no more. Only a few relics remain. A young Calgary lawyer liberated the doorknobs and plates of the original doors when it was demolished. The cornerstone was installed in the wall of the main entrance of the new modern courthouse. And between the Court of Queen's Bench and the Court of Appeals buildings is a plaque set in a decorative carved sandstone lintel from the old courthouse, which briefly tells its story. Aside from these mementoes, only photographs and memories remain of the building that helped civilize the North-West Territories.

# LETHBRIDGE

Lethbridge was one of the settlements of the Territories that lobbied hard for a courthouse. The town had always felt slighted when it came to the administration of justice. Although founded nearly a decade later than Macleod or Calgary, Lethbridge established itself as a major centre with remarkable swiftness, and expected proper treatment at the hands of the government. The lack of scheduled court sittings, a justice of the peace, a resident judge or a place to hold the assizes were points of great resentment among the town's citizens. Despite the fact that Lethbridge soon overshadowed rivals like Macleod in population and wealth, it remained the Johnny-come-lately, passed over for the status of a judicial headquarters and without even a deputy sheriff or clerk like Medicine Hat. It was, however, successful in winning a courthouse. But even this proved a hollow victory. Residents hoped for an impressive building that they could proudly point out to visitors, but they did not reckon with a government more interested in providing basic services than satisfying civic ambitions.

## Lethbridge – The Early Days

Lethbridge, originally known as Coalbanks, was a town founded on coal. Its heritage also includes one of the first acts of British justice on the Canadian prairies. At the junction of the Belly and St. Mary's Rivers, not far from the future site of Lethbridge, American whisky traders had built the notorious Fort Whoop-Up in 1870 as a base for their operations. When the North West Mounted Police (NWMP) began their march across the prairies, Fort Whoop-Up was their ultimate destination, thus striking at the heart of the illicit whisky trade. On October 9, 1874, a detachment of the police appeared at the gates of the fort, led by Colonel James F. Macleod. The police deployed their artillery and took up battle formation. Riding forward with a small escort, Macleod found the post almost deserted, an anticlimax made farcical when the sole remaining trader tried to sell him the fort for $25,000![87] After dickering over the price, the police force retreated on its dignity and built a post further up the Oldman River.

Shortly before Macleod's arrival, an American trader by the name of Nicholas Sheran had begun exploiting the exposed coal seams along the Oldman.[88] The police at Fort Macleod were his first customers. The abundant coal in the area soon came to the attention of Elliot Galt, son of Montreal financier and politician Sir Alexander Galt. He had travelled through the area in 1879 in his capacity as the assistant Indian Commissioner. When the Canadian Pacific Railway decided to cross the Rockies via Kicking Horse Pass, the Galts decided the coal deposits would be commercially viable. A company was quickly formed with British investors, one of whom was named William Lethbridge. The North Western Coal and Navigation

Company began operations in 1883. The lack of a rail connection with the CPR was a problem that the elder Galt solved by obtaining a generous government subsidy to build a narrow gauge railroad to Dunmore on the main line. With the connection completed in 1885, the coal mines shifted into high gear. Galt laid out a townsite for the miners and the merchants who appeared to serve them, and on October 15, 1885, Lethbridge was born.

It was a true company town, and the Galts would be a dominant influence for the next twenty years. Although coal remained a vital part of the town's economy, Lethbridge soon took on a life of its own. Despite its location in the arid heart of Palliser's triangle, both ranchers and farmers soon began to make their way to the area. By 1891, the town was ready to incorporate. It had overtaken nearby Macleod as the major settlement of the area and indeed became a town a year earlier than its rival. Lethbridge's leading citizens showed themselves to be eager and energetic promoters of their community. Like their compatriots in Macleod and elsewhere, they worked to attract businesses and investment to their town. And like their neighbours and rivals, they showed a keen interest in the administration of justice and in the prospect of a courthouse.

## The Courts – and Courtrooms – of Early Lethbridge

The NWMP returned permanently to the district in 1885, when a detachment was posted in Lethbridge as K Division.[89] A barracks was built the following year. The courts soon followed. Lethbridge was initially part of the Judicial District of Bow River. After 1887, it was in the newly formed District of Southern Alberta of the Supreme Court of the North-West Territories. The town's judge was Colonel Macleod, based nearby in the town of Macleod. He first held court in Lethbridge in 1887.[90] On his visits to the settlement, the justice dealt mostly with the cattle rustling and liquor offences common throughout the Territories, but also the legal problems peculiar to a mining town. Lethbridge had large ethnic communities, made up of Italians, Germans, and Russians who had come to work the coal seams. Mostly male, prone to drinking, gambling, and fighting, the miners contributed a great deal of business to the courts. The only room large enough in the town for the court was in the Lethbridge Hotel, and the good justice presided there in true frontier style. As an outraged resident put it: "... his Honor[sic] might be entertained during the proceedings, by hearing the rattle of billiard balls and the jingling of the glasses used in retailing our four per cent across a bar over which a member of a totally different profession presides...."[91]

One citizen of Lethbridge who keenly felt the indignity of putting Macleod in a hotel storeroom was E.T. Saunders, who had served under the Colonel as a member of the police force. Along with his friend and later business partner, C.E.D. Wood, Saunders had left the NWMP but stayed in southern Alberta, going into the newspaper business. He co-founded the Macleod Gazette with Wood in 1882.[92] Three years later, the partners started the Lethbridge News. Saunders went to Lethbridge to run the newspaper there, and the following year he and Wood swapped shares in the respective enterprises. Saunders and Woods were staunch boosters of their respective communities, and both were obsessed with a courthouse. Saunders made a hall of justice for Lethbridge a burning issue through his editorials. He served as the unofficial mouthpiece for a clique of the town's leading citizens, including Elliott Galt, Dr. F. H. Mewburn, lawyer C.F.P. Conybeare, C.A. Macgrath, the first mayor, and merchant Henry Bentley.[93] It was a tightly knit group, which organized the first board of trade, pushed for incorporation, and lobbied incessantly for rail connections, bridges, better post office service, a land titles office, a customs office – and a courthouse.

There was a clear lack of facilities for the court in the town. In nearby Macleod, residents had built a town hall with the intent of renting it to the courts. Inspired by this example, some residents of Lethbridge tried through 1887 to form a joint stock company to build a public hall, for everything from dances to political meetings.[94] To the disappointment of Saunders, his fellow citizens showed little interest. The town remained without a decent place for the assizes. Although the new Supreme Court of the North-West Territories made regular visits to Lethbridge starting in 1888, the court continued to be held in the dining room of the Lethbridge Hotel or the orderly room at the barracks.[95]

The fact that other parts of the Territories were receiving some attention made the situation all the more irritating. The Dominion estimates in 1888 contained appropriations for courthouses and jails in Moosomin, Wolseley, Maple Creek, and Medicine Hat, a fact that did not escape notice in Lethbridge. Both Medicine Hat and Maple Creek were in the same district as Lethbridge but considerably smaller, which was especially galling. In response, the town started to aggressively lobby the Dominion government for equal consideration. The local members of the bar and the court officials had already put together a petition, approved by Justice Macleod, urging the Department of Justice to build a courthouse.[96] When a board of trade was formed in 1889, it tackled the issue head-on. At a February 1890 meeting, the board resolved to urge the Department of Justice to take action, and more memorials followed.[97] And once Lethbridge incorporated, it was one of the first items the new civic government considered. On February 3, 1891, the first town council met, and the courthouse issue was noted and slated for action. Meanwhile, the News turned up the editorial heat with a demand for the hall of justice on January 29, 1889. For the next two years the paper periodically ran editorials that either bemoaned the inadequate facilities, called for the immediate construction of the courthouse, or declared the citizens of nearby Macleod misguided in their energetic attempts to procure an edifice.

## Courthouse or Public Building?

Much to the chagrin of Macleod, Lethbridge got its courthouse first, but it was a Pyrrhic victory. The 1888 petition had not gone unnoticed in Ottawa.[98] The

Department of Public Works asked Robert Sedgewick, the Deputy Minister of Justice, if they should request an appropriation in the estimates for 1889. The ministry dragged its feet on the subject, although word filtered back to Lethbridge that the matter was being considered. This spurred the residents of the town on to more letters and petitions, and the town later sweetened their demands with an offer to provide the site for the courthouse. Pressure was also applied to the local MP, D.W. Davis, to do something about the situation. Davis was from Macleod, and there was clearly some suspicion that he was accordingly slighting Lethbridge. The News pointedly called on him to use his influence to get an appropriation included in the main estimates for 1891. "Mr. Davis is member for Alberta, and not for any particular section or part of it, and the News and the people of Lethbridge will hold him responsible for the proper discharge of his duty...."[99]

Matters reached a head shortly before the Dominion elections of 1891. In January, faced again with the sample room of Lethbridge House, Justice Macleod gave in to a rare burst of anger and refused to open court. The locals scrambled to find a new location, and put him in the old schoolhouse, recently replaced by a new building. But it was still makeshift:

> ...even that possessed none of the conveniences usually looked for in a modern Court of Justice, or any of the environments that add so much to the dignity of Canadian law, Judge, jury, lawyers, witnesses, prisoners, and spectators were forced to mingle together in the same crowded room.... Spectators and witnesses were forced to stand for two whole afternoons, the place being unprovided with seats except the chairs for the Judge and the lawyers.[100]

It was noted that Davis was present for the session of court and saw first-hand what Macleod and his officers had to contend with.

And immediately afterward, the Dominion election campaign began. Despite its disappointment with his efforts to that point, the *News* heartily endorsed Davis and the Conservatives. Its support mostly rested on the fact that the Conservatives were in power. The expectation was clear: that government spending would only come from supporting the government. In the following weeks, this point was made as often as possible. The promise had been made: a courthouse was coming, but in return it was understood that the citizens of Lethbridge would have to return a favour and vote Conservative.

It must have looked like a raw deal. Davis was elected in March, and the following September, when the estimates for the coming fiscal year were released, Lethbridge was still conspicuously absent. The editor of the *News*, James Macdonald, was immediately wroth. In a piece entitled "Government Procrastination," he made a prophetic threat: "Our citizens are heartily sick of the government's delay in these matters, and unless some steps are taken this year, the Government Candidate will scarcely poll many votes in the neighbourhood."[101]

Frustrations were clearly reaching a boiling point, and perhaps the government got wind of this. A sum of $7,000 was placed in the supplementary estimates for the year 1891 for a courthouse and customs office at Lethbridge. Far from pleasing the voters of Lethbridge, however, the announcement of the appropriation merely started a new storm of protest. The town didn't want just any building, they wanted something impressive, something $7,000 was not going to buy. It was matter of civic and national pride:

> We either want a building, which we shall be not be ashamed to point out to our nearest neighbours the people of Montana, and which will compare with the Court House erected in Benton and similar towns, or we want none at all. A miserable apology for a public building will neither do credit to our town, or elevate Canada in the eyes of our United States neighbours.[102]

The sentiment illustrates the importance of public architecture, especially courthouses, to the civic body. Someone, probably Davis during the election, had given the citizens of Lethbridge high expectations. It was even more outrageous to the citizens of Lethbridge that the proposed building would serve double duty, housing the customs office as well as the court.

The people of Lethbridge probably had the Department of Customs to thank that they were getting a building at all. The town's board of trade had also been pestering the government to do something about better facilities for the local customs inspector.[103] The customs service needed storage space, and because of the valuable goods kept in the custom inspectors' care, including money, secure premises were very important. Public Works had outfitted a large house in Macleod for the department, a facility Customs did not like. The department asked for something more substantial in Lethbridge, "a place of growing importance."[104] This extra pressure likely helped Lethbridge get a public building, which although a great disappointment to the local boosters, would be much more than most towns of the Territories could boast.

The bitterness over the small estimate placed for the Lethbridge public building did not soon dissipate. When the government approached the town council to get the title to the lots it had chosen, and which the city was to provide, the council was in no hurry to comply.[105] Conybeare, the town solicitor, received notice in April 1892 that an Order-in-Council had been passed accepting the site.[106] Upset at the amount in the appropriation, the council simply refused to send the title. It was a form of brinkmanship, but it worked. In June, the Honourable Joseph Aldric Ouimet, the Minister of Public Works, announced in Parliament that the Lethbridge courthouse would cost $20,000.[107] It was not until late in October that the council deigned to send a title to the site of the public building. Sensitive to the delicate situation, Ouimet wrote the mayor to thank him for the deed, reiterating that the building would be as expensive as promised.[108] Although it was too late in the year to think about beginning construction, the town felt that they had finally received some justice.

Once the plans appeared in Lethbridge, however, any feelings of relief about the structure evaporated. It was exactly what the citizens had feared. The *Lethbridge*

*News* did not mince words, calling it "parsimonious" and referring to its "extreme ugliness."

Undeniably, it was a very plain structure. Like all federal public buildings of the period, it was attributed to the Chief Architect, Thomas Fuller, but was probably never given more than cursory attention by him. Interestingly, Fuller's son, Thomas, drafted the plans, although he probably did not actually design it. Minor buildings were likely handed over to younger staff members as a form of their training.[109] This might explain what was perceived locally as the aesthetic shortcomings of the Lethbridge building.

The edifice was two storeys with a full basement, brick masonry walls on a stone and concrete foundation and wood joists for the floor and roof.[110] It measured fifty-three by forty-three feet.[111] The roof was done with galvanized iron sheets in a low-pitched mansard, the emblematic roof type of federal buildings well into the 1890s, with one small dormer on the rear.[112] The facade, facing Baroness Road, had two main entries, each surmounted with an arched transom window, and a central gable. Enclosed in the gable wall was a plaque with the legend, "Lethbridge Public Building" All the windows on the front were gently arched with sandstone sills and brick lintels, and there was an extra row of small openings for the caretaker's attic suite. The second floor windows on the sides and rear, which opened onto the courtroom, were much larger, arched and topped with brick voussoirs. In addition to the main entrances, there were two entrances on the rear, one on the side, and a sunken stair and door into the basement on the other side. There was virtually no decoration aside from the window treatments: it is clear that the department wanted a cheap, easy-to-build structure to fill the need in Lethbridge.

The building was expected to fulfil a lot of duties. It was truly a public building rather than the courthouse expected by the town. On the main floor the post office was to be placed on the right side of the building, while the left was given over to the customs office and the back to the offices of the Department of Inland Revenue. The left-hand entrance had a foyer with the main staircase to the next floor. Quarters for the court were restricted to the second floor. Most of this was used for the courtroom proper, well lit by the large windows and with a seventeen-foot ceiling that extended into the attic. Like the Calgary courthouse, the higher ceiling for the courtroom was a small but sophisticated touch. The judge's bench sat along the west wall. Along the north wall there was a room for witnesses and for the jury to retire, a barristers' chamber, and a judge's robing room. Above these offices, in a partial attic, the caretaker had his quarters. The basement was given over to the furnace, coal storage, and cisterns for drinking water. No bathroom facilities existed in the building; detached outhouses were provided.

There were no pretensions about the Lethbridge courthouse: it had only the barest connection to the decorous buildings designed under Thomas Fuller that could be found in other parts of the country. The dual entryway, centre gable and mansard roof were remnant elements linking it to the many delightful public buildings that had been constructed by the department in eastern Canada in the

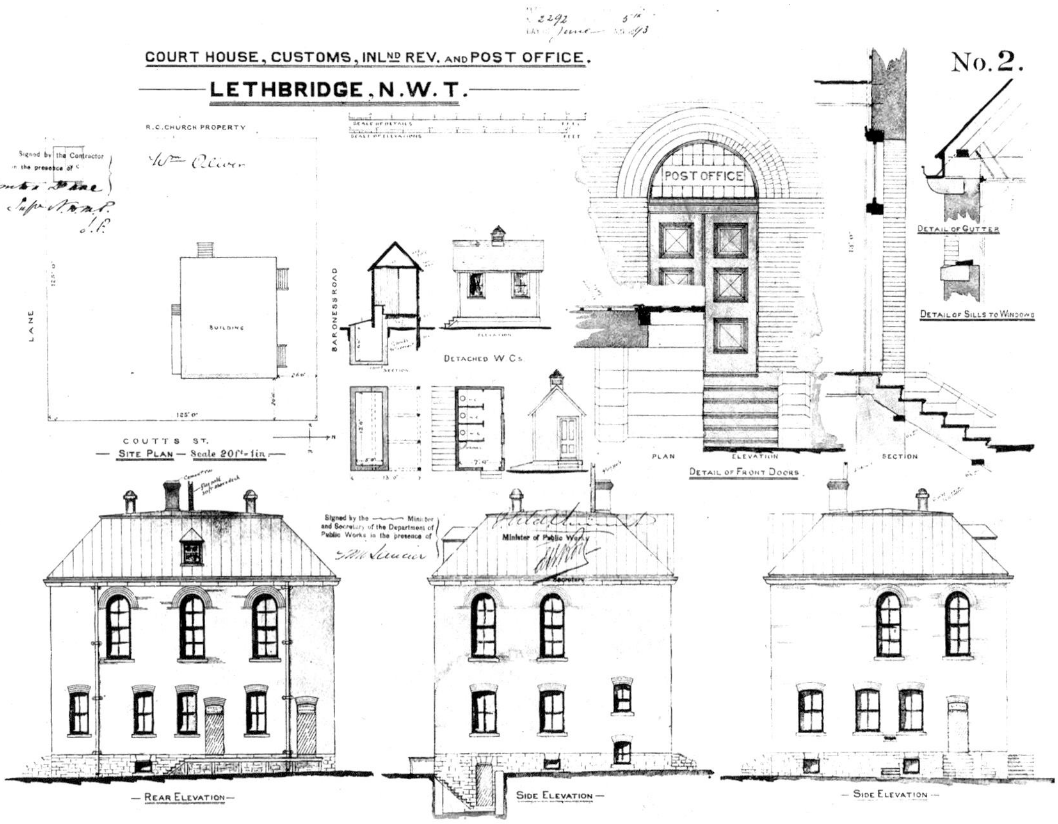


*Elevations, Lethbridge Courthouse and Public Building, [1893]. NA, C147159*

1880s. The disappointment and even anger of the residents of Lethbridge over their building was no doubt caused by comparisons to these structures. By the time the Lethbridge courthouse and customs office was begun, however, the Department of Public Works was feeling the pinch of recession like the rest of the nation. Most new public buildings became simpler and more restrained in appearance; in the Territories, where builders were less able and everything was still impermanent, the department was even less willing to spend money.

The town was pleased to note that the contract had at least gone to a local builder, William Oliver. He received notice of his good fortune at the end of May 1893, and signed his contract on June 5.[113] William Cluston, another local man, was appointed clerk of works. By the beginning of July, Oliver had begun work excavating the foundation.[125]

## WILLIAM OLIVER, BUILDER OF LETHBRIDGE

Upon his death, the contractor for the first courthouse in Lethbridge was called "in very truth a builder of Lethbridge."[115] Not only was William Oliver the leading contractor in the town for many years, but he had been a lead-

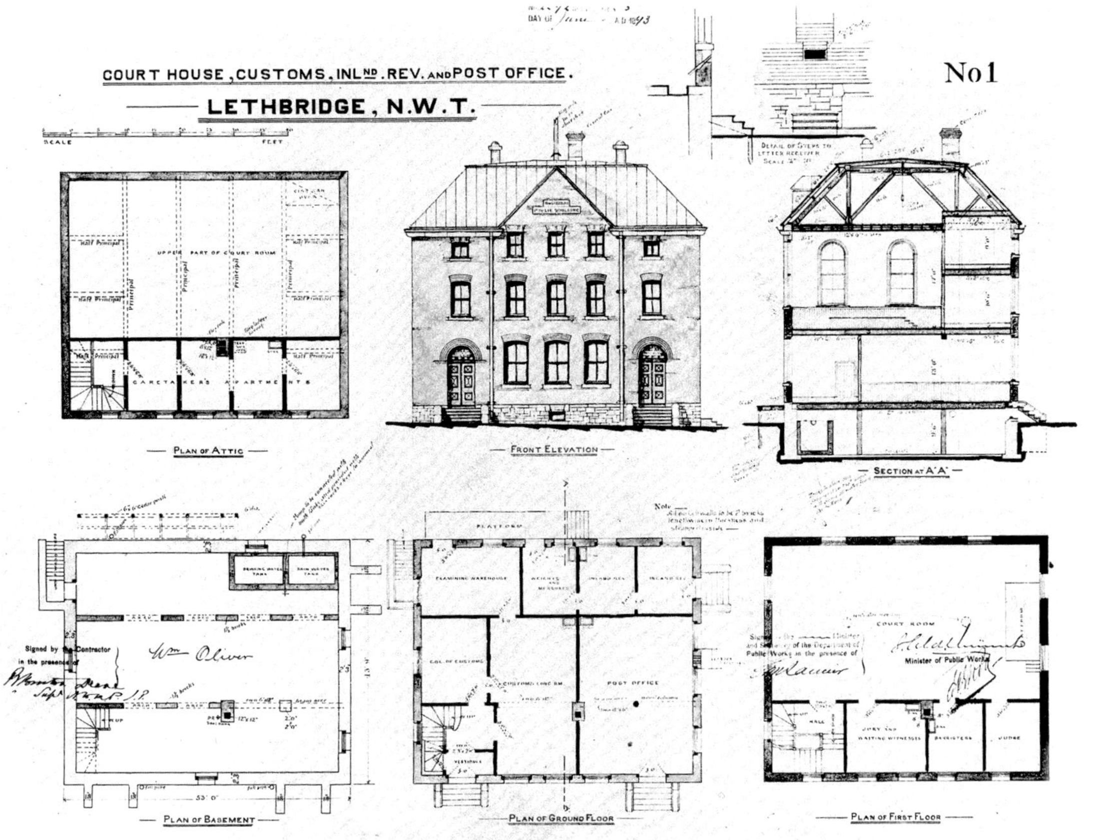


*Elevation and section, floor plans, Lethbridge Courthouse, [1893]. NA, C147158.*

ing citizen: mayor four times, alderman, member of the board of trade, and director for the local agricultural society.

Oliver came from Oxford County, Ontario, where he was born on December 26, 1860. He followed his father into the construction business. Like many young men of Ontario, Oliver came west to seek his fortune. With a set of carpenter's tools, he arrived in Winnipeg in 1882 and travelled west with the railroad until he reached the area of Regina and got a homestead. While proving up his land, Oliver also contracted. Building homes on Indian Reserves for the Department of the Interior brought him to Lethbridge around 1886. He began putting up workers' houses for the Alberta Railway and Coal Company, and within a couple of years was a general contractor and brick maker. Soon he was the town's biggest builder and a developer in his own right, owning several buildings and extensive real estate. Oliver took a keen interest in municipal affairs, running for town council in the 1890s and acting as mayor from 1901 through 1905, leading the drive to make Lethbridge a city. Not surprisingly, he was also a member of the board of trade. Oliver chose to retire in 1909, still a relatively young man, just as the building boom in the west was heating up.

Oliver was a natural choice for building the courthouse. Interestingly, he was a Liberal in political inclination, just like J.G. McCallum, contractor for

*William Oliver, Lethbridge Builder, Galt Museum Archives, P-1987-117-8000.*

the Calgary courthouse, at a time when the Conservatives ruled the country. It puts paid to any notion that Territorial public works contracts were necessarily doled out to party supporters. The courthouse may not have been the most lucrative project for Oliver. It was a long, drawn-out affair, taking over two years. Although he finished work on it in 1895, it was not the end of his involvement with domiciling the courts. In 1908, he rented rooms in his business block to the province to house the new sheriff and clerk of court for the Lethbridge Judicial District.

By January 1894, the building was well along, with the exterior completed and work proceeding on the interior. Even as the building approached completion, controversy raised its head once again. It had not gone unnoticed that the plans sent out to Oliver at the beginning of the contract showed a post office on the main floor. In smaller towns, the customs and post office were usually put in the same building, but no one had told the citizens of Lethbridge this.[116] For the third time tempers flared in Lethbridge over the courthouse. As far as the News was concerned, it was a violation of the original deal with the government: land in return for a $30,000 building that would only contain the customs service and the court facilities. The paper commented bitterly: "... it would be a breach of faith on the part of the Government to endeavour to thrust the Post Office into this building which is costing only $14,000."[117] The residents might have been more forgiving, but for the location of the edifice. It was deemed especially important for the post office to be right in the business district, and even a few blocks' removal was seen as a major inconvenience by residents.

Despite the angry protests, the Department of Public Works proceeded to send out plans and specifications for post office fittings anyway.[118] The town council was wroth, and protested to the Postmaster General, demanding compensation for the lots it had purchased for the courthouse. The matter remained a source of contention until well into the summer of 1895. The government delayed at first, but then awarded the contract for the post offices fittings to William Oliver.[119] His work was for naught, for in the end the town won. In the face of bitter opposition, the government dropped its plans for moving the post office. In the end the Dominion land office would move into the space intended for the postmaster.

Colonel Macleod, who put up with so much discomfort as the circuit judge in Lethbridge, never got to sit in the new courthouse. He had at least been freed from the hotel. After some fuss over the amount of rent the owners wanted to charge, Macleod had been allowed to use the town's Opera Hall, and he held his last session of the assize in Lethbridge there in August 1894. Then he was moved to Calgary and died before returning to the south. As for the courthouse itself, it was not used for the sittings of the court until 1898 because no furniture or fittings had ever been provided.[120] Oliver received another contract to fit it up properly, including the installation of electric lights, and Justice Scott finally opened his court there in December.[121] Even then it was not a very successful space. With several different government offices in a small building, it was crowded. And among other problems, the layout did not allow the judge private access to the courtroom. As C.F.P. Conybeare, the town's leading lawyer noted: "... the judges and bar of this district have always expected that a spiral staircase would be erected from this room to the floor above. If any case of importance is on and the court room crowded, it is scarcely consistent with the with the dignity of a judge to have to elbow his way through at throng of sightseers in order to reach the bench."[122]

It seemed that the frontier would never leave in Lethbridge. The whole saga of the courthouse left a legacy of lasting bitterness in the town. The Dominion's policy in the North-West, especially in the tardiness in supplying public works, goes a long way in explaining why the Conservatives were turfed from the Territorial seats, replaced with Independent Liberals, in the 1896 elections. The Conservative candidate, Thomas Cochrane, lost the Alberta seat to Frank Oliver. Alberta was on its way to becoming a Liberal stronghold, which it would remain until 1921. Unfortunately, when the provincial Liberals addressed the problem of court accommodation in Lethbridge, they were scarcely more successful than their federal predecessors.

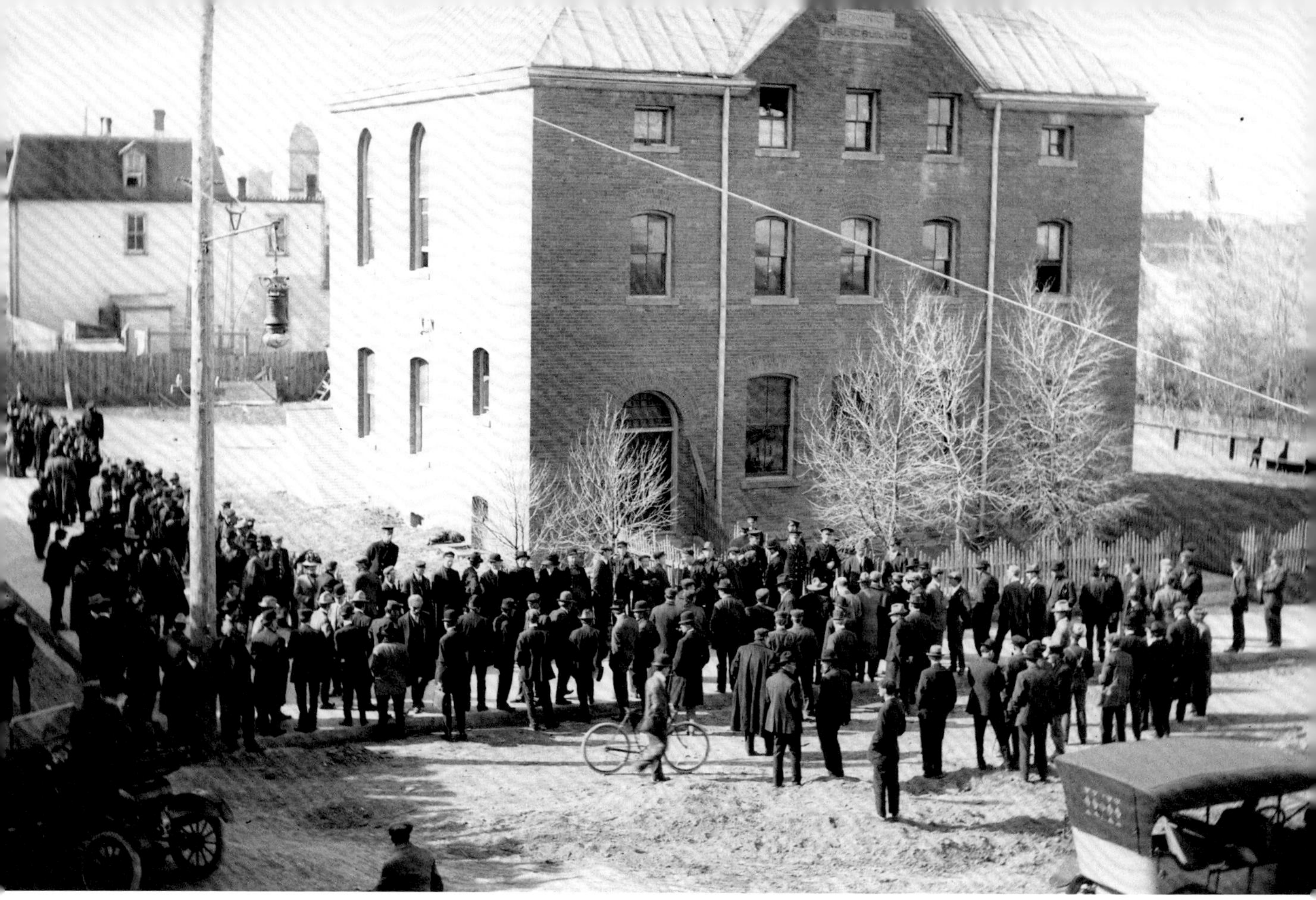

*Courthouse no longer: Lethbridge Dominion Land Titles Building, 1914. Galt Museum Archives, P-1964-127-4000*

## Epilogue

A new courthouse for Lethbridge, built by the province of Alberta, was opened in 1911. By this time, the Territorial building was no longer used by the courts, which had been suffering the indignity of renting the Caledonia Hall for sittings since 1908. The federal government decided to retain ownership of the Lethbridge building after the province was formed in 1905. Three years later, it decided it needed the upper floors for the local Dominion land office and asked the court to leave. The building originally built as a courthouse served as the public building for Lethbridge until the completion of the new post office in 1914.

According to local historians, the building was fitted out as an isolation hospital during an outbreak of typhoid in 1916. After the end of World War I, the federal government turned it over to the City of Lethbridge for the use of the Great War Veteran's Association, the forerunner of the Canadian Legion, as a meeting hall. A 1919 Order-in-Council mandated this use in perpetuity, and the Prince of Wales himself presented the hall to local veterans. The Legion added an extension in 1949, the Memorial Hall, and continued to use the building until 1977. By that date the venerable structure was in need of major repairs, and the Legion elected to move to a new building. The city decided to sell the building to a car dealership, splitting the proceeds with the Legion, and stipulated its demolition. Ironically, the first hall of justice outlasted its successor by some twenty-six years.

# MEDICINE HAT

The hall of justice that was finally built in Medicine Hat in 1900 was another example of the government's parsimonious policy toward courthouse construction in the Territories. It was undoubtedly the plainest and cheapest of the five halls of justice built in Alberta during the Territorial days. The need for more courthouses was clear as the immigration boom on the prairies began at the end of the century, but the Dominion wanted to build simple inexpensive wooden buildings. Medicine Hat, unlike other Alberta towns like Calgary, Lethbridge, Macleod and Red Deer, did not have the vocal civic boosters to look out for its interests. While Macleod and Red Deer managed to derail the government's intentions and get more substantial courthouses out of the Liberals, Medicine Hat found itself with a small building that could have been mistaken for a schoolhouse.

## Medicine Hat – The Early Days

Perhaps more than any other city of Alberta, Medicine Hat was a creation of the Canadian Pacific Railroad. Late in 1882, a few squatters pitched their tents on the flats by the river, anticipating the arrival of the railroad.[123] A canvas city sprung up when CPR construction crews arrived in the spring to build a bridge across the Saskatchewan River. The North West Mounted Police abandoned Fort Walsh in the Cypress Hills the same year, and posted part of the detachment there to Medicine Hat.[124] Erecting barracks at Police Point, the Mounties tried to keep order among the multitude of railway workers, who attracted whisky traders, gamblers, and prostitutes as well as respectable merchants. The first trains crossed the bridge by the summer of 1883, but the CPR decided to make the settlement a divisional point and Medicine Hat quickly took on a more permanent air. By the following year, frame buildings began to replace tents, and in 1886 a brickyard was opened.[125] Although the construction crews soon moved on, by 1891 the town had a respectable population of several hundred.

Like the rest of the Territories, Medicine Hat stagnated with the economic recession of the 1890s. The expected flood of settlers did not materialize, and the area suffered a severe drought to the discouragement of the few hardy homesteaders already there. Cattle ranchers had better luck, and Medicine Hat became an important centre of the free-range ranching economy. And there was always the railroad, which kept the town going during the hard years. The decision by the CPR to put its repair shops in Calgary and to move the divisional headquarters there in 1899 was a great blow to local boosters. However, with the new century and an immigration boom, things picked up for the little prairie town. As a civic body, Medicine Hat remained unorganized until relatively late. A board of trade was formed in 1887, but soon faltered and vanished.[126] It did not reappear until

1900. Incorporation did not take place until 1898, when the need for fire protection and other basic services became acute. This affected the way the town approached its needs for the administration of justice, especially courthouses.

## A Temporary Courthouse

The courts came early to Medicine Hat. By the time the town appeared on the map in 1883, the North-West Territories had been organized into judicial districts. Medicine Hat was placed in the Bow River District, and in October 1883, Colonel Macleod visited the town to hold court.[127] When the Supreme Court of the North-West Territories was organized in 1887, Macleod recommended that Medicine Hat, which was in the provisional district of Assiniboia, should be made headquarters of a separate judicial district.[128] The Territorial council, in its wisdom, left it in his bailiwick, the Judicial District of Southern Alberta. Medicine Hat had two assizes each year for the superior courts. The town and its sparsely settled hinterland had an unusually law-abiding population. Dockets, both criminal and civil, were small, and court was often cancelled for lack of criminals to try.[129] In spite of this, Medicine Hat got a deputy clerk and deputy sheriff in 1891, due to the long distance between it and the judicial headquarters at Fort Macleod.[130]

Medicine Hat was barely more than a tent city when the Dominion government decided to provide it with a large immigration hall, anticipating the settlers the railroad would bring. With funds allocated for immigration halls in Calgary and Medicine Hat for the 1884–85 fiscal year, the Department of Public Works gave the contract for both buildings to M.P. Zindford on November 28, 1884.[131] The contractor started work immediately, and had the two facilities finished within several months. The expected stampede of immigrants did not materialize and the immigration hall, far from greeting weary settlers with a bed and hot meal, stood empty. It was put to use by the townsfolk as a meeting place, and hosted the courts on occasion. In 1889 the NWMP quartered two constables in the building as a town detachment, and the west side of the main hall was fitted as a temporary courtroom.[132] Some space remained reserved for any immigrants who did make an appearance. The Department of Justice soon cast its eye on the hall as a permanent home for the court. Accordingly, the Deputy Minister of Justice, Robert Sedgewick, approached the Department of Agriculture in the fall of 1890.[133] The matter was soon arranged, and when the police officially took over the building and made it their new headquarters the following year, it also became the site of the town's assizes.[134]

More than two years passed after the 1890 agreement, however, before the Department of Public Works actually called for tenders to renovate the shed. The conversion was one of four courthouse projects undertaken by the Dominion government in the district of Assiniboia, which included small, wood frame facilities combining a courtroom, police bunkhouse and jail for Moosomin, Wolseley, and Maple Creek.[135] Ten thousand dollars was allocated in the 1888–89 fiscal year

*Medicine Hat with Immigration Hall to left of railroad tracks, c. 1885. Glenbow Archives, NA-2003-13*

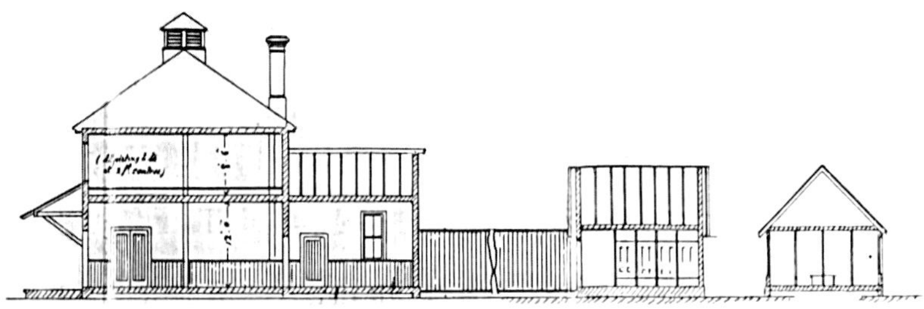

*Elevation, Medicine Hat Immigration Shed, 1884. NA, C148376*

for the new buildings. The Moosomin courthouse, originally planned as a $3,500 structure, used nearly all of the original appropriation.[136] Another $15,000 had to be assigned by Parliament in 1890 for the three remaining court facilities. Deputy Minister Sedgewick felt strongly that the Moosomin edifice had been far too lavish for the immediate needs to the district and wanted to get all the courthouses built as cheaply as possible. At Medicine Hat, the government stuck to its plan and converted the immigration hall, and if the townspeople had been entertaining any hopes of a more elaborate structure, they soon were disillusioned.

Renovating the shed was not a simple matter. First it had to be moved: the police complained that it was too close to the railroad tracks.[137] Anyone crossing from the west side might not see an oncoming train. The CPR agreed that there was potential for a serious accident. They had also leased their property to the government to encourage the building of an immigration shed. Now that it was no longer in use as such, the company wanted the shed relocated and the land returned. The Department of Public Works purchased three lots nearby in block A from John Niblock in May 1892. The building inspector and clerk of works in Winnipeg, D. Smith, was sent out by the department several months later to make arrangements to shift the building and then renovate it. Arriving early in January, he took tenders for the move from local contractors before giving it to Harry Yuill for $475.

The energetic Yuill also got the contract in March for creating a barracks and courtroom in the old hall.[138] Part of the upper floor was kept for the occasional stray settler; the rest held the bunks of the police and private quarters for the sergeant in charge of the detachment. The lower hall was to have a courtroom twenty by thirty feet, two cells, and a mess hall for the Mounties.[139] It cost the government $685.[140] The new courtroom was destined to sit unused for several months. The fall assizes of the court in November was cancelled: there were no cases on the docket. In light of this, the government's decision to convert the shed instead of building a proper courthouse seems eminently reasonable. A year later, again in the fall assizes, there was only one case waiting for the honourable Justice Rouleau.

The citizens of Medicine Hat seemed willing to put up with the makeshift courthouse for the time being. Although Medicine Hat did not lack for civic boosters, they were not well organized. A nascent board of trade was stillborn in 1887, and it was not until 1898 that the town was finally incorporated. Even the local Conservative and Liberal Associations were quiescent. Unlike other towns, the civic elite of Medicine Hat did not pull together effectively to promote their home. Instead the townspeople spent most of a decade divided into two feuding camps over prohibition.[141]

Medicine Hat also did not have good relations with the local MP, Nicholas Flood Davin. Some of the local worthies gave the Regina newspaperman some rough handling at one 1894 town hall meeting over his efforts – or lack thereof – on behalf of the town, including the dearth of public works.[142] His challengers included William T. Finlay, who would later be involved in some electoral shenanigans involving courthouses in Medicine Hat. The customary vote of confidence at the end of the meeting was challenged and voted down, thirty-five to twenty-seven. This was perhaps not calculated to obtain the most conscientious lobbying on the part of Davin.

---

A CASE OF SEDUCTION

"A case which had created a large amount of interest was tried before Judge Macleod on Monday and Tuesday. It was brought by Fanny Small against Donald Walker, the charge being seduction under promise of marriage. It is the second case under the clause of Thompson's [Justice Minister Sir John Thompson] new criminal code which makes it a criminal offence for a man over twenty-one years of age to seduce under promises of marriage, a woman under twenty-one."[143]

It may have been only the second such charge before a court, but it was far from the last. Charges of seduction would become common in the courts of the North-West Territories, and the province of Alberta would produce its own legislation, the *Seduction Act*, which allowed parents of underage girls to sue a seducer for damages. It was the kind of legislation that was seen as very important in controlling moral behaviour, especially the licentiousness of young men, taking advantage of what prevailing opinion of the day saw as the naïveté of young women. But it was not just about morality; it was also a means to prevent the unwelcome social consequences of pregnancy out of wedlock and to ensure that fathers took some fiscal responsibility for their children.

*A frugal Liberal: Honourable J.I. Tarte, Minister of Public Works. NA, PA-13027*

"The greater part of the other evidence is unfit for publication," reported the *Medicine Hat Times*, but the newspaper could relate that Reverend C. Stephens and W.T. Finlay had testified for the "girl's reputation for chastity previous." The courtroom in the shed was full and waited in "breathless silence" as the jury filed back in after two hours of deliberation. The jury pronounced that Walker was "guilty of having promised in June, 1892 to marry Fanny Small and also in November of the same year both previous to seduction but [we] are of the opinion that he then intended to marry the said Fanny Small." Walker's lawyer immediately asked Macleod to reserve judgment so that he could argue before the court en banc in Regina against the justice's interpretation of the statute. Macleod, perhaps uncertain himself about this new law, agreed.

Infighting may have kept Medicine Hat from energetically pursuing a courthouse, but it did not prevent some animosity on the part of the public toward the government about the makeshift quarters in the immigration shed. It boiled over shortly before the 1896 Dominion elections. In August, the News bitterly commented: "About the only thing that the town of Medicine Hat has received in recent years from the Dominion Government in the way of public works is the makeshift courthouse – a combination court room, barracks, immigration hall and lock up."[144] The lack of proper furniture for the courtroom was particularly infuriating: "There is no seating accommodation for a jury, no witness box, no seating accommodation for witnesses, or for court attendants. As a court room it is altogether a shabby outfit."[145]

The townsfolk had a chance to bring the state of the courtroom directly to the attention of Joseph Israel Tarte, the new Minister of Public Works in the government of Sir Wilfrid Laurier. Not long after the election of the Liberals in 1896, Tarte took a tour of the Territories. The minister only spared a half-hour for Medicine Hat, taking advantage of the regularly scheduled stop of the CPR. Arriving on the evening of November 9, Tarte was taken to the courthouse, where he was pointedly shown around the courtroom and judge's chambers.[146] Those present, including the executive of the district's Liberal Association, asked the minister for proper furniture. No fool, Tarte quickly assented. The Hatters also requested that honourable minister provide a land office and a customs office for the town. Assured by

Tarte that the shed would be properly equipped for the court, the local citizenry was placated. As it turned out, they would have an entirely new courthouse sooner than they expected.

## The Territorial Courthouse

Tarte's interrogators could not know that soon the town would have no courtroom at all. One of the greatest dangers to any prairie town in the nineteenth century was fire. Shortly after three o'clock in the afternoon on Friday, May 28, 1897, the constables quartered in the immigration shed realized to their horror that a fire had somehow started under the flooring.[147] A gang of men tried to rip up the floor and get at the flames, but by the time they could come to grips with it, the entire ground storey of the hall was alight. Beating a hasty retreat, the police and their helpers could only watch as the fire leapt to the nearby police stables and Sanderson's Livery Stable. There was not even a volunteer fire department in the town; fortunately the efforts of a makeshift bucket brigade and the presence of a CPR water tower kept the flames from other nearby buildings.

A week later the *News* commented on the wonderful irony when, as promised, the courthouse caretaker received permission from Tarte to buy new furniture. The destruction of the courthouse was a perfect cudgel to back arguments for establishing municipal government. As the *News* pointed out: "We will not get a decent government building in Medicine Hat until the town has some system of fire protection. The government does not insure its buildings, but it makes very rigid enquiries regarding fire protection, etc., before any steps are taken in the way of substantial public works expenditures."[148] Within a year, Medicine Hat was incorporated as a town.

The loss of the immigration shed was a serious one, and the Dominion government could not deny the need to replace it; nonetheless, it took almost three years to do so.

Unknown to the people of Medicine Hat, the government had moved relatively quickly in the aftermath of the fire. The blackened ruin of the old shed had hardly cooled before E.L. Newcombe, the Deputy Minister for Justice, contacted Justice David Lynch Scott in Calgary.[149] He wanted the judge's opinion on the requirements for a new courthouse. Scott was only too happy to forward some specifications. The learned jurist, quite familiar with the assizes at Medicine Hat, requested a courtroom of twenty by thirty-four feet, small rooms for the judge, jury, barristers and witnesses, and offices suitable for a clerk and sheriff and a strong room for storing documents. Scott's suggested building was relatively small, just what the government wanted. Both the Departments of Justice and Public Works felt that a modest building would be ample for the little prairie town. Newcombe passed along Scott's letter directly to the Secretary of Public Works with his support of the judge's suggestions.[150]

Although the plans for a new courthouse were well underway within six months of the fire, the project soon succumbed to the delays that plagued the Territorial courthouses. In part, it was due to all the consultations that had to be carried out. Not only did the Department of Justice have to decide how large a building they needed, the justices of the Territorial court also had to be consulted. This was a wise decision: the judges were the best qualified to estimate the needs of the court, and the ones most likely to complain if the building was not up to snuff. But it meant that plans and suggestions had to be passed back and forth between the two departments and the judges, which quickly ate up months of time, even for a small and simple building like the proposed courthouse. The Justice and Public Works ministries also had to settle between themselves just how much money was to be spent.

The Department of Public Works also had to wait for the money to become available. There does not seem to have been a contingency fund for Public Works to replace a building destroyed in a fire or other natural disaster. Parliament had to make funds available, which meant waiting for the next budget. An appropriation for Medicine Hat was made in June 1898 for the Estimates of the upcoming year, much to the relief of the town.[151] Six thousand dollars was slated for the new building – not an enormous amount, but it promised a much better court facility than the old shed. The Medicine Hat appropriation would also be the start of a surge of more courthouse construction in the Territories.[152] The Minister of Justice, David Mills, had become much more conscious of the lack of facilities in the North-West, at least in part because of the Medicine Hat project. He would announce a new construction program in the fall of 1899. As for Medicine Hat, it would be more than another year before tenders were called. It was an unwelcome and somewhat inexplicable delay. The appropriation for the 1898–99 fiscal year was allowed to lapse; a revote for $4,000 was necessary the following spring to get building started.[153]

Before construction could start, the location of the new courthouse had to be chosen. The department had decided to build it on the site of the immigration shed, on the corner of Main and North Railway Streets. It was, however, still NWMP land. The police had decided to put a new barracks on the property to replace the lost shed, and had actually begun moving some buildings there from Police Point. The residents of Medicine Hat objected strongly. The town wanted to see the courthouse on the main street facing the CPR station, not a barracks building, and were perhaps afraid that there would be even more delays if a new site had to be found.[154] A wire early in April to Tarte from the local Liberal Association stopped construction in its tracks. The police were persuaded to transfer the land to the Department of Public Works, and the barracks was moved to the rear of the block.[155] Tarte's quick response gained him a measure of popularity in Medicine Hat. With word several weeks later that a new appropriation of $4,000 was available and that the Department of Public Works was calling for tenders, the minister was forgiven for any past transgressions, real or imagined. The News was moved to pronounce that "Public Works Minister Tarte is not half as bad a fellow as he is made out."[156]

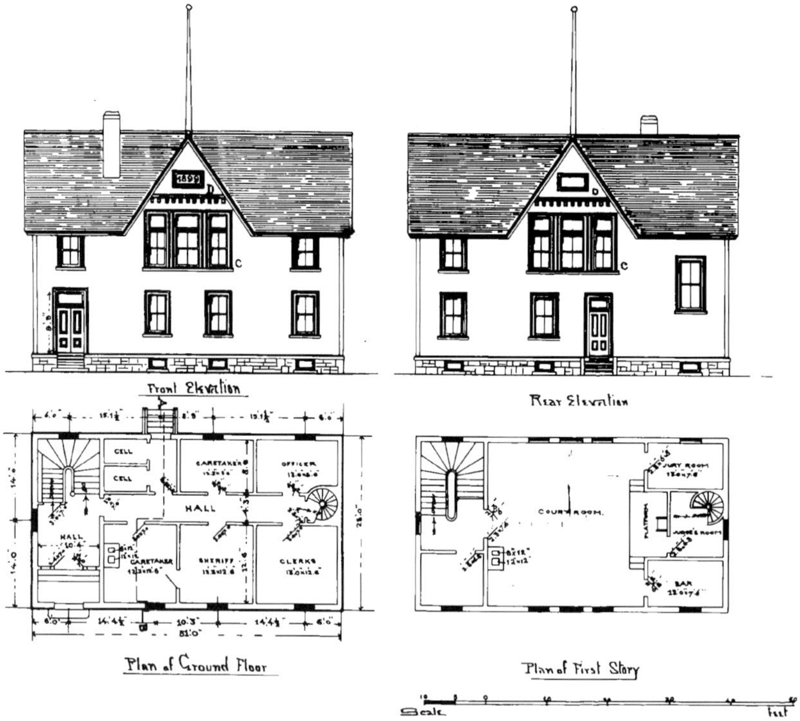


*Elevations and floor plans, Medicine Hat Territorial Courthouse, 1899. NA, NMC45509*

As for the courthouse itself, the building was a modest structure, designed under the aegis of David Ewart, the Chief Architect of Public Works, and most likely executed by one of the subordinate architects on his staff. It was a two-storey, wood frame building on a stone basement, slightly larger than had been initially planned, measuring fifty-one by twenty-eight feet. The main facade faced Main Street, with the entrance offset on the left side. Once inside, visitors could proceed directly up the staircase to the second floor, or turn left down a hallway to the offices. In layout it was very much like the plan that Scott and Rouleau had seen two years earlier, with five offices on the ground floor, a courtroom, judge's chambers, and rooms for the jury and barrister on the first floor. There was a nifty spiral staircase in the plans between the first floor and the judge's room. The extra floor space was put to good use to provide two cells for prisoners awaiting trial. In the absence of sewage service, there were detached latrines out behind. The rectangular, wood-sided building had a gable roof, with a cross gable on the long facade. A date plaque reading 1899 was prominent in the cross gable.

With its gable roof, wood construction and lack of architectural elaboration, the building had a decidedly residential appearance, and there has been a suggestion that it was indeed built with an eye to other uses, once the courts outgrew their modest home. The structure, like the courthouses built earlier at Moosomin and Moose Jaw, was an utterly pragmatic attempt to fill a need without committing the government to a major expenditure. The building was divorced from any of the symbolic elements used to embody judicial dignity. The Calgary and Regina courthouses, although relatively plain structures, were unmistakably public buildings that even untrained eyes might figure for a hall of justice. Not so Medicine Hat. Ewart hoped to use it as a model for other Territorial courthouses. When

Schoolhouse or courthouse? Medicine Hat Territorial Courthouse. MHA, 209.3

the Department of Justice decided to proceed with five more courthouses in 1900, Ewart used the Medicine Hat plan as the basis for the new designs. It was not, however, well received.

As far as the residents of Medicine Hat were concerned, the planned structure was too small, and it was wood, a major point of contention. The courthouse simply was not what the Territorials hoped for. As the *News* pointed out:

> Either a brick building or a stone building gives, we think, a better impression of permanency. To impress upon travellers and visitors the idea of permanency and lasting confidence in the future is as much a duty of the government as the individual ... we are getting over the pioneer idea that anything will do, and are putting up a class of building which are in themselves permanent advertisements of the town and the North-West. The government can well afford to take a leaf out of the people's book, and bank a little on the future as well as upon the present.[157]

Undeterred by criticism, the department proceeded with the courthouse as planned. Only two bids had been received for the building: Charles Purmal, a local builder, was given the contract on his bid of $6,403.30.[158] William Knox of Prince Albert was appointed the clerk of works, a surprising choice, as a local man – usually of the persuasion of the ruling party – was given the position as a rule.[159] Purmal signed his contract on August 2, 1899, and began excavating the foundation on September 11.[160] By December, the building's exterior was nearly finished, and work continued on the interior fixings.[161] In early February the department called for tenders to install the heating, a hot water system that used a coal furnace.[162] The contract was awarded to local hardware dealers Williamson and Macintyre in March. This met with the approval of the News, which noted that all the work on the building had been done by men from the town, reflecting well on government policy and on the quality of the local craftsmen.[163]

Sentiment in the town had not been favourable toward the courthouse, but by the time it was finished, the residents were prepared to make the best of it. The *News* praised the work of the contractors, saying that: "Together they have built us the Court House, which is without doubt the best and most substantial frame building in our town."[164] The shiplap walls were covered in wood siding, and the whole building was painted white. Inside, wood trim and wainscoting of Douglas fir complemented the bronze fixtures and white plaster walls. "People of this district will no doubt appreciate the work of the Department of Public Works in giving Medicine Hat a useful, substantial and ornamental building," the *News* opined; the courthouse was "a credit to the community."[165] Although inclined, as a supporter of the Liberals, to make the best of the situation, the paper still damned the courthouse with faint praise. But it was with some pride the following June that the paper reported the national flag was flying over the courthouse, as the first sitting in the building of the Supreme Court took place, Judge Rouleau presiding.[166]

## Epilogue

The Territorial courthouse in Medicine Hat had an unkind but not unexpected fate. It succumbed to the wrecker's ball in 1969. It came close to being saved, but unfortunately the preservation of historic buildings was not a great priority at the time. An important link to the past was lost, and a significant architectural treasure.

A new provincial courthouse was opened in 1920. No longer needed for the courts, the old Territorial building was immediately put to good use by the Great War Veteran's Association, which leased the building in 1923 from the provincial government as a clubhouse and meeting hall.[167] Several years later, after a squabble with the government over funding for an extension, Premier Brownlee decided to give them the whole building.[168] The province transferred it to the organization for the sum of one dollar on June 12, 1929.[169] A brick addition was built shortly after World War II and expanded in the 1950s.[170] Finally, the organization decided it needed a new, modern building. The Legion was not insensitive to the historical character of their headquarters. They looked into donating the building to Heritage Park in Calgary.[171] It was an excellent idea: the park was an outdoor museum dedicated to preserving Alberta's frontier heritage by obtaining or replicating historic buildings as part of a village on the banks of the Glenmore Reservoir. The courthouse would have fit in well.

In the end, the Legion decided that moving it there was beyond their means, and efforts to find a sponsor for the project were unavailing. Reluctantly, they hired a contractor, Paul Stober Construction, to knock it down.[172] The company began its work on October 6, 1969, and by the end of November, it was gone. The carved date plaque, bearing the legend 1899, was kept and displayed in the Legion's new headquarters.

# FORT MACLEOD

Of the Territorial courthouses built in Alberta, Fort Macleod is the only surviving example. Built between 1902 and 1904 by the Dominion Department of Public Works, the Macleod courthouse remained in service as a court facility until 1971 and witnessed almost sixty-seven years of hearings, trials and litigation. It opened less than a year before the creation of Alberta and Saskatchewan, one of the last halls of justice to be built under the Territorial regime. From the inception of the town of Macleod, the leading citizens had lobbied hard for a courthouse. Their campaigns are the best illustration of the role of the local gentry in obtaining such an edifice for a community. The saga of the Macleod building amply demonstrates the symbolic and practical importance attached to a courthouse by the growing communities of a newly settled land.

## Macleod – The Early Days

The administration of justice in what would become Alberta started at Fort Macleod. After neutralizing Fort Whoop-up, headquarters of the notorious whisky traders, a contingent of the NWMP under Colonel James F. Macleod established a fort further west on the Oldman River in the autumn of 1874, almost in sight of the Rocky Mountains. It was the first outpost of law and order to be found in the region. A small hamlet soon appeared by the fort. The continued presence of the NWMP detachment gave the village an importance out of proportion to its size. The grasslands of southern Alberta and the excellent terms offered by the Dominion government for leasing grazing acreage also attracted many would-be ranchers to the area. The ranching community was a small and scattered clientele, however, and the settlement grew slowly. It did not incorporate until 1892, when the name was changed to Macleod to give the town an identity separate from the police post.

Macleod struggled against a certain amount of adversity. The original townsite on the banks of the Oldman was prone to flooding, so the fort and hamlet moved in 1885 to higher ground. Civic boosters lobbied hard to have the Calgary-Edmonton Railroad extended south to their district, but when the line reached Macleod in 1892, the company did not enter the existing town. Instead it built a station two miles away and surveyed a new townsite, hoping to entice the citizens of the existing village to move. They proved stubborn, and Macleod remained a short wagon ride away from its rail station. Railroads would cause more anxiety in the town a few years later: there were doubts as to whether the Crow's Nest Pass line of the Canadian Pacific would go through Macleod, and the town fought hard to ensure it did. The CPR made Macleod a divisional point, thus ensuring a certain measure of prosperity and stability – although the station remained outside town until 1907.

The boost from the railroad was important. The country around Macleod was not very suitable for farming, and the ranching industry suffered many ups and downs. Changes to government leasing policies ended the age of the vast open range ranches, and Alberta's harsh winters often wiped out struggling ranchers. The worldwide depression of the 1890s injured the cattle industry and reduced new settlement in the district to a trickle. By 1901 Macleod was considerably smaller than both Lethbridge and Medicine Hat, its main commercial rivals in southern Alberta. For more than a decade, there was an air of uncertainty about the future of Macleod. The town responded with some of the most aggressive boosterism to be found in the Territories, which involved every possible civic improvement, including courthouses.

## Macleod and the Courts

From the beginning the courts and the administration of justice was central to the town of Macleod. The fort was not only the base for law enforcement in the region but also the site of the first courts by virtue of its commander's judicial powers. Colonel Macleod was made a Stipendiary Magistrate in 1876, doing double duty when he became Commissioner of the NWMP, and continued on as a judge after retiring from the police in 1880. As Stipendiary Magistrate, Macleod was based in Fort Macleod, although he built a home for himself and his family in nearby Pincher Creek.[173] In 1877 the Territorial Council created the Judicial District of Bow River, a territory that stretched from British Columbia across the southern half of the Territories to past Maple Creek, with the Colonel as the resident judge stationed at Fort Macleod. After the magistrate's courts became courts of record, Charles Edward Dudley Wood of Macleod was made the first clerk of court for the district. Thus the village became the judicial centre for all of southern and central Alberta.

In 1886, the town became the seat of the new Judicial District of Southern Alberta for the Supreme Court of the Northwest Territories. Stipendiary Magistrate Macleod became Supreme Court Justice Macleod, with his jurisdiction now covering the southern portion of the District of Alberta and the eastern precincts of the District of Assiniboia. The town of Macleod had the advantage over other settlements in the Territories of being a judicial headquarters from the beginning, with a resident judge, clerk of court and sheriff, a fact that did not escape the residents of other growing communities like nearby Lethbridge.

## The First Courthouse

As the main base for the NWMP and the headquarters of the region's judge, the court at Macleod was busier than the size of the town warranted. The assizes soon outgrew the police barracks. Throughout the Territories, the magistrates held court in any decently sized room they could find, and sometimes in indecently sized rooms. At Macleod, the judge resorted to using the Methodist church and the local schoolhouse for sittings of the court.[174] Faced with this and other pressing needs for public facilities, the people of Macleod took matters into their own hands. A group of leading citizens formed a joint stock company late in 1885 to provide a town hall, which would be rented for different civic functions.[175] It was a popular idea. The Macleod Improvement Company, as it was named, quickly set to work on their hall, hiring local contractors Scott and Merrill and building on a donated lot on Main Street.[176] By the middle of January 1886 they had a foundation finished. With mild weather, they were able to finish the building by February, despite fierce Chinook winds. As the Gazette remarked of the new hall: "It would blow over bodily before it would break up. It has in fact already stood some to the severest winds we ever experience in this country."[177] The building was twenty-eight by sixty feet, wood-framed and wood-sided, and painted white. The lower room stretched the entire length of the hall, with a movable partition. The upper floor, accessible by an outside staircase, was rented to the Masons for a meeting hall. A piano was installed in the lower hall in anticipation of dances and theatricals.

It quickly became Colonel Macleod's courtroom for the assizes. Whether upon the request of the judge or through the generosity of the Macleod Improvement Company, the lower hall was fitted with railings, a witness box, and other sundries to transform it into a court of high justice for the sitting of April 21, 1886.[178] Judge Macleod must have been pleased to have use of the new hall. The judge and lawyers wore gowns to impart a suitable atmosphere for the occasion. It was a popular event for the townsfolk as well, and the hall was filled with spectators. The improvised space was "unanimously voted about the best courtroom in the territories."[179] It would serve as the town's courthouse for nearly two decades.

It was ironic considering that of all the towns in the Alberta District of the Territories, Macleod was without a doubt one of the most tenacious, even strident, in pursuit of a courthouse. The settlement quickly developed a sense of entitlement as the most important community in the immediate area. Constructing public buildings to reflect this was high on the agenda of the town's promoters. One of the foremost boosters was Charles Edward Dudley Wood, an ex-mounted policeman who founded the town's first paper. Within months of starting its presses in 1882, the Fort Macleod Gazette called upon the Dominion government to provide public buildings for the district, including a post office, a jail, schools, and a courthouse.[180] Charles C. McCaul, one of Fort Macleod's first practising lawyers, suggested a petition for a courthouse in 1884.[181] It was the start of a long campaign for the Gazette and its supporters.

The residents of Macleod had good arguments for a proper courthouse. Once the town had been made the centre for a judicial district, there was a firm conviction that the court must be properly housed. "As the headquarters of the District Court, Macleod is surely entitled to some public buildings. At present there are no offices for the Clerk of Court or Sheriff, no Judges' chambers or Court House."[182] Under such conditions there was always fear for the records of the court, especially from an untimely fire. The clerk's office did catch fire in 1897, and the papers inside were nearly destroyed.[183]

Aside from practical concerns, the dignity of the court was a consideration. As settlement increased and the machinery of justice became more regular, the makeshift facilities that served the NWMP and the stipendiary magistrates were no longer considered adequate to present a proper image for the court. Certainly informed opinion, in the form of the *Gazette*, presented such sentiments. "We are not advocates of wigs, and scarlet and ermine, nor of cocked hats, spurs and javelin men, but we do believe that our Courts of Justice should be held with fitting accompaniments, or at least, should not be brought into contempt."[184] To settlers from eastern Canada or the United States, accustomed to courts housed in imposing buildings with a certain grandeur, the presentation of justice was important, and this sentiment was expressed over and over again in the Territories.

A proper courthouse was also vital to secure the judicial headquarters and court offices for Macleod. The one drawback of being the first and sole judicial headquarters in the Alberta district was that every other town wanted the court officials, including the resident judge. One way to get them was to lobby for additional appointments; another was to get them moved from somewhere else. The townspeople of Macleod spent a great deal of time fending off attempts to have their judge removed. Calgary and Lethbridge were the worst offenders. The former had already vaulted well past Macleod as a place of importance. From a nearly abandoned police outpost in 1882, Calgary fast became the major centre of the region, and the town's growing and politically influential legal community desired Macleod's resident magistrate. It was not long before the Calgary approached the Dominion government to have Justice Macleod moved north. As recounted in an earlier chapter, the two settlements fought a spirited battle that ended in the appointment of Jeremiah Travis to Calgary – a definite victory for Macleod. The construction of the Calgary courthouse late in 1889, however, must have seemed like a defeat. Upstart Calgary now had the fine courthouse Macleod felt was rightfully theirs.

The town soon faced a much greater threat to its position. At the beginning of 1889, nearby Lethbridge began agitating for better court services. Although Lethbridge was already larger than Macleod, it did not have a regular sitting of the Supreme Court. Soon the Lethbridge News was also calling for a courthouse. At first the Gazette offered lukewarm support: "We join with the News in the demand for court buildings in Lethbridge.... But if a necessary building will only be supplied now at one place, that place should be the headquarters of the court, Macleod."[185] The News, under the direction of Wood's former business partner E.T. Saunders, had the temerity to disagree. It claimed Lethbridge obviously had priority for a new courthouse, as Lethbridge had no facilities for the court while Macleod had its town hall.[186] The Gazette retaliated that Lethbridge had much better rooms available than the arrangements in the hall, and reiterated that as the seat of the judicial district, if anyone got a courthouse, it would be Fort Macleod: "Everything is in favour of building a handsome, permanent courthouse at Macleod."[187]

The editorial war continued on into the spring of 1890, with both sides presenting figures to show that their part of the district had the most court traffic.[188] The argument grew nastier, as the citizens of Lethbridge began calling for the removal of the judicial offices to their town, and Macleod retaliated by advocating the local Dominion lands office should join the court. The boards of trade of the respective towns weighed into the contest as well. The citizens of Macleod were shocked and disappointed when the Dominion government approved a public building, including court facilities, for Lethbridge. At least they had the comfort of knowing that Lethbridge was quite unimpressed with its new building.[189]

Another blow followed soon after. The government decided to move Justice Macleod to Calgary to join Rouleau, citing the much greater workload in the Judicial District of Northern Alberta.[190] The removal of their justice confirmed the worst fears of the residents of Macleod, and made a courthouse all the more crucial.

## An Unwanted Courthouse

Macleod was not completely ignored when it came to court facilities. When the citizens of Fort Macleod built their town hall in 1886, they had cheerfully rented it to Justice Macleod, optimistically expecting to see a proper courthouse in the not-too-distant future. In the same round of planning that produced the Lethbridge public building, the converted immigration shed in Medicine Hat, and several small courthouses in Saskatchewan, the Dominion decided to provide more permanent facilities in Macleod by renting the hall outright. It was a move forced upon them by the Macleod Improvement Company, which wanted to lease out the building as shops. Justice Macleod intervened personally, requesting that the Justice Department either rent the old town hall or negotiate an arrangement with the local Oddfellows Lodge, which was about to build a temple and was keen to rent out part of it to the courts.[191] The Department opted for the Improvement Company hall and agreed to lease it in November 1893.[192] Now that it had the whole building, the department renovated it to provide an office for the Clerk of Court, judge's chambers, and a room for the barristers, at last providing some permanent court offices. The town lost its only public hall, and it was the end of dances and theatricals in the building. In an ironic twist, several months later Justice Macleod kindly and with the great gratitude of the town council allowed them to use the courthouse for their meetings.[193]

The hall was never adequate, and its lacks further fuelled the demands for a proper hall of justice. By the time a new century had dawned, the old courthouse had become a scandal to the citizens of Macleod:

> The old court room at Macleod is a thing of beauty and a joy forever. The sign outside the building is very suggestive. One might pass it a hundred times and never notice its inscription for time and age has done their share to despoil the work of art. The Macleod Improvement Co. and such is the nature of the work aspired to by the company within.
>
> The court room proper is a four cornered enclosure much larger than a bed room and ever so much more cheerful(?). It is lighted by five openings in the walls called windows, and the flashes of rhetoric and wit from the 'learned friends.'
>
> Directly in the line of the two doors where any draught of air will surely pass, is thoughtfully arranged the judge's throne ... separating the court proper from the ordinary rabble is a beautiful example of the fence builders' art, hand coloured and strengthened on each side of the centre gate by two supports in natural iron. These are placed so every fourth man who ventures inside the bar on his way to the jury and witness stand trips over them. By that means the witness always manages to swear before he enters the box as well as after.[194]

No town fought so hard as Macleod to obtain a proper courthouse, nor left as good a record of its struggle. It is instructive to examine their efforts in closer detail.

Macleod had a major strike against it. There was a great deal of uncertainty about the future of the town. When the Calgary-Edmonton Railway reached the district in 1892, the company tried to co-opt the town by establishing a new townsite and station several kilometres away. Even Justice Macleod had his doubts about the settlement's long-term prospects. Although the justice did not want to move his judicial seat, he also thought it would be unwise for the government to build a courthouse in the town with the climate of uncertainty.[195] A major problem for the Dominion in responding to demands for public works was deciding which towns in the Territories would actually amount to something and be worth the investment. There was a great deal of scepticism in Ottawa about Macleod. "The position of the town is a very unsettled one ... it must be a matter of grave consideration whether, in view of the construction of the Crow's Nest Pass Railway, the commercial centre of that portion of the Territories may not be moved from Macleod. It must be remembered that Macleod is no longer the seat of a Judge, Judge Macleod's successor, Judge Scott, being located in Calgary."[196] So wrote the Deputy Minister of Justice in 1897. The townspeople of Macleod would have been horrified to know that the very thing they feared – that loss of the judge would mean the loss of the judicial district and a courthouse – was a very real possibility.

If the citizens of Macleod divined the doubts of the Ottawa bureaucrats, it may have simply galvanized them to lobby even more energetically, and they kept at it for almost a decade. The Gazette had been busy with editorials for some time, but in the spring of 1894 a more concerted effort involving the town council and board of trade began. The council first met with MP D.W. Davis, a resident of Macleod, ostensibly on railway issues but also asking him to urge the erection of court building.[197] In November, councillors Grady, Anderson, Barker and Mayor Bleasdell formed a committee "to frame and circulate a petition praying that the Dominion

Government do grant us a Court House and Jail in the Town of Macleod."[198] The petition was circulated to all the nearby villages and towns, such as Pincher Creek, Cardston, and Meadow Creek. This was a tactic that would be used again in the years that followed.[199] The committee was also charged with obtaining letters from Justice Scott, Justice Rouleau, Senator James Lougheed, Frederick Haultain and other political notables, who gave their support to the petition.[200] It was sent to Ottawa early in the new year.

The loss of Justice Macleod was still a fresh wound, and from the beginning, demands for a new resident judge were part of the campaign for a hall of justice. From a practical point of view, the judge was even more important than the courthouse. Macleod's departure caused a great deal of inconvenience in the district. Even though there was still a sheriff and clerk in Macleod, all applications to the judge in chambers either had to go to Calgary, or be presented when he arrived in the south. This caused extra expense and delays for litigants and interfered with the judge's ability to deal with the cases on the docket. Two Macleod lawyers, Harris and Burns, wrote the Lieutenant Governor in September 1894 to complain bitterly.[201] Even the Lethbridge News wanted a judge in Macleod rather than no judge at all.[202]

It quickly became obvious that letters and petitions would not be enough. In 1896, the first of several delegations from the town visited Ottawa. They received many assurances from the government, but no action. A second delegation followed the first in 1897, and then, goaded by Wood and the Gazette, the town organized a third.[203] The four members were all ex-NWMP officers: the redoubtable Wood, now a town councillor; Colin Genge, rancher, contractor and owner of the Queen's Hotel; David J. Grier, also a hotelier, rancher, pioneer wheat farmer and future Mayor of Macleod, and James W. Bell, an Irish rancher who had come to Macleod on the original march west. Grier and Genge were both prominent Liberals: Genge would have the honour in 1909 of being the last Liberal ever elected to the Alberta Legislature for the Macleod constituency.

They set out for Ottawa in January 1898 and arrived on the 24th.[204] The delegates arranged meetings with the Minister of the Interior, Clifford Sifton, as well as the Ministers for Justice and Public Works, David Mills and Joseph Israel Tarte. What they heard was not encouraging. Mills informed them that the Department was unwilling to authorize a resident judge or courthouse without "exceptionally compelling need." Tarte claimed that Parliament was extremely unwilling to spend money on public works at the moment. It was not just empty rhetoric: under the new Liberal administration of Laurier, the amount of money spent on buildings had been drastically curtailed for reasons of economy.[205] Discouraged but not defeated, the delegates took with them the understanding that the needs of Macleod did not loom large in the thoughts of Ottawa's mandarins. Wood, for one, used the trip as a call to arms. A fervent conservative, he swallowed his political partisanship to advocate working with the local Liberal committee in the greater interest of Macleod, and the local Liberals were happy to join the campaign.

With the Liberal association on board, a new strategy was adopted: putting pressure on Frank Oliver, the Liberal MP for the Alberta District. In April 1899, town council wrote Oliver and drew his attention to the many past promises they had received from himself and from Ottawa about the courthouse.[206] Frank Oliver was to prove a good ally for Macleod, despite the town's predilection to support the Conservatives. The town council pestered him mercilessly about the courthouse, but Oliver not only gamely passed on their resolutions to the appropriate ministers, he added his own strong voice on their behalf. He was quick to point out to Mills, the Minister of Justice, that the future of Macleod was much more certain after the completion of the Crow's Nest Pass Railway.[207] At times Oliver must have wondered why he bothered, for he also was on the hot seat every time there was a setback. When a call for tenders in Medicine Hat to build a courthouse was received in May 1899, a terse letter was sent immediately to Frank Oliver: "Why has Medicine Hat [received] a Courthouse and Macleod has nothing in Estimates?"[208] The council promised Oliver a "strongly worded" missive from the Macleod Board of Trade.

In October 1899, another delegation met with Justice Minister David Mills in Calgary.[209] The minister was evasive: he now agreed with the delegates wholeheartedly about the courthouse, but tried to shunt responsibility for the matter to the Department of Public Works. Simple forgetfulness, he told them, an oversight that would be corrected, probably in the next year. The delegates received assurances from Mills that the construction of a courthouse was now imminent. Although the citizens of Macleod might have been sceptical – and with good cause – Mills actually took their demands quite seriously. The constant peppering of letters and petitions and appearance of delegations was having its effect. Despite the brush-off Mills had given the 1898 delegation, he had written not long afterward to Tarte. Citing the amount of legal business and also the incidence of serious crimes in the district, he stated "that in my opinion it would be in the public interest to build a courthouse at Fort Macleod in the North West Territories."[210] Mills came away from his tour of the west in 1899 impressed with how fast things were developing. Besieged by constant requests for courthouses, he decided that it was time his government responded. In another letter to the Department of Public Works he stressed the importance of a courthouse in Macleod.[211]

## The Dream Becomes Reality

After all the years of lobbying, Macleod's turn finally came. The government had decided to go forward with a number of new courthouses in the Territories, and on June 29, 1900 the Gazette could report that "The sum of $5000 appears in the supplementary estimates for a new court house for Macleod."[212] The announcement was a source not of pleasure but of more anxiety for the town. As in Lethbridge back in 1892, the size of appropriation was greeted with some alarm, as it did not promise a very large or impressive building. The anxiety was reinforced when the town was sent plans of the Medicine Hat courthouse as an example of the government's intentions.

The kind of courthouse was just as important as having a courthouse. Macleod wanted as splendid a building as they could get and as they felt they should have. It demonstrates again that the residents of the Territories had strong preconceptions – and expectations – about courthouses. The smaller wooden building in Medicine Hat was not the sort of permanent and imposing building that the citizens of Macleod expected for the courts. The residents, inspired no doubt by Calgary's courthouse, clearly felt that only stone would give a hall of justice an appropriate appearance. The town council and the *Macleod Gazette* repeatedly requested a stone edifice from the Dominion government. Frank Oliver proved a valuable ally in this respect, also urging that the building be more substantial.

Surprisingly, the Department of Justice was of the same mind, despite its desire to keep costs down. David Mills had told the Macleod delegation two years earlier he wanted stone edifices, and had been sincere. He clearly had the same feeling expressed by the residents of the Territory – that courthouses should have a certain monumental quality to bolster the authority of the courts, and this meant stone. On his visit to Macleod, E.G. Conklin of Winnipeg, appointed by the Department of Public Works to look at site for their proposed courthouses, noted – or more likely had his attention drawn to – the abundant supply of sandstone in the area. The local Liberals even went so far as to suggest to him that "the Government should give five hundred ($500.00) dollars towards opening up the quarry on account of the site [of the courthouse] being at no expense to you."[213] To further fan the flames, George W. Dawson, Inspector of Penitentiaries for the Department of Justice, came out to the Territories in the autumn of 1901 to examine the various courthouse and jail sites that had been picked out by the Department of Public Works. Dawson was also a strong believer in stone for public buildings, and strongly advocated the material. He too saw the sandstone outcrops near Macleod, and claimed them "to be much superior to Calgary sandstone."[214] None too discreet, Dawson's opinion was well received in the town.

The Chief Architect's office initially knew none of this. Ewart had thought he would be asked to produce a small and economical building along the lines of Medicine Hat or Moose Jaw, and had sent out a set of plans of the former to Macleod at the request of the Minister of Public Works. The hostile reception given the Medicine Hat plans had not gone unnoticed in Ottawa, and in the fall the Department of Justice formally requested stone for the Macleod courthouse. Ewart's reaction to this sudden change is not recorded, and his staff produced a set of plans by February 1901. The new design was a far cry from Medicine Hat's simple little building. The architect had created an imposing two-storey stone edifice, vaguely Romanesque in style and resembling the Calgary courthouse. It was intended to serve double duty as a jail, with a one-storey wing tucked unobtrusively to the rear. It was everything the citizens of Macleod could desire.

Meanwhile, in Macleod the citizens waited expectantly for the announcement of tenders. The town council kept up the pressure, writing the Ministers of

Justice and Public Works repeatedly asking for plans of the building.[215] There were some promising signs, including requests from the Ottawa for a plan of the town and information about sources of stone.[216] Then the plans of Ewart's stone hall of justice were sent to Macleod in March 1901, and were prominently displayed at the A.Y. Young Stationery and Drug Store.[217] They came courtesy of former mayor A.F. Grady, in Ottawa acting as a delegate of the Macleod Board of Trade.[218] He had gone to discuss the railway situation but took the opportunity to buttonhole the ministers concerned about the promised courthouse. Frank Oliver took him to see the Minister of Public Works and the Chief Architect. Oliver asked Ewart for a copy of the plans, which Grady then mailed to Macleod. They described a two-and-a-half-storey building, with dimensions of seventy-six by ninety-five feet, and Grady was informed that the building was budgeted for $40,000 and that tenders would be called for within two or three weeks. Not only was Macleod going to get its long anticipated courthouse, it would be a true palace of justice.

It looked again as if promises had been made only to be broken. By the summer of 1901, there was still no sign of action on the courthouse. And indeed, through the fall, there was no announcement for tenders. By December, the only activity was the appearance of a departmental underling from Ottawa, who took away samples from the local stone quarries.[219] Suspicion grew that the courthouse was being used as an election sop, and the government had no intention to actually build:

> We were really foolish enough to believe at one time that the government intended to build this court house, but presume we should have known better.... What is the matter with Oliver's pull, by the way. He has been in parliament now for five years, and he has done a considerable amount of talking in the house but we cannot at the moment call to mind that he has done anything yet for Macleod except act as the servant man of the local Liberal committee in getting or trying to get, officials fired, and needy Grits appointed. We shouldn't wonder if the Court House will be kept on ice until the next election comes around, to be dangled to our dazzled vision with the assurance that it will be dropped into our watering mouths – if we are good![220]

The delay had little to do with elections or indeed with Macleod at all. Designing even the modest courthouses intended for the Territories was a slow process, mostly due to the tardiness of the Department of Justice. In the fall of 1900, after being bombarded with queries from Macleod and their parliamentary advocate Frank Oliver, the Minister of Public Works rather testily directed his people to get on with it.[221] The Chief Architect's office, however, was waiting to hear from the Department of Justice as to its requirements for the five proposed Territorial courthouses. Newcombe, the Deputy Minister of Justice, in turn had to ask the Territorial justices for their input, which involved sending out floor plans from the old Moose Jaw courthouse as a possible model for the new buildings and waiting for judicial feedback. It took until the end of October before Newcombe could tell the Chief Architect what his department wanted.

Ewart immediately ran into another snag. His staff could not complete the plans without knowing where the building would be situated and the characteristics of the site. However, the town of Macleod decided that it wouldn't choose a site until it saw the plans. The local Liberal association argued that the town could not decide on a location if they did not know what kind of building to expect. By March 1901, the town had relented and settled on the public square, a block of land that had been reserved in the townsite for civic and other government buildings, as the best spot for a hall of justice. E.G. Conklin visited soon afterward on his tour, and was shown around the town by the executive of the Liberal association.[222] Not surprisingly, he agreed with their choice of the square.[223] Macleod had decided to follow the model of a courthouse square common in North America, a choice that would not be uncontroversial.

One obstacle was removed, but others arose. Once the plans went to Justice, they sat for months awaiting approval.[224] The Minister of Justice decided that he wanted to speak to George Dawson in person before making any final decisions, and the Inspector of Penitentiaries would not return to Ottawa until late in October, too late to realistically start building. Macleod was destined to wait almost another year before construction finally got under way. On February 17, 1902, the Dominion government released the estimates for the coming year, and Macleod received a much increased $12,000 for a courthouse and jail, but there was still no call for tenders.[225] A visit by Frank Oliver to Macleod a few days later threw some light on the cause of the delay. He blamed George Dawson. According to the parliamentarian, Dawson's report had created a monster: "He had very large ideas, and his recommendations and suggestions involved so much more expenditure that ... it probably hung up the whole business."[226]

It must have a bitter pill for the boosters of Macleod to have their building delayed because someone in the government wanted exactly the sort of grand courthouse they desired. It was unfair, however, to pin the blame on the Inspector of Penitentiaries. The Department of Justice had wanted an impressive stone edifice but developed cold feet when it realized how much it was going to cost. Despite pronouncements to the contrary, the department now opted for a cheaper building. Ewart and his staff had to return to their drafting tables

Thus the Department of Public Works was not ready to proceed until the fall of 1902, when new plans were finally completed. After all the years of fuss, the call for tenders was only a small item in the local column of the paper, announcing plans were available from John Ryan, town assessor, and that the competition would close on September 4, 1902.[227] The town had little comment about the award of the contract to Patrick Navin of Cranbrook, British Columbia.[228] An experienced builder, Navin had erected the hospital in his hometown but had also done work east of the Rockies, including the Catholic Church in nearby Pincher Creek. This was not his first or last major government contract. Navin had worked for the department before as the contractor for the post office in Lindsay, Ontario, and later built the Dominion public building in Moose Jaw.[229] Little is known about his tender for the Macleod courthouse and what competition he might have faced, but the lack of any uproar in the town likely means that no local contractors bid on the project. Liberal party stalwart Colin Genge was named the clerk of works. The building would not be finished overnight, and Navin made arrangements to move his family to Macleod from Cranbrook.[230]

With the contract signed and work about to begin, controversy arose again over the site of the building. Although it was more or less accepted that the government square would be used, some residents were aroused when two local Liberals, John Ryan and A.F. Grady, apparently on their own authority, began staking out a spot for the courthouse. An acrimonious town meeting resulted, which said more about the factions among the citizens of Macleod than any pressing issue on the location: the controversy was essentially whether the courthouse should be on the edge of the square or in the middle. The matter was referred to the Department of Public Works, which passed it right back to Frank Oliver. Oliver essentially left it in the hands of Grady, who had precipitated the whole crisis. It left little doubt that the local Liberals were calling the shots.

The town had a further surprise waiting for it: the new courthouse was not going to be the stone hall of justice it had expected. David Ewart, having been instructed to drop the more elaborate stone building, reverted to the Medicine Hat model, but in a more substantial brick version.[231] Ewart described the building in his 1903 annual report:

> On October 8, 1902, a contract was entered into for the construction of this building, which is to be of brick, 2 1/2 stories, with stone dressings and on a stone basement, measuring 56 feet by 43 feet, exclusive of projecting porches. The partitions, floors, roofs and stairs are wood excepting the cell partitions which are brick and the basement floor which is concrete. The ground floor contains 2 vestibules, 2 stairways, a passage, 2 brick vaults, a guard room, a sheriff's office, a clerk's office, a storeroom, a kitchen, 3 cell for prisoners and 3 projecting porches. There are 4 entrances, 1 in front, 1 in rear and 2 on the right side. On the first floor, midlength, is the court room occupying all but 16 feet at either end and extending up into the attic. At one end of the court room are rooms for judge, jury and bar, and at the other end a room for witnesses. In the attic the space at the rear of the court room is finished as a spare room.[232]

One major change, suggested by Dawson in his report, was the elimination of the jail wing. Cells were retained in the new design, but they were not for prisoners serving their sentence; they were meant only for holding defendants for trial.

The new design was certainly dressier in brick than the frame version in Medicine Hat. Compared to contemporary courthouses in eastern Canada, however, it was still a utilitarian building with little architectural decoration.[233] It resembled some of the smaller post offices produced by the Dominion government. It did not any strong pretensions to a distinct style, using some basic elements of several then current. The cross gable roof, with decorative brick corbelling under the some of the eaves, gave it a domestic appearance with a passing resemblance to the Queen Anne Revival style.[234] The utilization of Queen Anne elements was uncommon in public buildings, but not unheard of, especially for town halls in smaller centres.[235] The Macleod building, however, eschewed the picturesque elements seen in most Queen Anne buildings for a formal symmetry of the elevations and the solid projecting porch that helped proclaim it a public building, imparting as well a sombre quality more suited to its purpose.

*A booster's dream: front elevation, Macleod Territorial Courthouse. NA, C148375.*

The Romanesque treatment of the second floor windows, which opened into the courtroom on the side elevations, enhanced the formal quality of the building. The four windows on the facade and the three on each side were each topped with a brick arch with radiating voussoirs, blind on the front windows. Missing were the classical decorative elements common to public buildings of the period. The main entrance had a basic porch, with an arch over the door and a minimal cornice and entablature the only features. The two entrances on the east side had projecting porches with gable roofs and pediments. Sandstone was used extensively for simple decoration. The windows had sandstone sills and lentils, while the exterior walls had several stone courses. It was an edifice with few affectations, which, perhaps not incidentally, also meant it was cheaper and easier to build. And while a substantial and attractive building, it was not really what the residents had had in mind for a courthouse.

The Macleod building was very much the result of trying to reconcile conflicting aims. On one hand, once the stone courthouse had been abandoned, Ewart had been instructed "to prepare plans for [a] cheap or inexpensive building."[236] On the other hand, when he did, it was immediately suggested that "the exterior of the courthouse be modified so that the building might look more impressive," which is exactly what Newcombe said when presented with a new set of plans in the spring of 1902.[237] Even as the Macleod courthouse was being conceived, talk of autonomy and provincial status was in the air. The resemblance of the courthouse to a school may not have been accidental. The department, as one historian suggests, may have looked upon the Territorial courthouses as temporary, and therefore built them in a style that might be more easily adaptable to other uses.[238]

A last-ditch effort was made to rescue the palatial stone courthouse. Just before the spring construction season of 1903, the Gazette encouraged its readers to lobby the government.[239] The indefatigable Frank Oliver protested the use of brick and tried to persuade Public Works by writing the minister. The decision,

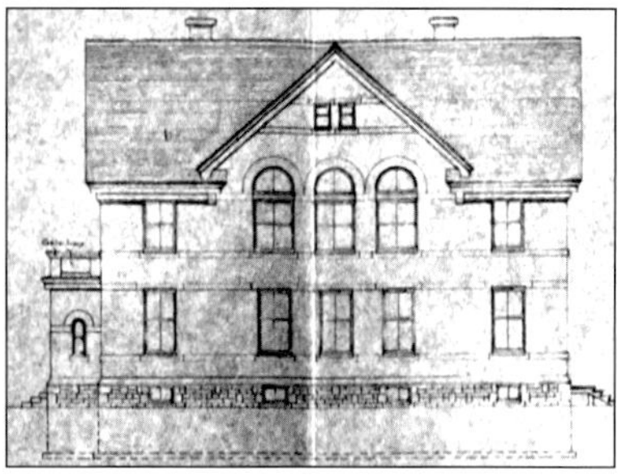

Macleod Territorial Courthouse, c. 1903. NA, C148377

however, was immediately referred to Ewart. The Chief Architect held firm. "I have already reported on this matter to the effect that I did not consider it advisable to depart from the plans and specifications as per contract."[240] With those words the matter was closed.

C.E.D. Wood left Macleod in 1903, selling the Gazette to interests that backed the Liberal party.[241] Navin was allowed to start his contract in peace, and in April 1903 he began work on the concrete and sandstone foundation. Both Genge and Navin were probably happy not to have the Gazette watching their every move, for construction was not trouble-free. A sudden snowstorm in May destroyed stockpiles of bricks waiting for the kilns and led to a shortage, delaying work on the superstructure considerably.[242] Navin also found that the highly touted local sandstone crumbled too easily and could not be used for the trim on the building. He had to make a trip to Calgary and ship stone down to Macleod. At this news, there was likely considerable relief in the Chief Architect's office that the stone courthouse had been cancelled. In August, there were some difficulties over the roofing. The town of Macleod had declared a fire limit that encompassed the business thoroughfares and also the courthouse site. All buildings within the limit had to conform to what was considered "fireproof construction," and the wood shingles specified on the law courts did not qualify. Painted steel shingles were used instead.

Navin had turned out to be fairly reliable contractor. There were major drawbacks to having planning for federal buildings centralized in Ottawa, especially when building in the Territories. The architectural staff rarely had the benefit of actually seeing the sites of buildings, and although emissaries from Public Works, including assistant architects, might perform tours to inspect works in progress, these were few and far between. Ewart had himself visited Macleod, but over a decade previously. During construction, the department depended on the clerk of works to keep things on track, but they were political appointees and not always reliable. Genge was reprimanded early on for not filing monthly reports. When Navin quoted what Ewart considered a very high price for galvanized steel shingles for the roof, the Chief Architect was instantly suspicious. After he decided on painted shingles, Ewart pressed the minister for quick approval: "I recommend that they be authorized, so as not to delay the work and give the contractor excuse for claims on account of delay."[243] Ewart's fears were groundless. The roofing was one of the few problems the department had with Navin, who would stand in stark contrast to the contractors for the nearly identical Red Deer courthouse.

Once the courthouse was open, little more remained to be said. The edifice cost almost $24,000.[244] The Gazette gave a very critical reception:

> This was the first session of court in the new building, and while it has been known all along that the building was frightfully mis-planed [*sic*] it was most fully recognised Tuesday morning. Barristers' room all crowded, main room so completely full that there is really no room for an advocate to cross the floor with out disturbing

> all others, Clerk hemmed in so that one must reach over two tables to pass documents or almost interrupt Court to speak with him. The worthy sheriff stuck on the end of a platform so narrow that the utmost caution is required in order not to fall off. It's all too bad, It would have been much easier to have built the rooms larger and less of them.[245]

*More imposing: Macleod's larger brick version of the Medicine Hat design. NA, PA-53102*

Not much was said about the building by other journals of the day; the *Calgary Herald* dwelt on the first court appearance of Justice Harvey, but made no remarks about the debut of the courthouse.[246] Predictably, the *Lethbridge News* had no comment at all. As for the judges and lawyers, there was nothing recorded in the way of praise or criticism of the building. One may conjecture that after years of visiting the makeshift offices of the sheriff and clerk, attending the judge in his hotel room for chambers, and conducting trials in the cramped and dingy confines of the old town hall, the legal community of Macleod was not complaining.

## SHERIFFS AND CARETAKERS

One of the more contentious issues about courthouses in the Territorial Period was who had authority over them. Built and maintained by the Department of Public Works, they were used by Department of Justice. It took some time to settle who actually controlled the courthouse from day to day. Much of fighting was between the caretakers, who were employees of Public Works, and the sheriffs, appointees of the justice ministry.

Superficially, the matter was quite simple. Up to 1899, the Department of Public Works controlled the buildings. At that point, the two ministries decided that the sheriff, as the senior administrative official of the court, should have authority over the building and its uses and the caretaker would take direction from him. The reality was more complex. The building caretakers were sometimes surprisingly prominent members of the community, who got the jobs through their political connections, and frequently did not like taking orders from the sheriff. Both the sheriff and the local bar also had a tendency to treat the caretakers like lackeys. The Territorial Law Society requested that caretakers look after the law libraries in the courthouses, but also suggested that they should act as messengers while court was in session.[247] The Department of Public Works was willing to let them assist judges, but decided that it was just a bit beyond the pale to allow the local lawyers to use their employees as clerks and message boys.[248] There were also the judges to consider. They tended to think they had final say in the courthouses and sometimes had odd ideas. Justice Scott, who was a bit of a dandy himself, insisted the caretaker in the Edmonton courthouse should have a special uniform. However, the caretakers were not just janitors; they were more like building superintendents. Among other duties they were in charge of the heating of the buildings, which was a sizable responsibility. The Department of Public Works considered them valuable employees charged with ensuring the courthouses were kept in good repair.

Nowhere was the problem more acute than in Macleod. Duncan J. Campbell, the sheriff, was a prickly sort who had a strong sense of his prerogatives. John Ryan, appointed caretaker for the old courtroom and continuing on in the new courthouse, was a local Liberal who had been the town assessor and also the caretaker for the town hall. He, of course, had a starring role in the courthouse site controversy. The two never got along. Campbell complained many times that Ryan was not doing his job properly and did not keep the court building in proper condition. Matters reached a head shortly after the new courthouse was finished. In December 1904, Campbell sent a letter to the Deputy Minister of Justice. In it he complained that Ryan was "insolent and uncooperative," and refused to take orders on the grounds that the sheriff had no authority over the courthouse.[249] He also noted that Ryan had been dismissed from his post as town assessor for "impertinence." A big bone of contention was the care and cleaning of Campbell's own office and his inability to get into the building after hours.

The matter ended up on the desk of David Ewart. He was quick to remind his employee "that it is your duty, as Caretaker of the Building, to be as polite and gentlemanly to the public and to the officers, as it is possible to be."[250] At the same time, he gave Ryan a chance to answer the charges against him, and regarded some of the sheriff's complaints as trivial: "As regards the caretaker attending to your ink bottle, pens, etc, I do not think he has anything to so with such matters."[251] Part of the problem remained the vagueness of the sheriff's powers. Ewart asserted that Ryan's duties were not the concern of the sheriff, and if the latter had any complaints about the maintenance of the building, they were to be passed along to the Department of Public Works through the usual channels. As far as the Chief Architect was concerned, Campbell had complete authority as to the proper use of the building, but not the ability to order the caretaker to look after it. That was the Chief Architect's prerogative. To Campbell this meant he had no authority at all, and he said as much when complaining again in the spring about the state of his office.[252]

The feud between Ryan and Campbell was never resolved. The province of Alberta adopted a similar policy toward the control of courthouses, although the final authority of the sheriff and Department of the Attorney General eventually became accepted. This didn't help Campbell. His rival died soon afterward, but much to the sheriff's chagrin, Ryan's son William was hired in his place.

## Epilogue

It was not long before there were calls to replace the Macleod courthouse. The Dominion transferred the building to the province of Alberta in 1906 pending purchase. There was hope in the town that there might be a new courthouse in the not-too-distant future, hope fuelled by comments of the provincial public works minister and other government officials. The Attorney General's office was none too impressed with the facility it had inherited. On a 1908 visit, the Inspector of Legal Offices, A.Y. Blaine, did not mince words: "The Court House is a very poorly planned Building, and a great deal of space is wasted. I should think that the most satisfactory way of dealing with the matter would be to erect an addition to the Court House...."[253] The inspector recommended, at the very least, major changes to the existing floor plan. Prospects for a new building ended in 1910, when Alberta bought the existing courthouse outright for the sum of $27,807.29.[254] It was clear that while Macleod remained a convenient headquarters for a judicial district, the volume of court business did not merit a new building immediately or likely in the near future.

Some changes were needed to keep the courthouse useful. On the building's tenth anniversary the department undertook some limited renovations. J.S. Lambert, a Macleod contractor (and future mayor) was hired to install a safe and

*Civic function: Blood First Nation at Macleod Courthouse to meet Prime Minister Laurier, 1911. Glenbow Archives, NC10-29*

convert the building to natural gas from coal and update the boilers.[255] After contemplating eliminating the judicial district of Macleod altogether – much to the alarm of residents – the government reluctantly decided on a major renovation in 1924. Although stopping short of an addition, some extensive interior modifications were made.[256] Space was increased for the law library, maintained by the local benchers of the Law Society. The quarters for the judges, the witnesses and the lawyers were expanded. The lavatory was moved on the main floor to the rear of the building, with a new office for the district judge next to it. A vault and a small cell adjoining the clerk's office were removed, and the space devoted to the library. The department carried out the changes with local labour under the supervision of the provincial architect. It was the last major renovation the courthouse would see for the next fifty years.

Macleod remained a sleepy cowtown between the wars, but as in the rest of Alberta, the booming economy of the 1950s brought new life to the district. The provincial government now had the funds to look at some much-needed infrastructure. In 1963, the construction of a new courthouse for Macleod was put in motion. The Calgary architectural firm of Beatson Stevens was commissioned late in 1964 to design a $150,000 building, including courtrooms for the Supreme Court, the District Court, and the Police Court.[257] Arrangements were made for the town of Fort Macleod to buy the territorial courthouse for a dollar. More historically minded than many locales, the town wanted to renovate it for use as a town hall or a museum, a not uncommon use for decommissioned courthouses. Macleod, however, remained low on the list of priorities. It was not until 1970 that Gillette

Construction broke ground for a new structure, now designed by David Kehoe of Calgary.[258] The new one-storey building was placed unobtrusively to the east of the original courthouse. A simple, modern design, the only reference it made to the Territorial building was the brick facade.

The Territorial courthouse saw its last sitting of court on May 14, 1971. In October the new courthouse opened for business with a sitting of the Supreme Court, Justice A.J. Cullen presiding.[259] The business of the court was a far cry from the days of Horace Harvey. Instead of dispensing frontier justice to cattle rustlers, Cullen considered several motor vehicle accidents and two divorce cases, and remanded two defendants on charges of breaking and entering. Happily, the old courthouse became the town hall for Fort Macleod. With almost no exterior modifications or renovations, it has continued in this role right up to the present. Declared a National Historic Site in 1982, it preserves an important part of the heritage of Alberta.

*Civic function: dedicating cenotaph, 1922. Glenbow Archives, NA3251-16*

# EDMONTON: THE COURTHOUSE THAT NEVER WAS

Edmonton presents one of the puzzles around Territorial courthouse construction. It was always the second city of the Alberta District after Calgary, the centre of a vast hinterland that stretched into the far northern reaches of the Territories. Yet Edmonton never saw a courthouse, a case of stunning neglect for a town that in 1891 had over two thousand residents and was the oldest, if not the most populous settlement in the Territories. The mystery is deepened by the fact that from 1896 onward, the MP for the Alberta District was none other than Frank Oliver, Liberal, publisher of the Edmonton Bulletin and booster extraordinaire. Oliver was accused more than once in his political career of favouritism toward the north and the town he made his home. Yet as Lethbridge, Macleod, and even little Red Deer received halls of justice, Edmonton made due with inadequate rented quarters that raised the ire of judges and lawyers alike.

To a certain extent, the citizens of Edmonton were authors of their own loss. The town made a conscious decision to focus their energy on civic improvements other than a courthouse. There was never the kind of organized campaign, bringing together civic government, business and legal interests, and the local political bosses that was seen elsewhere. Ironically, the need for a courthouse was not lost upon the Dominion government. When the Departments of Justice and Public Works decided at the dawn of the twentieth century to provide better accommodations for the courts in the Territories, Edmonton was there on the list. The town of that era never saw its hall of justice built, but once again, it was due to local circumstances.

## Edmonton – The Early Days

Edmonton has claim to being the oldest settlement in the province. The fur traders of the Hudson's Bay Company had established an outpost on the banks of the North Saskatchewan River in 1795. The first Edmonton House was built near modern Fort Saskatchewan, a stone's throw away from Fort Augustus, run by the rival Northwest Company. After the supply of local firewood ran out, both companies abandoned their original trading posts in 1802 for a more defensible spot upstream. The Northwest Company and Hudson's Bay amalgamated in 1821, and so did their Edmonton posts. By 1867, the year of Confederation, Edmonton was the largest and most important settlement in Alberta, with a permanent population of perhaps 150 souls.[260]

As a trading post of the Hudson's Bay Company, Edmonton was to some degree an outpost of law and order, but the company was never successful as an enforcer of the peace, being first and foremost interested in commerce. The arrival of the North West Mounted Police established the proper observance of the law. On

October 27, 1874, "A" Division under Inspector Jarvis arrived at Edmonton House after a harrowing journey from the south. The police did not stay beyond their first winter and erected Fort Saskatchewan downstream from Edmonton. It was a more strategic location, where the banks of the river were lower and therefore a possible crossing point for a rail line. Rumour had it that Jarvis and the Hudson Bay factor, Richard Hardisty, had not enjoyed each other's company that winter.[261] It meant that the nearest police presence was some twenty miles away from the settlement.

With the arrival of government railroad surveyors in 1872, the settlement's destiny appeared to be certain. It was on the original route of the Canadian Pacific Railway, and would be one of the major cities of the North-West Territories, perhaps soon to rival Winnipeg. Shock and consternation followed when the CPR chose the southern route through the Rocky Mountains over Kicking Horse Pass. The tiny hamlet and dilapidated police fort of Calgary suddenly took centre stage and grew by leaps and bounds, largely at the expense of Edmonton. When the expected rush of settlers did not materialize after the completion of the CPR, Edmonton suffered more than the south. The ranching industry provided a boost to Calgary, while the superior agricultural land of the parkland of central Alberta remained mostly unsettled. The village, with a population of around three hundred, stagnated until the middle of the 1890s and the Klondike Gold Rush. When a rail line was completed to Edmonton from Calgary in 1891, instead of crossing the North Saskatchewan River, the railroad established a rival town, Strathcona, on the south bank.

Despite the CPR setback, Edmonton was still destined to become an important city. It was the gateway to the north, it still played a role in the fur trade, and it became the heart of a rich agricultural district. By the turn of the century, while not quite yet challenging Calgary's commercial predominance, Edmonton was not far behind. While Calgary had over four thousand souls, Edmonton and Strathcona together could account for almost three thousand.[262] Yet Edmonton continued to wait for a proper courthouse, and waited even as much less populous centres such as Medicine Hat, Fort Macleod and Red Deer received permanent structures from the Dominion government. The neglect of Edmonton was inexplicable.

## Edmonton's First Courtrooms

With the arrival of the NWMP, the machinery of justice was established in the region, if not at Edmonton proper. Jarvis was a justice of the peace by virtue of his rank and three Stipendiary Magistrates had been appointed for the Northwest Territories. The nearest was Hugh Richardson, appointed in 1876 and based in Battleford. From here, he travelled on circuit to Edmonton, holding his first court in the area in late 1877.[263] Edmonton became part of the Judicial District of Saskatchewan. Judge Charles Borromee Rouleau replaced Richardson at Battleford in 1883.[264] Judge Macleod would sometimes make the long journey north from his district in southern Alberta, as did Judge Jeremiah Travis during his short tenure as the fourth magistrate, based in Calgary.[265] After the Riel Rebellion and the sacking

*Cramped quarters: Edmonton's first schoolhouse and sometime courthouse, 1882. PAA, B3894*

of Battleford, Rouleau went to Calgary. When the Supreme Court of the North-West Territories was organized in 1887, Edmonton was placed in the Judicial District of Northern Alberta. The learned Justice Rouleau remained Edmonton's judge, but only on circuit from Calgary. Edmonton did not receive a resident judge. Nor was the town high on the list for a courthouse: while Calgary received a substantial sandstone edifice in 1890, there was no move to build anything comparable in the north.

Early Edmonton had much the same problems as other hamlets in the Territories in finding a place to hold the court assizes. For one visit by Justice Richardson in 1881, the Chief Factor Richard Hardisty kindly lent the use of his sales room at the Hudson's Bay post the session.[266] Visits by a magistrate were, however, few and far between, much to the annoyance of the community. Despite the infrequent assizes, finding a place for the court remained a problem, and Hardisty's generosity could not always be counted on. In November 1881, future Edmonton mayor Matthew McCauley decided the hamlet needed a permanent school and teacher and organized a private subscription to raise the money. Keenly aware of the lack of any public facilities in the area, the organizers intended the structure to serve as a hall for dances, meetings, and as a place for the assizes of the district court. The first sitting of Judge Richardson in the schoolhouse took place on June 15, 1882. It was a mutually beneficial arrangement: the school struggled until the Territorial government started providing funding with the School Act of 1885. The court paid a rent that was very useful.

### FIRST TRIAL IN THE SCHOOLHOUSE – THE NOTORIOUS SQUATTER CASE OF 1882

One of the most famous stories of early Edmonton involved a squatter and a little vigilante justice, and ended up before Magistrate Richardson in the little schoolhouse. By 1882, more and more people were coming to Edmonton, and as the area had not yet been surveyed, many grabbed land wherever they wanted. This upset the previous residents who could not yet get title for land they had claimed for years. One squatter, Joseph Bannerman, built a shack on land belonging to the Methodist mission of the McDougalls. A group of leading citizens, including Mathew McCauley and Frank Oliver, decided matters had gone too far, and paid Bannerman's shack a visit at the end of February.[267] They picked it up and put it on sleds, dragged it over to the escarpment overlooking the river, and pitched it over the bank. An outraged Bannerman sued them, and it came before Richardson at the assize in the summer of 1882.

The judge decided that the matter merited a jury trial. The six defendants pleaded not guilty, and both they and the plaintiff represented themselves. The defence of the six was straightforward: they did not deny throwing the shack down the bank, they simply argued that they were within their rights. McCauley had an understanding with the McDougalls over the use of the land; he had warned Bannerman that he would remove the shack, and the latter had got his just deserts. Richardson's charge to the jury dwelt on the law in regards to rights of ownership, and concluded that until an owner was legally dispossessed, under common law one had to right to forcibly resist encroachment. Not surprisingly, the jury hastened to agree and found for the defendants.

As more settlers came to the region, however, teaching and judging could no longer coexist. Although the court only sat in Edmonton three times a year, classes had to be cancelled to accommodate the court schedule. More importantly, the grant from the Territorial government was calculated on the basis of the number of days that students were in school. The board trustees, deciding they lost more money cancelling classes than they made in rent, gave the court its notice in October 1886.[268] Edmonton's first school and sometime courthouse still survives. Sold in 1904 when replaced by the McKay School, the original building was moved and converted into a five-room bungalow. Rediscovered decades later, it was bought by the city of Edmonton in 1980 and restored to its original site and condition.

Ejected from the school, the court led an itinerant existence. The Supreme Court of the North-West Territories was inaugurated at Edmonton in the Stewart and Bannerman general store on May 14, 1887, Justice Rouleau presiding.[269] Two years later, Rouleau was holding his court in a room above Ross's Saloon.[270] While it was not calculated to enhance the prestige of the court, litigants may have found this convenient, especially the losers. Surprisingly, the makeshift and undignified quarters of the court, and the obvious need for new facilities, did not create the immediate public outcry seen elsewhere in the Territories, nor did the fact that

Edmonton had not been given a resident judge in the reorganization of the courts, only a deputy sheriff and clerk.

## Distractions

Edmontonians had something else on their minds: railroads. Getting a rail connection to the CPR's main line was of the highest importance to the town and absorbed the energy of local boosters. The local board of trade was formed in 1889 to assist in the endeavour. After the Calgary and Edmonton Railway Company was formed in 1890, there was a move to incorporate the village as a town, with the aim of increasing its bargaining clout with the railway.[271] Shortly thereafter, Edmonton got its wish. In 1891 the Calgary and Edmonton railway was completed, and although the town was not on the main CPR line, there was now a regular rail service to the district. There was one small catch: the railroad stopped on the other side of the river, across from Edmonton.

It was abundantly clear that the town's next priority was a bridge to ensure its businesses were not cut off from the rails. The campaign for a traffic or rail bridge was prosecuted vigorously for the next seven years. There can be no doubt that the same energy spent in Macleod or Lethbridge pursuing a courthouse was expended in Edmonton on the bridge. A proper domicile for the court may have been a valuable symbol of permanence and stability in a frontier community, but in Edmonton's case, getting the rails across the river was vital to the town's continued well-being.

In fact, it was felt in some quarters that any lobbying for a courthouse might jeopardize the bridge. Nicholas D. Beck, crown prosecutor, town solicitor and future provincial Supreme Court Justice, reminded his audience of this at a public meeting with the Honourable T. M. Daly in Edmonton during the summer of 1893. Along with the matter of a resident judge, the subject of a courthouse came up. Beck had done some backroom lobbying for a courthouse, speaking directly to Sir John Thompson, Conservative Minister of Justice, in 1892. He had not pursued the subject more aggressively "because he felt the question of the bridge should come first, and feared that if the court house was pushed too much, it might retard both."[272]

Even when public buildings did appear on the town's agenda, what the residents wanted first and foremost was a land titles office. A temporary office had been located in Edmonton, but there was some suspicion that the government was going to move it across the river to the rail terminus. Edmontonians became agitated when the permanent building promised by the government still had not appeared by early 1892. As the Bulletin commented: "If there is a delay ... it will prove that someone is working against us in this matter and will be all the more reason why we should be on the alert and active to protest our best interests as a town."[273] It proved a remarkably accurate prediction. The Dominion government tried to move the office to Strathcona in June 1892. It prompted a riot: an armed mob of townsfolk seized the effects of the office and faced down a detachment of Mounties sent to restore order. To ensure the office would stay, a permanent building in Edmonton for the offices was deemed of the utmost importance. The fight over the land titles office soured Edmonton's relationship with the Dominion and left a lingering suspicion of the government's motives in the town

In all the controversy, the courthouse was pushed aside. The matter of a courthouse would not to surface again until the low level bridge was finally begun in 1899.

## Robertson Hall

The town had decided a courthouse was not the most pressing issue at hand, but the judge still needed a place to do his work. Deputy Sheriff Walter Scott Robertson jumped in to fill the gap. Like some of the other early sheriffs and clerks of court in the Territories, Robertson was an entrepreneur first and an officer of the law second. Robertson farmed, ran a general store in partnership with Macdonald and John Cameron, and dealt in real estate and insurance. One of his speculative ventures was Robertson Hall.

Much like the school, the hall was built to serve a number of purposes. Constructed by local contractor A.F. Degagne, the building was a modest forty-five by sixty-five feet, two storeys high, wood framed and sided.[274] With two stores on the ground floor, the entire second storey was given over to combined theatre and ballroom. It was equipped with a stage, raised four feet, and two small dressing rooms. A proscenium arch was later added, with a curtain and scenery backdrop imported from Chicago.[275] It even had a small gallery that could seat twenty. The entrance was up an outside staircase from the street. The main hall could accommodate up to five hundred. It immediately put Edmonton on the map for touring theatre companies. Dances were regularly held in the building, and within days of its completion in September 1892, a grand ball was held in support of Edmonton's athletic teams. With an interior painted in blue, white, and gold, the hall was lauded for its "bright and pleasing appearance."[276]

The hall was soon put to use as courthouse. On May 8, 1893, Justice Rouleau held the Supreme Court in the building.[277] The Dominion Department of Justice paid a fee of five dollars for each sitting of the court, apparently not seeing any conflict of interest on the part of Sheriff Robertson.[278] By day, a different kind of drama would be played out in the hall. The court was itself a form of diversion from the drudgery of frontier life, and what better place for it than the town's opera house?

## THE TRIAL OF WILLIAM BELL

The first assize of the Supreme Court in Robertson Hall presented a trial guaranteed to pique the interest of the townsfolk. Regina vs. William Bell on the charge of manslaughter led off the criminal docket on May 12, 1893.[279] It was a case of frontier justice meeting the law of the Queen. William Bell was part of an armed posse hunting for a man named Mickelson near Red Deer. Mickelson was wanted for a murder that had been committed in Strathcona a few days previously – an American named Skaadunt had been shot and robbed and the evidence pointed toward the victim's companion, Mickelson. He was spotted walking along some railway tracks by a neighbour of Bell, who sounded the alarm. A group of local farmers went after Mickelson. He was found by his pursuers four miles from Red Deer, armed to the teeth. Ordered to halt, Mickelson ran instead and a pitched gun battle broke out. The eight-man posse somehow managed not to shoot each other in the melee and killed Mickelson. The inquest into the shooting decided that Bell was responsible for the fatal bullet. He was charged with manslaughter and committed to stand trial in Edmonton, the closest assize.

Sidney S. Taylor, as counsel for the defence, argued that in common law the "hue and cry" gave the posse the authority of a magistrate's warrant, and that Bell had a duty to apprehend the suspected felon. Shooting him became justifiable homicide when Mickelson refused to surrender and clearly intended to violently resist arrest. Taylor was very confident in this argument. When he pointed out to the jury that it had not been absolutely proven that Bell had fired the fatal shot, he told the six good men *not* to acquit him on those grounds, because Bell had been within his rights to shoot Mickelson. As the *Bulletin* related: "He pointed out that it would be an extraordinary state of the law that would punish any well thinking citizen for upholding with his best endeavors [sic] his country's laws and bringing a murderer to justice"[280]

Rouleau spoke strongly against the lynch mob in his charge to the jury, reminding them that there was a proper authority for enforcing the law. He did, however, agree that the dead man had been a dangerous character, and also raised the possibility of reasonable doubt that Bell had killed Mickelson. It was very clear to the jury; they took hardly a minute to come to a verdict of not guilty.

*Judicial landlord: Edmonton Sheriff Walter Scott Robertson. PAA, B3891*

The court did not exclusively use Robertson Hall. On some occasions it would use the town council chambers in the fire hall.[281] The need for proper fire protection prompted the construction of the building in 1894. With good frontier pragmatism it was fitted with a room for council meetings and an office for the town clerk, and served as the town hall until the Civic Building was completed in 1913. When Robertson Hall was not available, the court might sit in council chamber, as happened in 1898. After the town set up a police court in 1900, presided over by Magistrate Cowan, it usually sat in the fire hall. On at least one occasion, the court had to scatter when the firemen scrambled to respond to an alarm.[282]

Robertson Hall may have been available but was hardly satisfactory as a courtroom. Among other deficiencies, there were no permanent offices for the court officials, which had to be rented elsewhere. Alex Taylor, the deputy clerk, kept his records in his office as the postmaster. Local advocate Sidney Taylor complained bitterly about the hall and gave a vivid description of its inadequacies in a letter to the Deputy Minister of Justice in 1896, calling it: "… simply a hall where entertainments and dances are held, is very cold and has no Barristers room, Jury room or any thing of that nature, except by use of the stage and this is extremely cold ... the building is very noisy and frequently the Judge has to stop the work of the Court and order the Constable to go down and stop the noise…."[283] Nicholas Beck, the crown prosecutor, sent a similar litany of complaints to the department.[284]

Taylor tried assiduously to interest the government in renting space in a new business block he was building, an endeavour in which he had the support of Senator James Lougheed, Justices Rouleau and Scott, and Beck. Robertson was quite aware of Taylor's plans, and made his own offer to renovate the hall as deemed necessary – the extra income from renting the hall to the court was clearly important to the sheriff.[285] In the end, Robertson need not have worried: Taylor's offer was deemed too expensive. The Department of Justice was excessively cost-conscious and didn't even want to buy Rouleau office furniture: "Edmonton is not the seat of a judge and I should suppose that there would be no necessity for buying a desk and chair for the judge's chamber."[286] In such a climate, it is hardly surprising Edmonton remained without a courthouse.

## The Resident Judge

As with every thriving town in Alberta, Edmonton desperately wanted its own judge. Although Edmonton was the second city of the region after Calgary, it remained part of the Northern Alberta Judicial District, and depended on the services of the justice at Calgary. The trip north by stage, however, was long and arduous and easily delayed by bad weather. Once the two cities were linked by rail in 1890, travel was expedited, but as Edmonton and region grew, the state of the courts remained a burning issue.

Rumours circulated in 1893 that a new district was to be created, with a boundary around Innisfail and its headquarters most likely in Edmonton.[287] Nothing immediately materialized, but over the next year the rumours persisted and expectations rose in Edmonton that a resident judge would soon be installed. It became a charged issue as Edmonton got wind of the efforts of Calgary to get a new judge stationed there. Word came via the Calgary Herald that J.R. Costigan, a lawyer of Calgary, had been informed that the Department of Justice intended to move Judge Macleod from the Southern Alberta Judicial District to Calgary.[288] More importantly, there would be no new judge, and no judge in Edmonton.

The issue of a resident judge cut deep in the towns of the North-West Territories, as has been amply demonstrated with other courthouses. The citizens of Edmonton were outraged at the state of their courts and angry about the preference shown to Calgary. The Bulletin[289] argued that the business of the courts for the north had exploded, and there was a desperate need for a resident judge. The Bulletin was not alone in complaining about the state of the court and the lack of a judge. The town expressed its outrage at a public meeting May 9, 1894, passing a resolution demanding a resident judge from the government.[290] The local legal fraternity was well represented, and to a man complained about the endless delays in the courts, especially the constant postponements of court dates. The Edmonton Board of Trade also stepped into the fray, passing similar resolutions at a meeting on May 17.[291] To underline the serious need, the Bulletin carried this item in its issue of May 31:

> Judge Rouleau left for Calgary on Tuesday's train after having sat two weeks and three days, during which he disposed of 4 criminal and 28 civil cases in court besides a large number of cases in three days of proceedings in chambers. Five civil cases and one criminal case were put off until next court on account of the impossibility of the judge remaining over to try them, and a very large number were set down for trial at next court that could have been disposed of at this court had the Judge been able to remain, while a still larger number could have been set down had there been any probability that they could be taken up.[292]

The efforts of the town were in vain. No new judge was appointed for Edmonton or anywhere else. After the death of Justice Macleod in 1894, David Lynch Scott was elevated to the Territorial Bench to replace him, but Scott was placed in Calgary. He and Rouleau continued to make the long trek north several times a year.

## A New Home – The Sandison Block

By the end of the decade, the need for a more permanent location for the courts had become a scandal. One solution was to rent a permanent space in one of the substantial commercial buildings that had been built in the town by this point. Sidney Taylor had tried to interest the government in his building three years before, but now matters were reaching a crisis. Justice Rouleau had finally had enough of the facilities at his disposal. In 1899, another lawyer, H.C. Taylor, cousin of Sidney Taylor, suggested that the government rent space in a block being erected by a local entrepreneur, Charles Sandison. In support, Rouleau fired off a scathing letter to the Department of Justice:

> Enclosed I have the honor to forward a copy of a letter sent to Mr. Oliver M.P. by Mr. H.C. Taylor, on behalf Mr. Sandison. I endorse every thing he says in it, and I may add besides that unless better quarters are given to me to hold the Court at Edmonton, I will be obliged to refuse to hold it in such a barn as the present room, where I am exposed to injure [sic] my health.[293]

*Justice, then a few groceries: 1899 Sandison Block. Glenbow Archives, NC6-375*

Sandison was an Edmonton pioneer who had gone into real estate. In 1899 he built his most ambitious commercial building to date, a two-storey brick block on Jasper Avenue. Designed by Edmonton architect F. Deggendorfer, the building was to have a thirty-foot frontage with plate glass windows.[294] The brick building rested on concrete footings and the Bulletin remarked on the full-size basement. The J.H. Morris & Company general store was to rent the main floor. By the beginning of October 1899, the $8,000 building was mostly finished, with its main tenant open for business at the end of the month.[295] The paper opined that it was "undoubtedly one of the most substantial additions to the business buildings of Edmonton."[296]

Pressured not only by the local bar but also by its own judges, the Department of Justice agreed to rent space in Sandison's new building. The court moved in time for the December assizes, inaugurating the new location on December 19, 1899.[297] The new court facility was still rather small, not even occupying the whole of the second floor. In the front were four rooms, serving as the judge's office, a room for the barristers, a library and a jury room.[298] One large room served as the courtroom. The offices of the sheriff and clerk remained in other quarters; Alex Taylor, the clerk, had his office in the post office, where the judge also frequently held chambers.[299] The papers pertaining to each case had to be carted back and forth to the Sandison block during trials. The first session of court in the unassuming new space, presided over by Justice Scott, was appropriately lacking in excitement. Scott dealt with one charge of theft, giving the perpetrator three months, heard motions in chambers, and disposed of a civil suit involving a horse. After dealing with this small docket, Scott hurried back south, and the new courtroom sat empty until February.

The Supreme Court's new headquarters in Edmonton created surprisingly little public comment. While it was an improvement on the opera house and dance hall, Sandison's block was far from an imposing monument to justice. However, the town was starting to stir. Now that a new bridge across the North Saskatchewan was under construction, attention could be turned toward a proper hall of justice. In June 1899, the board of trade, the body in Edmonton most concerned with a courthouse, decided to set up a committee to start a campaign.[300]

## The Courthouse that Never Was

Despite years of neglect, the government did take the demands for new courthouses in the Territories seriously. Justice Minister David Mills, in particular, underwent a change in opinion by 1899, announcing plans that fall to build a number of courthouses in the Territories.[301] The year before, the Minister of Justice had suggested a courthouse at Macleod with his colleague, Public Works Minister Tarte, and the two clearly discussed the needs of the North-West Territories. Mills officially approached the Department of Public Works in October 1899 about a courthouse for Edmonton, citing the "really pressing" need and also asking for a jail as part of the building.[302] Ironically, considering that the Department of Public Works was busy arranging to rent the Sandison Block, Mills wanted to get a courthouse built as soon as possible to avoid the expense of moving to another temporary location and fitting it up for a court.

Once again, designing the courthouse was a slow process, mostly due to the tardiness of the Justice Department in deciding what it wanted. E.L. Newcombe, the Deputy Minister of Justice, had promised to gather information for the new buildings immediately, but it was nearly a year before he finally contacted the Territorial justices for their opinion. It was not until early October 1900, after some pointed enquiries from Public Works, that the Deputy Minister finally got the recommendations of Rouleau and Scott.[303] They suggested a courtroom of at least thirty by fifty feet, separate rooms for the jury, witnesses, barristers and prisoners, and offices for the clerk of court, the sheriff, and themselves. They also suggested cells for up to twenty prisoners. Newcombe, for his part, felt the Edmonton building should probably be stone or brick rather than the wood-frame construction proposed for all the other new courthouses.[304] A year after Mills had first requested a hall of justice for Edmonton, Ewart and his staff could start drafting. By late December, plans had been prepared for the Edmonton courthouse and gaol and sent to the Department of Justice for their approval.[305] It was quick in coming: "The plan seems to me to be a very good one and to meet in all respects what the judges asked for."[306]

It was no secret that a courthouse was on the way, and in no time at all the citizens of Edmonton were debating where it should go.[307] Anxious to make sure the courthouse was built, Justice Rouleau strongly recommended property owned by David McDougall, of the Morley missionary family, which the town had already tried to buy for a public market. The judge wanted the government to buy land before the railroad was extended into Edmonton proper, which he feared would raise property values greatly. McDougall's asking price of $10,000 was too steep for the Department of Public Works, but Rouleau convinced him to consider a government offer of $6,000.[308]

McDougall's property, consisting of a section of River Lot 8 along McDougall Street and subdivided as block X (now south of Jasper Avenue on the east side of 100th Street) was also the choice of the Edmonton branch of the Territorial Law Society. As Nicholas Beck wrote to Rouleau: "All the profession here think this property to be, not only the best, but the only suitable site for a Court House."[309] The lawyers liked the fact that the courthouse would face the road down to the new bridge. The town council supported the selection, but had reservations about the presence of old coal shafts under the property.[310] The local Liberals, however, stepped in to ensure that the matter would become controversial. The Young Liberal Association, backed by Frank Oliver, opposed the choice as "not a suitable or safe site," perhaps because of its proximity to the river escarpment.[311] If there was a deeper conflict, such as competition for a lucrative land deal, is not known. Two powerful elements in Edmonton, however, had drawn up battle lines.

The sites for the five new courthouses were already a concern for the government. To keep costs down, the Department of Justice wanted to use either government or donated property and to avoid purchasing land.[312] The Department of Public Works needed locations suitable for building sizable edifices. Both departments knew that there was the possibility of considerable controversy over each site. To avoid getting drawn too deeply into local politics, Public Works decided to send an agent west to look over building sites and purchase suitable property. He would visit Macleod and Red Deer as well as Edmonton. E.G. Conklin of Winnipeg was appointed and came out to the Territories in the spring of 1901.[313] He arrived at the beginning of April in Edmonton. The location of the courthouse was clearly a sensitive matter: although the town council was told by the Secretary of Public Works that Conklin was coming, the agent took care to slip into Edmonton unannounced.[314] Conklin took a good look over the town before letting on that he had arrived.

While Conklin wanted a chance to see the possibilities in Edmonton without town councilmen and real estate agents buzzing around him, he was not wholly impartial. His instructions were clear: "Consult Mr. F. Oliver M.P. of Edmonton re the site there ... and at other places, deal and consult as much as possible with parties friendly with the Dominion Government." The agent met Frank Oliver even before setting foot in Edmonton, as the MP had stopped in Winnipeg on his way to Ottawa and seen Conklin there.[315] Following his instructions, the agent's first official call in Edmonton was on Charles W. Cross, President of the Liberal Association.[316] Conklin had spied a block on Elizabeth and Rice Streets he thought would be suitable, while block X remained a second possibility. The Liberal Association, never happy with the McDougall Street location, supported Conklin's first choice. Meanwhile, the town council, anxious to meet with Conklin once his whereabouts was known, appointed a committee of the mayor and two councillors to follow him about.[317] There was still lasting suspicion of the government from the land office debacle nine years before, and the town council wanted to make certain it had a say in the location of the courthouse.

The government agent was a canny negotiator and kept his hand close to his chest. The agent liked both sites, but preferred the Rice and Elizabeth street location, which was also cheaper. Town council approved, and it also seemed the first choice of the townspeople. Conklin was sensitive to public opinion. He satisfied himself there was no coal shaft under either property, as the subsidence of old coal mines was already a problem in Edmonton. Conklin wrote to Tarte, the Minister of Public Works, on April 13 to report his choice.[318] Some of the property owners along Rice and McDougall, however, were holding out for higher prices than Conklin was willing to pay. To keep them guessing, he spread rumours with the help of gullible town councillors. The mayor and committee heard from Conklin that the Rice Street block was the site; councillor Morris, in the meantime, was told by Conklin that he was going to buy block X if the owners of the Rice Street site did not come down in price.[319] Then councillor Brown was told that block X was the agent's preferred choice. Conklin left town after arranging to have local realtors pursue the desired lots if they came down in price, planning to return in ten days.[320]

As it turned out, no site was purchased and no courthouse was built. Money was available for land and to start construction. Plans had been prepared and approved. The ministers involved were behind the project. Yet, as was the case with almost all the Territorial courthouses in Alberta, delays began. The sudden death of E.G. Conklin before the end of April was the first complication, as he had not yet actually purchased any property.[321] The Department of Public Works decided to defer the decision on a site to Frank Oliver, who also became ill and was unavailable for several months. But more critically, the Department of Justice decided to review the plans again. It is unknown exactly why, or if any changes had been made, but they were dutifully sent off in June 1901 for the perusal of the Minister of Justice.[322] Ewart waited two months for a reply, only to be told that because the designs involved jails, the department needed to consult with one of its inspectors of penitentiaries before coming to any decision. The delay caused a great deal of strain between the two ministries.

In the end, there was an unlikely villain behind the cancellation of the Edmonton courthouse: Frank Oliver. He was never happy with the fact that the edifice was to be a jail as well as a courthouse. In Oliver's opinion, the combined edifice would be too large to place downtown in the desired location, and would entail considerable expense to the government for suitable land. More importantly, a jail would fail to enhance the most important part of town:

> The kind of building suitable for a court house and public offices should properly be an ornament to the business portion of the Town and should be conveniently located. A jail is necessarily anything but an ornament and should not be located in the business portion of the Town.[323]

Oliver took it upon himself to get the project changed. He tackled the Deputy Minister of the Interior, the Minister of Justice and Tarte, the Minister of Public Works, advocating a separate jail and courthouse.[324] The government was sympathetic to Oliver's argument, but did not want to spend the extra money two buildings would entail.[325]

Oliver's response was the jail first, the courthouse, second. The rented quarters in the Sandison block were adequate if uninspired, but Edmonton lacked any sort of a jail – the closest was at Fort Saskatchewan, where prisoners were kept in the NWMP barracks. Conditions there were atrocious, and the NWMP comptroller, Fred White, was quite concerned about the need for a better facility.[326] For his part, Oliver warned that "there are all the elements of a grave scandal" in the lack of jail accommodations for the growing little city.[327] The MP promised that he "would strongly press upon all Departments of the Government" the need for a jail first and the importance of building a separate courthouse. In one sense, he was successful; the jail was begun in 1903, well away from downtown.[328] But the courthouse was dead, and it would not be resurrected.

Of course, the citizens of Edmonton had been promised a courthouse and they were not about to forget. A few tentative inquiries by the town were made in 1902, but it soon became clear that whole matter had been shelved.[329] The board of trade tried once again to start a lobbying campaign, in February 1903.[330] As in the past, the courthouse boosters immediately ran afoul of significant civic indifference. The town council for Edmonton was lukewarm to the idea; busy with negotiations with the government over other matters, it viewed the courthouse as an unwelcome intrusion.[331] A month later, it finally considered sending a delegation to Ottawa, after a public meeting had overwhelmingly called for action.[332] The council decided against an actual delegation, instead voting to leave the matter up to Frank Oliver.[333] The member was not impressed, and wrote back to George Kinniard, the board treasurer:

> I very highly appreciate the confidence expressed in me by the council's declining to send down a delegation, but would have been much better pleased to have been relieved of a share of the responsibility by the presence of a delegation. However I will do the best I can....[334]

Oliver and the board did not give up, but as the movement for provincial autonomy began to pick up steam, the Dominion became very reluctant to make any commitments. Edmonton would have several more years to wait.

## The Resident Judge – Again

Although Edmonton lost out on a courthouse, as compensation it did finally get a resident judge. On August 25, 1901, the honourable Charles Borromee Rouleau died. He had been greatly respected as a judge, and his death threw the courts into disarray. Five judges for the entire Territories was already clearly insufficient, four was neglectful. Amazingly, for almost six months this was the situation. Scott in Calgary was expected to look after all of Alberta, jumping back and forth between Macleod, Calgary, Edmonton and points between, assisted by the other judges when possible. By January 1902 there was an enormous backlog in Edmonton. Scott was not able to clear the criminal case calendar, and civil cases were left untouched.[335]

In response to this judicial crisis, in February 1902 the town communicated with Oliver and the Department of Justice to urge the appointment of a resident judge.[336] It was propitious timing. Arthur Sifton, the Territorial Treasurer, and Frederick Haultain, Territorial Attorney General as well as Premier, suggested that the judicial districts should be reorganized as part of appointing a successor to Rouleau.[337] Haultain thought it was time to add a district in Alberta, which would retain the name Northern Alberta and be headquartered in Edmonton. The government reckoned that an entirely new district was not necessary, as a deputy sheriff and clerk were already at Edmonton. It did decide to move Scott north after stationing Thomas McGuire, the chief justice, in Calgary, where he was later joined by Rouleau's replacement, James Prendergast.[338] The Bulletin, while not effusive, was pleased by the appointment: Scott had already been the de facto judge for Edmonton for several years.[339] On May 14, attended by the Edmonton Bar, Scott opened his first court as the resident justice.[340]

Scott's appointment also led to a change in venue for his court. The new resident judge soon let the Department of Justice know his displeasure with the

*Nicer digs: new Sandison Block, c. 1903. PAA, B5554*

court's accommodation. In August 1902, he fired off a letter to E.L. Newcombe, the Deputy Minister for Justice, demanding better facilities and proper furniture.[341] He harangued Newcombe again in October, and in February of the following year, complaining about his cramped office space.[342] The deputy minister tried to pacify the judge, forwarding Scott's concerns to the Department of Public Works with his own urgings that something be done.[343]

With a hall of justice on hold indefinitely, the best the department could do was move Scott to an adjacent building just built by Charles Sandison,[344] even though it had just spent a considerable sum renovating the courtroom above the J.H. Morris Company.[345] Once again the court was installed on the upper floor and received more room, including some office space. The new building had a more imposing appearance, but was still a far cry from a proper courthouse. It was to become famous for stifling heat in the summer months and near freezing temperatures in the winter. It would be Edmonton's courthouse until 1912.

# RED DEER

It had no court offices and was not a judicial headquarters, and yet the hamlet of Red Deer somehow got a courthouse where other larger and more important towns in the Territories failed. Like the earlier and almost identical courthouse in Macleod, the building in Red Deer was constructed largely due to persistent, organized and united civic lobbying. The circumstances around the building of the Red Deer Territorial hall of justice demonstrates just how important good connections to the ruling government could be. The Red Deer Liberal Association was central to the push for a building, and their activities show how much influence the local association could wield in the design and the construction of the building. In Red Deer, the association chose the site, appointed the clerk of works, and may have even helped to ensure that a local contractor got the job. The presence of prominent Liberals on the Red Deer Board of Trade and the town council further extended the influence of the association. As in other towns in the Territories, a clique of leading citizens was at work, all the more effective because it brought together political groups and civic bodies.

## Red Deer – The Early Days

Once Fort Calgary and Fort Macleod were firmly established, an increasing amount of traffic began to follow the old Indian trails to Fort Edmonton. One obstacle on the Calgary-Edmonton trail was the Red Deer River, and a good ford was soon found about six kilometres west of the present city limits of Red Deer. It was also a sheltered camping spot, and in short order a small settlement sprang up. A trapper and jack of all trades by the name of Addison McPherson had maintained a small shack in the vicinity for years, and in 1882 one of his business partners, Robert McClellan, built a house at the crossing. Other prospective homesteaders soon joined him, and the arrival of the CPR in Calgary in 1883 boosted traffic going north to Edmonton. Soon the little settlement could boast a store and a small frame hotel. During the 1885 Rebellion, a detachment of NWMP took over McLellan's house and turned it into a barracks, establishing Fort Normandeau.

Despite a promising start, the crossing was not destined to become Red Deer. In 1882, a group of Ontario Methodists had formed the Saskatchewan Land and Homestead Company and bought several large blocks of land for colonization purposes, including 180 sections near Red Deer. In 1884, Leonard Gaetz, a retired Methodist minister and a director in the company, decided to try his hand at homesteading and promoting the district. He established a model farm a short distance from the crossing, and acted as the company land agent, the Dominion land agent, and the postmaster, and also bought the general store. Gaetz proved an indefatigable booster of the rich agricultural potential of the area, writing

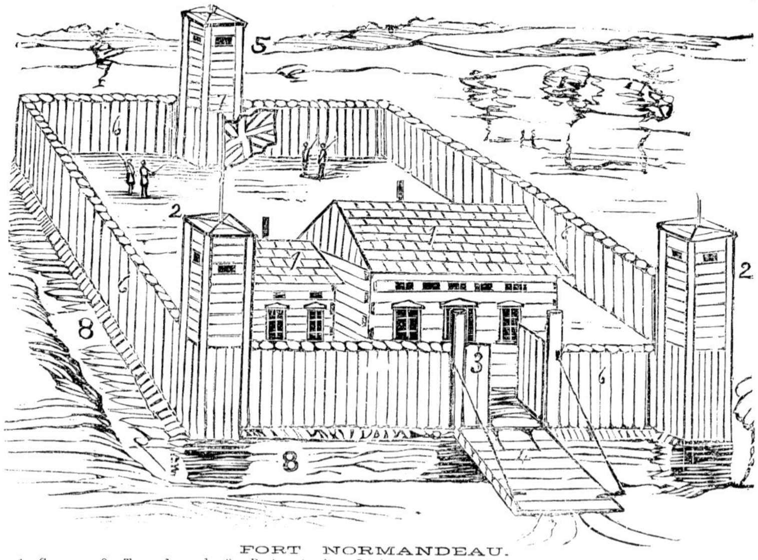


FORT NORMANDEAU.
1.—Casernes. 2.—Tours de garde 3.—Portes. 4.—Pont-Lévis. 5.—La plaine. 6.—Palissade. 7.—Bastion. 8.—Fossé.

*Law on the frontier: Fort Normandeau, c. 1885. Glenbow Archives, NA-485-3*

pamphlets and newspaper articles extolling the virtues of Red Deer River land. He became the father of modern Red Deer when the Calgary & Edmonton railroad was announced. The canny clergyman offered the railroad an interest in his extensive holdings if they would put the line across his land and survey a townsite there. The C&E was amenable. Suddenly the railway was six kilometres away from the crossing. Not surprisingly, many of the original settlers elected to move to the new townsite. Gaetz and his extensive family became the settlement's leading citizens, contributing several mayors and prominent businessmen.

Rail service brought a rush of new residents, but the hamlet stagnated in the severe recession of the early 1890s. A village overseer was elected in 1894 and a board of trade formed the same year. With better economic conditions, Red Deer began to grow again as a new century approached. Although the townsite only had an official population of 323, the Territorial government allowed Red Deer to incorporate as a town in 1901, perhaps in recognition of the burgeoning countryside around it. The great immigration flood that the northwest had been waiting twenty years to see finally materialized, and carried the new town along with it.

## The Courts in Red Deer

The establishment of Fort Normandeau brought not only law enforcement but also the administration of justice to the Red Deer district. The fort's namesake, Lieutenant J.E.B. Normandeau, and his detachment of soldiers soon left, but in 1886 a permanent force of thirteen NWMP was stationed there. By virtue of his rank, their commander, Inspector T.W. Chalmers, was a justice of the peace who could act as a local magistrate. The first civilian justice of the peace in the area was appointed in 1885, and was none other than Robert McLellan.[346] Once the village of Red Deer was established it was only a matter of time before some sort of courtroom was necessary. The police could use the barracks, but this was inconvenient at best for the civilian justice of the peace, living ten kilometres away in the new townsite.

By 1895, Red Deer and district was populous enough to merit a sitting of the Supreme Court of the Territories. Justice Rouleau, the senior judge, decided that central Alberta needed a regular assize and chose Red Deer "because I consider that place more central ... being the end of the division of the C&E Ry, between Calgary and Edmonton."[347] It was not a popular choice in nearby Innisfail. The lawyers and civic leaders there immediately sent a petition off to the Lieutenant Governor of the Territories, stating that their town had more people, more legal business, and more lawyers than any other town of the immediate district. Rouleau remained unconvinced, telling the governor, "the court at Red Deer may not suit the lawyers as well as Innisfail, but I believe it will be more suitable to the litigants in general."[348] Obligingly, the Lieutenant Governor added Red Deer to the scheduled sittings, with a judge to visit the village the third Tuesday of February and the first Tuesday of May and of October.[349]

Like recent settlers elsewhere in the Territories, the locals scrambled to find a place for the assizes. Red Deer lacked a town hall that could be used, but the local school board trustees had recently finished construction of a lovely two-storey brick school, and had anticipated the needs of the community beyond education. Not only was the building available for entertainment and dances, but they had fixed a rent of $5 per day for the court, light and heat included.[350] When Justice Scott opened his court in Red Deer on February 25, 1895, he did so in instructive surroundings.[351]

Scott and Rouleau used the upper classroom for the next three years. The school had not been intended as a courthouse, however, and the sittings soon interfered with classes for the children. As had happened years before in Edmonton, the school board eventually decided the rental from the court was not worth the trouble, and by 1898 the judges were forced to find other quarters. Various halls were rented over the next few years, including a room in the Alberta Hotel.[352] It was not a satisfactory arrangement. The secretary of the local board of trade complained to the Dominion government that the quarters "greatly detracts from that solemnity and dignity which characterises a British Court of Justice."[353]

## A Liberal's Courthouse

Red Deer did well out of the Dominion's program of courthouse construction in the Territories. It is surprising, considering Red Deer itself was not much more than a village when the Department of Public Works announced in 1903 it would build a courthouse almost identical to the one under construction in Macleod. The official population of the village in 1901 was only 323, although Red Deer would incorporate later that year.[354] By the time the new Red Deer Courthouse and Land Office was finished in 1906, the town had grown to nearly fifteen hundred souls. But even if Red Deer itself was small, it was situated in the heart of a rich agricultural district, and the town, an important junction on the Calgary & Edmonton Railroad, was placed almost exactly halfway between the province's two largest cities. The placement of a court building in Red Deer was a happy coincidence of government policy and the efforts of active civic boosters. The town already had a sitting of the Supreme Court, and the Department of Justice clearly believed it was a strategic location to serve the needs of the region. The civic leaders of Red Deer, however, also mounted a campaign to ensure the town would be given due consideration.

Although Red Deer lacked a properly constituted town council until 1901, it had other bodies to state its case. The Red Deer Liberal Association was particularly active – and effective. The board of trade also lent a persuasive voice. As was often the case, incorporation came straight out of these bodies, and the membership of the first town council, the board executive and the association executive overlapped to a significant degree. The Liberal executive in 1901 included lawyer George W. Greene, John J. Gaetz, one of the good reverend's nephews, and George W. Smith, the district's first schoolteacher and later a mayor and MLA. The Liberals acted as if they were the town council, and later as if they were the local agents of the Department of Public Works. The association considered a courthouse to be of particular importance because of the dismal quarters available in the village for the assize, and organized a petition in Red Deer during the spring of 1900 that was duly sent to Frank Oliver, the Liberal MP for Alberta, who passed it on the Dominion government.

The petition came at a timely point: just before an election. An item was placed, with Oliver's strong urging, in the Estimates for 1900-1901, for $5,000 toward a courthouse in Red Deer.[355] The Liberal Association appreciated the importance of persistence. Even while passing an appropriation for Oliver's work, the association also asked him to appeal for "immediate action in regards to the construction of the Red Deer court House." And taking action was important. John J. Gaetz, the secretary of the association, warned Oliver that "the local Conservatives are making a strong canvass of that, claiming it is only a dodge to catch votes and that after the elections are over, nothing more will be heard of it. The committee strongly recommend [sic] that proceedings be instituted at once to show the earnest [sic] of the appropriation ... such a movement would not only greatly assist us in our canvass but materially contribute to your popularity in this district."[356]

---

THE BAR IN THE BAR

Although no one was very happy about the poor quarters for holding court throughout the Territories, judges and advocates could still sometimes see the humour in dealing with frontier conditions. F.C. Jamieson recalled one evening in the Red Deer Hotel with Judge Scott:

"There were a number of stockmen in the sample room of the hotel which was used as a court room. It was separated from the bar by only a one-inch board partition. The bar was full of men. Mr. Justice Scott was taking down the evidence in his beautiful handwriting. The loud talking and laughing in the bar made it difficult for him to hear the witnesses. Finally he said: 'Will one of you gentlemen go in and ask those men to make less noise so that I can hear the witnesses.' A big fellow went out, and in a minute we heard a loud shout from him in the bar: 'Hi there, you devils make less noise. Judge says he is going to raise hell with you if you don't.' The judge smiled at the form his message took, but went on writing."[357]

It is not recorded whether bench and attending lawyers ever took advantage of their proximity to the bar to procure refreshments.

The justice ministry took the request from Red Deer quite seriously, thanks to Frank Oliver's support. The Department of Justice had already decided in 1899 that more courthouses were needed in the Territories, and thanks to its strategic position Red Deer was added to a list that included Edmonton, Macleod, Carnduff, and Yorkton. The Department of Public Works also regarded the issue as important. Both J.I. Tarte, the Minister of Public Works, and William Mulock, Postmaster General and acting Public Works Minister during the summer of 1900, instructed department staff in no uncertain terms to finish the courthouses with dispatch. Mulock was quick to send a memo to the deputy minister after receiving another note on the Territorial courthouses from Frank Oliver: "I wish all the buildings mentioned in Mr. Oliver's letter proceeded with at the earliest moment. Please obtain all necessary information from the various departments concerned, and act without waiting for further instructions."[358]

Ironically, David Ewart, the Chief Architect, was all ready to start drafting, and two days before Mulock's missive had sent a query to the acting minister about the requirements of the Department of Justice.[359] Ewart also suggested placing the new land office recently requested by the Department of the Interior in the building, acting on a suggestion from Oliver. L.F. Taylor, a department architect, was put in charge of producing plans.

While Ewart and his office got busy, the Department set about finding a site for the proposed building. In order to keep costs down, the Deputy Minister of Justice, E.L. Newcombe, wanted to use government land wherever possible.[360] Nothing was available in Red Deer, and the owners of the townsite were not interested in donating land, so the Department of Public Works had to buy a property. The local Liberals quickly stepped in to choose an appropriate spot. The association executive picked out lots 10 to 29 in block 18, a parcel of land bordered by Mackenzie, Ross and Mann Street on the edge of the existing business district. Frank Oliver was duly informed, and E.G. Conklin looked at the site on his western tour in 1901 and approved it as the best location available.[361] Conklin's report was later sent to the local association, who not surprisingly pronounced that it "has been very satisfactory to the Comm[ittee]."[362] The association urged that the site

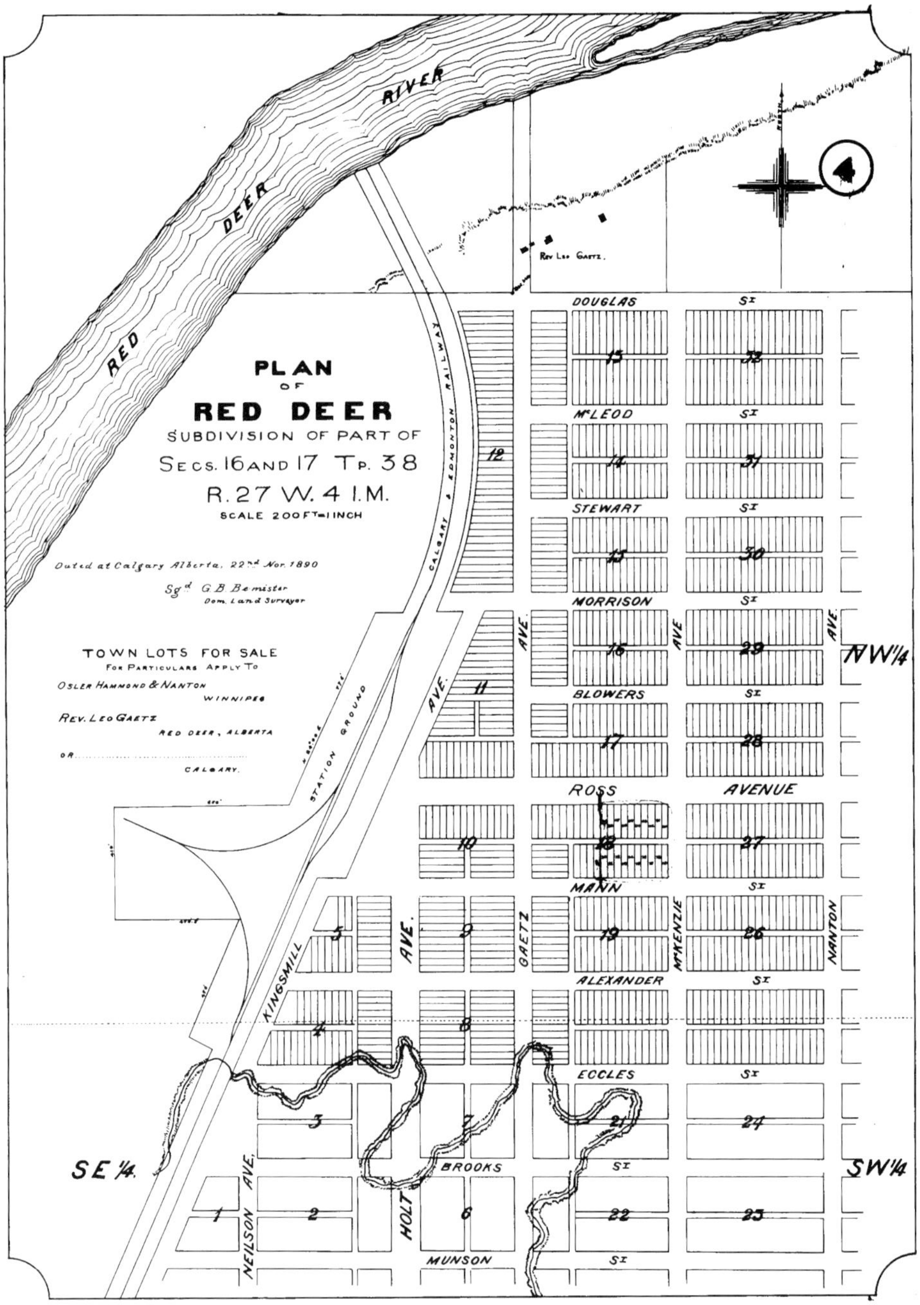


*Prime real estate: site for the Red Deer Territorial Courthouse. NA, NMC45566*

be purchased immediately. In fact, an Order-in-Council had already in passed in August 1901 to buy the lots for $830, but it wasn't until the spring that Red Deer found this out.[363] But if the purchase gave hope for the swift erection of a courthouse, the town was to be disappointed.

A certain amount of dissension had arisen between the concerned departments over the design of the building, which was no doubt a major source of the delay. Ewart, in the absence of any other directive, had his staff prepare designs for both Macleod and Red Deer modelled on the recently finished courthouse at Medicine Hat. Thus, both the law courts at Macleod and at Red Deer were originally planned as wood-framed and sided buildings that looked more like a country schoolhouses than courthouses. Ewart, taking his cue from the size of the appropriations and the concern of the Department of Justice over the expenditure, no doubt felt it was an expedient way to provide cheap court accommodations.

It did not take into account the ambitions of growing towns. In Medicine Hat the residents had objected to the use of wood. The citizens of Macleod unequivocally condemned the Medicine Hat plans, and it was certain the people of Red Deer would follow suit. The government itself had already raised their expectations. Conklin had noted that good building stone was available in his report, a document circulated in Red Deer. In 1901, the Inspector of Penitentiaries, George Dawson, was in the Territories looking at proposed jail sites. While there he looked at the proposed courthouse sites and reported to the Minister of Justice. Dawson also noted the available stone and decided that both in Macleod and Red Deer, stone should be used for the courthouse, and was indiscreet enough to let the townsfolk know his thoughts. And the Minister of Justice himself, David Mills, had gone on record as favouring stone construction for the new courthouses.

In his report in December 1901 to Newcombe, Dawson stated that "it would be a mistake to build the courthouse and lockup in wood."[364] The deputy minister concurred with the inspector. The residents of Macleod had, by this time, seen plans for their courthouse and vociferously objected to wood construction. The citizens of Red Deer followed suit, and Frank Oliver squarely backed them up.[365] Ewart later made reference to the "strong objections" made about the use of wood for a courthouse.[366] At the time, the Chief Architect reported that stone or brick would increase the cost of the building from around $10,000 to about $15,000 or $16,000, a broad hint that they were going to be too expensive.

The drawings that had been prepared were scrapped, and Ewart waited for instructions. It was a long wait, as the Department of Justice mulled over what they wanted to do at Red Deer. Ewart was not directed to begin a new design until the spring of 1903. Ironically, when the revised plans were prepared, there was no stone to be seen on the building outside of the windowsills. Instead, as Ewart had done in Macleod, the department compromised and decided to build a brick edifice. It was likely a matter of cost. The original Macleod contract had been for a stone building costing $13,000, but estimates had climbed to almost $40,000. Public Works had hoped to build three courthouses in the Alberta District for about that amount of money. The building stone at Macleod had also been found wanting, and this probably made brick seem like a less problematic material. Despite the hopes of local boosters, the two buildings would be brick. In April 1903, Ewart instructed his assistant Taylor to prepare a new set of plans for the Red Deer courthouse.

The building Taylor drafted was almost identical to the one in Macleod. It had the same cross gable structure and returned eaves to suggest a pediment. The exterior, however, was further simplified. Simple square-cut portals, two large central windows flanked by two smaller ones, replaced the Romanesque arcade

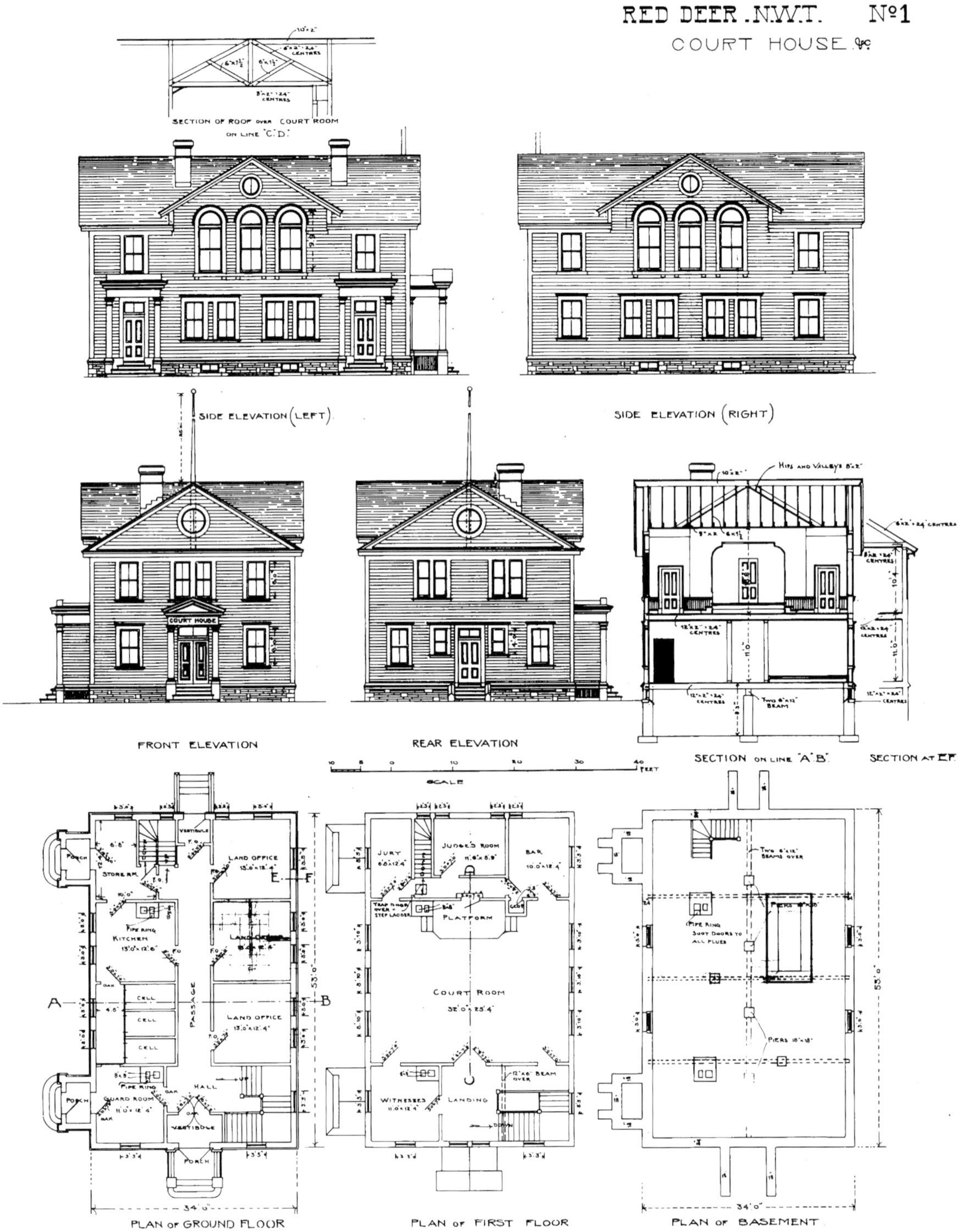


*Judged inadequate: first elevations and floor plans, Red Deer Courthouse. NA, NMC45563*

of arched windows on the second-storey facade used in Macleod. The simple cartouche with the legend "courthouse" was moved from above the door to between the second-storey windows and the attic windows. The Red Deer structure retained the arched windows on the sides of the building, as well as the two side entrances complete with small projecting porches. The building was entirely brick with sandstone sills and lintels and rock facing on the foundation wall; the stone stringcourses used at Macleod were eliminated. It was a simple and pleasing building, but with a decidedly residential appearance. The regular, symmetrical design signified it was a public building, but certainly did not suggest the awful majesty of the law.

Although the Macleod and Red Deer courthouses looked the same on the outside, they were quite different internally. Macleod's building was the seat of a judicial district, was used strictly as a courthouse and was planned to accommodate court offices as well as a courtroom. Red Deer was still part of the North Alberta Judicial District, and the two justices, Sifton and Scott, were in Calgary and Edmonton respectively. There was no deputy sheriff or clerk of court as there was in Medicine Hat. A permanent courtroom with facilities for witnesses and juries, rooms for the judge and barristers to prepare for the assize, and some holding cells for prisoners awaiting trials would serve the needs of justice in Red Deer. Thus, although the edifice would bear the legend "courthouse," only the second floor was turned over to the courts. It was laid out identically to Macleod's, with a courtroom, witness room, jury room, robing chamber, and judge's office. Cells were located in the basement and on the main floor, although once construction was underway the latter were eliminated.[367] The first floor was given over to the Department of the Interior. This ministry had been agitating for a building for the local Dominion Land Office, and the Department of Public Works had advocated putting it in proposed courthouse from the beginning. It was a disappointment for the citizens of Red Deer, who of course hoped for two buildings, but was accepted as a reasonable compromise.

Of more concern in Red Deer was whether the town would ever see the promised courthouse. Over two years passed after the original appropriation and purchase of the site with no sign of construction, and the natives were getting very restless. The local Liberals kept up a steady stream of correspondence to the authorities.[368] Frank Oliver threw his support behind them, and finally the town council, board of trade and Liberal Association made an all-out assault on the ramparts of ministerial indifference at the beginning of April 1903.[369] All three bodies drew up resolutions and the gloves were off. The local Liberals, led by George W. Smith, got right to the point, warning that "very great and widespread dissatisfaction exists and adverse criticism of the Government by its warmest friends and supporters is increasing on account of the delay." They also demanded "a much larger expenditure be made" due to the increasing population of the district and ended by urging "in the interest of both public and the government that these works be undertaken at once."[370] Thinly veiled threats seemed to work. The Minister of Justice wrote to assure everyone that immediate action would be taken, and memos passed back and forth between the ministries in Ottawa.

By April 16, less than a week later, Ewart finally had his marching orders: a brick courthouse and land office for Red Deer. Once the decision was made to proceed with the building, the Chief Architect's office soon had the matter in hand. Taylor and his drafting staff had the edifice drawn up in early May: all they really

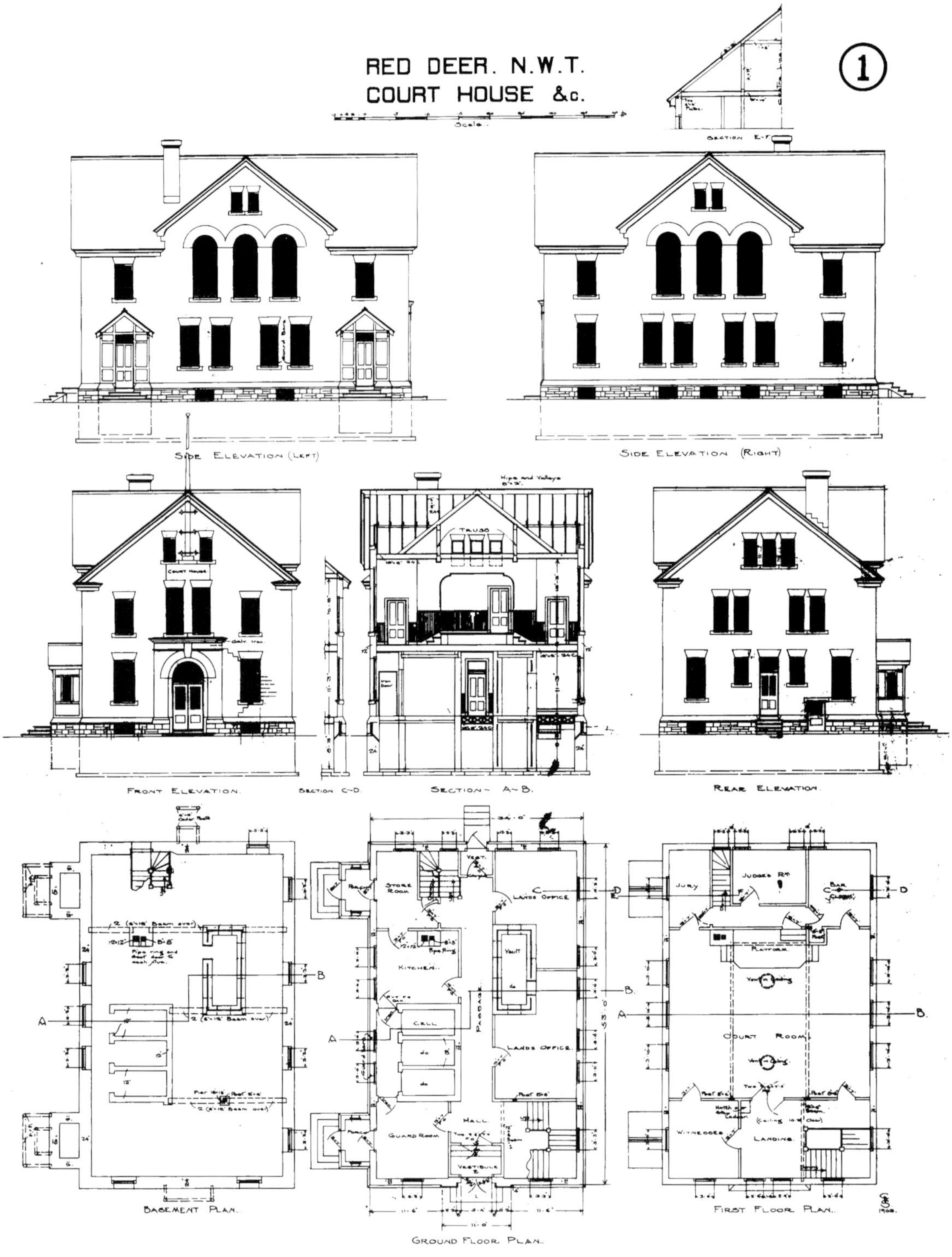


*An improvement: elevations and floor plans, Red Deer Courthouse. NA, NMC17027*

had to do was modify the existing Macleod blueprints.[371] The plans were sent to Red Deer and Calgary at the end of June and a call for tenders followed.[372] Patrick Navin, busy working on the Macleod courthouse, put in a bid, as did two Red Deer contractors and, perhaps more surprisingly, two companies from far-off Ottawa.[373] The department signed a contract on September 7, 1903 with local builders Andrew

Tait and George A. Johnson of Red Deer.

The influence of the local Liberals with regard to the courthouse was graphically illustrated by the events surrounding the appointment of the clerk of works. Originally the department hired Hugh Clarke, another local builder.[374] Paul Paradis, the district engineer in Calgary, was his immediate supervisor. Something went amiss as Clarke abruptly quit in March 1904.[375] The Liberal Association immediately set to choosing a new nominee for the position. Bizarrely enough, Hugh Clarke was one of the three candidates, and in an impromptu election by the association, was nominated as their choice for clerk.[376] In due course he was again appointed by the Department of Public Works.

Why he resigned in the first place was anyone's guess, but the whole incident demonstrates to what degree the local supporters of the ruling party became the de facto eyes and ears of the government. They could dictate, or at least strongly influence, matters like placing a building, buying property, or hiring personnel. In the case of Clarke, it can be speculated that he may have resigned for personal reasons, or out of some conflict with Paradis, but was likely talked into reapplying to guard local interests as perceived by the Liberal Association. Ironically, there was some criticism in Red Deer over the choice of Clarke: some residents felt he was too much of a newcomer to merit the work.

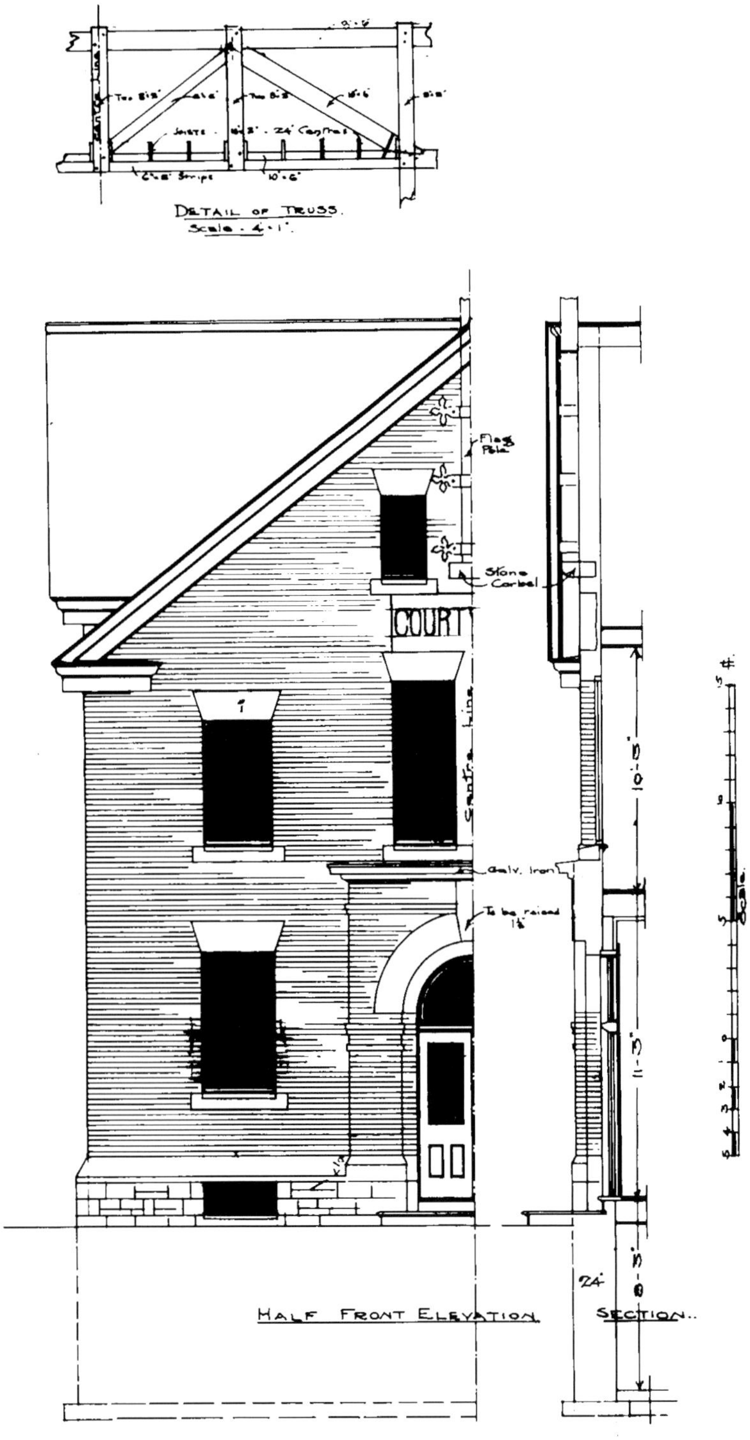


*Architectural details, Red Deer Courthouse. NA, NMC45565*

Clarke's original resignation may very well have had to do with problems on the building site. Progress on the courthouse was slow. Tait and Johnston were to finish their contract by November 1904, but by May they were still working on the basement.[377] A scarcity of brick didn't help: local manufacturer William Piper couldn't keep up with demand, and there were acute shortages as well in Calgary.[378] And there were changes to be made in the original plans. While the judges of the Territorial Court had been consulted years earlier when the Department of Justice had first decided to build a series of new buildings, none of them had seen the plans since. Chief Justice Arthur L. Sifton personally examined the nearly finished Red Deer courthouse in November.[379] He was immediately concerned with the lack of space for court officials, feeling they would be appointed in Red Deer in the near future and that it would be ridiculous if offices had to be rented for them outside the courthouse. He also criticized the amount of space dedicated on the main floor for a guardroom, kitchen and the three cells, deeming them unnecessary: he thought the guardroom could be turned into a judge's office. A library in the attic, such as existed at Macleod, also struck Sifton as a good idea. The justice's comments were sent to Charles Fitzpatrick, the Minister of Justice. Ewart, the Chief Architect, did not find Sifton's suggestions unreasonable and was eager to please the judge.[380] While the kitchen and upper cells were done away with, however, it did not create more room for the court – the extra space would be occupied by the land office.

If changes to the plans caused delays, problems with the contractors created more. Toward the end of 1904, a dispute broke out between Clarke and the contractors over the specifications. Tait and Johnston were not following the plans, and would not take direction from Clarke. Ewart promptly sent L.F. Taylor on an inspection tour, much like Ewart himself had done ten years before, and he visited Red Deer to deal with the situation.[381] It was not the last problem with the contractor. In the spring, Ewart instructed Clarke to "deduct from the final estimate what you consider would be fair value to do the work" if the contractor would not comply with his instructions.[382]

While the contractor struggled to get the building completed, a crisis in court facilities had arisen. In May 1905, as the new building moved closer to completion, Peter Talbot, the MP for Strathcona, presented a request to the Department of Public Works to use the facility for the next assizes.[383] The court was experiencing great difficulties renting quarters in town. The building was not quite ready in time for Justice Harvey's May assize, but the following January, with no other rooms available in Red Deer, another request wended its way through the new provincial as well as the Dominion bureaucracies to use the almost finished building.[384] It was a strange situation: the courthouse was still the property of the Dominion although the provincial government expected that they would be purchasing it in the near future. The provincial Attorney General's department had recently been organized, but the administration of justice was still mostly carried out through its federal counterpart. Thus the request had to go through four different departments! Harvey, who had inaugurated the Macleod courthouse a year and a half previously, entered the new courtroom on January 22.

*More suited: Land Titles Office and Post Office, Red Deer, c. 1912. RDDA, P-361-1*

Public reaction to the new courthouse was lukewarm. Somewhat perversely, the local paper, the *Red Deer News*, criticized it as being too attractive. The reporter covering the Brobeck murder trial, the first in the building, for the *News* found no fault with the layout or size of the court facilities, but was concerned with the atmosphere created by the new edifice. He was quite prepared to concede the decor of the interior was pleasant, but that was the problem:

> The room has a newly finished appearance which does not inspire that feeling of awe which a person feels upon entering the stone and oak court houses of the older provinces, and where also the dim light even at midday adds to that solemnity of feeling. On the contrary the new courtroom was quite bright and, but for the character of the proceedings, even cheerful. The light from the side window falls on the polished panels and the white plaster with pleasant effect.[385]

The writer illustrated nicely a point raised earlier in this book: that residents of the Territories had strong associations with regard to court. In this case, the *News* correspondent waxed nostalgic for the atmosphere that he thought better befitted the sometimes grim business of justice.

The courthouse may have been finished and in use, but the Department of Public Works was not finished with the contractors. The builders had deviated so much from the original specifications that in the end the department refused to pass the final estimate and pay out the contract.[386] Complaints also flooded into the department from Red Deer merchants and the local Bank of Commerce about unpaid bills and loans. Public Works would insist that Tait and Johnston fill out a statutory declaration detailing their expenditures so the department could determine what to do about paying creditors. Not only had the contractors deviated from the contract, they still owed their suppliers over $6,600.[387] Their original low bid must have seemed like a poor bargain.

Perhaps more than any other town in the Territories, the citizens of Red Deer were sensitive to the role of the courthouse, not just in providing a place for the machinery of justice, but also a face. And it was to be a stern and solemn visage, giving physical form to the abstract notions of the law and symbolizing its power. A central argument used by advocates of a courthouse was that temporary quarters "detracts from the solemnity and dignity which characterizes a British Court of Justice,"[388] and that maintaining this character for the courts was vital on account of the "many different nationalities"[389] that were flooding into the district. For at least some of the town's opinion makers, a proper courthouse would bolster the rule of law, providing a domicile for the awful majesty of the court. On this score the Red Deer edifice was a disappointment.

## Epilogue

As in Macleod and Medicine Hat, the courthouse in Red Deer looked more like a schoolhouse or a post office. The latter would indeed be its fate. After barely six years of service, it would be converted into the Dominion public building and eventually the town's post office. In 1912, the local member of the provincial legislature, E.E. Michener, a Conservative, persuaded the Borden administration to establish a customs office in Red Deer and also build a new post office. The federal government, still the owners of the courthouse, asked the court to move out and promptly established the customs office in the vacant space. World War I intervened before the proposed post office was constructed, and in 1918, much to the dismay of the city, the Dominion building was pressed into service. Despite continued campaigning for a new facility, a $2,000 brick addition was added to the old courthouse in 1930, cementing its function.

In 1949, the federal government finally committed to a new post office building, much to the delight of the city fathers and local chamber of commerce. Their success spelled doom for the 1906 courthouse. The most expedient course for the federal government was to use its existing property. There was ample space, and indeed it was not even necessary to tear down the old post office to start the new. But with a shiny new building in place, the old edifice was an eyesore to forward-thinking citizens. The city envisioned the land under the courthouse as a park;

business interests, including Canada Safeway, saw a parking lot.[390] In the end the latter option won the day. The city looked into the possibility of preserving the historic structure by moving it and converting it into a library. After considering several options, the city opted to instead use the old RCMP headquarters.[391] In 1951 the little brick courthouse was knocked down.

# CONCLUSION

By the time Alberta became a province, the courts had managed to move from hotels, schoolhouses and makeshift courtrooms in immigration buildings to a number of purpose-designed courthouses. The august justices of the Territorial court still dispensed justice in frontier conditions, but in a few centres at least they could look forward to working in proper quarters. With the exception of Calgary's stone hall of justice, the courthouses that had been built by the Dominion government were basic structures, solid enough, but not to be compared to the public buildings found in more civilized parts. They were better than nothing, but certainly not what the public in the Territories hoped for from their government.

As the saga of the five Territorial courthouses of Alberta makes clear, a hall of justice was considered an important amenity for every growing town and settlement. A courthouse was a mark of permanence for a new community that also brought with it important economic benefits: being a legal centre made a community that much more attractive to business interests. Contemporaries also worried that the law would be held in contempt if presented in a slipshod manner – a courthouse would give the court the proper dignity necessary to instil respect and even awe in immigrant populations who were not familiar with English law. As a consequence of these beliefs, and drawing upon examples common enough elsewhere, people wanted substantial and imposing buildings that were clearly courthouses: structures built in stone or brick and with some architectural merit, commodious enough for judge, court, and officers. The external appearance and internal finishings were part and parcel of giving the legal system a fitting home and creating a physical manifestation of the law. Thus, residents of Lethbridge were outraged by what they saw as an unattractive edifice, unfavourably contrasted to the courthouses built south of the border in Montana.

The desires of the Territorials ran counter to the very different priorities of government. Both the Macdonald Conservatives and the Laurier Liberals generally wanted to keep costs down in the Territories, and were reluctant to pursue large-scale building projects. Part of the difficulty was deciding if a location was worth investing in for the long term. Many of the towns requesting substantial courthouses and public buildings were hardly more than villages. At the same time, both administrations were inconsistent and could be influenced by strong public disapproval. The Conservatives, reflecting their nation-building ethos, were able to justify the sort of large courthouse requested by the Territorials in a place like Calgary or Regina, but elsewhere they tried to keep it cheap. Lethbridge, for instance, had to fight tooth and nail to get a court facility, and then to ensure it was a reasonable size. The Liberals also felt the pull toward more monumental buildings, but in the end decided that smaller and more inexpensive courthouses made more sense with political autonomy for the Territories on the horizon. Sometimes this was because the government itself did not know what it wanted – witness the events in Macleod, where a simple design was replaced by much grander one, and then again with something less expensive, with all the consequent delays.

Lobbying became the key element in determining where courthouses would be constructed. Although government still tended to build in centres that were either judicial headquarters or major centres, both timing and location could be influenced by civic campaigns. Despite its relative size and importance, Edmonton never did receive a Territorial courthouse, while Red Deer – which mounted a strong campaign – did, despite not even being a judicial centre. Macleod's long saga is especially instructive. Other locations in Alberta – Cardston, Wetaskwin, and others – tried to get a courthouse as well. In most of these cases, the local boosters must have known it was a long shot, and gave up quickly after getting an unequivocal refusal. The government could be swayed, but was also likely only to build in places that made some sense in terms of policy.

Outside their own control, the construction of courthouses – or lack thereof – infuriated residents of the Territories. With a small population and little representation, their aspirations could be ignored at length. In the larger scheme of things, this was not unreasonable for both the Liberal and Conservative governments. The west barely counted in the political balance, and with so many uncertainties about the pace and the course of development in the Territories, it is not surprising that politicians and bureaucrats both were reluctant to invest in expensive public buildings. And there were other edifices to consider beyond courthouses, such as post offices, customs facilities, even jails. Situations arose such as happened in Edmonton, where Frank Oliver – an indefatigable advocate of courthouses in other centres – derailed the building proposed for his hometown in order to secure other facilities.

The Territorial legacy in Alberta is the lone courthouse in Fort Macleod. It was lucky to have survived. The other buildings, small and unimpressive by later standards, were replaced as courthouses, although sometimes much later than was desirable. Once their original purpose was lost, the structures were largely forgotten, and their eventual demolition was not something that galvanized much protest. For all the fuss about their construction, there was little about their destruction. The exception was Calgary's building. Larger and more impressive than the rest, it had a stronger hold over the public's imagination and sympathies. Although it too was fated to disappear, it also made clear that Alberta's historic architecture was endangered and helped to save others.

# PART TWO
# THE FIRST PROVINCIAL COURTHOUSES
## THE LIBERALS REIGN, 1905–21

On September 1, 1905, Alberta and Saskatchewan became provinces. It was the dawn of a new era on the prairies. The two newest members of Confederation were about to witness a boom that would see their populations expand tenfold in less than a decade. The towns of the northwest were to become cities, the villages and hamlets would grow into towns. It was to be a golden decade of prosperity, and the two new provincial governments reflected the pride and optimism of the times with grand programs of public works. High on the list in Alberta were courthouses to contain the burgeoning legal business created by a roaring economy. And no longer would courthouses be simple utilitarian structures, derided as plain or inadequate. A government responsible to local voters put much more care and effort into buildings that were necessary and vital. A climate of frenetic boosterism gripped the province, characterized by massive real estate speculation and equally massive borrowing by governments to finance the infrastructure to serve the spiralling growth. A bust followed the boom in 1914, as a recession that had begun the year before was followed by war. A period of retrenchment followed, as the provincial economy continued to sputter until the mid-1920s, greatly affecting the construction of public works like courthouses.

## The Provincial Courts

One of the first priorities of the new governments of Alberta and Saskatchewan was dealing with the administration of justice. Like other provinces, under the British North America Act, Alberta had responsibility for its courts, which were overseen by the Attorney General's department. The two provinces decided to maintain the Territorial Supreme Court until they could prepare and institute legislation to create provincial court systems. For over a year and a half, the judicial status quo remained. The reorganization of the courts was vital, however, as the old Territorial system was badly overstretched, even with two additional judges, T.C Johnstone and C.A. Stuart, who were appointed in the fall of 1906. When the provincial Supreme Courts came into being the following year, all the justices stayed on. The existing Territories bench was split up, with a new judge, Nicholas Beck, appointed in Alberta to join Sifton, Harvey, Scott, and Stuart and round out the bench to five. All the sheriffs, clerks, and their deputies were also transferred to the new courts.

One of the first steps in reforming the courts was reorganizing the judicial districts. It was abundantly clear that Alberta needed more than two districts, and in the fall of 1906, five districts were established.[1] Macleod remained a judicial headquarters, its district bordering the Rocky Mountains and including the Crowsnest Pass. Lethbridge finally ascended to status of a full district, encompassing most of the southern part of the province along the American border. The new district of Calgary was substantially smaller than the old Northern Alberta District, but still stretched from the Rocky Mountains on the west to the Saskatchewan border on the east. It included Medicine Hat, where there was some dissatisfaction at not being made a judicial centre. Edmonton was the centre for the growing agricultural lands to the east and north, as well as the vast unpopulated reaches of northern Alberta.

There was a great deal of competition in central Alberta to be named headquarters for the fifth district that would inevitably be formed between Calgary and Edmonton. Although Red Deer may have looked like a more central location – and had a courthouse – Wetaskiwin, located just thirty miles from Edmonton, won out. The eponymous judicial district had an odd shape and incorporated Wetaskiwin's civic rivals Red Deer, Lacombe, and Camrose. As the population of the province grew, more districts were added: Athabaska in 1909, covering northern Alberta, Medicine Hat, Red Deer and Stettler in 1913, and in 1919 the Acadia District on the eastern margin of the province, later renamed Hanna after its centre.

The Supreme Court Act and the District Court Act, both assented to on February 11, 1907, established a new system for the province with a superior and inferior court. The Supreme Court was to have four puisne, or junior, judges and a chief justice. It would hear serious criminal charges as well as civil cases involving larger sums, by judge and jury or judge alone. Sittings of the court were set only for the headquarters of each judicial district – the justices no longer travelled on circuit in the way they had in the Territorial court. The justices of the higher court did not reside in the various judicial districts: by a 1908 amendment, the justices were stationed in Calgary and Edmonton. An assize of the court could be held at other points by an Order-in-Council. This was periodically done, especially in more remote areas of the province. The Chief Justice and the Attorney General determined when the expense of sending a judge was warranted. Twice a year at Edmonton and Calgary, the court would meet en banc for appeals. In October 1907, the Supreme Court of Alberta was inaugurated with a sitting for appeals in Edmonton.[2]

The District Court was created to satisfy demands for a resident judge in the major towns outside Calgary and Edmonton and also to expedite the majority of the business for the courts. It handled criminal charges beyond the summary powers of the police courts presided over by justices of the peace and police magistrates, and civil matters up to the value of $400.[3] A judge was appointed to each judicial district and had his office at the headquarter town, performing regular circuits to other points in the district to hold court. Larger centres in the districts could look forward to having a session of court every month. The lower court was meant to address the biggest complaint about the administration of justice in the Territorial days: lack of timely and inexpensive access for minor civil matters, especially small debts. As Attorney General C.W. Cross said in his speech to the house announcing the acts, "It is a matter of common knowledge ... that a very great number of cases in which parties feel themselves aggrieved are never brought to trial, because the amount involved would not justify ... an action at law which might have to be carried to a place some hundreds of miles distant from the place where the cause of action arose...."[4] The new inferior court was intended to bring justice to the people.

The Dominion continued to exercise its prerogative to appoint and pay judges. Throughout Canada, the federal government chose judges for all the superior courts and paid their salaries and expenses. While perhaps in theory a good idea, it had enormous drawbacks in practice. The reluctance of the Dominion to incur the expense of more judges caused constant shortages in the judiciary of Alberta. Both the Supreme and District Courts had a very difficult time keeping up with the growth of the province in the1910s. If a judge was sick or requested a leave of absence, the system almost broke down. The separation of the Supreme Court into trial and appeal divisions, along with a raft of new judges, eased the problem in the early 1920s. The District Courts were another matter. There were constant complaints about court sittings, especially in outlying regions like the Peace River where travel arrangements were more involved. And if the control of judges by the Dominion was intended to keep the courts at arm's length from provincial government, in effect it simply moved influence up one level. Judicial appointments tended to very much reflect the complexion of the ruling party in Ottawa.[5]

The shortage of judges led to the introduction of sub-districts in Alberta. This was not a new concept, and merely continued the system of appointing of deputy sheriffs and clerks. The sub-district did not get a resident judge, but was visited by the jurist of the district out of which it was carved. It did, however, get consideration for a sitting of the Supreme Court. The court offices were essentially district offices and were all intents and purposes autonomous. It was an attempt to expedite legal business but avoid hiring more judges, which remained a sticky issue between the Dominion and provincial governments. As Attorney General J.R. Boyle explained to the Grande Prairie Board of Trade in 1920: "There is no difference excepting in the name between a sub-judicial district and a judicial district, and the reason why sub-judicial districts are established instead of judicial districts is to avoid unnecessary appointments of Judges."[6]

Sub-districts were eventually formed around the towns of Bassano, Camrose, Grande Prairie, Taber, and Vegreville.

The explosive boom in the province quickly left the courts behind once again. By 1912, the situation was becoming critical. The federal government was finally persuaded to appoint William Walsh to the Supreme Court, and in 1914 three more judges – Hyndman, Ives, and McCarthy – joined the bench. The new faces helped, as did a 1913 reorganization of the court into two division, trials and appeals. Judges alternated between sitting for appeals or doing trial work: each December the justices were to choose four of their number to do the appeals for the coming years.[7] It worked so well that the government decided to formalize the arrangement, with each division having a permanent bench and identity. An amendment to the Supreme Court Act was duly proclaimed in 1919.[8] The actual establishment of the new court waited until 1921, as the federal government once again delayed appointing more judges.[9] By creating a separate appeals court (and hiring more judges), a major roadblock in the Supreme Court was removed: the court en banc could not sit frequently enough to deal with appeal work without removing trial judges from circulation and impeding civil and criminal assizes. The size of both benches increased, but the basic form of the Supreme Court remained the same until 1978.

---

### THE BATTLE FOR CHIEF JUSTICE

There is usually no shortage of egos on the bench of any court. The Alberta Supreme Court was no exception. The Court Act itself carefully established the order of precedence on the bench for ceremonial occasions, and the Chief Justice was the stand-in for the Lieutenant Governor of the province. He was also chief administrator for the courts, who made all the assignments for the judges to circuits and special sittings. It was a position of great prestige, the apogee of a jurist's career. And it was not free of controversy. When A.L. Sifton was appointed directly as Chief Justice of the Territorial Court in 1903, it caused great controversy – in the words of one historian, "it was widely regarded as crass Liberal patronage."[10]

This was nothing compared to the battle between Horace Harvey and David Lynch Scott. When Sifton resigned in 1910, Harvey, arguably the most able judge on the bench and a good Liberal, was named Chief Justice.[11] Scott, who had been appointed to the old Territorial court in 1894 by a Conservative government and was easily the most senior judge on the Alberta Supreme Court, was displeased. There was no particular precedent to say the most senior judge would be made the Chief Justice. But it still did not sit well. Scott had his revenge, however, when the Supreme Court was split into the trial and appellate divisions. The head of each division was named chief justice, but the leader of the appeal court was the Chief Justice of Alberta. Harvey continued on in the trial division while Scott was named to the appeal division by the Conservative government of Arthur Meighen, and Scott was now the province's Chief Justice.[12]

Harvey was just as prickly as Scott when it came to honours. The stage was thus set for a bizarre legal battle. Harvey decided to take the matter to the Supreme Court of Canada.[13] He argued that as the 1919 Act amended but did not replace the 1907 Act creating the Supreme Court, and ergo, since the new bipartite court did not replace the old court but was only a reorganization, he should continue as the rightful Chief Justice of Alberta unless his appointment was specifically revoked. The higher court agreed with him, and restored Harvey to his pre-eminence. But Scott, already robbed once, was not about to let Harvey get away with this legal legerdemain. He appealed to the Privy Council, which ruled in 1923 that of course Scott was Chief Justice – the 1919 Act made that pretty clear.[14] While the legal challenges went on, there was no end of problems with dealing with Scott and Harvey. For a time, they insisted on entering the room together in lockstep at official functions. Harvey had to take his defeat like a man, but Scott only lived to enjoy his post for a year, dying in 1924. His rival immediately moved to the Appeal Court and became Chief Justice of Alberta, reigning until 1949.

The growth of the judicial system drastically increased the pressure to provide new courthouses. The two went hand in hand. The creation of new judicial districts and sub-districts, with the consequent appointment of a resident district judge and offices of the court, made facilities of some sort imperative, while the expansion of the judiciary in Calgary and Edmonton had consequences for the new courthouses that were built there. In its judicial system, the province was hard pressed to keep up with the growth of the province. As will be made clear in the stories of the individual courthouses, Alberta would also have a difficult time providing the halls of justice to house its judges and courts.

## Courthouse Policy, Part One: Rutherford

Most of the factors at play in the Territorial period remained important in the early years of the province. Towns and cities still competed for the right to be declared judicial districts, which they fervently hoped would bring court staffs, resident judge and courthouse to their municipality. But it was now a different milieu.

Instead of dealing with far-off Ottawa and a bureaucracy reluctant to incur expenses governing the Territories, the voters of Alberta had their own government, made up of people imbued with their own booster ethic. For the first decade of Liberal rule, the notion that the province needed monumental public architecture for facilities like courthouses was not in question. The large cities did not put much effort into lobbying, on the assumption a new courthouse would be forthcoming as a matter of course. The smaller, up-and-coming towns, however, very much emulated their Territorial forebears in their strident demands, active campaigning, and competition with each other. Thus Vegreville cast a jaundiced eye at Vermilion an hour down the railroad, and Red Deer, Wetaskiwin, and Lacombe all jockeyed to be made the judicial headquarters for central Alberta. Much smaller towns like Gleichen, Claresholm, Nanton, and Edson all actively pursued courthouses.

The first order of business for the province was sorting out what would be done with the Territorial courthouses. When the Red Deer Territorial courthouse had been in the last stages of completion, it was clear to the provincial and Dominion governments that they would have to come to some sort of agreement about the buildings. In other provinces, courthouses were local or provincial responsibilities, and so the federal government agreed to turn three of buildings over to provincial control. The province paid rent on the buildings until they bought them outright in 1910.[15] The Lethbridge public building and the Red Deer courthouse were left out of the deal. The federal government maintained offices in these buildings and did not want to be rushed into constructing new public buildings in either centre. The province rented the space already occupied by the courts. With the other three Territorial courthouses, Alberta agreed to pay a substantial amount of money for buildings that were almost immediately obsolete and had to be replaced.

The Rutherford administration predicted in its first budget speech of 1906 that not many new courthouses would be necessary due to the Territorial legacy. It soon changed its tune and initiated many new buildings. Rutherford's government did not, however, promulgate a set policy toward building courthouses. The government officially proclaimed that courthouses were considered a vital public work, and declared that centres without courthouses would be first to receive them. It more or less stuck to this pronouncement, but not in a particularly coherent fashion or using any explicit criteria. While some centres like Edmonton that desperately needed courthouses were soon tackled, other towns like Fort Saskatchewan, where the need was less pressing, also got courthouses. Decisions were made directly in the Executive Council.[16] Sites were bought all through the province, sometimes in small towns like Claresholm and Vermilion where there was no immediate justification for building an actual courthouse. The practice hints at a grand vision, but it may have simply been a hedge against rising real estate prices and an easy way to please the local electorate. The government ended up with property in Camrose, Claresholm, Daysland, Edson, Red Deer, Vermilion, and Vegreville. It might be noted that at least three of these locations were in districts that were also represented by cabinet ministers, and that the Minister of Public Works himself, W.H. Cushing, personally chose most of the sites.

Outside the major centres, it was not easy to decide where to build courthouses. The provincial government had the same problem as had faced the Dominion. The province was still growing rapidly, and it was difficult to predict which towns were destined to become important, and how large a court facility would be best. Unlike the Dominion, the province was building for the future as well as the present. The success of the Liberals in doing so was mixed: three of the courthouses of Rutherford's administration – Cardston, Fort Saskatchewan, and Wetaskiwin – were destined to be underutilized. The Alberta government did better in this respect than neighbouring Saskatchewan, which built courthouses rather in excess of the requirements for the administration of justice.[17] After the first flush of optimism in the Rutherford years, the province tended not to build until conditions absolutely demanded it. This meant that some centres, like Medicine Hat and Red Deer, had to wait an excruciating length of time to get a proper hall of justice.

## Courthouse Policy Part Two: The Sifton Years

Under Premier Arthur L. Sifton, who took office in 1910, the government evolved a more definite policy for courthouse construction. It was tied directly to an expansion of the court system in the form of new judicial and land registration districts. Sifton, who was also Minister of Public Works until 1912, gave a full explanation for this more rigid policy in the legislature. Part of it was simple economics. The first series of public buildings started by the province had sucked the treasury dry and inflated the provincial debt. Another motivation for bringing down a clear policy was the incessant campaigning for buildings in every district. Sifton found the constant lobbying from the members of the legislature wearying and unrealistic, as well as excessively self-interested:

> ... the fact has been brought to my attention constantly during the summer ... that almost every settlement throughout the country would be delighted to have a court house built in it ... but the necessities of the legal business of this country do not yet require it, because it would be absurd to put up an expensive building in a place where a district judge goes once every two or three months for a couple of days to hold courts.[18]

Sifton could have been speaking about Cardston or Fort Saskatchewan, two courthouses built under his predecessor.

At the same time, the premier's comments were a bit disingenuous. Sifton's government came under criticism for using courthouses as political bribes, especially in Medicine Hat. The Sifton cabinet kept its policy both vague and flexible by some simple subterfuges. One strategy was passing items on the estimates for general public building without specifying the projects, as had previously been the case, thus making it hard for the opposition to know what the government planned.[19] And, of course, the government could always promise judicial districts to constituents with the understanding a courthouse would soon follow. However, Sifton's guidelines did cut down greatly on courthouse construction. Only the new Calgary courthouse was started under his administration's auspices, although a courthouse for Medicine Hat was planned and despite the fact that three new judicial districts were created.

The war ended courthouse construction for several years. As a measure of expediency, existing buildings in the town of Stettler and city of Red Deer were converted to serve as courthouses, but no new courthouses were built until 1917. Charles Stewart took over leadership of the Liberals in 1917 when Sifton stepped down. Although his administration built two courthouses, in Taber and Medicine Hat, due to the war and the recession immediately afterward, Stewart never had a chance to do extensive building before he was defeated in 1921. His government did not seem to have any particular plan for courthouse construction, following more or less Sifton's dictum of erecting them in established judicial centres where the need for a building was clear. In this spirit, Stewart's government may also have been intending to build courthouses in Red Deer and Vegreville, buildings that were not in fact erected until 1930.

## Patronage and Politicking

Political connections and lobbying had been important in the Territorial period, but under the Liberals, courthouse construction became more linked to political patronage. The exact role of patronage, however, is difficult to clarify. There was no effective opposition to the Liberals during their first two terms. The vast majority of the sitting members belonged to the ruling party. It is tempting to conclude that the cool dictates of policy, rather than the crass requirements of pleasing voters and winning elections, determined the new government's building priorities.

The reality was more complex. Deep divisions existed within the Alberta Liberals and party discipline was far looser in that era.[20] Many legislators considered themselves "independent" Liberals rather than "party" Liberals. The ruling Liberals essentially provided their own opposition. Members were far more likely to vote for the direct interests of their constituents, and in the absence of strong discipline, individual legislators arguably had more clout and used it to secure government spending for their constituencies. In competing for the judicial district and courthouse, the member for Wetaskiwin, A.S. De Rosenroll, was likely able to trade on his closer relationship with Premier Rutherford to secure the prize from fellow Liberal John Moore and Red Deer – the latter was a Rutherford critic.

The role of personal lobbying by members of the legislature appears instrumental in securing courthouses and judicial districts. At the opening of the Vegreville courthouse in 1931, Justice W.C. Simmons reminisced about his days in the legislature as the member for Lethbridge: "He told of the frantic efforts of all the members to get public buildings for their own constituencies. He and Mr. Holden had battled for buildings, but all that he had been able to get at that time for his constituency of Lethbridge was a jail."[21] Holden himself had talked at a Vegreville Board of Trade meeting about the horse trading that went on in reference to courthouses and other public works:

> Mr. Holden reviewed early history in connection with the Judicial centre. Back in 1911 when he was representing Vegreville, it was decided that both a Judicial Centre and an experimental farm should be placed along the Canadian Northern. Naturally both he, Frank Walker representing the Fort, and the Hon. A.L. Sifton representing Vermilion were out after these. Frank Walker was finally ruled out, because the Fort already had the gaol. Finally a saw-off between Hon. Sifton and he took place under which it was agreed and concurred in by government that Vermillion was to have the Experimental Farm, and Vegreville the Courthouse.[22]

This passage reveals a great deal about how members worked for courthouses, and also about how decisions were arrived at for locating them.

Aside from reflecting the influence of different legislators, there is also evidence that courthouses were parcelled out to sway the electorate. Cardston may have received the first provincial courthouse to keep the local member and electorate happy. In Medicine Hat, the Liberals promised a courthouse just before elections in 1909 and 1913, and when a Conservative was elected, the building was delayed. Despite the pressing need for a new building in Red Deer, the government was slow to provide one – the city was home of the head of the opposition Conservatives. A looming recession played a role in withholding these courthouses, but in 1918, despite wartime austerity, a courthouse was quickly erected in Taber. By coincidence, the sitting member for the area, who was also the Minister of Public Works, had just faced the electorate in a by election.

If political considerations were important in choosing where to build courthouses, patronage did not enter into design and construction. Contracts were awarded strictly on tenders and there was little sign of political favouritism. Like the Dominion Department of Public Works, the province managed to award contracts by and large to local builders, although it also chose to supervise a number of major projects directly, acting as its own contractor. Like good boosters, the government overseers were interested in encouraging local industry, and in the case of building materials tried to use nearby businesses. "We generally make it a practice to deal with the local firms, provided we can get an equal class of material and at a price not greater than we can obtain from outside sources," the department's structural engineer wrote in 1910.[23]

The success of local contractors in procuring the courthouse business is not too surprising: there was no shortage of builders in Alberta during the boom, and local men likely had some advantages in preparing attractive bids due to their connections with sub-trades and suppliers. After World War I, this policy changed. Courthouses tended to be built by larger contracting firms rather than strictly local builders. Bennett and White of Calgary, for instance, built the Medicine Hat courthouse, and the province was not afraid to get supplies from out of province if it was more cost-effective.

*Honest and able: John Stocks, the first Deputy Minister of Alberta's Department of Public Works. PAA, PA-965*

JOHN STOCKS

One of the most important figures in the early years of the provincial Department of Public Works was John Stocks. Appointed deputy minister of the department when it was formed in 1905, Stocks guided it through its birthing pains and in an astonishingly short period of time established it as an effective part of the civil service. He also established his own reputation for rock-solid integrity.

Born in Sherrington, Quebec, in 1858, Stocks joined a construction company in 1881 that soon afterwards merged with the CPR.[24] For the next twenty years he worked in the company's engineering department, becoming superintendent of construction and maintenance for most of western Canada. In 1901, he joined the Territorial Department of Public Works as assistant chief engineer and was deputy of the department when it was abolished by provincial autonomy. He was immediately recruited by the new government of Alberta as Deputy Minister of Public Works. Stocks faced an immense challenge, creating a department from almost nothing that would be responsible for surveys, roads, bridges, public buildings and their maintenance, as well as the sundry physical needs of other government departments. He rose to the challenge, and barely a year after the department was formed, it was undertaking major construction projects like the Calgary Normal School.

In an age where patronage was still very common, Stocks stood out for his unwillingness to allow politics to influence how he ran and staffed his department. His obituary mentioned that "he abhorred the patronage system." A.H. McQuarrie, the department's district engineer in Peace River, remembered reporting to Stocks in Edmonton just after the 1913 election. Stocks asked about complaints that McQuarrie had refused to take part in electioneering for the local government candidates. McQuarrie recollected their exchange:

"I was bold enough to tell him I had heard similar reports about him in the Edson district, even to the effect he would be fired because he would not take part actively in political affairs. He replied 'You can hear that right here in Edmonton. They can go right to it any time they like.'"[25]

Stocks resigned as deputy minister in 1915 and was appointed to the Alberta Utilities Commission. Early in 1917, he died suddenly of a heart attack.

Courthouse construction was the responsibility of the new provincial Department of Public Works. The transition from a territory administered from Ottawa to self-determination as a province was not easy. An entire bureaucracy had to be created in Alberta out of nothing. The provincial Department of Public Works needed a couple of years before it created its own architect's office in 1907. It also took about two years before the Attorney General's office and the Department of Public Works managed to figure out exactly who was responsible for what – more importantly, whose budget would be spent – in the administration of the courts and courthouses. John Stocks, the Deputy Minister of Public Works, had a running battle with Sheriff Robertson in Edmonton over the sheriff's office rent, which was largely due to a lack of clear lines of responsibility for approving changes to arrangements for accommodations.[26]

Once the Department of Public Works started erecting public buildings, it quickly organized its own design branch, modelled on the Chief Architect's Office of the Dominion. Why the government chose this route is unknown, but it may have felt it allowed more control over each building project. Of all the provinces, Alberta adopted the model of a government architect the most wholeheartedly, although Ontario had already set up an architect's office some years before for some building projects and Saskatchewan, Manitoba, and British Columbia would all follow suit before World War I. The architectural drafting staff was initially part of the Structural or Engineering Branch. Edward C. Hopkins was hired in 1906 with the title of Supervising Architect, but it was not until the following year that he was referred to as Provincial Architect and his staff as the Architectural Branch.[27] The branch was purely a matter of internal organization: it was never legislated in the Public Works Act. Not long after joining the department, Hopkins produced plans for the Cardston courthouse.

Hopkins left in 1907 after only a brief tenure, to be replaced by his chief draftsman, Allan Merrick Jeffers. Perhaps much more so than his counterpart in the federal government, Jeffers was chief designer for the province. Although his staff carried out the detailed drawings necessary for construction, the unified nature of the designs produced under Jeffers makes it clear they stemmed from him. Jeffers had a distinct style:

> The building in its general appearance will give one a feeling that it is substantially built of masonry structure, free from ostentatious carvings, and yet with its massive entrance columns and pavilions of the administration and legislative wings breaking the plain wall surfaces, and the low dome which surmounts the whole it will make one feel that a conscientious effort has been made to produce a simple pleasing structure, and yet one that is in keeping with a large monumental public building of this character.[28]

Jeffers' description of the legislature building, which he designed, expresses the aesthetic sensibility he also brought to his courthouses. Born in Rhode Island in 1875, Jeffers had studied at the Rhode Island School of Design.[29] During his training he had been thoroughly indoctrinated with the principles of the Beaux-Arts or "Academic" style of classical revival.[30] After a brief stint in the military during the Spanish-American War, Jeffers went into politics, elected to the Rhode Island legislature at the age of twenty-three. In 1902 he began his career in architecture with the firm of Ford, Bacon, and Davis. A few years later he came to Alberta to join the new Provincial Architect's office as senior draftsman. When the first incumbent, Edward Hopkins, resigned in September 1907, Jeffers replaced him, thirty-two years old and a relatively untested architect.[31]

Jeffers' courthouses were examples of Beaux-Arts classicism. Based on the teachings of the Ecole des Beaux-Arts in Paris, it was a very popular style in the Edwardian era. It has been described as a system of architecture, rather than a style.[32] It stressed proportion and harmony in design with a rich decorative vocabulary derived from classical architecture. Architects could choose from a number of different classical revival styles for a building's ornamentation. Interiors featured grand rotundas, hallways, and staircases, as well as what were sometimes elaborate decoration in plaster, marble, and stone. Beaux-Arts buildings could be distinguished from older classical revival buildings by their much larger scale and composition that focused the building upon a monumental entrance. Beaux-Arts was considered particularly well suited to public buildings. A 1908 editorial in Construction, an early Canadian architectural journal stated: "As regards the style of architecture of the West, it must, of course, be based on classic ... lines, the foundation of all good work in our public structures."[33]

The use of Beaux-Arts brought courthouse design in Alberta into the mainstream of architecture. Jeffers had plenty of models for Alberta's legislature and courthouses in the United States, where Beaux-Arts buildings had proliferated by the early twentieth century. The major designs produced by the department under Jeffers almost all conformed to the style. For this he received some criticism, especially in regard to the legislative building. Beaux-Arts, with its frequent use of French Renaissance and Baroque detailing, had become identified as an American style. Architectural critics in Canada preferred the so-called Edwardian Classicism. Less rigid in its design principles, it used English Renaissance or Baroque decoration, and was thought to be an "English" style more suited to Canada. The difference is difficult for a layman to spot: as architectural historian Harold Kalman puts it: "The distinction between English and French Renaissance sources provided a very real issue at the time, though it may seem moot to our own distant eyes."[34]

In reference to the courthouses, the debate was indeed a moot point, as they did not feature extensive adornment. A "simple pleasing structure" summed up Jeffers' personal taste. The entrances of his courthouses received most of the elaboration, but even this was limited, consisting of a pediment with dentilated cornice, ionic columns for the portico, fanlight windows, stone voussoirs and surrounds for windows and doors, and perhaps a relief carving of the arms of the province. The rest of the building was left almost unadorned. Jeffers preferred simple, straightforward lines to his buildings, and they were heavy, solid buildings that impressed mostly through their mass and stern, austere appearance. The Calgary hall of justice went to an even greater extreme in this regard. The buildings that resulted sometimes disappointed contemporaries. The Wetaskiwin courthouse design was thought of as "plain," and the Calgary courthouse was derided as "unadorned."[35] Considering the vast colonnades, domes and other features found on the courthouses in Winnipeg and Vancouver, it is not difficult to imagine that some Albertans were disappointed in their province's monumental architecture.

Jeffers was also a great believer in standardization. Whether on his own initiative, or in consultation with W.H. Cushing, the Minister of Public Works, the Provincial Architect tried to use each of his courthouse designs several times. The same plan for a medium-sized building with one courtroom was used at Wetaskiwin and Lethbridge and intended as well for Medicine Hat. The same design produced for the Edmonton courthouse was originally supposed to be used as well in Calgary. The attempt to use standardized designs is intriguing. It indicates that the provincial Liberals remained concerned with economy in public buildings, and may also explain Jeffers' predilection for a more minimalist style of Beaux-Arts.

Jeffers left rather abruptly in 1912. His successor was his chief draftsman and assistant, Richard Palin Blakey, which gave the branch continuity. Blakey continued the use of Beaux-Arts in his tenure, but also introduced newer styles like Mission Revival to government architecture. The renaissance-style Medicine Hat courthouse was the finest building produced by Blakey in his twelve-year career as Provincial Architect. He was destined to oversee designs for only three courthouses: Taber, Medicine Hat, and the police barracks and courthouse at Blairmore.

Born in Sunderland, County Durham, England on June 18, 1879, Blakey attended the Bede Collegiate Institute and then apprenticed with architect George Thomas Brown.[36] He worked in the north of England for several years before coming to Canada around 1906, going first to Winnipeg and then settling in Edmonton. Blakey began his career with the Alberta Department of Public Works in 1907 as a draftsman. He was made a permanent member of the staff of the Provincial Architect's office in October 1907, and soon became the Assistant Chief Architect. In 1911 he joined the Alberta Association of Architects and the Royal Institute of British Architects. The mantle of Provincial Architect fell on his shoulders on January 1, 1912, after A.M. Jeffers resigned. Blakey inherited a number of unfinished projects from Jeffers, including the legislature building. He did not have a chance, however, to put his mark on the province as his predecessor had. In 1913, the province cut back on construction, and the Medicine Hat courthouse was one of the few major edifices designed entirely under his aegis. After leaving government service himself around 1925, Blakey had a very successful private practice with his brother William. He died in Edmonton in 1963.

Blakey's architectural proclivities were quite different from Jeffers'. When Blakey was able to design a grand hall of justice in Medicine Hat, he created a building that was positively roccoco compared to Jeffers' courthouses. There are strong similarities in Blakey's three courthouse designs, which make it clear that the Provincial Architect determined the style of the buildings of the department. A 1913 design for a courthouse and land titles building at Medicine Hat, while still relatively unadorned, used decoration from Italian Baroque sources and a complex H-shaped plan that contrasted strongly to earlier courthouses. Blakey was open to the styles coming from the American southwest: his police barracks and courthouse in Blairmore was a Mission Revival building. A police building in Drumheller showed both the Spanish Revival influences as well as similarities to the Medicine Hat courthouse. Blakey also set the agenda for the courthouses that would be built later by the province. When the drafting staff at Public Works needed to produce courthouse designs at the end of the 1920s, they went back to Blakey's models.

Under both Jeffers and Blakey, Alberta's courthouses continued to conform to the basic and almost universally accepted conventions for these structures. Courtrooms were on the upper storeys, offices on the main floor, holding cells and storage in the basement. The early provincial courthouses were modern buildings in terms of technology. While the smaller buildings still used load-bearing, brick masonry walls, the courthouses in Calgary and Edmonton had steel frames and concrete floors. They were proudly proclaimed "fire-proof" buildings in the lexicon of the day. The courthouses also featured up-to-date electrical, heating, plumbing, and ventilation systems. At the same time, some of the buildings, especially Jeffers' designs, were not entirely successful from a functional perspective. Poor acoustics bedevilled all of his buildings, especially the Wetaskiwin and Lethbridge courthouses, and the architect also had a difficult time anticipating the future needs of the judiciary. There were many complaints about crowding in the Edmonton courthouse from the day it was finished, while other buildings stood half empty.

With the exception of the first courthouse at Cardston, finished in 1908, the early provincial halls of justice were also intended by and large to serve only the judiciary, and the buildings constructed before World War I did not include other government offices, nor were they generally open for use by the local community. By the early 1920s, however, some buildings had sufficient vacant space for other provincial offices, usually including the local offices of the Alberta Provincial Police. Some buildings, like Wetaskiwin, would eventually include most of the local provincial government offices. This evolved to the point that the last courthouse designed and built under the Liberals, at Medicine Hat, had space allocated for other departments at the planning stage. In the case of the courthouses at Cardston and Taber, the local community was also allowed to have some use of the buildings, although this was generally strongly discouraged.

After it was formed in 1905, the province of Alberta lost no time in building new courthouses. The Liberals wanted courthouses that properly expressed the vitality of the new province of Alberta – proper public architecture that would satisfy the collective ambition of its citizens. As will be shown in more detail with the courthouses at Cardston, Wetaskiwin, Edmonton, Lethbridge, Calgary, and

Medicine Hat, the government's ambitions were not always fulfilled. The building boom in the province made construction slow and expensive, and the changing fortunes of war and recession in the end forced the Liberals to abandon several proposed buildings and left a serious legacy of public debt for future governments.

# CARDSTON

It was the first courthouse built by the new province of Alberta. A substantial stone edifice done in the Richardson Romanesque style, the Cardston courthouse was an oddity among the court buildings of the early provincial period. It is the legacy of the shadowy figure Edward C. Hopkins, Alberta's short-lived first Provincial Architect. The Cardston building was old-fashioned in appearance and design even before it hosted its first assize in 1908. And the fact that the small southern town was even chosen for a courthouse was extraordinary. Other, much more populous centres in the province desperately needed new courthouses, but Cardston was first on the list. It invites speculation as to the true motives of the new Liberal administration of Alexander Rutherford. There are no smoking guns to prove that political opportunism was at work, but it is suggestive that the area's new MLA, John William Woolf, was one of Rutherford's supporters and also a well-respected member of southern Alberta's large Mormon community.

Thus Cardston, although never the headquarters of a judicial district or even a sub-district with attendant court officials, was granted a substantial courthouse. The building was also an oddity in the way it was open to the community. For a period of ten years, it was the de facto town and community hall. It was a stunning exception to the government's usual policy, and suggests a proprietary interest in the courthouse on the part of the community, unique in the province.

## Cardston – The Early Years

The town of Cardston has what is surely one of the most interesting histories of any locale in Alberta. It was founded by the eponymous Charles Ora Card, a leader of the Mormons in Utah. Card first came to Alberta in 1886, ostensibly to find a place for a new colony of the Church of Latter Day Saints. After scouting the area south of Macleod, Card returned the next year with a small group of immigrants and squatted on a site on Lee's Creek at the edge of the Blood Reserve. By the fall of 1887, a townsite had been properly surveyed and registered. At first named Lee's Creek, the settlement quickly became known as Card's Town and then Cardston. More settlers drifted in, and while Cardston did not exactly boom, it grew steadily.

The hamlet got a boost when the Alberta Irrigation Company struck a deal in 1897 with the Mormon Church to build an irrigation canal on the St. Mary's River.[37] The company would supply the money; the church would provide the expertise and manpower to build it, as well as homesteaders to take advantage of the newly opened agricultural land. The Mormons had a great deal of experience with irrigation in their Utah homeland. By the end of 1898, the people of Cardston were sufficiently numerous to become a duly incorporated village.[38] Barely a year and a half later, with an official population of 639, Cardston took the next step and the

Territorial Council declared it a town on July 2, 1900.[39] Charles Ora Card was the first mayor.

Although the population of Cardston was certainly not limited to devotees of the Church of Latter Day Saints, the latter always had a strong presence. Despite their excellent qualities as settlers, there was a certain amount of suspicion from neighbours and the authorities directed at the Mormons of southern Alberta. To a large extent it was due to the Church's doctrines concerning polygamy. In the United States, the Mormons were forced by government pressure to formally deny that polygamy was a tenet of the Mormon faith. In 1889, a delegation including Card went to Ottawa and petitioned Prime Minister John A. Macdonald himself to allow the Mormons of Alberta to quietly practice polygamy.[40] While the Dominion welcomed the homesteaders with open arms, multiple wives were out of the question, and to make the point clear the Criminal Code was amended in 1890 to expressly forbid polygamy. The NWMP were not above sending officers to predominantly Mormon settlements like Cardston and Raymond to spy on families.[41] Sometimes suspicion flared into open prejudice. Superintendent Sam Steele of the NWMP reported to his superiors that: "The intelligence of the Mormons is far below average of the settlers of any country; there are some sharp, shrewd men among them at the head of affairs but the remainder are, as a rule, steeped in ignorance and as perfect slaves to the Church and Elders as it is possible for any community to be."[42]

In point of fact, the Mormon settlers in Cardston and district were some of the more prosperous and law-abiding in the North-West Territories. Ironically, the police always had a strong presence in the area. Due to its proximity to the Blood Reserve and the International Border, there was a relatively large detachment nearby at St. Mary's from 1882.[43] Two constables were stationed in Cardston itself from 1898 onward.[44] The town was quite happy to have them, despite any overt prejudice against the Latter Day Saints. When a rumour surfaced in 1898 that the detachment would be moved to the post at St. Mary's, the Cardston Record was quick to suggest that instead the other post be shut and the police be moved to Cardston.[45]

## Cardston and the Courts

Cardston may have only achieved status as a town in 1901, but its residents lost little time in agitating for better court services. The town was not on the circuit for the Judicial District of Southern Alberta, so all matters for the Supreme Court had to be dealt with in Lethbridge or Macleod. As was usually the case, this did not sit well with the local movers and shakers, and the board of trade and local Liberal Association leapt into the fray. A petition was duly organized in November 1901 and sent off to Horace Harvey, then Deputy Attorney General for the Territories, demanding not only more sittings of court but also a deputy clerk and sheriff.

Harvey ignored the demand for court officers but included an assize in Cardston for 1903 – henceforth, the Supreme Court would visit in April, July, and

A man of influence: Cardston MLA John Wolff. Glenbow Archives, NA-114-13

November.[46] As always, the problem immediately arose of where to put the court. With commendable foresight, even before the good citizens of Cardston lobbied for a deputy clerk, they had been busy trying to get a courthouse built by the Dominion government. As with other towns, the local Liberal Association and the board of trade were right in the forefront. They requested that Frank Oliver, MP, present their pleas for a courthouse, customs house, and post office to the government.[47] It was the general shopping list of all growing towns. Cardston sweetened the demand with the usual offer of a free site if the Dominion would see its way clear to erecting a building worth at least $6,000. Oliver threw his support behind the request to Joseph Tarte, the Minister of Public Works.

Although Oliver's influence helped a great deal in persuading the government to build court facilities at other points in Alberta, it only extended so far. The request from Cardston was politely dismissed.

Thus when the court started visiting the town, it used whatever facilities were available, including the tithing office of the Mormon congregation.[48] As was true in other jurisdictions, halls and other spots were also rented. And as usual, no one was particularly happy with the situation, not Justice Harvey, who became the resident judge for the district in 1904, nor the people of Cardston.

## The Courthouse

The situation changed quickly when the province of Alberta was born in 1905. Of foremost importance was the election of John W. Woolf as the new MLA. He was not new to politics; when an electoral district for Cardston was formed for the old Territorial legislature, Woolf had been duly elected as the member. In the new house, Woolf openly declared his support of the Liberals and the Rutherford government. It was assumed that Woolf had delivered the Mormon vote into the Liberal fold, to the extent that nasty insinuations were made about bloc voting in the house and in the press. There is no surviving documentation to show Woolf's exact role in delivering a courthouse for Cardston. That he had some part is certain. "I was instrumental in securing from the government many thousands of dollars for the construction of same [roads and bridges] including a steel bridge over Lee's Creek and the court house, both at Cardston," Woolf recalled years later for the Lethbridge Herald.[49]

The haste with which the government moved to build a courthouse in Cardston is surprising when cities like Edmonton still did not have a proper hall of justice. Pleasing the constituents was almost certainly a factor, but there were other reasons. Rutherford claimed the judiciary had complained about the lack of court facilities in Cardston, and by 1906, it was a thriving little town of a thousand. This was not inconsequential by any means, and it was the largest centre near the international border. This in itself may have been a good reason for putting a courthouse in the town, to impress American visitors with the virility and progressiveness of the new provincial government in classic booster style.

Once the decision had been made, the government wasted little time. An appropriation was passed in the province's first budget for a site in the town and to start construction. The courthouse was one of the first major public buildings to be undertaken by the province; the other was the Provincial Normal School, or teacher's college, in Calgary. The first Provincial Architect, Edward Colin Hopkins, designed both buildings. He was appointed on March 27, 1906 and was barely in office a year before being dismissed after his parliament building design did not come up to snuff.[50] A.M. Jeffers, his successor, stated in his 1908 annual report that Hopkins had designed the Cardston courthouse, and construction had begun under his supervision in November 1906.[51]

Hopkins did not find it easy to produce a satisfactory plan and went through several designs before settling on the final building.[52] All were in the Romanesque Revival style and closely resembled each other. Originally, he wanted a much bigger edifice, two storeys with the courtroom on the second floor, as was traditional in courthouse design. It had the same large arched windows on the facade, a cornice and a large parapet above, as well as a complex window treatment on one side elevation around another entrance. The proposed building had two entrances on either side of the facade, each with a small projecting porch.

This first design was not intended, however, to be a pure courthouse, but instead combined facilities for the court with office space presumably for rent. The left entranceway, with the legend "chambers," led onto the main floor, while the right, marked "courthouse," had a stairway to the second floor. There was no direct access, however, between the two floors: there was no entrance from the first floor to the main staircase to the second, and another staircase at the rear of the building went straight down to the holding cells in the basement. The main floor was given over to offices, and it appears from the plan that they were not intended for court. One large suite was even marked as "insurance office." The separation of the main level from the rest of the building invites speculation that offices would have been available for rent, likely to members of the local bar.

The design never saw the light of day. It may have been too expensive, or deemed excessive for the needs of Cardston. Another possibility was that the Attorney General's department might have decided to eliminate offices not intended for the use of the court. As a rule, the early provincial courthouses were intended only for the superior courts, and other uses were strongly discouraged. The Department of the Attorney General may have decided against having the floor

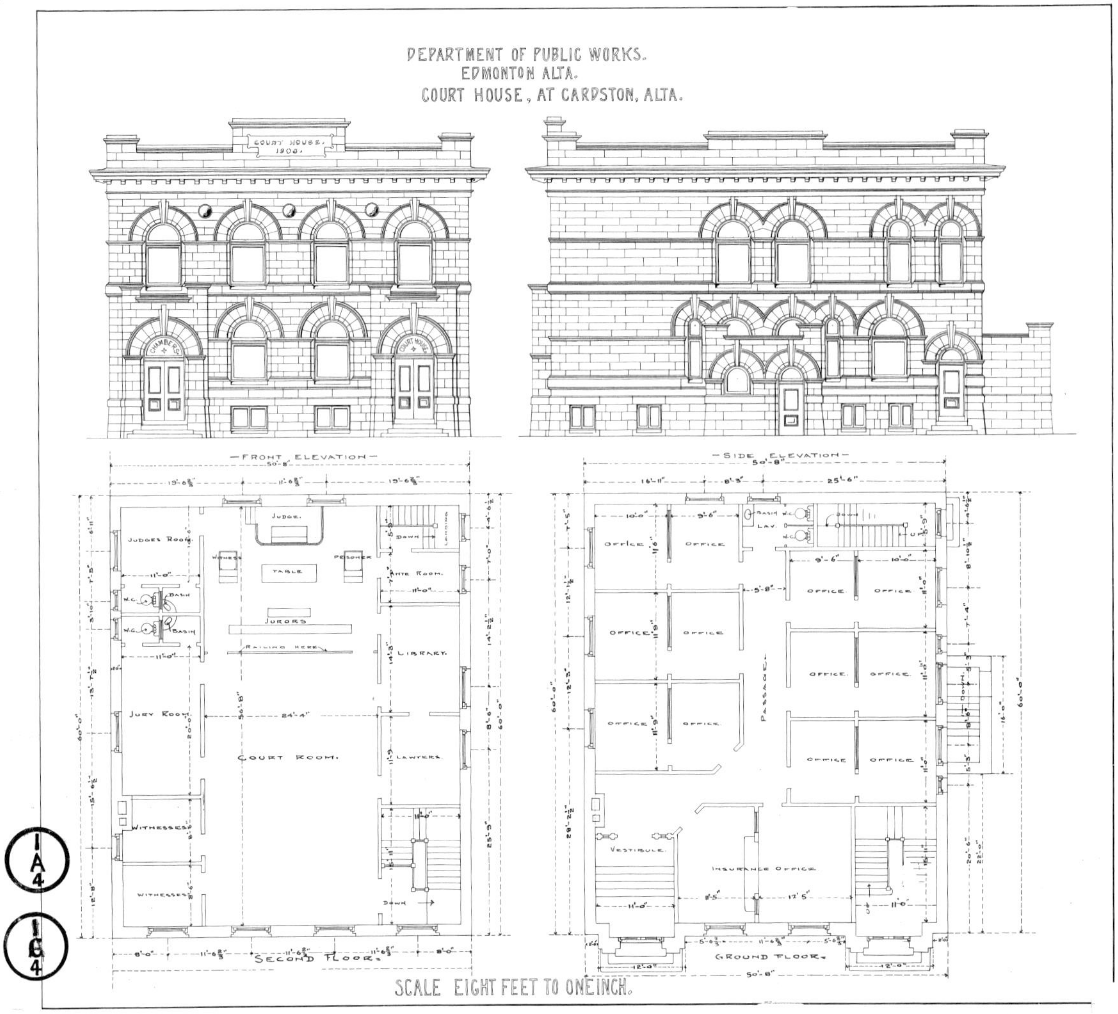


*Elevations and Floor Plans, Rejected Design, Cardston Courthouse, c. 1906. PAA*

of offices. The second design produced by Hopkins was essentially the same as the design for the courthouse that was built, although the main entrance was moved the left to the right side of the facade. The offset entrance was another quirk of the building: every subsequent provincial courthouse had a central egress in the facade. A small protruding porch housed the double doors, with a stone architrave and a fanlight. The facade had an arcade of three windows, recessed with stone arches and prominent keystones. The main floor windows on the sides of the building were given the same treatment. A partial cornice of metal wrapped around the sides of the building, adding a more contemporary classical touch to the building. There was a small stone and metal parapet on the roof. A date stone in the centre of the facade completed the decoration.

The building had a full basement with concrete and masonry foundations. Originally, the caretaker was to have a suite in the basement, while the police would have their offices and also jail cells. The main floor layout was very simple. The entrance was offset to one side of the building, and a vestibule led to a lobby where

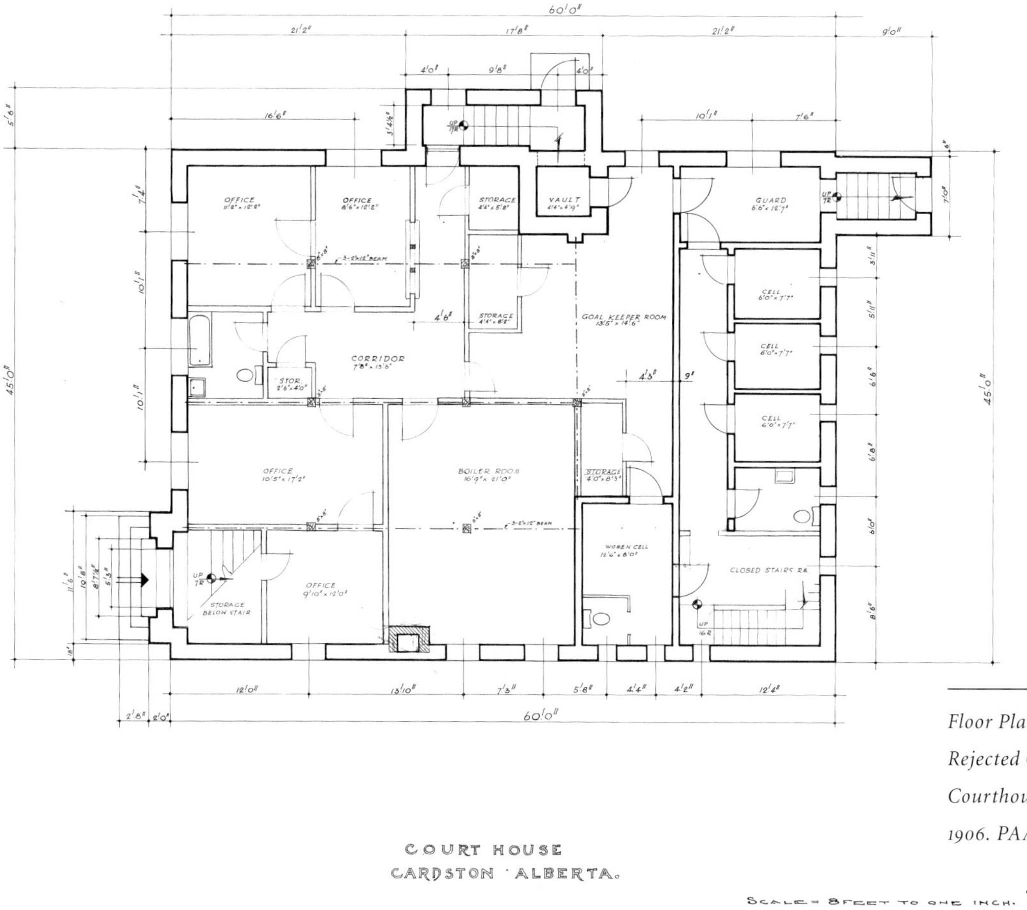


Floor Plan, Rejected Cardson Courthouse, c. 1906. PAA

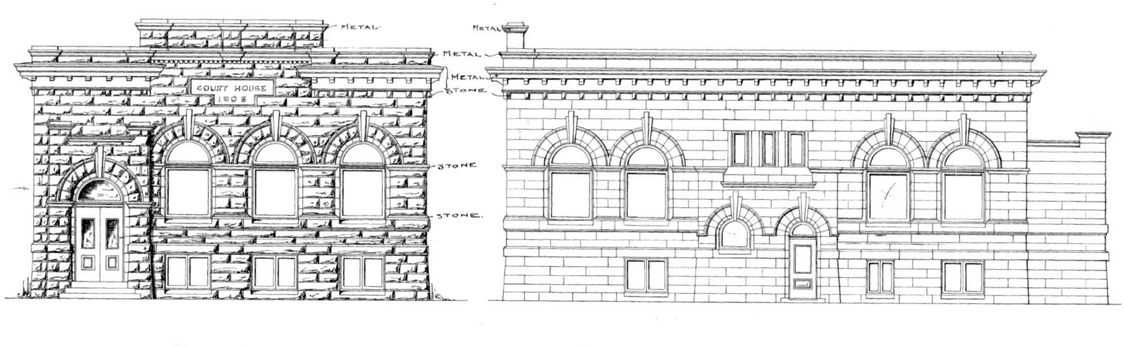


Elevations, Cardston Courthouse, 1906. PAA

one could enter the large courtroom. The various offices and chambers necessary to the functioning of the court lined the east and west walls of the courtroom. There were small offices for the clerk of court and the judge; a waiting room for the witnesses and a retiring room the jury. The interior finishing was simple, with plaster walls and extensive woodwork, using birch for the main floor and fir in the basement. "As this structure has but one principal story no attempt at elaborate stairs or other finish work was considered necessary to add to the beautifying of its internal features," commented Jeffers in his 1908 annual report.[53]

Unusual Design: Floor Plan, Cardston Courthouse, 1906. PAA

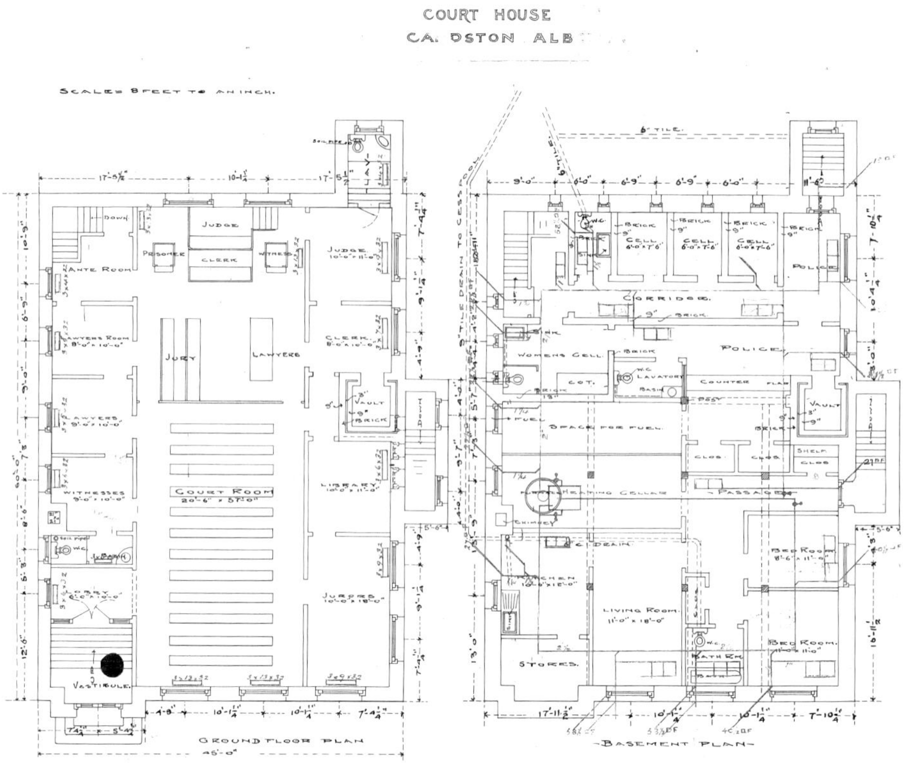


In its internal layout as well as appearance Cardston was quite unlike any of the early courthouses of Alberta, including the Territorial buildings. The single-storey plan was unusual, all the offices and private areas, including the clerk's office and library, open right off the main courtroom. Even the earlier Territorial court buildings attempted some separation of the different functions, generally putting the courtroom with witnesses, barristers' room, jury room, and judges' robing room on one floor, and all the court offices on another. The Cardston courthouse was in some ways, however, more reminiscent of a meeting hall, and there has been speculation that it may have been a local design.[54] It does seem clear that the building was never intended to serve as the headquarters of a judicial district, and was not designed with the thought that it would someday house a complete set of court offices. This is borne out by a comment by John Stocks, the Deputy Minister of Public Works, in correspondence dealing with the NWMP detachment in the basement. Stocks stated that the "court room will seldom be occupied."[55] Hopkins may have merely been lacking in sophistication, but his Normal School design belies that. He may quite intentionally have produced a small and simple building but with an imposing appearance that would please local interests.

W.H. Cushing, the Minister of Public Works, came to Cardston to find a location for the courthouse. Throughout his term, the minister personally attended to the politically sensitive matter of picking out building sites. In the case of Cardston, choosing a site was relatively trouble-free. Cushing arrived in August

1906 on a tour of southern Alberta and decided on a location next to the Assembly Hall for the Mormon Church.[56] The new edifice would face south from its position on Centre Avenue, between Main Street and 1st Street. The government paid $250 for the land.[57]

Local opinion was pleased when the contract was given to Samuel Newton, a local contractor and sometime draftsman. Newton has, in fact, been credited with having a hand in the designing of the courthouse, although there is no documentary evidence to show this. He was a talented stonemason, however, and was a fine choice for the building. The government asked for tenders at the beginning of September 1906, and the contract was awarded soon afterward. Newton began work on the excavation in November.

When work began again in the spring, the courthouse rose quickly from the ground. The misnamed "Limestone Quarry," owned by two local doctors and managed by Newton, provided easily accessible sandstone.[58] At first construction proceeded well. The structure was closed in by the end of 1907, and according to the Department of Public Works' annual report, "finished with the exception of placing wood finish and painting."[59] It turned out to be a big exception. The courthouse would not be ready until well into the spring. In his report for 1908, the Provincial Architect complained that "the progress on the building was slow, there being several contributary[sic] causes, and the taking over of same by the Department was not effected until May of this year."[60]

---

### SAMUEL SMITH NEWTON

Originally from London, England, Sam S. Newton was already a contractor and draftsman of great experience before coming to Cardston. His obituary in 1954, when he died at the ripe age of ninety-five, ascribed almost every major building of early Cardston to this prolific builder.[61]

Trained as brick mason, Newton had cut his teeth as a craftsman on the fabulous temple of the Mormons in Salt Lake City. After a stint as a builder in the Yukon during the gold rush, he emigrated to Alberta. As an experienced stonecutter, he thrived in Cardston. Aside from the courthouse, Newton built the Cahoon Hotel, the Spencer Block, the Tithing Office and Tabernacle of the Latter Day Saints. When the famed Cardston Temple was constructed in the 1920s, Newton was one of the contractors and supervised the quarrying of granite for the edifice in Nelson, British Columbia. The courthouse, however, remains his landmark building and the craftsmanship of the stonework for the building was of the highest order. In later years, Newton did some other small contracts on the courthouse.[62]

Newton was not just a talented builder. Self-educated, he read and travelled widely, and was an enthusiastic musician who led a number of bands, orchestras, and choral groups. A prominent and active member of the local

*Civic landmarks: Cardston Courthouse and Latter-Day Saints Assembly Hall, c. 1910. CDMA*

Mormon congregation, he also participated in civic politics as a councillor and general raconteur. Newton delighted in sending satirical letters lampooning town council to the local newspaper, and was well known as a self-appointed building inspector, quick to bring attention to any shoddy construction around Cardston.[63]

Almost all the courthouses built before World War I tended to be protracted affairs. Under Jeffers, the Department of Public Works would not set high standards for efficient construction. Cardston, at a year and a half, was actually one of the quicker jobs. Courthouses were somewhat more elaborate than most buildings, but many large commercial structures in Calgary and Edmonton, complete with expensive finishing materials, were built in a third of the time of the courthouses in these two cities. When time for design and letting tenders is allowed for, it might take over four years for a courthouse to be finished.

The first assize in the new edifice was very much an anticlimax. In June, a party from Lethbridge including Judge Roland Winter, Sheriff Malcolm Young, the Clerk of District Court Irwin, and C.F.P Conybeare for the Attorney General, as well as future Supreme Court Justice W.C. Ives, came out for the day.[64] Only two cases were on the docket, assault charges that were immediately adjourned when the defence counsel did not show up. Once completed, the courthouse tended to fade into the background, a civic landmark to be sure, but one that only entered the public consciousness when a particularly juicy trial was to be had. Thus we are provided with little insight as to the effectiveness of the building in its judicial function. It cost the government the tidy sum of just over $22,000,[65] a fair amount of money for an edifice that they did not think they would use very often, and indeed did not. Cardston would never be the centre of a judicial district with a resident judge or a regular sitting of the Supreme Court. This raises the suspicion that it was indeed a politically motivated building.

The Department of Public Works decided on one major change even before the building was quite completed. Instead of housing a caretaker in the courthouse, it decided that the whole basement would be turned over to the RNWMP detachment, which would then look after the building. Inspector Taylor of the police came up with the idea when the public works inspector for Cardston asked him if the police were going to get quarters in the building.[66] It immediately found favour with the department, and the police readily accepted John Stocks' offer of space, which gave them a fully equipped detachment with living quarters, cells, and office space. A stable was built out behind the courthouse for the police horses. Having the police in charge of the building saved the department the bother of hiring and supervising a caretaker.

The Alberta Provincial Police took up quarters in 1917 after taking over from the federal force. In the 1920s, even more of the courthouse would be given over to the provincial police. The courtroom would be partitioned and more living accommodation created for the constables on the main floor. After the APP disbanded and the RCMP took over policing duties again, the detachment abandoned the living quarters in the courthouse. The partition remained, but the sleeping areas were once again turned into offices. The Cardston detachment set an early precedent for housing the police in courthouses, something that would become more and more common after World War I.

## Courthouse or Community Hall?

As a rule the Department of the Attorney General was very possessive toward its courthouses. In busier centres, frequently not even the local police magistrates and justices of the peace were permitted to use the courthouse for their work. Police courts were the responsibility of the municipalities, and the town or city had to provide their own facilities. Usually, if the District and Supreme Court did not have large sittings, the police magistrate might be welcome to use the local courthouse. But organizations outside the government were not welcome, especially in the early years. Cardston was a major exception. There was never any difficulty with the courthouse being available for the local justice of the peace for police court. Even the district's liquor inspector began using it within months of opening for hearings on liquor offences. This was not unreasonable, as this use still fell within the purview of the Attorney General.

A literary society, however, was a different matter. At the end of January 1910, a local group met in the courthouse and organized itself as the Canadian Club, advertising "Meetings every Thursday evening at the Court House."[67]

Permission had come directly from the Attorney General's department, and it was not the first or last time that office would be so obliging.[68] In 1911, the secretary of the Cardston Agricultural Society wrote Sheriff Young in Lethbridge with the following request:

> We are showing a wrestling contest here during the Cardston Agricultural Fair. If the weather is bad we would desire to hold it in a building with some seating capacity. Can we arrange to hire the Court House here for the bout, should it storm? This is a clean contest and exhibition for a purse offered by the association.[69]

Although this was refused, the courthouse was used for other social events: the local Imperial Order of the Daughters of the Empire had a fundraising dinner in the building in 1918 that included dancing, and the town held a ball and dance in the courtroom as a farewell to the army units stationed there during the war.[70]

In 1918, the courthouse took on an even greater role in the community. Unable to raise the necessary funds to build itself a town hall, the town of Cardston approached the Department of Public Works to use the courthouse.[71] In return for meeting space, an office and permission to use it for civic matters, the town undertook to look after the heating and lighting in the courthouse. There were conditions on the use of the building, and the understanding was clear that the town would not rent the space they used to other groups.

The undertaking of the town not to rent their rooms was soon abandoned. The Superintendent of Buildings, Daniel McDonald, was not amused when he found out that the town was subletting the council rooms. By 1925, the board of trade had its meetings there; the local Liberal Association used it for a caucus meeting (and this under an United Farmers of Alberta administration), and the school board had been granted a meeting room and record storage.[72] When a teacher wanted to use the building for Sunday school and was improvident enough to write directly to the Minister of Public Works, however, it caused some waves.[73] There were some words from McDonald to the council about the practice of renting out rooms to other groups, but the town was allowed to continue using the building. Perhaps to prevent the courthouse from being wholly taken over as a town hall, however, the department decided to change the layout of the building to provide more room for the Alberta Provincial Police detachment. In April 1926, the town was given its notice and their office was moved to the Spencer block.[74]

Although both the Dominion and provincial governments as a rule strongly discouraged non-judicial uses for courthouse, it is not too surprising that Cardston was an exception. There was a high percentage of American immigrants in the area, coming from a different tradition vis-à-vis courthouses. In many jurisdictions in the United States, where courthouses were the responsibility of the local county administration, local taxpayers often approved the financing of a courthouse through a plebiscite and therefore had a strong sense of ownership. The courthouse belonged to the people, literally. Numerous American courthouses played a role in their communities as meeting halls, often extended to social activities like theatrical performances or dances. The provincial government seemed to recognize that the courthouse had a larger role in Cardson than simply judicial.

After the town office left, the building was used much less for other purposes, but it was still host to other groups: the board of trade, for instance, was allowed to continue meeting there. Eventually the government began to crack down on the various and sundry uses of the courthouse. Part of the reason was discontent in Cardston itself at the loss of rental revenue when the courthouse was made available to different organizations. When W.D. Stacey, the Superintendent of Buildings, found out that the local irrigation district board was using the courthouse for meetings, he wrote a memo to the deputy minister:

> I think an important point with the Government is that in these towns there are public buildings for this purpose, whereby a man makes his living from rent received for these buildings, and the Government does not wish to take business from them.[75]

Stacey relented and allowed the district trustees to continue using the building for meetings, deciding it was "more or less under the supervision of the Government"[76] and legitimate business for the courthouse. The local returning officers could still use the courtroom for elections, but when the Cardston Health Society asked the courthouse caretaker for permission to use the building in 1947, they were turned down.

The government required the courthouse increasingly for its own needs. Inevitably, as happened with courthouses in smaller centres, Cardston became a de facto provincial building. The lack of activity in the courts freed up room for other offices. Cardston had not grown much since before World War I, and perhaps due to the Mormon presence was quite law-abiding. By the 1940s, Judge Jackson in Lethbridge was only holding District Court once or twice a year. Thus the presence of other officials of the provincial government did not interfere much with the operation of the courts. In 1944, the judge's office was commandeered for the police magistrate and his office in turn given to the local school inspector. The inspector joined the district agriculturist and the district engineer among others. The department actually went too far in its eagerness to accommodate other government offices. A few years later, Judge Sissons of the District Court complained about not having any place to robe and prepare for court.[77]

The Cardston courthouse has to be considered unique among Alberta's early courthouses. Not only did it have a singular design, almost a throwback to small rural courthouses of over a century earlier, but the way the community regarded the building was also something of an anomaly. Only in Taber, a similarly sized town where the municipal government had made a major investment in providing land for a small courthouse, did the community have similar access to the building for other activities. Although the citizens of Cardston arguably overstepped the boundaries with their courthouse, it remains that town had a very proprietary view of their court building, and that the government was most obliging in meeting their desires.

Cardston courthouse, Cardson and District Historical Society.

## Epilogue

Cardston remained a small town. The farm crisis brought on by the droughts in the early 1920s and in the Depression kept the town stagnant, and even in the oil boom of the 1950s it only experienced modest growth, reaching a population of 2,800 in 1961. Unlike in fast-growing centres such as Lethbridge, Red Deer, or Medicine Hat, there was little pressure in Cardston to replace the 1908 courthouse, and it continued in use until 1979.

By the 1960s there was a need for a major renovation: over the years the internal configuration in the building had been changed several times, there had been some severe leaks in the roof, and it was simply getting old. As part of a general upgrading of the province's courts and courthouses, in 1966 the edifice was revamped. The partition installed in the courtroom in 1926 was removed and the space restored to its original size. The RCMP left the courthouse to occupy a new building. New floor coverings were installed, the electrical and plumbing upgraded, and the whole building thoroughly cleaned and repainted. The appointments in the courthouse, including the woodwork and original judge's bench, were left in place, making the courtroom one of the most atmospheric in the province.

The expansion of lower court services eventually made the old courthouse obsolete. Cardston was slated for a new provincial building that would also include judicial facilities. By 1980, it was finished and the original courthouse became redundant. The local historical society had begun a campaign several years earlier to get the building turned over to the town for use as a museum.[78] There were fears that the old courthouse might be demolished, and the town supported a request for designation of the edifice as a historic site. Alberta Culture recommended it for historic status in the fall of 1978, and designation was duly given the next year.[79] Once the provincial building was completed, the courthouse was given to the town of Cardston. There was a degree of uncertainty as to what would become of it: the plan for a museum ran into snags, but in 1981 the venerable structure was turned over to the local historical society and lovingly restored.[80] The courthouse now affords visitors a chance to learn about Cardston's past through displays of artifacts from the pioneer era. In the basement, the original cells, complete with graffiti from seventy years of housing defendants awaiting trial, remain as reminders of the building's own history.

# WETASKIWIN

Wetaskiwin's courthouse was a landmark building. It was the second provincial courthouse to be built, but the first attempt by Allan Merrick Jeffers, appointed Provincial Architect in 1907, to design a structure for the courts. The building he produced was a template, a medium-sized edifice that could be replicated in the smaller cities throughout the province. It was a sophisticated design, combining all the necessary functions of the superior courts in a compact and efficient floor plan. The grand courtroom, however, captured the essential qualities contemporaries looked for in a hall of justice. With its high ceilings and extensive architectural decoration, it created the atmosphere of awe, fear, and trembling thought suitable for the courts and captured the elusive quality called 'the majesty of the law.'

For all of its imposing character, Jeffers' model was not a success: its execution in Lethbridge produced a less than adequate building, and a planned third in Medicine Hat was dropped. In Wetaskiwin, at least, the courthouse was quite successful, a temple of justice that served the town and the judicial district for over seventy years. It was a community landmark, used for ceremonial occasions of all sorts. For many years it also contained other offices of the provincial government, and for several decades the Wetaskiwin edifice performed much the same role as the county courthouses of eastern Canada and the United States. Standing alone on its square, the courthouse was the symbol of not just the law, but government as well.

## Wetaskiwin – The Early Days

The name Wetaskiwin is a corruption of the Cree word meaning, "place where peace was made."[81] According to the Cree and Blackfoot tradition, two great braves of the warring tribes made peace at a meeting in the hills near the present city in 1867.[82] The Cree signed Treaty Six in 1876, and the Samson Band was established on a reserve nearby at Hobbema.[83] Samuel Lucas, the Indian Agent for the Hobbema Agency, was the first white resident in the district. In 1880 he was joined by his brother Frank and his family on a nearby homestead.[84] The Oblate fathers of the Roman Catholic Church, who had been ministering to the Cree for decades, did not forget them on their reserve and established the mission of the Lady of the Seven Sorrows there in 1884.[85]

Like many prairie towns, Wetaskiwin was a child of the railroad. In 1891 the Calgary and Edmonton Railway was completed. Prior to the railroad, travel between the two centres had been by horseback, cart or stage along a well-established trail. Frank Lucas turned his homestead into a stopping house within a day's travel of Edmonton. At a point near where the trail and rails intersected, the C & E set up siding number sixteen. On the advice of Father Albert Lacombe, the famous Oblate missionary, the company decided to survey a townsite at sixteen that the priest christened Wetaskiwin.[86] The proximity to the reserve was an opportunity for enterprising merchants, and the rich agricultural belt of the parkland was sure to quickly attract settlers. Within a short time eager homesteaders did appear, including several large groups of Scandinavians.[87] In 1896, an Italian nobleman, Anthony Sigwart de Rosenroll, appeared in the little hamlet along the railway.[88] Looking for investment opportunities, he opened a creamery and a lumberyard and began dealing in real estate. He was soon the district's leading citizen and its member for the Territorial legislature.

Rosenroll was not the only businessman attracted to the townsite. Stores, hotels, a post office, and banks all sprang up. Bob Edwards, famous for his satirical journal, the Eye Opener, started the first newspaper, known as the Free Lance, which lasted four years.[89] By 1899, Wetaskiwin was large enough to be made a village under the Territorial ordinances. Two short years later, its population standing at 550, it lobbied for incorporation, which was granted. As the immigration policy of Interior Minister Clifford Sifton made itself felt, the population of the town and district grew rapidly. Although Edmonton was just over the horizon, Wetaskiwin emerged as an important regional centre in the parkland, rivalling Red Deer. By 1906, civic boosters wanted all the advantages of cityhood. Led by Rosenroll, now an MLA, they successfully lobbied the Rutherford administration to become Alberta's fifth city.

## Courts and Courthouses

Despite the town's modest size and recent origins, the citizens of Wetaskiwin had big ambitions. As early as 1903, the townspeople demanded permanent court facilities from the federal government.[90] The local Liberal Association asked Frank Oliver to take their demands to Ottawa.

Oliver, as was his wont, forwarded the application with expressions of his support to the two relevant departments, Justice and Public Works. The latter deferred to the decision of the Minister of Justice, David Mills. He was not favourably impressed. Although granting that the town was a growing centre in excellent agricultural country, he speculated that "increased railway accommodation that is to be provided in the Northwest in the immediate future, … may have the effect of creating some other far more important centre than Wetaskiwin."[91] Furthermore, Edmonton itself, a scant thirty miles away, still did not have a proper courthouse, and the minister suggested that perhaps this took a certain priority. The Secretary of Public Works was officially told that the minister proposed to "make further enquires" but that "it will not ... be expedient to make provision of the courthouse this season, but the matter will be taken into consideration at an early date."[92]

The citizens of Wetaskiwin were not necessarily out of line in requesting a courthouse – just very optimistic. The town was actually larger than Red Deer, which had just successfully convinced the government it needed one. The courts were quite busy. With the stationing of Justice David Lynch Scott in Edmonton, northern Alberta became de facto if not de jure a judicial district, and Scott had been visiting Wetaskiwin since 1902.[93] In 1903 there was talk of appointing a police magistrate: the NWMP were finding that the justices of the peace in the district were hard to corral for trials.[94] In September 1903, several accused were released for lack of a judge to try them. Horace Harvey, Deputy Attorney General for the Territories, advised Rosenroll, the Territorial representative, that he would like a police magistrate in the town.[95]

*High drama: Angus Opera House, used by the courts. WCA 89.17*

The town tried one more time to get a courthouse, proposing once again that the government build a public building that would include a post office, land office, and customs office. A resolution from the town council setting out the pressing need for all these was sent to Peter Talbot, MP for Strathcona, early in 1905. Talbot replied two months later, but had to advise the town that with provincial autonomy in the works, it was highly unlikely the federal government would consider building anything.[96] The council changed tack. Courthouses might no longer be a federal responsibility, but post offices would remain so. Moderating their demands, they decided that a post office was really their highest priority, and communicated this to Talbot.

## The Provincial Courthouse

Thus matters stood. The Dominion government, trying to minimize its expenditures as rumours of autonomy buzzed around, was quite satisfied with completing the courthouse in Red Deer. In Wetaskiwin, the Territorial court continued to rent space for the assize, including a hall owned by town councillor Gould above his general store, the Oddfellows Hall, and later the new Angus Opera House. Wetaskiwin grew rapidly into a bustling little centre of over two thousand, and in 1906 lobbied the provincial government for city status. Wetaskiwin's early ascendancy to this exalted rank was partially due to A.S. Rosenroll, who had been elected to the provincial assembly in 1906. He was a leading booster of the district, not surprisingly given his widespread business interests. Rosenroll was a close friend of Alexander Rutherford and was a strong supporter of his administration. Although he never was given ministerial rank, Rosenroll wielded a certain amount of influence in the Liberal Party. This was to stand Wetaskiwin in good stead when it was time to hand out courthouses.

Although Wetaskiwin was also named the headquarters of a judicial district in 1906, thus increasing the merit of building a courthouse, it had not been a foregone conclusion that the city would be the headquarters for the central parkland. A

*New "courthouse": Heric's Hall under construction, 1901. WCA 81.31/20 C*

number of towns desired that honour, including Red Deer to the south, which already had a courthouse. Rosenroll, according to some accounts, fought hard to get the district headquartered in his town and was by and large responsible for winning it for Wetaskiwin.[97] A delegation was sent to Edmonton from Wetaskiwin under his care in at the beginning of September 1906, as the cabinet and the Attorney General debated how to best organize the province for the administration of justice. By what mechanism Cross decided to portion out the province into districts is unknown, but the Judicial District of Wetaskiwin was announced on September 5 by Order-in-Council. There was surprise and consternation elsewhere in the new district. The fact the home city of the district was in the far northwest corner did not please the residents of Lacombe or Red Deer, where feelings ran high about the decision. We do not know what effect the personal intervention of Rosenroll might have had, but it was likely quite important. The citizens of Wetaskiwin were very protective of their new honour: when they thought the government was going to split up the new district to provide for Red Deer, no time was lost in getting Rosenroll to write in protest.[98]

The fact that the member for Wetaskiwin had large business interests in Wetaskiwin did, however, cause some degree of friction. Not everyone in Wetaskiwin loved Rosenroll, whatever his efficacy in the legislature. The Rutherford administration had announced in its first budget speech on May 8, 1906 that it would buy property for a hall of justice, which was also the first public indication a courthouse was being considered for the city.[99] W.H. Cushing, the Minister of Public Works, headed to Wetaskiwin on August 17.[100] One of the blocks of property the minister looked at was block 62, located in the section of Wetaskiwin east of the railroad tracks, consisting of eleven lots, nine owned by K.A. Gullickson.[101] Cushing must have expressed interest in the land, for only three days later Rosenroll wrote to tell him that the owner wanted $400 per lot. Within two days, Cushing wired back his assent to the purchase, and all eleven lots were sold and transferred to the government. By August 29, the property was in the possession of the Department of Public Works, and a cheque had been issued to Archilles Schmid, Rosenroll's partner in a real estate company.[102] It was a large block of property, which would eventually provide a lovely park-like setting for the courthouse.

It appeared all a little too cozy for the Wetaskiwin Times. The paper objected strenuously to the fact that the citizens of Wetaskiwin had had no chance to review the choice of location.[103] The fact that the land was in east Wetaskiwin, on the other side of the C&E tracks from the business section, was immediately unpopular and fuelled suspicion that it was a sweetheart deal. Although the president of the local Liberal Association had been on the initial inspection tour, along with two prominent Conservatives, this was deemed insufficient representation. The newspaper's reporter claimed that only two sites were examined, one of which was Rosenroll's lumberyard, and that the Gullickson deal only went forward because some private individuals had contributed money toward the deal, as Cushing refused to pay the $400 per lot asking price. Referring to "cat in the bag tactics" by "one clique," the paper demanded an explanation in its pages from Rosenroll. The reply was swift in coming. Rosenroll categorically denied any special arrangements or even trying to direct Cushing toward any one property, saying that "the minister made his own selection as he has done in other places, without allowing any interference."[104] Moreover, he took the Times to task for not bothering to interview him about the matter.

In the fracas over the site, the fact that the *Times* felt that the Liberal Association executive should have been consulted over the purchase is most interesting. Indeed, the paper implied that the decision should be in hands of the association: "Why was the Liberal Executive not consulted in this matter? Of what use is the Executive unless it is to consider matters of this kind – which by the way, has not been taken into the confidence of the member since his election?"[105] Although one must be cautious in ascribing too much to the scribbling of one newspaper editor, it speaks volumes about the attitudes of at least some electors toward the government. Although the Rutherford government made great play on being nonpartisan, there were clearly expectations from its supporters that with Liberals in power, local Liberals would call the shots when it came to important decisions like where to build courthouses. This should be no surprise, as it was very much a continuation of Territorial days, when the Dominion government quite openly looked to its local supporters for advice and approval.

## Design and Construction

Some in Wetaskiwin feared the furor over the site would delay the construction of the courthouse, but the Department of Public Works was apparently unconcerned. The first set of drawings was completed in August 1907, and revised in November, just before construction began. The Wetaskiwin edifice was the first designed by Allan Merrick Jeffers. Trained in Beaux-Arts classicism at the Rhode Island School of Design, Jeffers brought this sensibility to his work for the province. The four major courthouses designed by Jeffers were all classical revival structures. He tended toward the severe with his designs, with only subdued decorative elements concentrated around the entrance of his buildings. Simplicity was the hallmark of a Jeffers courthouse.

For Wetaskiwin, Jeffers started with a cruciform footprint. The facade of the courthouse was about eighty-seven feet wide and the main part of the building was approximately eighty-four feet deep. It was a relatively modern building in construction, with a concrete foundation and load-bearing brick masonry walls. The building faced north on its site, with a west and east wing each of two storeys. The central component was three storeys high with a hip roof. The main entrance had a grand portico. Two engaged brick piers and two sandstone Ionic columns placed *in antis* supported the pediment, emblazoned with a carved relief of the coat of arms of the province and the building's date stone. The double doors, which were relatively small, and a large fanlight window on the second floor were contained in a prominent brick arch. The doors were surmounted by an arched transom window, with a carved stone pediment set on brackets above. Four arched windows, two per floor, flanked the doors, with brick and stone voussoirs.

The rear entrance was a mirror of the front. The columns were not used, but there was another pediment, and while there was only a single plain door, there was a large arched window above to let light into the stairway to the courtroom. Aside from the front entryway, the windows were all square cut, with stone sills and brick voussoirs, including the smaller windows for the attic storey. A cornice defined the top of the second floor. It was a very plain building in most regards, weighty and solid, asserting its presence more through a stern visage than architectural fripperies. The entire building used pressed brick as a finish, with most of the stone details, including the foundation wall, in Calgary sandstone. Jeffers was not averse to saving some money, however, on his stone trim. The plans called for the pediments and cornice to be galvanized iron like the roofing material, painted to resemble sandstone – it was a common enough practice on contemporary commercial structures. For architectural decoration that was well above street level, painted tin or iron could be substituted for stone, and in fact on some American courthouses the entire cupola or tower might be metal.

Internally, the Wetaskiwin courthouse had a clever design, another hallmark of Jeffers' court buildings. The main corridor ran the length of the building to the rear, where the grand staircase to the courtroom was located. The rear doorway gave more direct access to the stairs. This allowed, in theory at least, for a more unobtrusive entrance of spectators if officials so desired. A cross-corridor allowed access to the two wings. On the west, or left as one entered the building, were the offices of the Clerk of the Supreme Court and the judges' chambers, on the other side the District Court clerk and the sheriff. Both clerks and the sheriff had a general office as well as a private office. There was more office space along the corridor as one travelled toward the main stairs. Each wing also had a set of stairs to the second floor.

The heart of the building was the courtroom on the second floor. The vast, high-ceilinged courtrooms found in many British Columbia courthouses, which one author has compared to churches, may have influenced Jeffers. In any case, he put a great deal of effort into designing a space that would create a suitable atmosphere to project the majesty of the law. Rising right up to the attic, with a twenty-five

Front elevation, Wetaskiwin Courthouse, 1908. PAA

foot ceiling, it was grand space. Clerestory windows and a large skylight directly above the judge's bench introduced more light into the room. The walls were decorated with engaged plaster pillars of the Ionic order, and the ceiling had plaster beams. There were oak panels throughout the room, as well as maple flooring, with fanciful wood pediments over the doors and windows. Local tradition claims that the courtroom finishing was done by local Swedish craftsmen. The public entered the far south end of the courtroom. On either side of the judge's bench were doors to the hall. The judges, lawyers, witnesses, and jury could enter the courtroom from the axial corridor. One wing had the jury room, the other the witness room, with entrances right into the courtroom. The judges' offices, law library, and barristers' rooms lined the corridor. The officers of the court, as well as others involved in trials, could get into the courtroom without having to rub shoulders with the general public.

*Rear elevation, Wetaskiwin Courthouse, 1908. PAA*

*Side elevation, Wetaskiwin Courthouse, 1908. PAA*

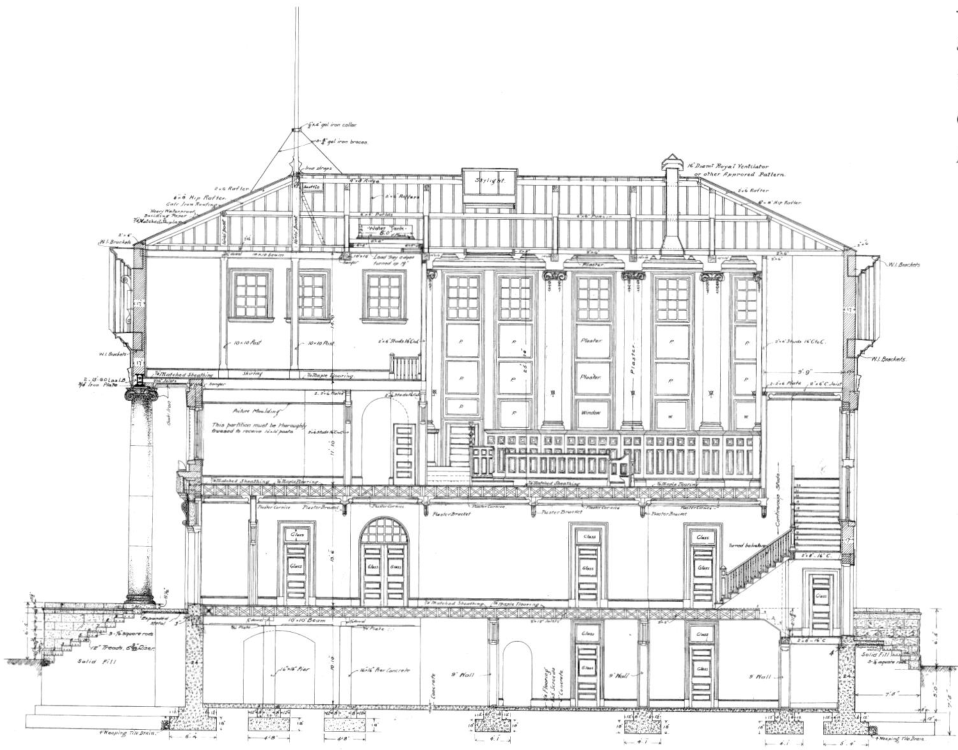

*Section, Westaskiwin Courthouse, 1908. PAA*

The Supreme Court justice had an apartment on the attic floor for his visits. A stair led down to the second floor just behind the courtroom. The judge was not the only one staying in the courthouse. An apartment was set up in the basement for the caretaker and his family, who could also look after the judge's needs when he stayed. There was even a kitchen. The basement also contained two cells for prisoners awaiting trial, while the rest of the floor was given over to storage. Egress to the basement was somewhat limited, with only one stairway in the west wing. The building as a whole had a well-worked-out floor plan, allowing fair access for the public to court offices and the main courtroom, while also giving the court the ability to move from office to courtroom out of sight of the spectators. However, like most efficient and compact designs, it had one significant drawback. It was difficult to add to without radically altering the building.

Construction could not happen fast enough for the citizens of Wetaskiwin. The contract was soon let to D.J. McLaughlin, an Edmonton contractor active in Wetaskiwin who had recently built the new Merchant's Bank (where the court offices were located). According to Jeffers' report for 1908, his was the lowest tender.[106] Surprisingly, there does not seem to have been any fuss about the job going to an outside contractor, but the city was exceedingly proud of the Merchant Bank building, and so may well have regarded McLaughlin as one their own. The foundation was excavated before winter.[107] Work began again in the spring with the stone masons shaping the blocks for the foundation walls and the trim.[108] Rosenroll meanwhile

Ready for the final touches, c. 1909. WCA, 84.59

was kept busy fielding concerns over the orientation of the courthouse on its site, and the quality of the brick to be used for the external cladding. The residents were keeping a sharp eye on the progress of the building.

At the end of 1908, the Post reported with great pride that "The new Court House, now nearing completion is a magnificent structure and reflects great credit upon both architect and builders."[109] It was actually not quite done. Although McLaughlin had been able to close the building up by end of the year, the interior finishing work was delayed by lack of building supplies. The construction boom had begun to take hold in the province. It was not until August 1909 that the building was finished, ready for the Supreme Court assizes of the fall session. When completed the edifice cost a substantial $74,706, with another $1,600 spent on furniture.[110] As was usually the case for new courthouses in the province, no special notice was taken of the completion of the building. It was as if the ruling Liberals did not want to draw attention to their new temples of justice: rather strange behaviour for a political party. But the fact remains that no Alberta courthouse was opened with formal ceremonies until the late 1920s. Sometimes the local papers hardly even noticed the building had been occupied. Such was the case in Wetaskiwin, where the Conservative-leaning Post did not deign to report on the building's opening or the first court.

While no great to-do was made about the opening of the courthouse, it was instantly a landmark building. Although Wetaskiwin had a town hall and several large churches, no other public building could compare with the courthouse, with its imposing architecture and landscaped environs, as a public space. It soon became the prime location for ceremonial occasions in the city. Perhaps the courthouse's finest moment was during the visit of the Governor General of Canada in 1930. The importance of the courthouse as a civic icon was well emphasized when Lord Willingdon came through the town at the beginning of May. The city literally rolled out the red carpet – having borrowed one from the Department of Public Works that reached from the courthouse door to the street – as well as flags and bunting to decorate the building itself. With great pride, the city clerk for Wetaskiwin reported to the deputy minister that the Governor General and his aide de camp had singled out the courthouse for its attractiveness and the decorations.[111] The courthouse was put to the same use again just two years later when Willingdon's successor, the Earl of

Postcard perfect: finished courthouse, c. 1909. WCA 78.15/S8

Bessborough, came calling. Asking to borrow the decorations again, the City Clerk mentioned that the courthouse "makes such a splendid background for the presentation of the address of welcome."[112] For a small city like Wetaskiwin, a building like the courthouse, set on its manicured lawns, remote and magisterial, could occupy a special place above and beyond its mere function.

To some extent, the Wetaskiwin building imitated the American courthouse not only ceremonially but in function. As with other courthouses in the province, over time more and more provincial offices moved into the building. Initially, the province, like the Dominion before it, was adamant that halls of justice were not to be used for other purposes. A need to economize after World War I found the provincial government using surplus space in court buildings for other departments, thus avoiding paying rents. The era of the ubiquitous provincial building was still several decades away, but courthouses in smaller centres generally became de facto public buildings.

In the case of Wetaskiwin, the building turned out to be far larger than the court needed. In the early 1920s, many of the judicial districts amalgamated the District and Supreme Court Clerks and Sheriffs. "The office accommodation [sic] in the Court House at Wetaskiwin is unnecessarily extensive, and I have directed that the room formerly occupied as a District Court office be closed," wrote George Henwood, the Deputy Attorney General (and former Wetaskiwinite) in 1929.[113] Court officials were replaced over the years by the district home economist, the local driving tester, the local inspector of highways, the fish and wildlife inspector, and the district agricultural office. Standing alone on its well-kept grounds, and containing most of the provincial offices in the town, the courthouse was both the symbolic and physical presence of government. The increasing use of courthouses for other government departments even influenced the design of later courthouses, such as Medicine Hat and Vegreville, where from the outset it was assumed that not only the courts would be housed there. Wetaskiwin was, however, perhaps the most versatile of the provincial court buildings, functioning not just as headquarters of the court but even as much-needed apartment space.

---

CAMROSE

The creation of a sub-judicial district centred on the community of Camrose in 1918 ignited a fair amount of controversy. Other towns in the province looked on enviously, and snidely insinuated that the fact the sitting member for the district was a cabinet minister had more to do with it than judicial requirements. The opposition Conservatives loudly criticized the move, claiming the sub-district would move most of the business of the Wetaskiwin judicial district to Camrose, where there was no courthouse, from Wetaskiwin, where there was – and which had cost over $70,000 to build.[114] The Liberal member for Wetaskiwin, H.J. Montgomery, joined the conservatives in opposing the move. It seemed ridiculous that Camrose, only twenty-five miles from the judicial centre, needed its own court offices.

Nevertheless, the government held firm to their policy. The Honourable George P. Smith, member for Camrose, replied to the critics that due to the way the rail lines ran, it was surprisingly difficult for people around the town to get to Wetaskiwin, and he cited the circumstances around the creation of a district at Stettler to bolster his argument. However, the province, while happy to establish deputy clerk and sheriff's offices in Camrose, was not in any hurry to build a courthouse as they had just begun in Taber. Instead, it leased quarters. In February 1918, the Department of Public Works signed a five-year lease for the old Camrose Canadian Club.[115] Built in 1908, it had been the pride of Camrose before World War I. A number of the leading citizens of the town had banded together to form a Canadian Club, a debating and speech-making society then all the rage throughout the country. With an infectious booster spirit, the new club decided to erect their own building. It would have a large meeting and banquet hall, as well as a billiards room, library and reading room. Completed at a cost of $4,600, Camrose could trumpet it had the only Canadian Club in the country with "its own premises."[116]

Ironically, the clubhouse looked more like a hall of justice than some of the later structures built by the province for court purposes. It was a simple wood-frame building with wood siding, but the builder, Mr. Allan, a member of the club, added Classical Revival touches that gave it great deal of dignity. The entryway was enclosed in a projecting porch with two Tuscan order columns *in antis,* with a second floor balcony. A simple pediment surmounted the doors onto the balcony, while a dentilated cornice and a stepped parapet topped the roof. Although hardly uncommon architectural decoration, one has to wonder if the courthouse then in the course of erection in nearby Wetaskiwin influenced the builder at all. In any case, the Canadian Club had a very dignified presence for a small building, and had it been done in brick or stone, could have easily passed as a purpose-built courthouse.

It was to serve in this role for many years. In 1931 the government decided to buy the building outright, and contemplated an addition on the rear, going so far as to draw up plans for it.[117] It was not built, however, and several years later, at the end of 1935, the new Social Credit government of William Aberhart took a hard look at the judicial districts and decided to abolish the Camrose sub-district in the interests of economy. Although a Treasury Branch moved into the vacant court offices, the building continued to host the District Court until 1957. The government then built a new provincial building, including courtroom, and the old clubhouse was moved and turned into a public library.

As was common in the other courthouses in the province, the RNWMP and then the APP were headquartered in the Wetaskiwin building for several decades. The city had its own constables, but the transport and guarding of prisoners awaiting trial in the courthouse cells was entirely the responsibility of the Mounties and then the provincial police. For many years, a constable also served as an orderly for the court, his presence helping to maintain order. It made sense to have the local police detachment in the courthouse, and in Cardston, the police barracks was in the courthouse right from inception. Originally the Wetaskiwin courthouse did not include detachment offices. By 1929, it was clear that there was enough room, and space was made available on the main floor for the police.[118] Unlike in Cardston, the police constables never actually lived in the courthouse; the caretaker lived on the premises until the late 1950s. The RCMP remained in the courthouse until 1945, when a new detachment building was finished, more suitable to the needs of local law enforcement. Their offices were immediately converted into a permanent courtroom for the local police magistrate.[119]

The rather relaxed attitude the department took toward the use of the courthouse as living quarters was perhaps the most surprising. In Red Deer, Lethbridge, Medicine Hat, and other courthouses, no matter what provincial departments might have offices there, the Attorney General's office was adamant against the judge's suite being used by anyone other than the visiting judges. But just as the department had been remarkably lenient in Cardston, it chose to ignore its own rules in Wetaskiwin. It was entirely due to the much lesser demands placed on the latter courthouse. Thus, Judge Lees, while sitting as District Court judge, had occupied most of the rooms of the rather large suite on the third floor, as "they had been vacant ever since the building was occupied," according to D.E. McDonald, the Building Superintendent of Public Works.[120] After Lees retired in 1934, he began renting the rooms as his personal accommodations. He was not alone in the courthouse, however. The Clerk of Court, Simpson, had also moved into the courthouse, utilizing two empty offices as living quarters.[121] The department decided that he at least had to be charged a small rent. The courthouse had become, it would seem, a judicial flophouse. The suite was rented right up to the middle of the 1950s.[122]

The caretaker and his family also lived in the courthouse for many years. One of the unique characteristics of the early provincial courthouses was the provision for a resident caretaker. This had not been a feature of the smaller Territorial court buildings, nor was it ever used again after Jeffers' tenure. Both he and his predecessor, Hopkins, felt that the courthouses in smaller centres should have such quarters, and Cardston, Wetaskiwin, and Lethbridge had suites in the basement. Edmonton and Calgary, presumably as large buildings with more than one janitor, did not provide accommodation. Their reasoning is unfortunately lost to us, but the architects may have felt it would result in better care of the building and that free quarters would be an enticement for good staff. In Wetaskiwin, the caretaker's suite was in the basement, and featured several rooms, including a kitchen. This was handy, allowing food to be prepared for any prisoners as well as for the visiting judge if he so required. The quarters meant that a great deal of room, however, was used for a non-essential purpose. In Lethbridge the quarters became storage quite quickly; only in Wetaskiwin did a resident caretaker grace the courthouse for any span of years.

*A ceremonial moment: call to the Bar, 1961. WCA 85.23-95, used by permission of the Wetaskiwin Times.*

Even with the good work of the caretakers, however, the Wetaskiwin courthouse gradually grew dingier and dingier. Inevitably, the roof leaked. For some reason, courthouse roofs had a propensity to leakage. Almost all the early provincial buildings had problems at one time or another. Wetaskiwin was no exception. By 1927, the building inspector for Public Works reported that both the east and west wings had water stains down the walls on the second storey.[123] Despite several attempts at repair, a good driving rainstorm still meant water getting into the building, and as usual it was the judge's suite that seemed the worst affected. Inevitably, this damaged the plaster walls. In 1928, there was even more water damage when one of the water lines on the second floor broke. As the building aged, the windows did not seal tightly, permitting a great deal of dirt to enter on the wind. The sheriff and judges all noticed how difficult it was to keep the dust down in the building. But it was the Depression that did the most damage. All maintenance, from cleaning to repairs, was cut down to the absolute minimum. The war continued to restrict maintenance work. It was hard on the building, with its constant stream of traffic. Justice Howson wrote to William Stacey, the Building Superintendent, in 1947 to complain about the appearance of the court, especially the painting and the woodwork; Chief Judge Kerr of the District Court expressed similar sentiments, especially about the furniture in the judge's chambers and quarters.[124]

Matters came to a head by 1955. There were constant complaints from the judges on the state of the building. Doors and windows were loose, screens had disappeared, the exterior brickwork needed re-pointing, and the carpets and flooring required repair and replacement.[125] Even with the renovation work done a few years before at the insistence of Justice Howson, the building needed painting. The acoustics in the courtroom were a particular bone of contention. In Lethbridge, the poor acoustics had been noted in the very first trials held in the building, and the same problems arose in Wetaskiwin. Justice J. Boyd McBride, never one to mince words, noted: "For many years when I was practising at the Bar everybody avoided going to Wetaskiwin if they could do so because the acoustics of the court room were so bad."[126]

His complaints were given immediate attention, with Chief Architect Ron Clarke inspecting the building and the courtroom. In a rare moment of sensitivity, not characteristic of the era, he recognized the unique character of the room, especially its high ceiling, and was unwilling to damage the building's most attractive feature. Clarke recommended against a suspended ceiling, advocating acoustic tile and other remedial measures. His report was filed and forgotten for a year until Justice McBride pointedly reminded Arthur Arnold, the deputy minister, of their previous exchange. Harold Brettelle, the maintenance supervisor, took a look at the building in November 1956.[127] He found even more problems, with plaster in danger of peeling away, and worn-out heating and plumbing. A $5,000 renovation of the courtroom turned into a $45,000, then $60,000 revamp of the whole building.

Arnold took matters in hand, contacting H.J. Wilson, his counterpart at the Attorney General's office, to ask about his department's intentions as to a courthouse in the Wetaskiwin area.[128] The green light was given to renew the existing building. Sheriff R.V. Roberts contributed his wish list of renovations, and in May 1957 work began. Roberts' suggestions included some major changes. The caretaker's suite in the basement was to be done away with, and the police magistrate was to be installed with a new courtroom at his disposal. It was quickly discovered that all the basement walls were load bearing and could not be removed, so the offices for the Fish and Game Inspector and the Driving Tester were moved to the basement and the magistrate put on the main floor of the building. The judge's suite, rarely if ever used, was removed and the library shifted to the third floor, while a judge's bedroom was installed next to his chambers and office, and the barristers' facilities enlarged. The plaster walls were removed and replaced, and the old maple flooring covered in sturdy linoleum in most parts of the building. When the department was done, the building was almost as good as new, if somewhat less attractive, and would serve well for another twenty years.

### THE GUNS OF AUGUST

One striking feature of the Wetaskiwin courthouse is the two vintage artillery pieces that guard the main entrance. They have been a part of the landscape of the courthouse for decades, so much so that their origin has been forgotten. By the 1950s, even the Department of Public Works and the Attorney General had no idea who had presented the guns to the government and how they came to be in front of the courthouse.[129]

The answer was simple. After World War I, the Dominion of Canada came into the possession of a great deal of captured German weaponry and had a vast surplus of its own arms. The federal government decided that they would make fine displays in the cities and towns across Canada and appointed A.G. Doughty, the Dominion Archivist, as Director of War Trophies. Wetaskiwin was allotted two field guns and six machine guns as its share of the booty. In June 1920, Doughty advised the city its trophies were on the way. City council immediately struck a committee to find a suitable spot for them.[130]

It turned out to be a more complex task than anyone had imagined. The school board and the manager of the Bank of Commerce were asked if they would display the guns, and at the beginning of December one was placed at the Alexandra School and one on the east side of the bank, facing the railroad.[131] Boys are drawn to artillery as to candy, however, and within two weeks it was clear the gun could not stay by the school. The children took great pleasure in moving it and climbing on it, and council feared an accident. The garden by the CPR station was the next choice, but the railway was not interested. Slightly vexed, the committee next approached the province.[132] Would the Attorney General allow the guns to be placed on the courthouse grounds? The answer was yes, and in May 1921 the guns were trundled over to the courthouse.

Wetaskiwin was not the only city to station their trophies on the courthouse grounds. Cardston also put their allotted gun in front of the courthouse, although over the years it has disappeared. As to Wetaskiwin's six machine guns, their fate is a mystery.

## Epilogue

Unlike its sister courthouse in Lethbridge, demolished in 1952, Wetaskiwin's building has enjoyed a kinder fate. The city took some time to live up to its early promise: the population remained around two thousand until well after World War II. While Wetaskiwin remained the centre of the judicial district, its courthouse did not suffer problems with overcrowding for many years. It continued in use as a courthouse up to 1983, a span of seventy-four years. Only the Court of Queen's Bench building in Medicine Hat has had a longer career.

Civic landmark: awaiting the Governor General, 1930. WCA 88.7/197P

Eventually, however, the courts in Wetaskiwin outgrew their venerable building. The city itself grew much larger in the 1960s and by 1971 had a population of over ten thousand. The court system had also become much more complex. Specialized traffic courts, family courts, and juvenile courts had been added to the old magistrate's court, and judicial business in the district had increased to the point that the old building was not up to the task. In the aftermath of the Kirby report in 1975, the government was decided that a new court facility was required in Wetaskiwin. Some court functions had already moved into the provincial building. Fortunately, even before the Attorney General requested a new courthouse, the province had already decided to make the old one a provincial historic site. It was officially designated on March 15, 1977. There would be no uncertainty as to the ultimate fate of the Wetaskiwin courthouse. The federal government added its own designation as a national historic site in 1984, along with a plaque in front of the building.

To declare a building a historic site does not, however, necessarily keep it a viable structure. Like other courthouses, the Wetaskiwin building became the home of a museum, the Reynolds Alberta Museum. That organization outgrew its home by 1993, and the courthouse has sat vacant ever since. It is not an ideal situation: empty buildings have a way of falling apart, victimized by vandals, lack of care and attention, and frequently end up mysteriously burning down. Mindful of this, the provincial government put the building on the market in 1994 and has been looking for a suitable buyer and adaptive reuse ever since. The courthouse in Wetaskiwin does have friends, however. A group of concerned citizens formed the Old Court House Society in 1995 after public meetings with representatives of the Department of Housing and Public Works. At the time of this writing, this group of worthies is still working to ensure an important part of their city's and the province's history is preserved for future generations.

# EDMONTON

When completed in 1912, the courthouse of Edmonton was a true temple of justice. The building's Beaux-Arts facades commanded a fine location on the corner of May Street and McDougall Avenue, across from a parcel of open land slated to be the civic square for the city of Edmonton. The two-storey courthouse had not one, but two imposing entrances, massive porticoes each with a monumental pediment, supported by a row of six Ionic columns. Within the tympanum of each pediment was a sculpted relief of the coat of arms of the province. In contrast to the entrances, the rest of the building was simple, almost severe, with simple keystones over the gently arched main floor windows, a course between the two storeys, a small cornice, and the suggestion of pilasters, continued from the second floor through the cornice and low parapet above. The building was clad in smooth Calgary sandstone; the steps to the entrance were British Columbia granite.[133] Panelled bronze doors set in arched doorways guarded the inner sanctum of the law.

Inside, a corridor led directly from the McDougall Avenue entrance to a central staircase, lit from above by a skylight. It was set in a grand rotunda square, with a second-floor gallery of columns and arches. The four courtrooms and the courthouse library opened onto the gallery. The interior was sumptuous. The staircase itself was marble with ornate iron railings, and the building was finished throughout with oak and marble.[134] Each of the four courtrooms – one for the Supreme Court Criminal, the Civil Court, the Appeal Court and the District Court – was panelled in oak. The large windows of the library and reading room overlooked the May Street entrance. On the main floor there were offices for the administration of the courts and rooms for chambers. In the basement were cells for felons awaiting trial and offices for a detachment of the Royal Northwest Mounted Police. Nothing was overlooked: a chamber for the barristers to robe themselves in their gowns, rooms for juries to deliberate and witnesses to wait, and offices for the Sheriff, the Clerk of Courts and judges. For the first time, Edmonton's courts and court officials were gathered under one roof.

The building had been long awaited. It was the first proper courthouse built in the capital: overlooked by the Dominion in the Territorial days, Edmonton waited until 1912 for a proper domicile for the courts. The new courthouse was by far the grandest built in the province up to that time, and remained so for fifty years. In both appearance and function, it was the epitome of what a courthouse was supposed to be, and exemplified the attitude of the Liberal administration of Alberta toward public buildings. No longer were letters, petitions, and delegations necessary; the government was as committed to impressive public works as the next booster. Ironically, the opening of the Edmonton courthouse was scarcely noticed in the capital's press. For all of its magnificence, perhaps it was overshadowed by the even more majestic legislature building, opened shortly after the courts took up residence in their new quarters. Once again, Edmontonians seemed curiously indifferent toward their courthouse.

*Top of main staircase, interior of Edmonton Courthouse, 1912. Glenbow Archives, NA-1328-64229*

*A temple of justice: interior of the newly completed Edmonton Courthouse, 1912. Glenbow Archives, NA-1328-64228*

Edmonton came into its own on September 1, 1905, when Governor General Earl Grey officially proclaimed the province of Alberta in an elaborate ceremony at the Thistle Rink. Under Alexander Rutherford's Liberals, Edmonton, a city since 1904, would be showered with largesse, at least in the eyes of the rest of the province. It had been the centre of power for the Liberal Party in Alberta for years. Within a year, Edmonton had been declared the capital and a university had been established in Strathcona. Plans were being drawn up for a magnificent legislature building overlooking the North Saskatchewan River. Soon, not one but two transcontinental railroads had reached the city, and the government was busy granting railway charters for new lines to the northeast and northwest, turning Edmonton into the rail hub of the province. And if Calgary was still slightly larger and richer, Edmonton's prospects seemed better, surrounded as it was by the best agricultural land in Alberta. A population that stood at just 2,626 in 1901 had grown to 24,900 in 1911, with another 5,000 in Strathcona, and showed no signs of slowing.

Edmonton had desperately needed a new courthouse before becoming capital of the province; now the explosive growth of the city made it absolutely imperative. The courts were extremely busy, and the court system itself was vastly expanded. In 1907, the government was ready to implement legislation to replace the Territorial courts with a provincial system. Edmonton was finally given a proper role in the administration of justice: half the bench of the Supreme Court were stationed in there, as well as two District Court judges for the Edmonton district, and still another District Court judge for the Athabasca District established in 1909. There were also all the other new personnel of the court, from District Court clerk and sheriff to the court reporters and stenographers, for whom there was no space at all in the existing quarters. Yet the province would be seven years old before a proper hall of justice was finally ready. When the first sitting of the Alberta Supreme Court en banc took place in October 1907, it was in the rather less than decorous surroundings of the Sandison Block.[135]

Some steps were taken immediately to secure the new Edmonton building. Alarmed at the rising value of land, in the summer of 1906 the government moved to acquire a site for a suitable edifice. It required a special warrant from the executive council, as no money had been budgeted for the purchase. On September 1, the Attorney General, C.W. Cross, officially requested that Public Works buy the land; the minister for the department sent the same recommendation to the Lieutenant Governor, and the council authorized the purchase of lots 68, 69 and 70 in river lot 6 from George Stockton.[136] It cost the government $27,000, more than the whole Cardston courthouse, but it was a prudent decision.[137] Had the government waited until they were ready to start construction, the price would have been far higher: the great prairie real estate boom was about to begin. The price tag attracted little adverse comment in 1906, but later there would be some awkward questions raised in the Legislative Assembly.[138] At the 1909 Conservative convention, a former provincial auditor tried to stir up controversy by charging that the Rutherford government had paid exorbitant prices for both the courthouse and university sites, among other financial irregularities.[139]

A site having been chosen, Edmonton's hall of justice inched closer to realization. For its second budget in 1907, the Rutherford government gave prominent place to the courthouse, asking for $20,000 to begin construction and projecting a final cost of $80,000.[140] It was a surprisingly small amount of money, about what would be appropriated for Wetaskiwin's courthouse. It was clear that the Department of Public Works did not know how large a structure they would be building or how much it was likely to cost. The department and the recently established Provincial Architect's office were still very much learning the job. The first departmental architect, E.C. Hopkins, had been fired after only a year, and his replacement, Allan Merrick Jeffers, had only taken over in the fall of 1907. It is not surprising that there were difficulties in getting up to speed, and the amount of work that the architectural staff undertook was prodigious. Thus Jeffers' staff were able to only complete sketch plans for "a typical four room Court House building to be erected at Edmonton" before the end of the year.[141] Inexperience clearly slowed them down. John Stocks, the deputy minister, commented in his 1907 report: "The preparation of plans for the above buildings [including courthouses for Calgary, Edmonton, and the Calgary Land Titles office] has entailed a very considerable amount of labour, as it was necessary to make so many changes before we could seem to arrive at the design most suitable to the requirements in each case."[142]

Despite the original optimistic announcement from the government and excited reports in the newspapers at the beginning of the year, there was no chance of work on the Edmonton courthouse getting underway before 1908. It was not the best start, and William Cushing, the Minister of Public Works, tried to mollify local opinion early in the new year by declaring in a Bulletin interview that "a new courthouse ... was needed more now than the new parliament buildings" and put it high on the government's list of priorities for the new year.[143] More importantly, the courthouse would be "a splendid edifice, worthy of the capital," and for the 1908 budget speech Cushing's department had upped the estimate for the building to $200,000, with $50,000 allocated for that year alone.[144] Here, at last, would be a courthouse of which Edmonton could be proud.

---

FORT SASKATCHEWAN

Among the early provincial courthouses, the edifice at Fort Saskatchewan, completed in 1909, was something of an oddity. Like Cardston, the town was not the centre of a judicial district or even a sub-district. It was also very close to Edmonton, and would seem an unlikely candidate for a courthouse. It was, however, to be the location of the provincial prison for the north and thus occupied a unique position in Alberta's justice system. It also had an active member of the provincial legislature, Frank A. Walker, who lobbied hard to get a courthouse placed in the most important town in his riding. This happy coincidence meant that like Cardston, Fort Saskatchewan received a courthouse long before many larger and more important towns.

Fort Saskatchewan had a long association with law and order. G Division of the North West Mounted Police had chosen to build a post there in 1875 instead of Edmonton. The barracks of the police became the *de facto* prison for northern and central Alberta. In the early part of the century, its manifest shortcomings led local parliamentarian Frank Oliver to remark about the "scandal" of prison accommodations in the area and led to the building of a jail in Edmonton – and the postponement of its Territorial courthouse. The Edmonton jail was soon inadequate, and the provincial administration decided to return the prison to Fort Saskatchewan. Due to its long association with the administration of justice, the town had long had a sitting for the Territorial Supreme Court, but under provincial auspices was only on the District Court circuit.

On February 25, 1909 the *Fort Saskatchewan Reporter* ran the headline "Court House Assured," announcing the decision of the government to build one in the town. Without reservation, the paper gave the credit to the efforts of Frank Walker, commenting that: "we are confident that all our fellow citizens; be he Liberal or Conservative, must appreciate a member who will fight for his constituents, as Frank has undoubtedly had to fight, in order to secure this magnificent gift for the fort."[145] The local boosters, as always, saw it as proof of their town's importance. The perspective of the Department of Public Works was somewhat different. Whatever the influence of Walker, the courthouse itself demonstrates that the decision was a pragmatic one. It was the most utilitarian of the five courthouses designed by A.M. Jeffers. A simple two-storey, hip-roofed building, it had brick masonry walls over a concrete and stone foundation. It conformed to the standard courthouse design with courtroom and adjunct chambers on the top floor, and offices on the first floor.[146] Although room for cells was planned in the basement, they were omitted due to the proximity of the barracks. Architectural decoration was limited to a stone course and stone window surrounds, and arched voussoirs around the main floor windows and entrances with a keystone.

More remarkable was the speed with which the building was completed. Jeffers and his staff began drafting in June 1909, and the building was ready for occupation in December.[147] Although a modest size, thirty-two by forty-eight feet and an uncomplicated design, this was quite a contrast to Jeffers' other courthouses and also to the comparably sized Territorial buildings. The department carried out construction itself, using local labour under the supervision of J.W. Johnston.[148] The stone and brick were also locally procured, with the brick made right in the town by the Fort Saskatchewan Brick Company.[149] It was also an inexpensive building, costing only $9,384.81, with land provided out of the NWMP reserve.[150] Clearly, it was important to the government to supply a court building quickly and cheaply. If the Fort

Pragmatism or politics: Fort Saskatchewan's under-utilized courthouse. PAA, A8248

Saskatchewan building was built as a political move, however, this would seem counterproductive. The courthouse may have been erected in anticipation of the construction of a major penitentiary at the town and also to serve the large NWMP detachment still stationed there.

If so, they turned out to be misplaced priorities. Although a substantial new prison was built in 1913–14, the police moved their detachment to Edmonton into commodious new barracks. The courthouse never saw much traffic from the prison or the town and district. Eventually, the main floor was turned over to the Alberta Provincial Police as a residence, and later the bursar of the penitentiary used it as quarters.[151] By 1948, the residential uses of the building had almost usurped the judicial functions. When the police magistrate complained the tenants had locked off the bathroom in the basement, the resident, G.H. Reimer, wrote to the Department of Public Works to say the bathroom had been installed by previous tenants and was for their personal use, and he and his wife wanted their privacy.[152] Soon afterward, the police court moved into the town hall. Fort Saskatchewan was

Almost as shown: architect's sketch used on postcard, Edmonton Courthouse. LASA, 5-G-70

one of the first courthouses abandoned by the province, and in 1971 was turned over entirely to the town of Fort Saskatchewan to be converted into a museum.[153]

Next to the legislature building, the Edmonton courthouse was the most important structure designed by Allan Merrick Jeffers. A true temple of justice, it was one of the buildings the government proudly held up as an example of their extensive public works program. The Edmonton hall of justice epitomized Jeffers' preferred style, which relied on monumental entrances and simplicity in architectural decoration. Although Jeffers was hardly the only architect of the time who used a subdued decorative scheme, it was certainly characteristic, and anticipates the later phases of Beaux-Arts classicism, usually called the neo-classical revival, where monumentality and severity largely replaced ornate decoration. In his annual report for 1908, Jeffers left a few thoughts on the Edmonton edifice that give some idea of his preferences: "The general treatment of the exterior, which produces a purely classic effect, leaves nothing wanting from an architectural standpoint. There is just sufficient detail in the entrances and cornice to agreeably relieve the broad, simple lines of the facade."[154] The austere quality of Jeffers' work is obvious on all his courthouses, taken to its final extreme in the Calgary courthouse, his last design.

The Edmonton building was in some ways quite different from his earlier courthouses at Wetaskiwin and Lethbridge. Jeffers evoked the image of a temple with its grand Grecian entrances. The two porticoes of the building represented an idiosyncratic aspect of the courthouse that showed Jeffers did not follow any rigid principles, but could show imaginative responses to certain design problems. Rather than one grand entrance and primary facade, facing the open public square, Jeffers harmonized the courthouse to the corner site. He gave the building two

*Tourist attraction? Postcard view, Edmonton Courthouse. LASA, 5-G-71*

entrances and two facades, thus providing it with a strong presence on each of busy streets of its location but sacrificing the symmetry beloved of Beaux-Arts buildings. One of the grand classical porticoes faced north onto May Street, the other east onto MacDougall Avenue, allowing the building to make an impression on the man on the street – both streets.

Jeffers likely oversaw the design personally, with the drafting of the plans carried out by Richard Blakey, the assistant provincial architect, and other staff.[155] The Provincial Architect spent a great deal of time over the design of the working spaces of the courthouse, striving for efficiency:

> The arrangement of the second floor is especially worthy of comment. Here the four courts are so placed as to be entirely separate from each other, the civil, criminal and district courts each being provided with a an individual jury room conveniently situated. Located between the criminal and district courts are rooms for male and female witnesses, each being separated from the other by a third room, to be used for the accommodation of lawyers interested in the court proceedings.[156]

The interior arrangements of the courthouse did not quite reach the level of sophistication that would be seen in the 1914 Calgary courthouse, but was nevertheless impressive. One drawback that would become obvious over the decades was the lack of a secure and relatively private connection between the holding cells in the basement and the courtrooms on the second floor. Jeffers took advantage of the most up-to-date building technology for the building. Underneath the masonry cladding was a steel-and-concrete frame and reinforced concrete floors and roof. In the lexicon of the day, it was a "fireproof" building. It would also cost the government almost $280,000.[157] A significant part of the expense was the opulent

*North and east elevations, Edmonton Courthouse, 1908. PAA*

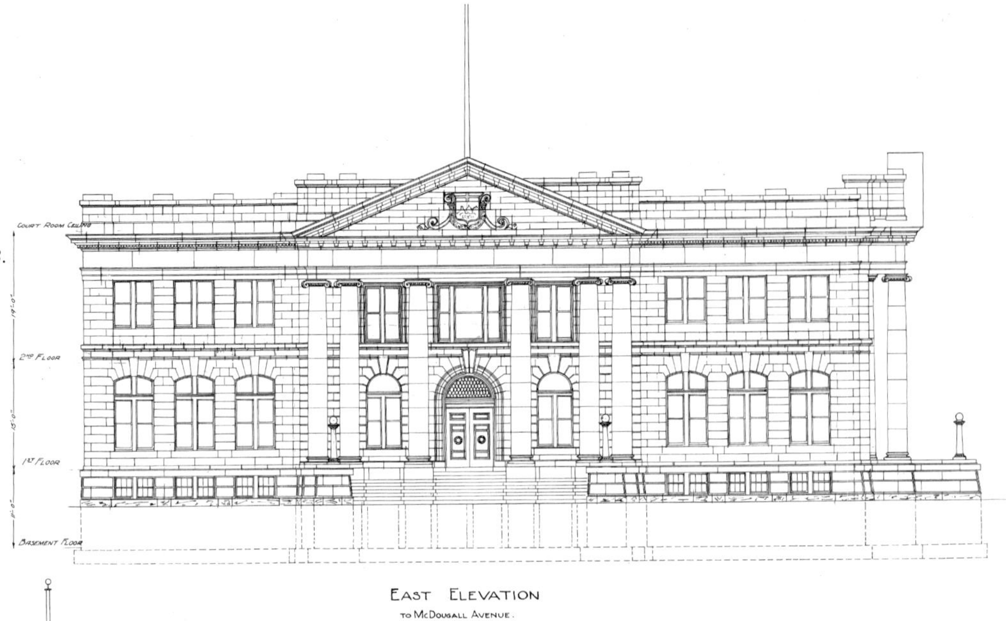

interior of the building which, true to the Beaux-Arts style, featured rich materials like marble and expensive hardwoods, as well as a great deal of decorative plasterwork.

The Department of Public Works advertised for tenders on May 8, 1908.[158] The following month, a sketch of the proposed building was released to the press, and the Bulletin regaled its readers with a long description of the plans, noting in loving detail the architecture and interior decor.[159] The department let the main contract on July 18 to Manson and Dunlop, the contracting firm of Edmonton alderman Robert J. Manson.[160] Manson had been appointed the Clerk of Works for

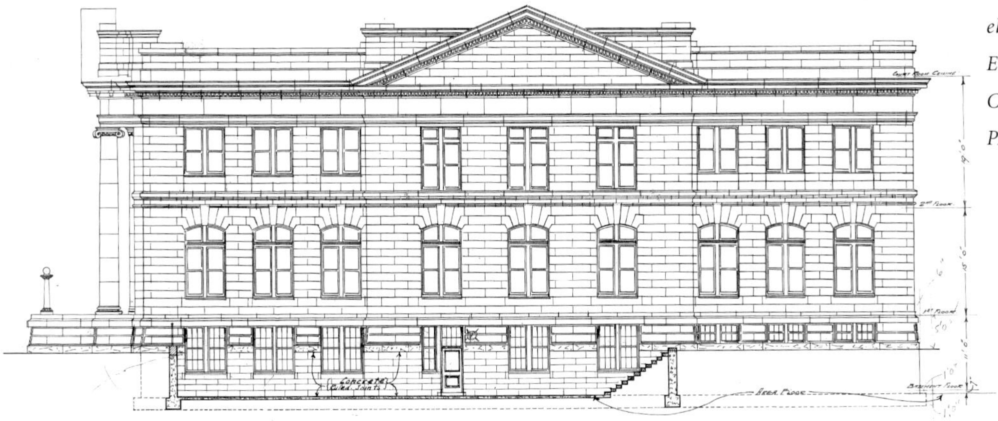

WEST ELEVATION

SOUTH ELEVATION
TO LANE

*West and south elevations, Edmonton Courthouse, 1908. PAA*

the Edmonton jail in 1903, and probably had strong Liberal Party connections.[161] The firm was to do the lion's share of the work on the courthouse, including the excavation, the foundation, and the masonry work, valued at $165,000. The Structural Steel Company received the contract on tender for the steel framework of the building, and later the department awarded contracts for the interior finishing and for the plumbing and heating.[162] Supervision of the construction of the courthouse came directly from the Provincial Architect's office.[163]

*Sections, Edmonton Courthouse, 1908. PAA*

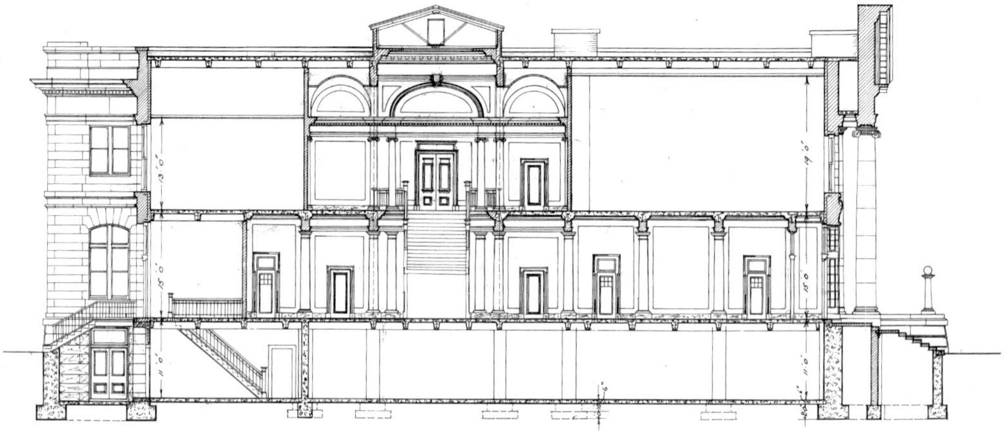


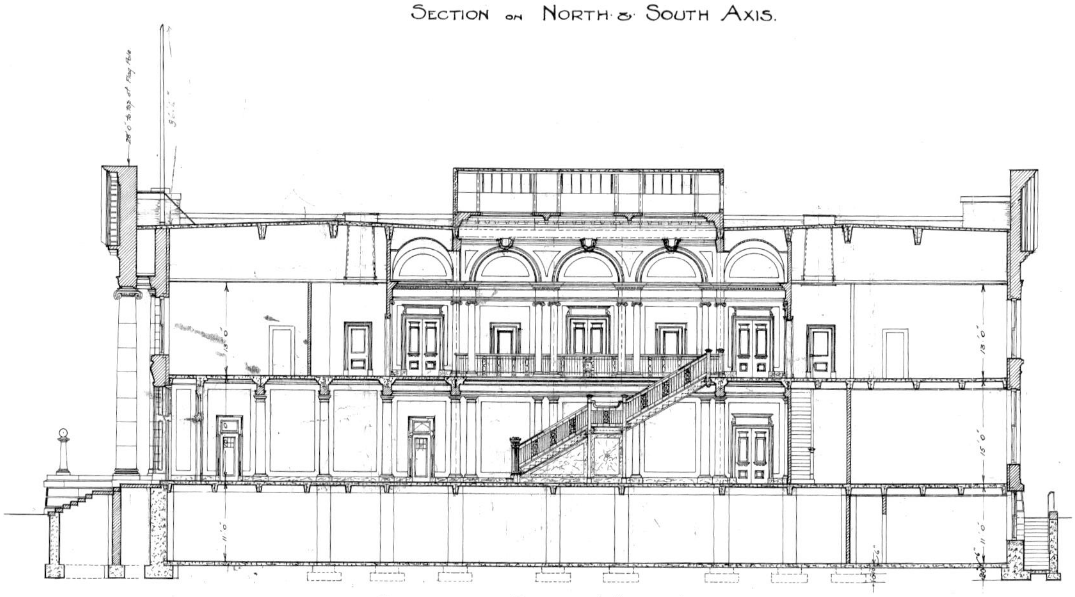


## CONSTRUCTION

Construction began in the fall of 1908 with the excavation of the foundation.[164] After the winter, work resumed on the foundation. In June, cranes were erected to put the steel frame in place and masons had begun to prepare the stone.[165] By the end of the building season, the exterior walls were done up to the second floor, before the supply of sandstone from the quarries at Calgary ran out.[166] Originally, construction was expected to take two years. By the building season of 1910, however, the great construction boom on the prairies had moved into full swing. The supply of building materials and skilled workers became very tight. Although Manson did not have any technical problems, the project was delayed due to problems procuring sandstone. The government was consuming massive amounts of material in its own building program. The Annual Report of the Public Works Department for 1910 noted the slow progress of the courthouse, "principally owing to the difficulty of the part of the contractors to secure stone."[167] There was also tragedy on the job site before construction ceased over the winter. In November a young stonemason, L.G. White, fell to his death while working alone in the building.[168]

In the summer of 1911, the Department of Public Works called the tenders for the interior plastering.[169] The government wanted the building finished and in service by the beginning of the new year.[170] There was some degree of urgency: the Sandison block was becoming intolerably cramped, with water leakage and cranky heating. One corner of the ceiling in the courtroom collapsed in December 1910, and there was a persistently squeaky door – a minor shortcoming, but one that drove the judges and members of the bar to distraction.[171] Once again, shortages of material slowed work on the new building. It was not until the end of 1911 that the exterior was completed and the roof put up. The plastering contract was given to W.B. Poucher, the heating, plumbing and ventilation to the firm of McKnight and Frost.[172] By March 1912, the interior still was not finished.

By this time Jeffers was gone and his assistant, Richard Blakey, had taken his place as Provincial Architect. The long wait for the Edmonton hall of justice as well as the legislature building may have hastened his departure. All of the courthouses built under Jeffers' supervision suffered from delays, but Edmonton was the worst: it took almost four years after the groundbreaking before the building could be turned over to the courts. To some extent, the problem was outside the control of the Department of Public Works and the contractors, because of the scarcity of building supplies. Within the government, however, a somewhat jaundiced eye may have been cast in Jeffers' direction. Premier Sifton, during a debate in the house over the merits of the government erecting its own public buildings rather than contracting them out, singled out the Edmonton courthouse as evidence of the inefficiency of using private builders.[173] The Department of Public Works would turn to day labour supervised by its own foremen to build the courthouse in Calgary.

## An Anticlimax

Despite its grand appearance, the courthouse was in the end overshadowed by the legislature building, figuratively if not literally. While the edifice taking shape on McDougall Avenue was no doubt eagerly awaited by the legal community of Edmonton, the tall dome of the legislature captured the public imagination. To some extent, this is not surprising. Although the courthouse was high on the list of public buildings desired by civic boosters, an "ornament to the town," it was also a specialized building with a very specific purpose. Many members of the public might never step between the doors. A sensational trial would focus attention on the courthouse briefly, but it was altogether a building easily taken for granted.

*Edmonton Exterior, Glenbow Archives, NC-6-324*

*(top right) Unlikely neighbours: residences around Edmonton Courthouse, c. 1912. Glenbow Archives, NC-6-80*

*(bottom right) Court is now in session: a rare view of a courtroom in Edmonton courthouse, 1925, Glenbow Archives ND-3-2911*

Of all the daily papers, only the Edmonton Daily Capital had much comment when the courts officially moved from the Sandison Block to their new home. The timing may have had something to do with the lack of press: the move took place during summer recess, without any significant trials scheduled until the fall. The Journal reported on June 19, 1912 that Judge Taylor would finish his District Court sittings in the new building, while the Bulletin stated several days later that the Supreme Court would conclude its business there as well, to avoid the sweltering heat in the old Sandison rooms.[174] Neither paper had much to say about the nearly completed building, although as the ally of the Conservative Party, the Journal made sure to mention the long delay in finishing the building.[175] When the judicial staff moved at the end of July, only the Capital bothered describing the architecture and interior of the new building.[176] The other papers were indifferent and made no mention of the move. As with all the early provincial courthouses, there was no ceremony to celebrate the opening.

The press showed no greater interest when the courts resumed their business in the fall. On October 15, the fall assizes of the Supreme Court opened, but no credit was given to the government for the fine new courthouse that now anchored Edmonton's public square.

McDermid 80

## An Inadequate Design

Within two years of opening, the new courthouse was already insufficient. The sad truth was that the building, for all its magnificence, had been designed too small, a problem with many of the early courthouses of Alberta. What followed were years of chronic shortage of office space. Jeffers and his staff had not sufficiently anticipated the expansion of the city of Edmonton and the ever-growing needs of the courts. By September 1914, the Department of Public Work's building superintendent and assistant sheriff were trying to find more space for the sheriff's staff.[177] A new judge, J.D. Hyndman, had just been appointed to the Supreme Court and would require an office.[178] A shuffle took place within the courthouse, with the District Court clerk moved and replaced by the sheriff and his staff. The losers in this game of musical offices were the court reporters, removed entirely and banished to the land titles building next door.

Moving the officials and administrators of the court was one thing; the judges were quite another. The justices were not unreasonable men, but they were overworked and inclined to be protective of their office space. They were what could be charitably described as not lacking in assertiveness. Blakey took a look at the courthouse and wrote to the Deputy Attorney General, J.D. Hunt, on October 19, 1914, with what he thought was a reasonable solution.[179] The District Court judge for Athabasca, Joseph Camillein Noel, was headquartered in the Edmonton courthouse. A strictly middling judge, his appointment probably owed more to his family's close ties to Wilfrid Laurier than outstanding legal acumen. [180] However, through some vagary of chance, he had been assigned a singularly large office. Blakely felt that after removing a closet, the room could be split in two to create the necessary extra space.

Noel clearly did not think much of the idea: shortly after Blakey came up with his plan, the district judge was looking for an office to rent – outside the courthouse, in the Macleod Block![181] Despite being a junior judge, Noel had no compunction about insisting on his prerogatives. Needless to say, John Stocks, the Deputy Minister of Public Works, would absolutely not countenance such an expense, as it undermined the whole rationale behind building courthouses in the first place. Stocks wrote directly to Horace Harvey, explaining the advantages of his department's plans and looking for Harvey's support.[182] The Chief Justice was not much help, pointing out that the other offices were too small, and thus making two offices of similar dimensions was not very desirable at all.

Justice Hyndman, meanwhile, was awaiting his office. On December 3, 1914, the Minister of Public Works wrote and apologized to the new judge for the lack of accommodation.[183] Stocks had clearly run out of patience by this point; no doubt under pressure from above, he ordered the partitioning of Noel's office to be executed at once – only to rescind the order two days later, after receiving a phone call from the Chief Justice.[184] Harvey, once again showing his active interest in all matters concerning the courts, had scoured the building and found another solution. He suggested using the stenographers' room for another office, presumably moving them elsewhere, perhaps to join the court reporters in their exile. Hyndman, in deference to his rank, would have first choice of office.

By the time the judges were fighting over their offices, a war was on, the boom was over, and with it the end of the government's great splurge on public buildings. As with many other courthouses in the province, a climate of fiscal chilliness meant there would be no significant changes to the Edmonton building for over forty years. After 1921, the successors to the Liberals, the United Farmers of Alberta, wrestled with huge deficits, and not long after the province's finances were brought under control, the Depression made itself felt. As the city of Edmonton slowly grew, the courthouse became more and more overcrowded. Offices were further divided and the cells in the basement were taken out for more space. As early as 1924, Blakey expected to have to move the library out of the building in the near future.[185] By 1928, conditions were so bad that the judges sent a memorandum to the Attorney General, complaining of the crowding and warning of the consequences if the matter was not addressed, and soon.[186] Every judge of the Supreme Court signed.

For a few brief years, there was hope the building might see an addition. The Brownlee government had just started building new courthouses and even undertook the design of an addition for the Calgary hall of justice. Edmonton's temple did not receive the same consideration. It was a much more awkward building to expand: the Calgary edifice had a large park behind it, but in Edmonton, the land titles building sat right beside the courthouse and there was no space for an addition. It would be another sixteen years before there was any relief.

---

### THE MCPHERSON WIFE-SWAPPING TRIAL

What exactly are a court and a courtroom? It seems clear from these pages that the latter can be where ever a duly appointed judge decides. Yet in the 1930s, the question was debated in the exalted presence of the Judicial Committee of the Privy Council in England, the last court of appeal for Albertans. Ironically, it involved a divorce action held right in the Edmonton courthouse.[187]

Oran L. "Tony" McPherson was an American from Kansas who had emigrated to Alberta in 1906. An active member of the United Farmers of Alberta, he decided to run as a candidate when the organization decided to contest the 1921 provincial election. A rising star in the new party, McPherson was promoted to cabinet as the Minister of Public Works after the UFA won its second mandate. McPherson's promising career was undone by his mad passion for Mrs. Helen Mattern. The minister and his wife, Cora, met Helen and her husband, Major Leroy Mattern, in Calgary in 1929 and became fast friends. At some point, their socializing took a bizarre turn. McPherson developed a wild infatuation for Helen, who returned his affections. Roy Mattern, meanwhile, had seduced a willing Cora. Within a short time, McPherson decided he wanted to be with Helen and allegedly proposed a wife-swap.

To make the exchange permanent would, however, require two divorces. Although laws in Canada had been liberalized in the 1920s, actual divorces were still regarded as somewhat beyond the pale by most respectable Albertans. For a minister of a United Farmers administration, it would be political suicide. McPherson, not to be deterred, set about procuring a secret divorce. While Roy Mattern and Cora obligingly went off to Regina under the discreet observation of a private detective, he brought his problem to the Attorney General, J.F. Lymburn. If McPherson's cabinet colleague was shocked and appalled, he decided to help anyway, perhaps hoping to avoid a public scandal. Bypassing conventional channels, Justice Tom Tweedie of the Supreme Court was persuaded to hear the action in the judge's library of the Edmonton courthouse. Tweedie, a bon vivant and man of the world, left the door open and claimed later that he had declared the room an open court before beginning proceedings, but the judge's library, a small room tucked away on the second floor of the courthouse, was not exactly a public venue. Tony and Cora McPherson had their divorce and shortly thereafter he married Helen Mattern.

The whole affair began to unravel when Roy Mattern declined to marry Cora. Showing his peculiar lack of common sense, McPherson not only refused to give his ex-wife any support, he also did not allow her access to their children. A woman scorned, Cora soon found Neil Maclean, an Edmonton lawyer and prominent Liberal with a particular dislike for the UFA. Maclean lost no time bringing a statement of claim against McPherson for fraud and collusion in the divorce action and challenging its legality on the grounds it had not been an open court. An inflammatory affidavit detailing the entire McPherson-Mattern affair was thrown out of court by Justice Frank Ford, but got much play in the newspapers. The courtroom was packed on May 8, 1933 for the sequel. Cora lost her action: Ford ruled that if Tweedie had called it a court, it was a court, and since Cora had been a willing party to the whole divorce, she could not very well claim damages.

Needless to say, the trial ended McPherson's political career. Maclean had reduced him to a sobbing wreck on the witness stand. Cora herself did not give up. Helped by several Edmonton lawyers, she pursued the matter all the way to the Privy Council. The law lords of England did not think much of Tweedie's impromptu courtroom, ruling that it was most assuredly *not* a properly constituted court, but declined to put the divorce action aside, on the grounds that a remarriage had taken place.

## Epilogue

The overcrowded courthouse meant that when the government turned its attention to court facilities again in the early 1950s, Edmonton was one of the first cities

Aerial view of new courthouse addition. PAA, J-84.

to have its needs addressed. Instead of building a new courthouse, however, the Social Credit government of Ernest Manning decided on an addition to the existing building. The extension would be as large as the original courthouse, costing over $700,000.[188] The land titles building, the courthouse's immediate neighbour, was promptly demolished to make way for the addition.[189]

Designed by Edmonton architect Neil C. McKernan, the extension was steel and reinforced concrete and clad in stone masonry.[190] The exterior appearance was thoroughly modern, austere with almost no decoration. The addition changed the elegant proportions of the original building, which looked positively baroque in comparison. One concession to the old courthouse was the use of sandstone salvaged from its demolished wall and the land titles building for the exterior cladding.[191] The addition provided four additional courtrooms and offices finished with green marble, oak, and terrazzo tiling. Construction began in 1952, and the new building was finished in 1955.[192]

The addition, however, only bought the courthouse a few years. By 1964, Justice S. Bruce Smith had convinced the government to consider a new courthouse.[193] Premier Manning and the City of Edmonton had already agreed that any new law courts would be part of the city's grandiose civic square scheme for downtown.[194] A location was picked out between 97th and 99th Street and 101st and

*Extension of service: Edmonton Courthouse addition. PAA, PA93/3*

103A Avenue, occupied by a number of small commercial blocks and a warehouse and gas station belonging to Woodward's Department Stores.[195] A land swap was arranged in 1966 with Woodward's.[196] As part of the agreement, the old courthouse was to be destroyed.

Edmonton's new hall of justice could at least claim to be the most imposing of Alberta's modern courthouses. From the start, the government was determined to design a perfect courthouse. The Edmonton firm of Bell, McCulloch and Spotowksi were retained as architects in September 1966.[197] The firm worked closely with an expediting committee and exhaustively canvassed the users of the courthouse and travelled North America to look at other modern facilities.[198] The Law Courts building of Bell, McCulloch and Spotoswki was a six-storey inverted ziggurat of reinforced concrete, designed in a style that has since been dubbed Brutalism. The building undeniably had presence. With twenty courtrooms and every amenity conceivable, when it opened in 1972, Edmonton once again had the most impressive and modern building in the province, another veritable temple of justice. A large annex was added in the 1980s, to relieve the inevitable over crowding.

As for the old courthouse, it was demolished sixty years, almost to the day, after the courts had moved there from the old Sandison block. A few voices were heard in protest, but it was too little, and far too late. The government kept much of the sandstone, using it to repair other buildings from that era that were allowed to survive.

*End of an age: Edmonton's courthouse succumbs to the wrecking ball.* PAA J-856

## LETHBRIDGE

The April 26, 1911 editorial in the Lethbridge Daily News was simply titled "Inadequate." The first sitting of the Supreme Court of Alberta in the city's new provincial courthouse was in session, and the public and the newspapers had finally seen the courtroom inside the imposing edifice. And although Justice David Lynch Scott put the best face on it, giving his compliments to the city on their new hall of justice, the courthouse had been judged – and found wanting. As the News reported:

> ... even as he spoke, half of the witnesses and the men who were concerned in the litigation or summoned as jurors, were standing. How such a colossal blunder could have been made, seems incomprehensible. The acoustic properties in the room are also very bad, the lawyers and witnesses finding it very difficult to make themselves heard more than a few feet away. The money that has been spent on this building has to a large extent, been wasted ... a great deal of unfavourable comment was heard yesterday...."[199]

It was not the sort of reception the government had anticipated. The courthouse in Lethbridge was part of a massive investment in public works with judicial facilities planned for every major city in the province. The new hall of justice was greeted with the same scorn as the Territorial building. The second courthouse was incomparably better than its predecessor but ran up against much higher expectations. It was only the third courthouse built by the province, nearly identical to the building started a year earlier in Wetaskiwin. The Provincial Architect, Allan Merrick Jeffers, tried with his first courthouse design to create a template that could be used throughout the province. The first two were built, a third, intended for Medicine Hat, was not, as the design was abandoned after its reception in Lethbridge. The city was left saddled with a courthouse that, while attractive, was not sufficient to the task. Lethbridge would wait over forty years for a replacement.

### Lethbridge in the New Era

The deep recession of the early 1890s slowed the growth of Lethbridge and district, but the introduction of irrigation in 1898 and the Dominion government's immigration policies soon brought thousands of settlers to southern Alberta. Lethbridge boomed like the rest of the Territories. In 1906, shortly after the founding of Alberta, Lethbridge became a city. Although still very much a company town, its economy had begun to diversify and it was the major commercial centre south of Calgary. Although the citizens of Medicine Hat might have differed, Lethbridge claimed to be the third largest municipality in the province and their claim was sound: the city had almost three thousand residents and was growing rapidly. It was clearly going to be the dominant city of southern Alberta. It had been a conservative stronghold through most of the Territorial days, and therefore was an important prize to the ascendant provincial Liberal party.

Now that Alberta was a province, the fate of the old Territorial courthouse was uncertain: it was not clear if the Dominion would sell it to the province. This was the general policy, but in both Lethbridge and Red Deer, the federal government held onto their buildings because they maintained offices of other departments in them. Lethbridge was thus a good prospect to get a new courthouse in the vast expenditures on public works that followed the creation of the province. However, it would be a case of one step forward, two steps back. The province began planning a new courthouse within two years, but in the interim the courts were forced out of the Territorial building. For over three years the administration of justice was once again carried out in the halls and theatres of Lethbridge, sharing space with fraternal clubs and vaudeville entertainment.

The elevation of Lethbridge to headquarters of an eponymous judicial district made a courthouse imperative. Becoming a judicial centre was, of course, a major victory for the town. Lethbridge had never given up on obtaining a resident judge. When a sixth justice, Horace Harvey, was appointed to the Territorial Supreme Court in 1904, the News immediately agitated to have him stationed in Lethbridge, making veiled threats about what would happen come election time if the government failed to do so.[200] Apparently Harvey himself agreed with the good burghers of Lethbridge, and dropped a few unkind remarks about his new home in Macleod. The paper commented a year after his appointment, with scarce sympathy, "it's too bad the judge could not be permitted to choose a more congenial place of residence, but he should have thought of that before he accepted the job."[201] Once Alberta was made a province, the city fully expected to be made a judicial centre. Attorney General C.W. Cross agreed and visited the city on the May 24, 1906, to make the announcement in person.[202]

While the citizens of Lethbridge could look forward to a resident District Court judge and all the other advantages of being a district headquarters, the new status created some headaches. As the new clerk and sheriff tried to get ready to start their duties, they were forced to look for office space. There was no room for them in the old courthouse. C.V. Bennett, the clerk, was on the receiving end of pointed enquiries from both the Attorney General's Department and the Department of Public Works when he submitted his accounts in December 1906, which included his office rent.[203] This was not withstanding the fact that Bennett had written Deputy Attorney General S.H. Woods several months before, after hearing of his appointment, asking about accommodations for his office. Woods had given him nine pages of sage advice on the supplies and furniture he would need, but neglected to say anything about office space.

Both Woods and John Stocks, Deputy Minister of Public Works, seemed surprised that Bennett was renting an office when the province was paying the Dominion government fifty dollars a month to rent the second floor of the old courthouse. It is one small example of the confusion surrounding the creation of a provincial administration: even though a provincial official had catalogued and evaluated all the facilities the province was taking over or renting, he had neglected to detail the exact arrangements of the courts in Lethbridge. Bennett was probably more than a little miffed, but the Department of Public Works rented a suite of offices for the court in the Oliver Block early in January 1907.[204]

Matters would get worse before they would get better. The provincial government had no set policy regarding courthouses in new districts, but there were high hopes in Lethbridge that a new building might be forthcoming. When Cross visited to announce the new judicial district, he was questioned closely about court accommodation at a meeting held with the constituency. He did not commit himself to a new hall of justice, and indeed thought it more likely the province would buy the old public building and turn it over entirely to the courts.[205] Ironically, considering how much the town had disliked the original courthouse, there was no great hue and cry over the idea – the board of trade passed a resolution asking the province to build a new courthouse instead, but also saw the potential advantages of the public building becoming the courthouse.[206] It would be a good opportunity to prevail upon the Dominion government for a new post office, and the town immediately began plotting to do just that.[207]

However, the Dominion government had no desire to hand over its Lethbridge property. The government had decided that the land on which the original courthouse sat was well situated and would be quite valuable, and unprepared to make a substantial expenditure for a post office, a land office, and a customs office in Lethbridge.[208] So the Dominion retained the public building, and in the middle of 1908 the court was asked vacate the second floor to create more office space.[209] Now the judge and library also had to be housed in rented offices, and halls such as the Caledonia were engaged for holding both the District and Supreme Court.

It was a ludicrous situation for the third largest city in the province. Fortunately, the provincial government, understanding they would not get the old courthouse, put a fairly high priority on a new building in Lethbridge. The Department of Public Works accordingly was already looking for a site in 1907.

## Finding the Perfect Spot

The positioning of the proposed edifice almost immediately became a matter of great controversy. A movement sprang up almost immediately to have it put on the city square, following the traditional practice of having the courthouse either in or facing a central public park in the heart of the town. Discontent had been brewing about the so-called public square in Lethbridge for some time. It had been set aside by the Galts and the Alberta Railway and Irrigation Company as a park for the enjoyment of the citizens of Lethbridge. As the city grew, the town fathers eyed it as a site for new public buildings, including the hoped-for post office, the courthouse, and their own city hall. The supporters of this scheme did not want to use the entire square, just parts of it, and hoped that the presence of civic architecture would lead to the proper landscaping of the space as a park. The City Beautiful movement then in vogue strongly advocated this kind of planning, especially grandiose civic squares

Complicating matters, the Alberta Railway and Irrigation Company still owned a large chunk of the square and had a proprietary interest in its use, although it was amenable to the wishes of the town. There was suspicion that some elements in the town welcomed the public buildings because it might mean the rest of the park would be opened up for businesses. The city council was itself divided: some councillors feared any development on the square would lead to its loss, others felt some monumental architecture would make it a showpiece.

Cushing came down himself early in January to choose a suitable location. Walking into a hotbed of dissension, after interviewing the various factions the minister diplomatically left the matter up to the town to decide, offering to accept their choice as the best choice. It removed the responsibility for an unpopular decision from his government, but it didn't do much to expedite matters. Opinion in the town swung against using the square. The board of trade executive and the city council met to try to hammer out a consensus shortly after Cushing left.[210] One option the council had shown Cushing on his visit was the site of the Forbes Presbyterian Church on Crabb and Dufferin Street, and several members of council and the board moved for it to be adopted as the preferred site. The idea of a popular plebiscite was tossed around but not adopted. Finally the two bodies agreed to the church site as the choice of the city, subject to the approval of the minister.

If the civic fathers thought that was the end of it, they were sadly mistaken. Once it became known that the church property would be suggested, there was immediately an outcry. Some souls still wanted to use the square. Cushing had also received the offer of an option of seven lots across from the RNWMP barracks on Dufferin Street, and a number of citizens came forward to back this location, even preparing a petition which was sent to the minister.[211] The petitioners included future senator W.A. Buchanan, owner of the *Herald*, the managers of the Union Bank and Bank of Commerce, and several prominent real estate men. The continuing doubt as to the legal rights of the city to the square ruled it out of contention, but the site across from the barracks emerged as a strong contender.

Much to the frustration of the city council, Cushing himself came out in favour of the barracks location. So much for his neutrality – "Mr Cushing says that he did not intend the impression to be given that the city could select any site and that the Government would accept it."[212] The minister's main objection was that the church property was rather small, would put the courthouse too close to the main business district, and the resultant noise would be a detriment to the building. The consensus within the council and the board of trade became increasingly fragile. At meetings in early February, councillors and board members argued again about putting the matter to a plebiscite, and even debated heatedly about which site they thought Cushing actually preferred.

Anxiety began to build that the squabbling over the site might delay the building altogether.[213] Mayor Henderson said as much at a February 4 board of trade meeting. He also reminded the board that the church needed to sell their property to raise enough money to build a larger facility. Although it seems unlikely that this argument swayed the board or council, a consensus was finally reached, and the city insisted on the church site. The deputy minister, John Stocks, formally announced on March 14, 1908, that the government had agreed to purchase the Presbyterian Church property.[214] The department had insisted that an additional adjacent lot be included in the deal, and W.C. Simmons, the local member, was able to arrange this as part of the sale.[215] The Department of Public Works paid a sum of $7,700 for its site, which comprised five lots of block 33, plan 4353S, at the corner of Crabb and Dufferin Streets.

## A Less than Successful Design

While the folk of Lethbridge argued about the best place to put their new hall of justice, the building was taking shape on the drafting tables of Allan Jeffers' architectural staff.

In basic layout, the Lethbridge and Wetaskiwin buildings were more or less identical, so much so that Jeffers used copies from the earlier building plans, simply crossing out "Wetaskiwin" and replacing it with "Lethbridge."[216] It had the same cruciform layout, but the exterior and interior were richer in decoration. The front of the building faced west onto Crabb Street, and the longer central portion of the building was three storeys with a hip roof, while the two wings were two storeys. As in all Jeffers' courthouses, the entrance dominated the facade. The troublesome cement stairs used in Wetaskiwin were upgraded to granite. Two massive engaged brick piers defined the porch, supporting a large pediment with a cartouche of the provincial arms. Stone Ionic columns *in antis* flanked the doorway, which consisted of double doors with fanlight transom window, with a stone surround consisting of two Doric columns with carved stone brackets and an open pediment.

Interestingly, Jeffers abandoned the hemispheric window above the main doorway found in the building's predecessor in favour of simple square-cut openings, but changed the clerestory windows to the courtroom to delightful round portals. The windows had stone surrounds with prominent keystones. Sandstone quoins were added to all the corners, front, sides, and back as well as more stone detailing on the attic storey. Jeffers also abandoned the arched windows used on the rear facade in his previous design. The exterior treatment was more lively than with Wetaskiwin, but the Lethbridge courthouse still presented a stern face to the world.

The layout of the building saw some changes. Cells, caretaker's quarters, vaults, general storage, and furnace room remained in the basement. On the main floor the south wing had the sheriff's office and district clerk's office, the north was given over to the District Court chambers and the Supreme Court clerk. As

Front (West) elevation, Lethbridge Courthouse, 1909. PAA

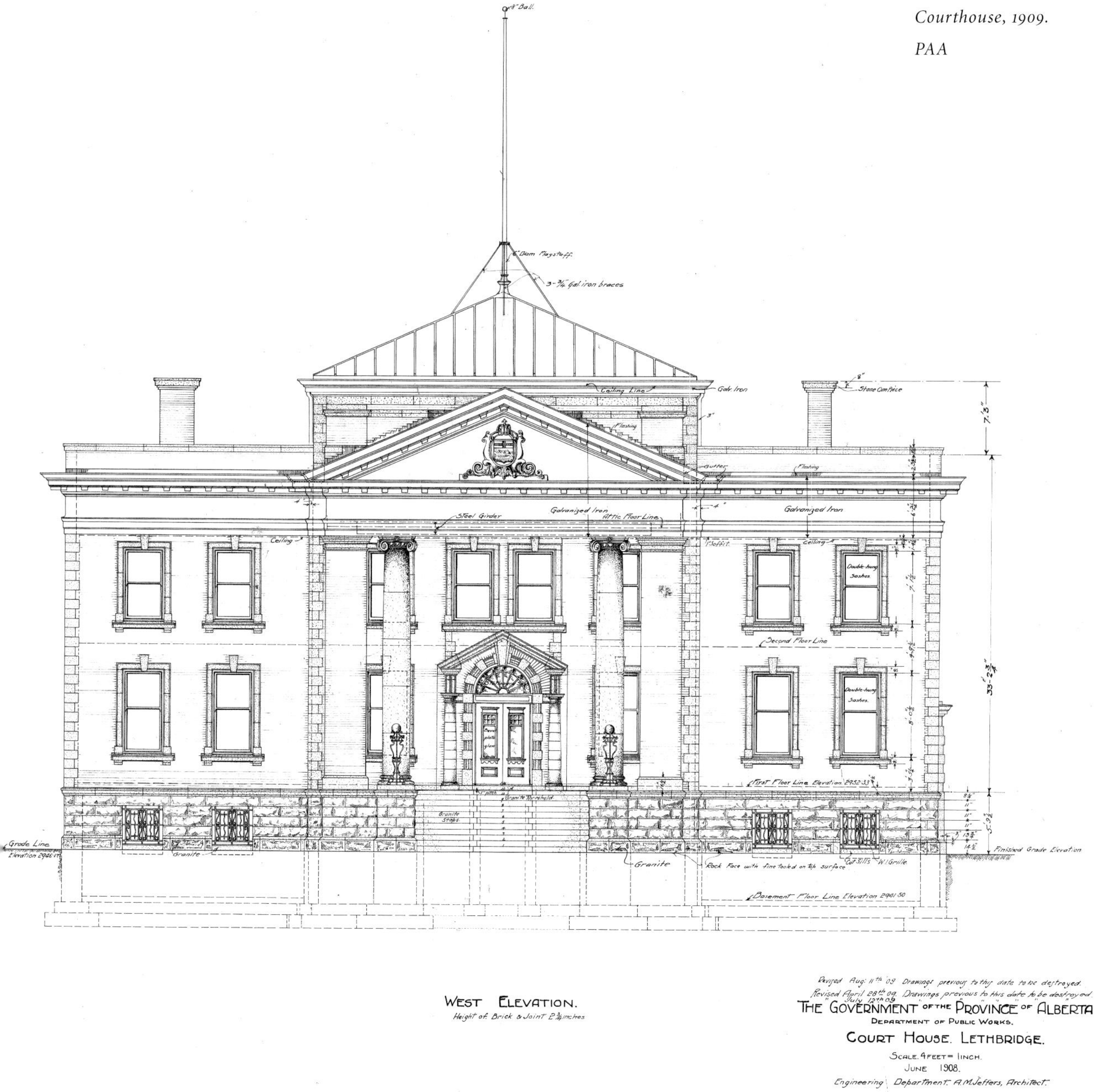

*Side (North) elevation, Lethbridge Courthouse, 1909. PAA*

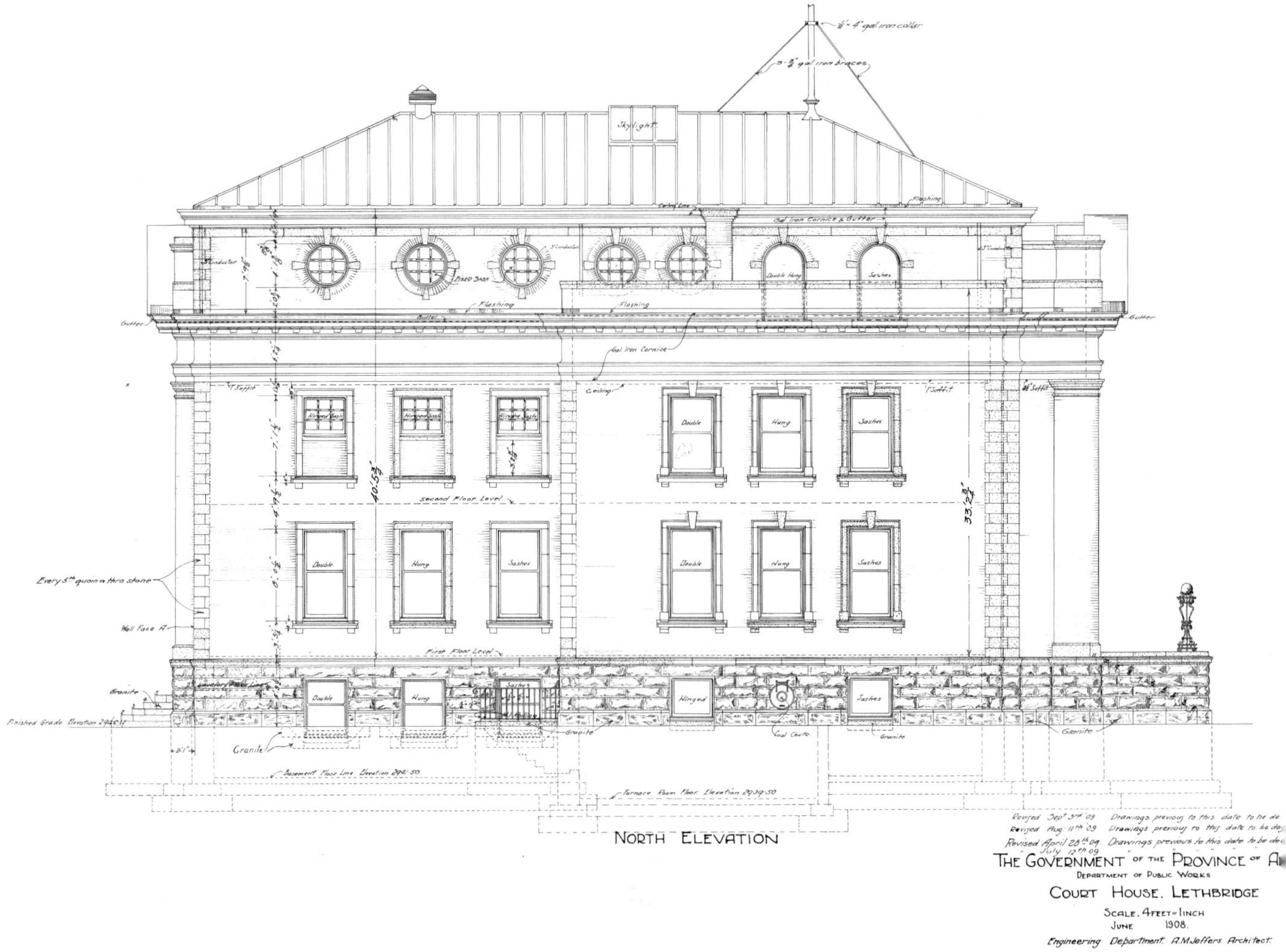

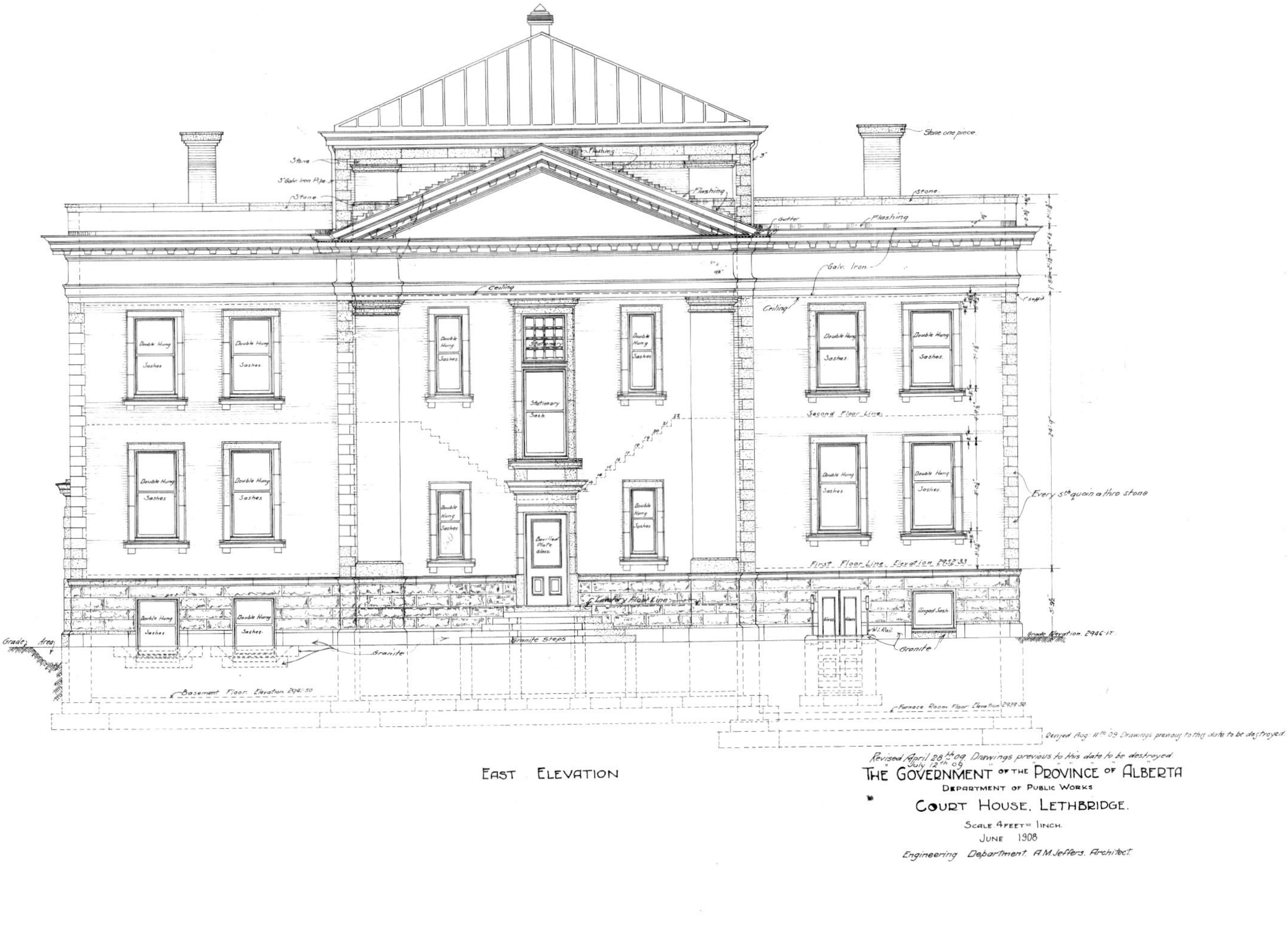


*Rear (East) elevation, Lethbridge Courthouse, 1909. PAA*

*Section (A-B), Lethbridge Courthouse, 1909. PAA*

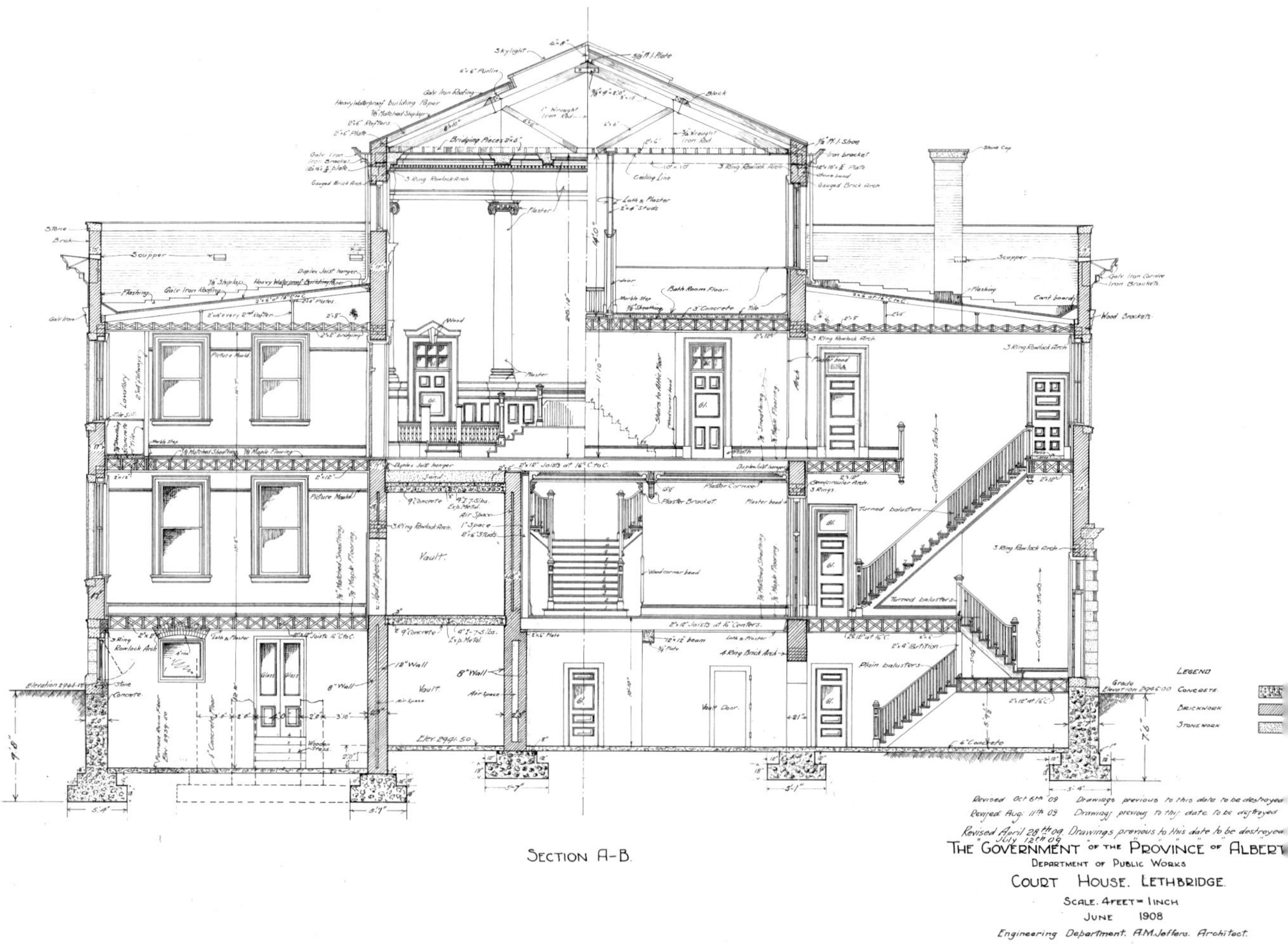

*Section (C-D), Lethbridge Courthouse, 1909. PAA*

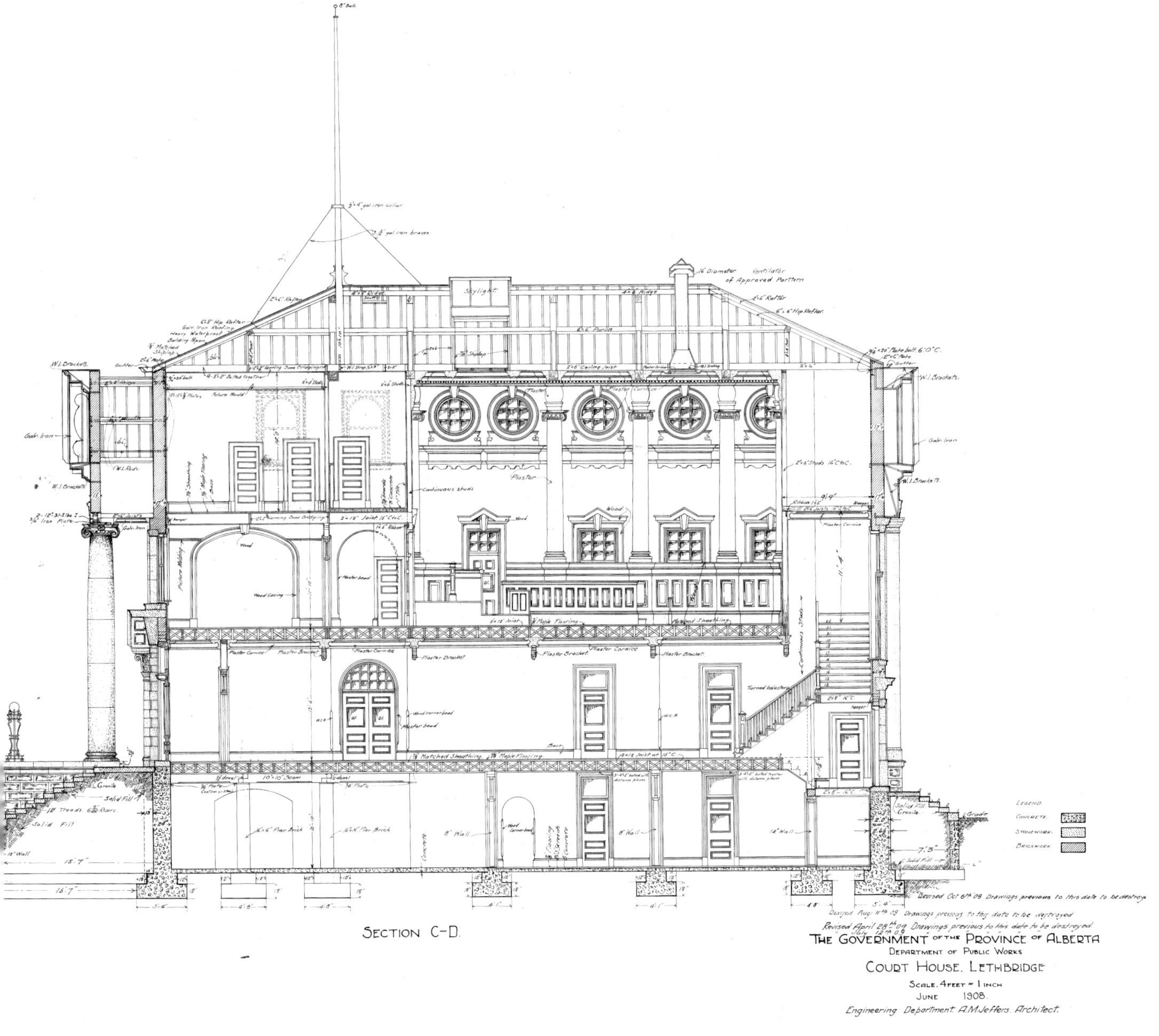

*Main floor plan, Lethbridge Courthouse, 1909. PAA*

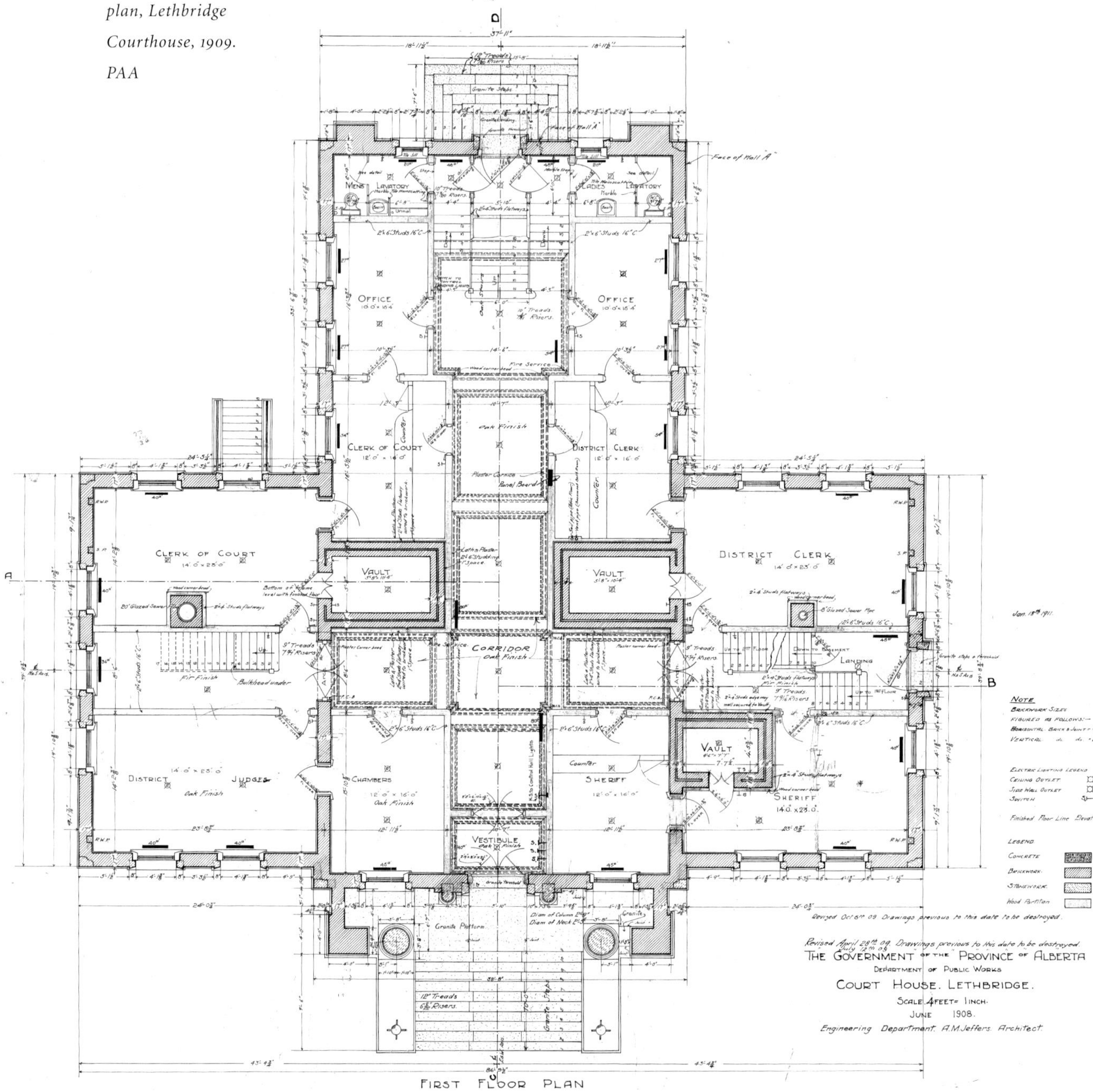

*The grandeur of the law: Lethbridge's new courtroom. LASA 61-G-39*

in Wetaskiwin, two axial corridors ran through the building. The main corridor from the front entrance led to grand public staircase at the rear of the building, which led to the main courtroom on the second floor. There were two more staircases in each wing. On the second floor, the library was placed at the front of the building, overlooking the entrance. The District Court judge's office was on one side and the Supreme Court justice on the other side, while the witness room and jury room were placed in the wings but entered onto the main courtroom. An attic storey contained a judge's sleeping quarters. It was a compact and efficient design, with one major drawback: it left little room for expansion.[217] The interior was decorated throughout with oak trim and plaster mouldings, with floors of polished maple. Jeffers drew back from using the extensive marble finishing that would be seen in his Edmonton and Calgary courthouses. That would have been, no doubt, too much of an extravagance for the smaller edifice.

The second-floor courtroom was the true glory of the building. Although sharing dimensions with its cousin in Wetaskiwin, the Lethbridge version was much more opulent. Jeffers spared no effort in creating an impressive space. Taking advantage of the attic storey, it had a twenty-five-foot ceiling. In addition to the main floor windows, there were round clerestory windows five on each side, as well as a skylight. The walls were lined with plaster columns surmounted with ionic capitals, and the ceiling had decorated plaster beams, while a cornice encompassed the whole room. The upper windows had elaborate plaster sills, the lower windows and doorways oak woodwork, including pediments above the doors. The floors were polished maples and oak wainscoting lined the walls. The judge's bench was against the west wall, with access to the hallway and stairway to his quarters, while public seating was at the east end by the main staircase. It was a magnificent space, with a degree of decoration exceeded only by the Edmonton courthouse. Sadly, it turned out to be an acoustic nightmare with the high ceiling and the many nooks and crannies, and the one courtroom took up an enormous amount of space.

JUSTICE THOMAS TWEEDIE – A LETHBRIDGE GHOST?

As a justice, Thomas Mitchell Tweedie brought a certain physical presence to the bench. A bon vivant, the judge was enormously stout, and the long stairs up to the top of the Lethbridge courthouse proved his undoing. At the time of his death in 1944, Tweedie had been Chief Justice of the Trial Division of the Supreme Court for just two months.

One of seemingly hundreds of Nova Scotia lawyers who came west in the early part of the century, Tweedie was born in River John on March 3, 1872, and received his law degree from Harvard in 1905.[218] He was one of the last advocates admitted to the Territorial Bar before it was absorbed by the two new provinces in 1907. The Maritimer quickly became a mainstay of the Calgary Bar, both in practice and at their dinners and social functions. Like many of his compatriots, Tweedie was politically active and was a Conservative MLA and MP for Calgary. Made a King's Counsel in 1913, Tweedie practised with A.A. McGillivray, one of the leading trial lawyers of his generation, until his appointment to the bench in 1921. He served on the Trial Division for just over twenty-three years, and became Chief Justice on August 16, 1944. A popular judge, his legal acumen was well respected, and his reputation even survived his involvement in the sordid McPherson wife-swapping affair. Tweedie had helped Oran McPherson, the Minister of Public Works in John Brownlee's UFA government expedite his divorce by holding court in the judge's library of the Edmonton Courthouse. When McPherson's wife challenged the divorce, the matter ended up in front of the Privy Council. Justice Tweedie took a great deal of good-natured chiding from his contemporaries over the affair.[219]

Tweedie's role in the McPherson scandal only bolstered his reputation as a man of the world. The confirmed bachelor, who lived in the Ranchmen's Club in Calgary, was a fixture at bar association functions for years. The justice loved a good dinner, and while in Lethbridge for the 1944 fall assizes of the Supreme Court, he was wined and dined by the local bar in congratulations for his promotion. Returning alone to the courthouse, he did not make it to the attic apartment but had a heart attack while climbing the stairs, and died a lonely death. The clerk of court found him early the next morning.[220] A great loss to the bench, Tweedie was generally mourned throughout the legal community and the tributes poured in. While the circumstances of his passing were somewhat macabre, Tweedie was evidently a soul at peace with himself, for no tales ever circulated of his spirit visiting the halls of the Lethbridge courthouse.

The province did not show itself to be much more efficient at building projects than the Dominion government in the Territorial days. The new courthouse took two full years to build. To a large extent, the long wait was the product of an overstretched budget and an overheated economy, which created difficult conditions for builders. No project could be carried out without funds being allocated for it in the budget, and thus could be no real start until the Estimates for 1909 were brought down: the legislature set aside $40,000 to begin construction. In February concrete was sent to the city for the foundations, but sat until spring.

Bon vivant: Justice Thomas Tweedie. LASA 97-005

The wait immediately produced political complications for the Liberals. The Rutherford government called its first election for the end of March. During a candidate debate in Lethbridge, W.C. Simmons had to account for the government's tardiness in getting the court building started. He blamed the spring floods, which siphoned off funds for emergency repairs for bridges and roads.[221] The Liberals were returned to government with an enormous majority, and any further criticism was silenced when Public Works finally called for tenders on May 5, 1909. Cushing gave his promise the building would be rushed to completion. The main contract was given to Lethbridge's own Smith Brothers and Wilson Construction, the city's largest building firm. The company was well equipped for project: it had won a $100,000 contract for Regina's city hall three years earlier.[222] Through its Saskatchewan arm, it would also build several courthouses in that province.

Construction began in June 1909. The Department of Public Works decided to put in the foundation itself, and a government crew finished the job near the end of the month before starting work on the new telephone building.[223] Smith Brothers got down to work in July. As with all the early provincial courthouses, progress was slow. Both skilled labour and materials were in great demand as the prairie building boom started. In 1909, supplies were tight, but progress was made on the Lethbridge building. By the end of the year, the sandstone basement walls and part of the first storey on the edifice had been completed, but already a shortage of building brick made it impossible to finish the exterior before winter.[224] The situation was not much better the following year, and to add to the builder's headaches, there was labour trouble. In April, all the carpenters in Lethbridge walked off the job for several days demanding better wages.[225]

It did not help matters that the government faced a major crisis in 1910, which paralyzed it for several months. The Alberta and Great Waterways scandal broke early in the year, and soon the Rutherford administration was in disarray. Cushing resigned in March 1910. Although the Deputy Minister of Public Works, John Stocks, was able and efficient, a great deal of routine, even trivial, decisions still went to the minister's desk or to the Executive Council, and Cushing's departure deprived the department of its leadership.

More disruptive was the financial disarray caused by the fall of Rutherford's government. The legislature only approved the estimates up to the end of May 1910, leaving the civil service, at least on paper, without authority to spend more money.

In the temporary estimates passed in March, there were reductions in many of the votes including public buildings – the Edmonton courthouse, for example, had its estimate reduced from $50,000 to $25,000.[226] It is difficult to gauge exactly what affect the furor had on the building projects of the department. The Public Accounts for the year do not show much money spent for construction, but later summaries of expenditures for the Lethbridge courthouse show that the government found the resources to carry on.[227] By the end of the year the courthouse was nearly finished.[228] The department anticipated having the building ready by January, but the interior finishing took several months to complete and it was not ready until the spring.[229] When the contractors finished with the building, it had cost $75, 905.91 – not including the site – and was well within budget.

The completion of the courthouse was a bit of an anticlimax. In March, Judge Winter held the first open court in the building, which consisted of one civil case that he adjourned, reserving judgment. The clerks of court and sheriff were happy to have proper offices at long last, and the bar association lost no time in moving the library and utilizing the new space for its meetings. But it became abundantly clear that the grand courtroom had some real problems. The first session was a busy one and featured several cases that attracted large crowds of spectators. There were complaints about the noise and poor acoustic properties of the giant hall and the lack of seating. The local papers roasted the Department of Public Works for the design. It was not exactly the sort of reception the government had hoped for. As was usually the case with the provincial courthouses, however, once the judges and court officials settled in, not much was heard about the building, even its shortcomings. For Lethbridge, whatever its problems, the new domicile of the courts represented an enormous leap in the quality of facilities available for the administration of justice.

Shortly after it was finished, it looked like the Lethbridge courthouse would be soon outgrown, much as would happen in Edmonton: within two years of completion, there was not enough office space for all the judges and court staff in the capital's hall of justice. The end of the great boom, however, solved the overcrowding problem. By 1917, far from being overwhelmed, there was enough room in the courthouse for officials from Public Works and the Department of Mines.[230] They were soon moved out to make room for the Alberta Provincial Police, who took over the entire basement in 1918 and eventually had offices on the main floor as well.[231] The amalgamation of the District Court offices with the Supreme Court clerk and sheriff in 1921 freed up even more space. Like other courthouses, but perhaps less than some, other provincial government departments were housed in the Lethbridge courthouse at various times. The hall of justice in Lethbridge was also able to absorb another resident judge in 1935 when A.M. MacDonald was moved from Macleod as part of an amalgamation of the District Court.

The Lethbridge courthouse spelled the end of Jeffers' attempt to produce a standard design for a medium-sized courthouse. The shortcomings of the courtroom and the lack of room for expansion were fatal flaws. When the government decided to delay the Medicine Hat courthouse in 1909, which was to follow the

*Civic attraction: Lethbridge Courthouse [c.1914]. LASA 5-G-72*

*A natural rallying point [c.1945]. Lethbridge Public Library*

same plans, the design was discarded. Soon Jeffers would be gone, and the province scaled back on the construction of new facilities for the courts. Of the five courthouses designed by the Provincial Architect, Lethbridge was probably the least successful. Although it gave yeoman service for over forty years, it was also the first building to be sacrificed when the government turned its attention again to courthouses in the early 1950s. The absence of any protest at its replacement and removal suggests that for all its attractiveness, the building never won the hearts of the Lethbridge bar or the citizens of the town.

The 1911 building had never been a success, and by the end of World War II, Lethbridge was almost four times larger than when the courthouse was erected, and growing fast. The city started an urban renewal project immediately after the war, a civic centre that was to include a new city hall, an auditorium, sports centre, and other public buildings. Hoping a new courthouse might follow, the city council reserved land and informed the provincial government it was available, and in 1947 the offer was formerly accepted.[232] It was not a commitment to build; not long afterward, the province spent a considerable amount of money renovating the existing facility.[233]

Once rumours surfaced that the courthouse might be replaced at a different location, however, the Department of Public Works began to receive discreet enquiries about the existing building. As offers passed over the desk of George Monkman, the Deputy Minister of Public Works, it occurred to him that selling the old building could fund the construction of a new courthouse. He estimated it would cost at least $225,000 for a new building, but with the city of Lethbridge offering a free site, the sale of the land under the old hall of justice might recoup much of the outlay.[234] Within a short time Monkman had a suitable offer. On February 18, 1950, the province announced the sale of the existing courthouse to unnamed Toronto interests, making a new building a priority.

In an unprecedented move, the province retained the Lethbridge architectural firm of Meech, Mitchell and Meech to design the new courthouse. This was likely part of the land deal, to ensure the new courthouse would fit in well with the new city hall designed by the firm. It also reflected the Department of Public Works' lack of trained architectural staff – a number of commissions in the immediate post-war period went to private architects, a policy later reversed. Meech Mitchell and Meech made the courthouse the north anchor of the civic centre, situated on corner of 4th Avenue and 11th Street. The three-storey brick building was essentially Modernist in design, but with some subtle Art Deco style touches and a formal facade reminiscent of the austere classicism of the Depression years. Bird Construction, one of the province's major contracting firms, successfully tendered a bid of $399,555 for the structure.[235]

The new law courts were opened with considerable fanfare in September 1952.[236] No fewer than five judges, including Chief Justice Colin McLaurin, came down along with a crowd of distinguished lawyers from as far north as Edmonton. Senators, MLAs, and deputy ministers joined every important municipal official in Lethbridge to celebrate the occasion. Contemporaries were not so sure: at the official opening, the Deputy Attorney General remarked that "some persons are non-plussed by such modernistic buildings."[237] Even as the citizens and the bar of Lethbridge celebrated, a few blocks away the wrecker's ball was swiftly levelling Jeffers' courthouse.[238] Within days, nothing remained, and excavations began for a Woolworth's store, the temple of justice replaced almost overnight by a temple of commerce.

*The new face of justice: Lethbridge's post-war courthouse. GMA, P1989-1049-115*

*Current courthouse aerial view. GMA, P1993-1000-023*

Like the Territorial building, the 1911 courthouse is now a distant memory, preserved only in a few photographs and postcards. The 1952 courthouse was itself superseded by the end of the 1970s. A new building, located on the corner of 3rd Avenue and 4th Street South and designed to house all the provincial courts in Lethbridge, from Court of Queen's Bench to the traffic courts, was opened on June 1, 1983 to much praise from the assembled judges and politicians.[239] As for the previous building, it was rescued by the City of Lethbridge for civic offices at a nominal yearly rent of one dollar.[240] When Lethbridge decided to demolish its old city hall and build a replacement on the same site in 1996, the arrangement preserved a significant contribution of Meech, Mitchell, Meech to the city's architecture. With Lethbridge's first two halls of justice lost to the passing years, the 1952 building has become "the old courthouse," a monument to the optimistic years after World War II.

*Sleek and modern: courtroom in the new Lethbridge courthouse. Glenbow Archives, ND-20-221*

## THE TABER COURTHOUSE

Like Fort Saskatchewan, the hall of justice at Taber was a properly designed and built, if modest courthouse. And like the older edifice, it was destined to be under-utilized and abandoned to non-judicial functions at an early date.

Exactly why Taber got a courthouse is not entirely clear. A small community of fourteen hundred souls in 1916, Taber's economy was based on agriculture and coal. The latter industry may have something to do with the decision to build a court facility: coal-mining towns in Alberta often had reputations as rough places. Another, more compelling reason has been suggested: in October 1917, Archie McLean, rancher and long-time MLA, was made Minister of Public Works and had to stand in a by-election.[241] What better way to reflect the honourable member's new influence than by a public works project in his community? And what better way to make sure he was duly reelected? This may be considered a bit cynical, as there is no direct evidence the building was a bribe to the electorate. However, right after McLean's election in 1913, the local paper immediately called for a land titles office in town as a reward for being "the only Liberal riding from east to west across the south country."[242] The town wanted a land title office; Maclean instead informed the local board of trade that a combined courthouse and telephone exchange would be built soon.[243]

Taber's privileged position in the judicial system might also make one skeptical of the government's motives. The town was made a judicial sub-district in 1914 even though it was only thirty miles from the district headquarters, Lethbridge, by rail. After the court offices were created, Taber expected a courthouse in short order.[244] The town council tried to speed things up in the fall of 1917 by offering a free site, hoping to be allowed to use the building for council meetings and in return for some say on the design and appearance of the structure.[245]

Despite the poor economic conditions and shortages of material, the government decided to follow up on its promises. By the end of 1917 the Architectural Branch had designed a modest public building for the town. Assistant Provincial Architect J.B. Allan drafted two sets of plans while his boss was on leave, but on his return Blakey decided it was not sufficiently well thought out and revised it.[246] The Taber building was a simple one-storey structure, but of interest as it set the tone for the rest of the courthouses built by the province before World War II. It was quite utilitarian with a hip roof, with extensive use of stucco and brick trim. The entrance did feature a prominent porch, with a grand arched entry and transoms and fanlight around the door. Of concrete, hollow tile and timber construction, the building had a facade of fifty-two feet and was twenty-eight feet deep. It bore a resemblance to the cottage schools that were to come in vogue soon in the province.

Built by the contracting firm of Hotson and Depew of Medicine Hat, the courthouse was started in June 1918 and finished by November.[247] The final cost was $14,532.[248] The townsfolk, expecting something grander, were disappointed the building was only one storey and of plain appearance.[249] Once the building was in operation, it was soon criticized in the local paper for its small courtroom.[250] The courts and its officers were not the only ones who got new quarters. The APP were installed in the basement with cells for local miscreants. Probably because of the large outlay Taber had made in procuring a site – it issued debentures for finance the purchase[251] – the town got to use of the building for council meetings, and soon the community also used the courthouse for other things. The local curling club met there and it was even used by hockey teams from the nearby rink to warm up.[252]

The town might have regretted any unkind words about their house of justice when only fourteen years later the province decided to wrap up the sub-district of Taber and close the courthouse. There was immediate consternation in the town, and every organization that could muster pen and paper protested to J.F. Lymburn, the Attorney General.[253] He was told it was false economy and an unfair imposition on the people of Taber and district, especially due to the hardship of the Depression. J. Harper Prowse, a local barrister and later leader of the provincial Liberal party, also reminded the government that the town had donated the site on the condition it would be used for the courthouse, implying that perhaps there would be some legal

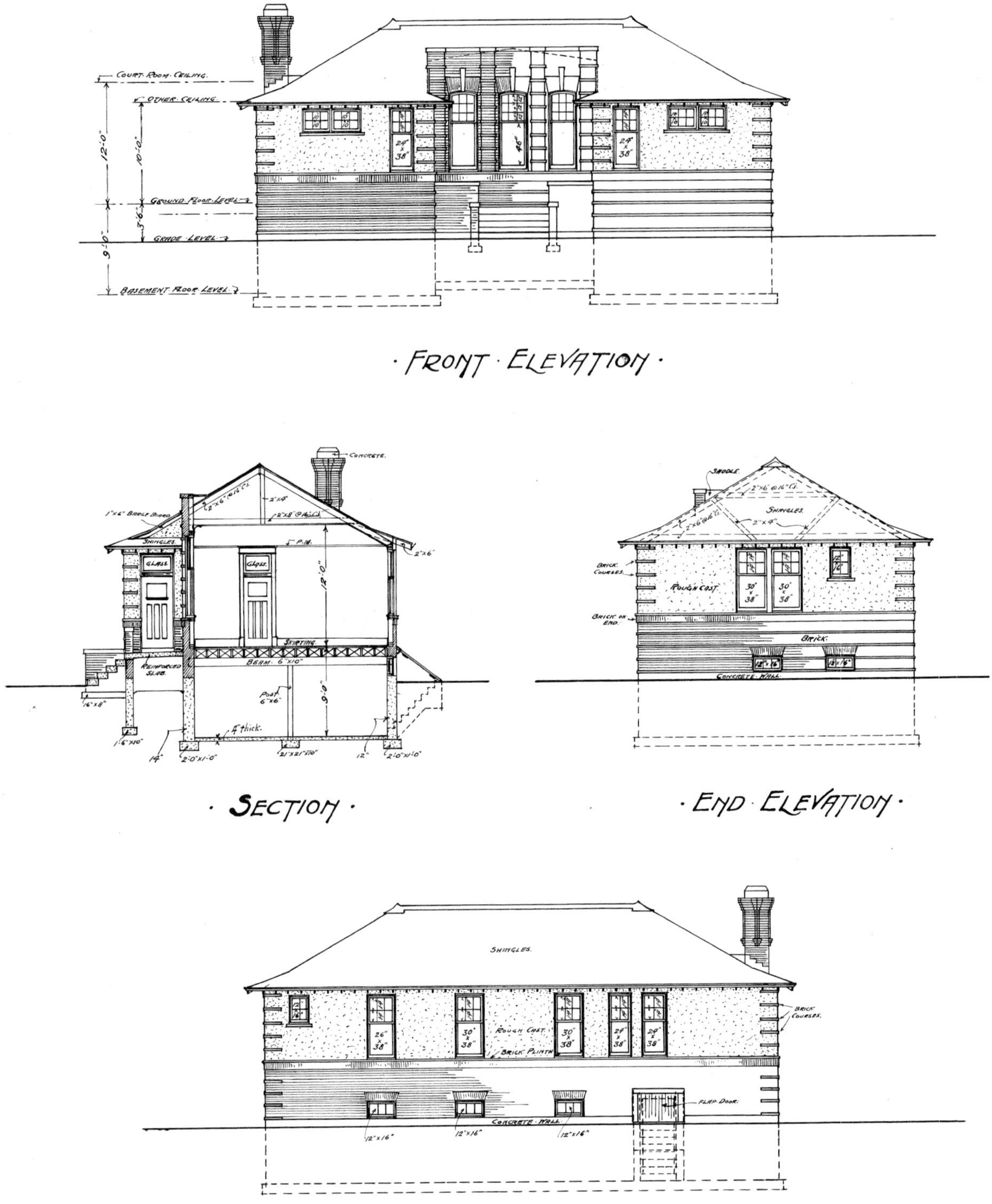


*The understudy's effort: proposed Taber Courthouse, 1917. PAA*

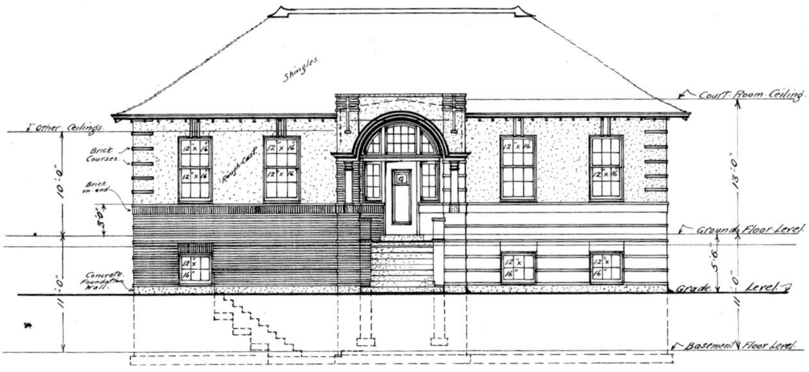


- FRONT - ELEVATION -

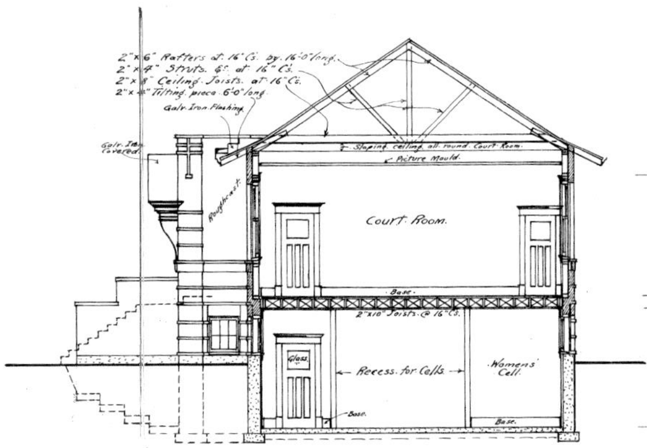


- CROSS - SECTION - "A"-"A".

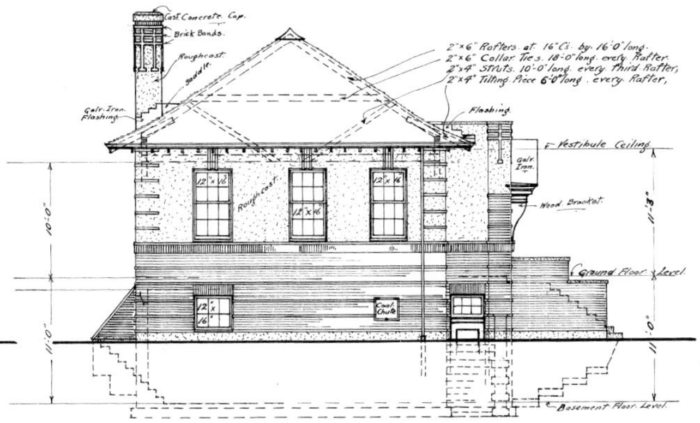


- END - ELEVATION -

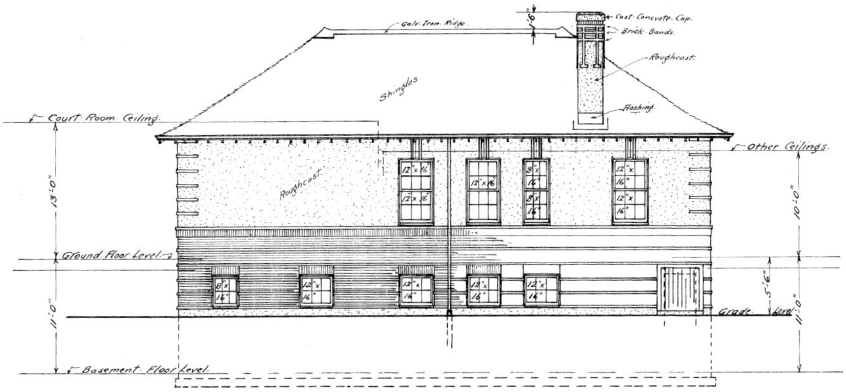


- REAR - ELEVATION -

*The master's touch: Blakey's elevations for Taber Courthouse, 1917.* PAA

nastiness if it wasn't. And the local UFA also weighed in to point out the extra expense it would mean to the district. Perhaps this last protest, coming from the grassroots of his party, scared off Lymburn. It was left to J.W. Hugill, the Attorney General for the new Social Credit government in 1935, to make good on the threat. Despite a new round of vociferous protests, he held firm.[254] As of January 1, 1936, the sub-district of Taber was no more.[255]

Although the court offices closed, the courthouse remained in use. The RCMP took over the barracks in the basement, and the District Court was still held in the courtroom. The extra office space was used for other provincial departments and also for the school district office and eventually the town offices. Finally, in the early 1950s, the Department of Public Works decided to sell the building to the town for $8,000, and in 1953 it became the Taber town hall.[256] It is worth noting that while the Taber building was designated a provincial historic resource, the town tried to get this rescinded in the 1990s due to concerns over what to do with the structure.[257]

# CALGARY

Calgary's second courthouse, built to replace the increasingly cramped and inadequate Territorial building, still stands, much as it was when finished in 1914. Its surroundings have changed dramatically. The land titles building that sat beside it has vanished; on the site of the old Territorial courthouse rises a modern structure, the Court of Queen's Bench building. The first courthouse in Calgary symbolized the end of the frontier, and the second symbolized another equally poignant ending: the finish of the ten-year boom that had transformed the city from a dusty cow town to a prairie metropolis. And if the Territorial courthouse was one of the first major sandstone buildings in Calgary, the provincial courthouse was one of the last, heralding the end of an era for the "Sandstone City."[258] The new Calgary court building also represented the end of Allan Merrick Jeffers' tenure as Provincial Architect. His last courthouse design was austere even by his standards, a fitting monument to the finish of the great boom and its infectious optimism.

## Calgary in a New Era

By the time the ground was broken for a second courthouse, Calgary had changed immensely. In 1901, the city had just over four thousand citizens, an increase of only several hundred from a decade before. By 1911, it officially had over forty-four thousand residents and was still growing. The political scene had also been transformed: the Liberal party had ruled the country since 1896 and the new province since its inception in 1905. Calgary, as a Conservative bastion, was not the darling of patronage it had been. Although barely twenty years had passed, the Territorial courthouse was a relic from another age, no longer a monolith of stone but just another building of the frontier days. Commercial blocks like the Burns Building were far more impressive, and Calgary's nearly completed city hall was now the architectural gem of the town.

Calgary's courthouse remained the largest in the Territories until well into the twentieth century, but it was nonetheless clearly inadequate. With only one courtroom and limited space, it could no longer keep pace with the volume of business in the courts. Not only was the courthouse too small, but there was a growing sense that it was too rustic to be a credit to a dynamic city. When the District Court and the Supreme Court Acts took effect in 1907, several more judges, another clerk of court, another sheriff's office and their staff all moved into the old Territorial building. It created quite a crisis. A.Y. Blaine, the new Inspector of Legal Offices for the province, visited in 1908 and was appalled by the conditions.

> At Calgary I found the Clerk of the Supreme Court and the Clerk of the District Court occupying the same office, a small room entirely inadequate for the

CALGARY, ALBERTA, SATURDAY, JUNE 21, 1913 UNSETTLED; MODERATELY WAF

T A SUCCESS---PELKEY TRIAL ADJOURNED TI

Scene In The Court Room At Pelkey Trial Yesterday



*A last view: courtroom of the old courthouse during the Pelkey trial. Glenbow Archives*

purpose. There is not room for the Clerks to do the work of the office, and the man in charge of the Chattel Mortgage Book and of the Lien Notes Book had these books at a table in the Library....

... It is necessary that a further Court Room be provided at once, as recently on several occasions there have been two courts in session at the same time, and this will be a more frequent occurrence in the future....

... After carefully considering the whole matter I am of the opinion that the only thing to do is to have a temporary addition added to the Court House.[259]

## A Long Wait

A replacement was in the works. Economically, Calgary was the first city of the province and its needs were too important to be ignored. The city was still regarded as a den of Conservatives, but the initial Liberal sweep of the province carried William H. Cushing, a popular and well-respected local businessman, into the legislature for the Grits. Cushing was made Rutherford's Minister of Public Works, giving Calgary excellent representation in cabinet. It was not the only town in dire need of a new courthouse, however: both Edmonton and Lethbridge were in worse situations. The capital, nearly as big as its southern sister, only had one small courtroom on the second floor of a commercial block to serve the District and Supreme Courts, while in Lethbridge the court was renting offices and holding assizes in various halls. Not surprisingly, the province gave priority to towns without courthouses over the centres that had Territorial buildings, whatever their inadequacies. So while Calgary saw the Normal School (teachers' college) started in 1907 and a desperately needed land titles building in 1909, a new courthouse would not be immediately forthcoming.

Calgary was fortunate in one respect: there would be no difficulties in finding an affordable site near the city centre, thus saving the city from the controversies that beset other courthouses in the province. The Dominion government had reserved the entirety of block 16 where the old building was situated. When the provincial government decided in 1906 that it would eventually purchase the Territorial courthouse, the block came with it. Four years later the province plunked down just over $40,000 for the Calgary facility, including interest and some rent charges, but it got a large parcel of land downtown.[260] Although the property was situated on the edge of the business district, the province avoided paying an outrageous sum for a new site, as land values were swiftly rising by 1910. The actual transfer of the title was not settled until 1918, even though the province had handed over a cheque in 1911 for the property. The land titles building was already finished by this point, and the new courthouse was started soon afterward on land to which the province did not yet have clear title. It never became an issue, but it was ironic considering the nature of buildings situated there.

The Provincial Architect, A.M. Jeffers, was apparently a great believer in standardized buildings. He intended his first courthouse design for Wetaskiwin to serve as a template for a medium-sized hall of justice, with one grand courtroom, suitable for the province's smaller cities. Jeffers' second design, for Edmonton's temple of justice, was to be the model for a larger facility, with a twin built in Calgary. The local Liberal newspaper, the Albertan, proudly ran an article in the summer of 1908 about the new Edmonton hall of justice. Along with a sketch of the building, it included the legend "The Calgary Court House to be Started in Few Months to be built from same Plans."[261] It was a premature announcement. Far from preparing to erect a similar facility, the Architectural Branch had in fact shelved plans for Calgary and was concentrating on the land titles office beside the old Territorial courthouse. The replacement building was still in the works, however. A power and heating plant built for the land titles office in 1909 was specifically designed to accommodate the future court facility. That spring, shortly after the provincial election, the Calgary Herald told its readers that "there is to be commenced this summer in Calgary the construction of a magnificent new court house, the cost of which will be $250,000 to $300,000."[262] The paper claimed that the government had also called for tenders.

Despite these promising signs, the awaited building stubbornly refused to materialize. In a memo dated December 28, 1909, the Public Works deputy minister, John Stocks, advised Cushing to delay construction, along with the courthouse in Medicine Hat and the land titles building in Edmonton.[263] Stocks felt that the department was stretched too thin with the construction on hand to realistically begin more projects. And he had a point. The Edmonton courthouse and the legislature building were considerably behind schedule, and although the Lethbridge courthouse finally opened in the spring of 1911, the jail in that city was still under construction. There were buildings for the provincial asylum at Ponoka and the university at Strathcona to be finished, and the telephone system was in desperate need of buildings. The Architectural Branch was clearly overwhelmed. Consequently, it was not until 1911 that the proposed Calgary hall of justice reappeared in the reports of the Department of Public Works. The government put a sum of $50,000 in the estimates for the year to begin construction.[264] The Provincial Architect started drafting plans, presumably late in the year, as they remained unfinished going into 1912.[265]

## Jeffers' Last Hurrah

Calgary's second courthouse would be the swan song of Allan Merrick Jeffers. More than any other one man, Jeffers had put his stamp on the early architecture of the province. Calgary was the fifth courthouse designed by Jeffers in five years, and it differed substantially from his earlier work. For Wetaskiwin, Lethbridge, and Edmonton, Jeffers had created Beaux-Arts-inspired, classical designs. If Jeffers had a distinctive style, it was his preference for simple, even severe, buildings, emphasizing "the broad, simple lines" of the facade. Decoration was usually minimal and used around the entrance, in essence focusing the edifice there. Calgary's courthouse would fit this description perfectly, but compared to his other buildings would be exceptionally austere.

There is some question as to whether Jeffers was responsible for the very subdued aspect of the edifice. He left government service at the beginning of 1912, before the drafting was complete. His replacement as Provincial Architect was his former assistant, Richard P. Blakey. With the abrupt departure of Jeffers, Blakey was left with several projects to finish, including Calgary's courthouse. How much of Calgary's hall of justice belonged to Jeffers and how much to Blakey is a matter for debate. A full set of drawings from February 1912 and signed by Blakey was used for the building, with some later modifications to the floor plans. Little remains of the earlier drafts produced under Jeffers, and it is difficult to say, from the remaining drawings, how different the final product was from his original conception. Blakey changed the front entrance appreciably, possibly to bring costs down, but probably left the rest of the building as he found it.[266] Jeffers quit in January, and construction began in the spring of 1912, which did not leave Blakey much time to make extensive changes to the Calgary designs. Furthermore, as is demonstrated by the Medicine Hat courthouse, Blakey was a far more rococco architect than Jeffers. Almost all the major courthouse designs produced under Jeffers were restrained; indeed, one complaint was that they were too plain.

In the case of the Calgary courthouse, the whole building, even the main entrance, was downright minimalist, to the extent of anticipating the so-called "stripped classical" style of the 1920s and 1930s. A simple rectangle, the structure was two storeys and 80 by 173 feet. Like Edmonton, it had concrete foundation, a steel frame and concrete slab floors with masonry walls, taking full advantage of modern construction technology. The exterior stone cladding was cut smooth and regular, with granite specified for the basement storey but sandstone for everything else. The building had a simple cornice below the roofline, and string-courses delineating each storey. The square windows had straight-cut, flush lintels and sills.

Only the entrance had even a hint of ostentation, but just a hint. It projected slightly, with two massive rusticated piers flanking the door and running through the cornice. On each pier, under the cornice, there was a decorative stone bracket. Jeffers' original design called for two engaged pillars characteristically placed *in antis*, similar to the entrance of the neighbouring land titles building, but without the pediment. Blakey changed this to two pairs of small recessed Doric columns above the main door, on either side of the windows overlooking the main entrance. The small, paired Doric columns would be a motif he would use on the Medicine Hat courthouse several years later, and may be Blakey's attempt to put a personal imprint on the building, rather than an economy measure as has been suggested. The doorway was a simple arch, with a small coat of arms for the province perched above. In the earliest drawings, a plaque of stone above the cornice, between the two piers of the entrance, was marked rough for future carving. Whatever cartouche was planned, it was never carried out, and the building remained unadorned.

Internally the courthouse was laid out on a simple axial plan. It lacked the grand rotunda of the Edmonton courthouse and instead had the main staircase placed immediately inside the entrance foyer, but what it lost in beauty it made up for in efficiency. A long marbled corridor ran the length of both floors. As had become standard practice, the offices of the clerks of court and sheriff were on the main floor, as were the judges' offices and the court chambers. The design very cleverly incorporated private stairs for the judges, leading from their offices to the four courtrooms above. The courtrooms, for the Supreme Civil, Criminal and Appeal Court and the District Court, lined the north side of the corridor. The learned jurists could enter directly from the stairs to the judge's platform in each room, or go to the judge's retiring room. The prisoners also had a special stair direct to the criminal court rooms from the basement cells. Jury rooms also opened directly onto the courtroom, but the witness rooms had to be put on the other side of hall with the barristers' lounge and the library. The basement was mostly undeveloped, with vaults, storage space, and the offices of the police detachment and cells for the accused awaiting trial. The interior treatment was not quite as opulent as Edmonton's temple of justice, lacking the extensive plaster detailing, but still calculated to uphold the dignity of the courts. Marble wainscoting, wood trim,

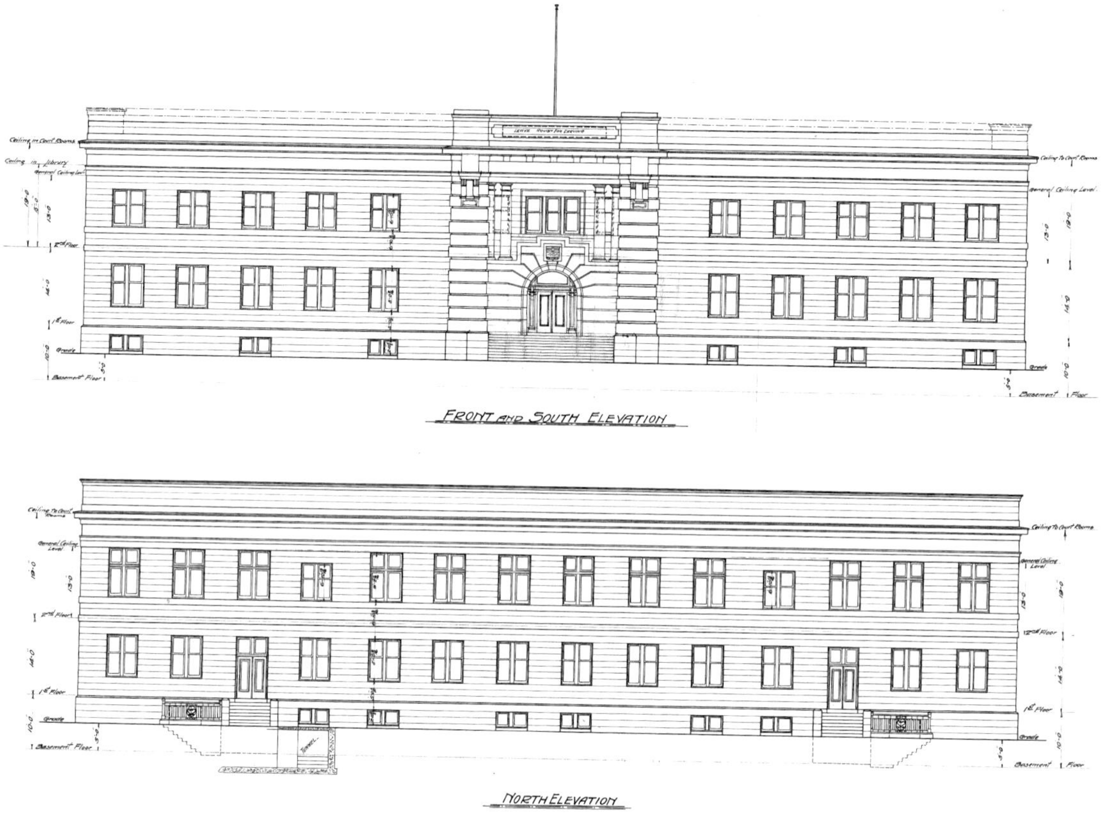


*Front and rear elevations, Calgary Courthouse, 1912, AI*

terrazzo tile floors, and elaborate plaster crown moulding made for attractive surroundings.

The severity of the building's exterior treatment can be seen as a development of Jeffers' austere classicism. It can also be seen, and usually is, as a response to concerns over the breakneck spending of the Alberta government. It is true that outside of the legislature, courthouses were among the most expensive buildings constructed by the province. The Edmonton courthouse, when completed in 1912, cost almost $280,000, and the new Calgary building was projected to be at least as expensive. The Department of Public Works had already cut back on its construction program once, delaying the Calgary courthouse. The concern over expenses comes through clearly in the Department of Public Works 1913 Annual Report. Blakey stated bluntly, "In connection with architectural work it has been our endeavour to design buildings of simple yet dignified character, giving due attention to economical construction and with a view of obtaining the maximum of accommodation for the minimum of cost."[267] Ironically, by the time it was complete in 1914 the newest courthouse ended up being the most costly at $279,932.31, a few hundred dollars more than Edmonton's hall of justice.

Whatever Jeffers' – or Blakey's – intentions, the new building did not find favour with the town fathers. At the beginning of June 1912, with construction already underway, Mayor J.W. Mitchell of Calgary had his first look at the plans. He

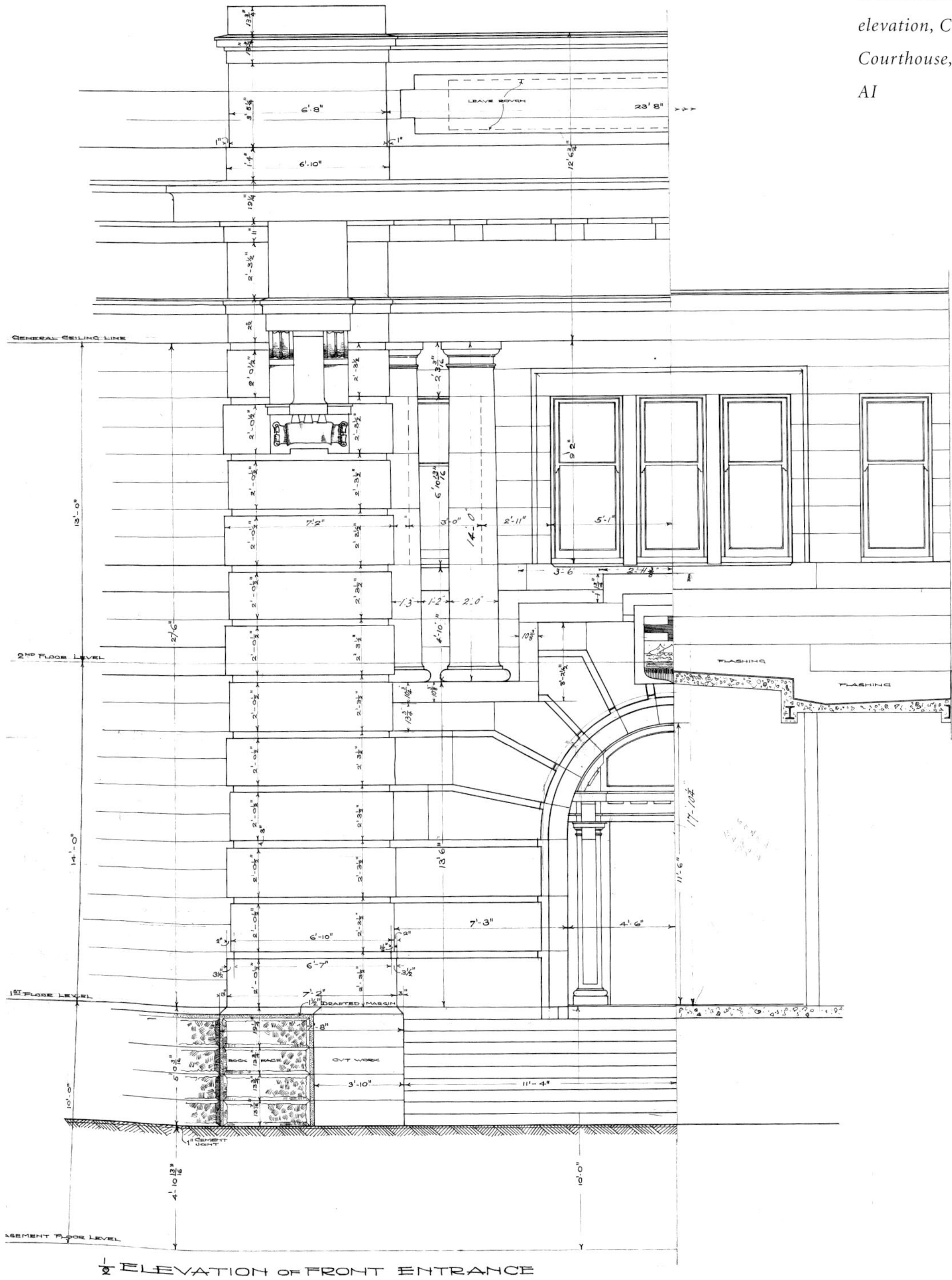


*Front entrance elevation, Calgary Courthouse, 1912, AI*

*Front entrance elevation, Calgary Courthouse, 1912, AI*

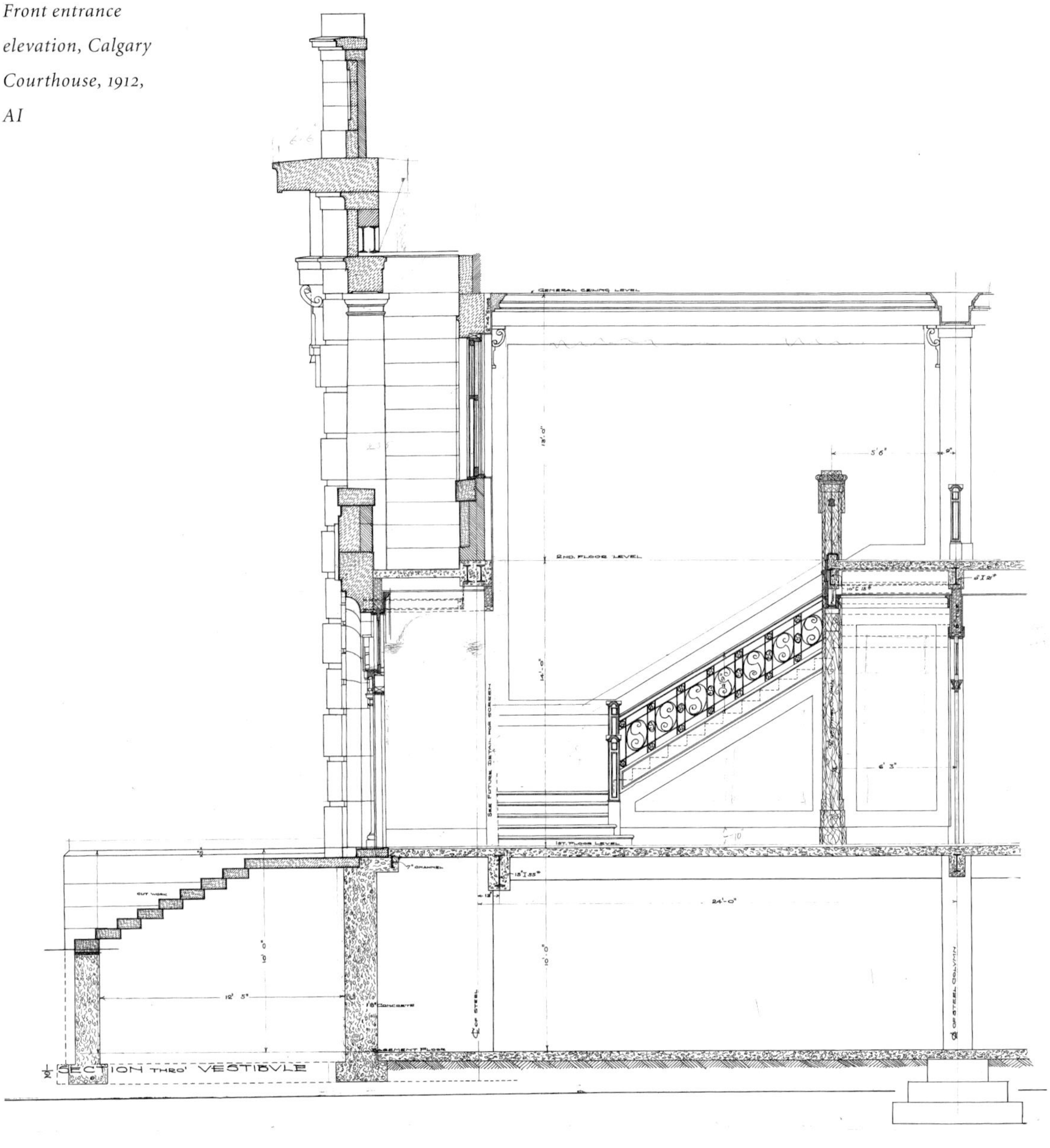


was shocked by the appearance of the building. It was not the twin of Edmonton's courthouse as had been expected. The mayor lost no time in bringing the matter to the attention of the alderman and city commissioners. In a memo circulated on June 5, he warned his colleagues that the new building did not measure up to expectations: "The plans do not indicate a very ornamental or picturesque building, or a building which in appearance would be half has [sic] handsome as the present Land Titles Office ... it is my personal view that the City of Calgary is entitled to a building more modern and fitting in design than the plans of the present structure would indicate...."[268]

*Site cleared for the new courthouse, 1913. Glenbow Archives, NA-3173-1*

City council agreed with Mayor Mitchell, and the city clerk duly sent a letter to the Board of Commissioners of Calgary, instructing them to contact the Minister of Public Works, Charles R. Mitchell, and arrange a deputation to discuss the courthouse.[269] If the delegates went, they were unable to change the department's plans. In August, the Honourable Minister came to Calgary himself on a tour of inspection. Pronouncing himself "well pleased" with the progress on the edifice, he reassured the sceptics, telling them that "When the Calgary court house is finished it will be a good building and a credit to the city. Work on the building is going along satisfactorily, and the citizens will have no complaint when it is ready for occupancy."[270] The *Albertan*, sympathetic to the Liberals, pronounced it "classic in design, massive, bold and dignified, with little attempt at elaboration, thoroughly in keeping with the nature of the building."[271] Jeffers would have concurred, but a great many Calgarians likely agreed with a letter to the *News-Telegram*, describing it as "A Glasgow tenement, and there you have it."[272]

Unlike previous – and subsequent – courthouses, the Department of Public Works did not hire a builder. Instead, it acted as its own contractor, utilizing a series of subcontractors while supervising the project directly. The department hired its own labourers, while presumably the subcontractors provided the skilled workers.[273] It was a shift of practice for the Architectural Branch. It underwent a name change to the Architectural and Building Construction Branch in 1913 and hired

*A suitable companion: the new courthouse rises beside the Land Titles Office, c. 1913. Glenbow Archives, NA-5467-33*

Daniel E. McDonald as Building Superintendent. Among his duties McDonald monitored construction activity.

On March 5, 1912, the Department of Public Works called for tenders on the structural steel framework.[274] Building permit no. 1378 was issued to the government by the city on May 23, 1912 and construction began soon afterward.[275] Dominion Bridge of Winnipeg supplied the structural steel, but local firms were still well represented on the job site. The Quinlan-Carter Company provided sandstone for the exterior from their Glenbow quarry.[276] Other stone came from the Western Canada Stone Company, including in all likelihood the granite for the basement storey.[277] Later, Calgary firms like the Flesher Marble and Tile Company and Macdonald and Ward, plasterers, took over the interior finishing.[278] By the end of 1912, the building exterior was completed, except for the front entranceway, and the roof had been put on, allowing work to continue inside.[279]

## Not Without Incident

Progress on the courthouse was swift, but not without incident. Barely a week after the Minister Mitchell's visit, two men died working on the superstructure of the building. A derrick, recently moved and not securely fixed, gave way and dashed three steelworkers to the scaffolding around the ground floor.[280] At the inquest, the foreman revealed that it was common practice not to fix the derricks in place. No government inspector had ever criticized the practice; and the foreman had not seen the city building inspector at the site even once. After a visit to the site of the accident, the inquest blamed the deaths on defective equipment and inexperience on the part of the workers. The *News-Telegram* thought the verdict, although reasonable, should be construed as a stern warning to the contractors making money hand over fist in boomtown Calgary. Siding with the common labourer, it called for comprehensive preventive measures on work sites, and opined that:

> The jury were merciful in their verdict, for they might have brought in one which must have been followed by a criminal prosecution.... Ignorance is no excuse for sacrificing life and existence, and immunity from injury, are as precious to the commonest laborer [sic] as to the most opulent contractor.[281]

The accident was not the only controversial moment. A month after the two workers were killed, the *News-Telegram* blew the whistle on the Department of Public Works after discovering that the sandstone used on the building was coming from Ohio.[282] This was an outrageous state of affairs in the "Sandstone City," which prided itself on the award-winning product of the local quarries. Although the government had contracted for stone from Quinlan-Carter, the quarry could not supply enough material. The legislature building, as it turned out, had also been started with home-grown product but was finished with American stone. Patriotic feathers were ruffled, especially as the government was the sinner. After the report in the paper, scathing letters were written by "Alberta First," a thinly disguised *News-Telegram* editor, castigating the government and denouncing the Ohio stone: "Now for the workman's viewpoint. The stone being imported means that the foreign quarrymen got the work while home quarries are shutting down and local quarrymen are idle. Teamsters, laborers and local merchants also suffer."[283]

The opposition Conservatives seized upon the paper's revelations. The mighty R.B. Bennett took a few shots at the government over the courthouse, igniting a small war of words in the local news journals. The *Albertan* immediately attacked the politician, claiming the builders were indeed using local stone.[284] The *News* did some investigative journalism, and gleefully published its findings:

> ... if the morning paper wished to get accurate knowledge on the subject it could have obtained the same from Deputy Minister John Stocks, of the public works department, or it could have gone to the customs office and ascertained that Ohio sandstone was imported for use in the construction of the courthouse.[285]

Mitchell, the Minister of Public Works, himself admitted it was not Alberta sandstone, explaining that the Glenbow quarry had simply run out of good stone and prevaricated by claiming the Palliser Hotel, then under construction, was also using imported material.[286] "Alberta First" took the minister to task over his statement about the Palliser: "Mr. Mitchell should take care to state facts; we expect our public men to do so."[287] (It would turn out the newspaper was wrong in this instance – the CPR was using Indiana stone.) As far as the shortage went, the writer asked readers: "Did the government send one of their practical men to find out and report on the truth of that claim? No. Did they give a chance to any other quarry man to supply the stone? No. Did they even take the trouble to find out if the foreign stone was at all the equal to our native stone?" The issue refused to go away. It was raised again in the legislature by Harold Riley in the spring of 1913. Now the legislature building was involved as well, as rumours circulated it too had been built with American stone. Riley demanded the government come clean not only on the extent and cost of any foreign building material, but also explain its relationship with the Quinlan-Carter quarry, particularly whether the purchase of stone had been by tender or not.[288]

It may all seem like a tempest in a teapot now, but in the climate of the day it was a deadly serious issue, and one with considerable political fallout. To civic boosters, it was vitally important that local workers and local materials be used. The government was held to an even higher standard, and expectations were that local contractors would get the work when a courthouse was built, and that local materials be used whenever possible. Ironically, the courthouse was one of the last major buildings put up with local stone in Calgary; the age of sandstone as the premier building material was at an end. In the future brick or Manitoba Tyndall stone, imported of course, would become the favoured material for building exteriors.

## The Long-Awaited Hall of Justice

As the fall assizes of 1913 drew near, excitement mounted in Calgary about the new law courts. In late September the Herald announced they would open in a week or two and interviewed Sheriff Graham at length about the new building.[289] The paper praised the modern conveniences, the interior decor, and the airy, bright new accommodations for the courts. The Sheriff even claimed that a cafeteria might be added to the building, an innovation well ahead of its time. Despite the newspaper's optimistic words, scarcely three weeks later, Graham was looking around town for a room to rent for non-jury trials of the Supreme Court.[290] The new courthouse would not be ready for "at least another two months." Although the local press did not go into details, it is likely the delay was simply a matter of the intricacies of the finishing work. The interior work for the early provincial courthouses always took longer than expected, partly due to the competition from the commercial sector for the same materials and workmen.

Calgary's "Glasgow tenement". Glenbow Archives, NA-1667-1

On a Monday morning in January 1914, Justice William Walsh took his seat on the bench of the crowded civil courtroom to applause.[291] He spoke for the entire legal community of Calgary when he expressed his delight at opening the long-awaited hall of justice. A good number of the city's barristers visited the new courthouse and were especially pleased with the library and the lawyers' room, while the judges assigned to Calgary came to inspect their offices and supervise moving their effects. Sheriff Fred Graham was perhaps the most pleased: "... a broad smile played over his features when The Herald representative entered his sanctum."[292] The sheriff especially looked forward to the first criminal assize, for which he planned to don his official uniform, including sword and cocked hat. The new courthouse, however, was not without some problems. Like the Lethbridge and Westaskiwin buildings, it too was bedevilled by poor acoustics. Graham, though otherwise satisfied with his new domain, told a reporter for the News-Telegram that "Something will have to be done to remedy this, and I will see that it is attended to at once."[293]

After the new hall of justice was finished, the fate of the old courthouse had to be decided. Even as far back as 1904, there had been suggestions it could be used as a jail. The Calgary Herald had then commented, "The present courthouse, it is urged, would make an excellent jail, its outside appearance being eminently suggestive of such an institution."[294] It was a practical suggestion, since Calgary lacked any penitentiary facilities and the old courthouse would be close by the new. The idea was resurrected as the new building approached completion. A number of other notions were thrown about; one rumour had the building earmarked for

*An appropriate use: Territorial Courthouse as RNWMP barracks and lockup. Glenbow Archives, ND-8-380*

conversion into offices for the government telephone service.[295] Then it was suggested that it should be made a prison for women. Finally the Royal North West Mounted Police took it over; the police had sold their barracks to the Grand Trunk Pacific Railway and needed a headquarters of their local detachment. The Department of Public Works converted the interior into offices and cells during the spring of 1914 at a cost of $3,670.[296] A yard was added for the prisoners that was also to be used "for the execution of murderers," according to the local paper. This alarming prospect never occurred: the last hanging in Calgary took place in 1914 at the police barracks. The sandstone plaque bearing the legend "courthouse" was replaced by another reading "NWMP," signalling the end of an era.

The new courthouse in Calgary was initially spared the problems with overcrowding that plagued the Edmonton courthouse, at least at first. There was room enough for the Public Museum to be placed in the basement in 1914, the same year judges were threatening to move out of the courthouse in the capital. On the tenth anniversary of the building, some alterations were carried out to give the appeal court and the law library more room.[297] Although complaints were not as vocal as in Edmonton, by the end of the 1920s, the need for more space was pressing. The museum was moved out in 1927, and several years later, the government contemplated erecting a large addition. It was part of an expansion of court facilities carried out by United Farmers of Alberta government of Premier John E. Brownlee.

The Calgary addition was a straightforward proposition, made simpler by the unadorned character of the building and the abundant land behind the existing courthouse to the north. The department had abolished its architectural office in 1924 as a cost-saving measure and replaced it with the Building and Maintenance Branch. A drafting staff still existed, under the supervision of Frederick H. Macdonald, which was capable if uninspired and simply copied the older building. A wing 113 by 52 feet was to be added along 5th Street to create an L-shaped building. Like the original, it was two storeys with a steel frame, but was to have hollow tile and brick masonry walls faced with sandstone. The window treatments and roofline were identical to those of the 1914 building. The first drawings were finished in November 1930.[298] A detailed floor plan was not included in the sketches: very likely the department did not yet know exactly what the Attorney General's department required. By this point, many courthouses in the province also housed other government offices. The provincial authorities may well have been planning to insert other departments into the courthouse, turning it into the local provincial building. A set of drawings was as far as the department proceeded. By 1931, it was obvious that the economy was not going to revive anytime soon. The expansion plans were dropped and never revived.

---

LASSANDRO AND PICARIELLO

One the most famous courtroom dramas in Alberta's history began in the Calgary courthouse but ended in the Supreme Court of Canada. The trial of Emilio Picariello and Florence Lassandro featured a volatile mix of racial prejudice, the politics of prohibition, and a last spark of chivalry. When it was over, the gallows had claimed two lives and the career of the province's leading criminal counsel, J. McKinley Cameron, lay in tatters.[299]

Emilio Picariello, known throughout the Crowsnest Pass as "Emperor Pic," had come to Canada from Italy. Like many of his countrymen and sundry other immigrants from Poland, Russia, and Germany, he found work in the coal mines of southern Alberta. The miners, mostly young men with few means of entertainment, boozed, gambled, and brawled, lending the region a reputation for lawlessness. Picariello himself graduated quickly from the mines to become owner of the Alberta Hotel in Blairmore. His success had a seamy side, however, for he was rumoured to be heavily involved in bootlegging. Emilio maintained a stable of six powerful McLaughlin cars, and not for Sunday drives in the country.

Prohibition had been implemented in Alberta in 1916 after a provincial plebiscite and reaffirmed in 1920. Many immigrant communities, particularly the miners of the Crowsnest, did not share the enthusiasm of Anglo-Saxon Protestants for prohibition. The Crowsnest became a hotbed of bootlegging and then rum-running from British Columbia government liquor stores to

Alberta and the United States, where prohibition was also in effect. It was an ongoing battle of wits between the local detachment of Alberta Provincial Police and these entrepreneurs. The police would try to catch the rum-runners with roadblocks on the only highway through the Pass. On September 21, 1922, Emilio and his son Steve were returning from Fernie, with father in a decoy car and Steve behind loaded with booze. They spotted a roadblock at Blairmore, and while Emilio blocked the road, Steve made his escape. The police got word back to Coleman a few miles down the road, where Constable Lawson attempted to stop Steve. A car chase and running gun battle broke out. Lawson wounded Steve in the hand, but gave up the pursuit when he had a tire blow out.

Word filtered back to Blairmore and to Picariello that Steve had been shot by the constable in Coleman. Without waiting to hear more, Emilio set out for the town. Accompanying him was Florence Lassandro. Her relationship to the Picariellos was never made clear, not even in the trial. It was assumed she was Steve's girlfriend, but she also was rumoured to be Emilio's mistress. The pair had two handguns, both legitimately registered in Picariello's name. Once in Coleman, they went to the APP barracks, a small house where Lawson and his family lived. The constable, now off duty, was fixing an axe when Picariello and Lassandro drove up. Lawson went down to the car, and talked with Emilio for about ten minutes. Witnesses reported that it was peaceful until suddenly, Lawson and Emilio seemed to be struggling. Then four shots rang out. It was later the contention of the prosecution that two shots from Emilio's weapon were wild, hitting the speedometer and the windshield, but that Lassandro shot Lawson twice. Picariello sped off, while Lawson crumpled in front of his terrified children. He died soon afterward. Picariello hid out in the mountains for a couple of days, but was soon apprehended, only to discover that his son Steve was fine.

The case was an immediate sensation, filling the newspapers of the province with lurid headlines. The preliminary hearing took place at the Coleman Opera House on October 2, 1922, before Justice of the Peace J.W. Gresham.[300] C.F. Harris of Lethbridge appeared for the accused. Two days of testimony provided ample evidence to go to trial, and Lassandro and Picariello were committed to the next session of the Supreme Court. J. McKinley Cameron, recognized as one of the leading defence lawyers of the era, took on the case. The government retained the services of future justice A.A. McGillivray, friend and former classmate of Cameron, and his partner Sam Helman. Cameron succeeded in having the trial moved to Calgary, citing the sensational newspaper coverage and the public feeling in southern Alberta over the case. When the court opened on November 27, 1922, Justice William L. Walsh presiding, the Attorney General of Alberta, John Brownlee himself, laid the charge.[301] The government thus served notice that it planned to make an example of the accused, and Brownlee remained in court for the entire trial.

It appeared to be an open-and-shut case. The prosecution called over thirty witnesses, including half a dozen to the shooting. Cameron elected to have his clients tried together. Gossip among the legal community later called this as a critical error. With separate trials, he may have been able to get Picariello convicted of manslaughter instead of murder, as he and Lawson had been physically struggling when he was shot, and Lassandro had fired the fatal bullet. Cameron could have also tried to get Lassandro's conviction reduced to manslaughter, playing on the jurors' chivalry and arguing she had fired in fear and confusion. Years later, Cameron told a colleague he had indeed wanted separate trials, but Picariello insisted they stick together, apparently out of fear that Lassandro would take the fall for what he felt was his crime. A less charitable interpretation was that Emilio hoped the jury would not convict them of murder because they wouldn't want to see a woman hang.

If so, the stratagem backfired. On December 2, 1922, after four hours of deliberations, the jury found both guilty of murder with no recommendation of mercy. Justice Walsh agreed with the verdict, and solemnly sentenced the two to hang. Cameron had not conducted a very active defence, trying his best to raise a reasonable doubt as to how Lawson was shot and by whom and keeping his clients off the stand. He saved his effort for the appeal, finding thirty-three points in Walsh's conduct of the trial to use as grounds. It was to no avail: the Supreme Court of Alberta dismissed the appeal four to one, with only Justice Beck dissenting. He called for a new trial on the charge of manslaughter. This was enough for Cameron to try the Supreme Court of Canada. On April 11, 1923, the high court also dismissed the appeal. Petitions and letters to Prime Minister Mackenzie King and the federal cabinet could not alter the fates of the condemned. Lassandro became the first – and last – woman to be hanged in Alberta on May 2, 1923, followed soon afterward to the scaffold by Emilio Picariello.

## Epilogue

Sometime in the mid-1950s the provincial government began to consider a new edifice for Calgary's courts. Like other older courthouses, the 1914 building was crowded, and items such as ventilation, acoustic insulation, and security could not meet contemporary standards. Meeting in the courthouse at the end of May 1956, the city's legal community drew up a resolution to urge the Department of Public Works to build a new facility for the courts, and soon. The lawyers also wanted an active part in the courthouse design: "When plans have been drawn up the Calgary Bar Association would be pleased to have a committee go over them with the architect."[704]

The bar got its wish and planning started for a new facility. The decision to build a new hall of justice did not bode well for its predecessors. The block of

"A department store": Calgary's third courthouse. PAA, PA-9312

(top right) Calgary's stately legal district: the 1914 courthouse, land titles building, and Territorial courthouse. Calgary Public Library, Local History Collection

(bottom right) Demolition of Calgary Territorial courthouse. Glenbow Archives, NA-2864-1134

land held by the government, containing the two courthouses and the land titles building, was simply too convenient. The Department of Public Works worked out a scheme in which the new facility would be built on the site of the Territorial courthouse, the land titles office would be moved into the 1914 courthouse, and the land titles building demolished to make room for a replacement. Finally, the 1914 courthouse would be razed and its location used for a building to house other provincial government departments.

The aggressively modernist tower that was to be Calgary's new courthouse was a problematic building. To the eye of an architectural historian it is a fine example of the International Style, with strong vertical elements and beautifully finished in granite and marble, but to contemporaries it simply did not look like a courthouse. The opposition Liberal party uncharitably called it "a department store."[303] There were many delays in construction, including a steel strike in the United States and problems with water in the foundations. Excavations for the foundation began in 1959, but the building was not opened until October 1962. The twenty-storey Elveden Centre, an office tower, only took eighteen months. Within a few years the five-storey building was overcrowded – fortunately, it was designed to be expanded by four floors, which was done in 1972. The Calgary building would be used in the planning of later courthouses as an example of what to avoid. It would also be the last courthouse designed by the architectural staff of Public Works.

The destruction of the Territorial building helped save the 1914 courthouse. When the government decided in 1962 that it would be too expensive to convert for use as a land titles office, it too was slated for demolition.[304] The well-publicized fight to preserve the city's first hall of justice had made the public much more conscious of the value of historic buildings. Calgary Conservative MLA Ernest Watkins

took up the fight to save the second courthouse, reviving the idea of converting it into a provincial museum of some sort. Fortuitously, oil millionaire Eric Harvie had just decided to set up his own museum in Calgary called the Glenbow, and was interested in using the old courthouse. The building was admirably suited for the purpose, and began a tradition that saw a number of old courthouses converted for the same purpose. The Glenbow received an excellent deal from the government, which paid to convert the building and built special displays and also threw in an annual operating grant.[305] The foundation took up quarters at the end of 1964.[306] The museum was housed in the courthouse for twelve years until, in need of more room itself, it moved to a new facility.

The continued inadequacies of the 1962 courthouse proved the salvation of its predecessor. Although in poor repair, the 1914 courthouse was destined to once again become a hall of justice. A more sensitive government declared it a historic site in 1978 and decided to refurbish it as the home for the Court of Appeal, relieving pressure in the new courthouse.[307] The stately old building was the perfect setting for the more deliberate and thoughtful proceedings of the appellate court. It meant an award-winning seven-million-dollar facelift by Calgary architect Gerald Forseth, a careful refurbishment that saw much of the interior restored while at the same time equipping it for the modern needs of the judiciary. By 1986, sombre, robed judges once again considered the arguments of opposing counsel in the oak-panelled courtrooms. Fifteen years later, the justices were forced to abandon the building due to a toxic mould in the ventilation system. As a new (and controversial) courthouse rises across the street, the building's ultimate fate is now in doubt.

# MEDICINE HAT

Of all the early provincial courthouses, Medicine Hat's hall of justice was the most contentious. Twice on the eve of elections, the town was promised a new building to replace its 1899 Territorial law court. Twice the promised edifice never materialized. The Medicine Hat courthouse was an example of how these prosaic buildings, as government largesse, could be used for partisan ends. Medicine Hat finally received a new court building in 1920, a veritable palace of justice on the banks of the South Saskatchewan River. Shortly thereafter, the incumbent Liberals were thrown out of office, swept away by the reforming tide of the United Farmers of Alberta, which pledged, among other things, to do away with partisan politics and patronage.

## Medicine Hat in the New Era

With the new century and an immigration boom, Medicine Hat grew rapidly, taking its place as the fourth largest city in the province. The discovery of commercially exploitable natural gas in the vicinity of the town in 1904 helped attract industries, as well as inspiring Rudyard Kipling's famous line about Medicine Hat as the city with "all hell for a basement."

As it turned out, possession of a Territorial courthouse was not necessarily a boon for Medicine Hat. The populace of the town was not especially pleased with the building, and it was the smallest courthouse built in Alberta by the Dominion government. It remained the home of the district's assizes for over twenty years, and after 1910, was clearly inadequate. But unlike other centres such as Edmonton, Lethbridge, or Wetaskiwin, Medicine Hat at least had an actual courthouse. This put it lower on the list for a replacement when the province took over responsibility for public works, sharing this dubious distinction with Calgary, Fort Macleod, and Red Deer. Up to the end of the first decade of the new century, Medicine Hat remained small enough that the court could make do. The population explosion that began around 1905 changed that quickly – by 1911, Medicine Hat had over 5,500 people and was still growing, a four-fold increase in the space of a decade.

Consequently, in 1914 the government set up a new judicial district, eponymous to its headquarters, the city of Medicine Hat. While a feather in the cap of local boosters, it also meant that more legal business than ever was being transacted in the little frame courthouse. With a District Court came a resident judge who had to be accommodated. It also meant more sittings of the courts, and more records to be kept. Although the permanent personnel of the court did not change – the deputy sheriff in the Judicial District of Calgary became the sheriff of both the District and Supreme Court, and the same was true of the clerk – space was at a premium. One enormous strike against the old frame courthouse was that it was not fireproof, although it did have a brick vault. Another blaze could have easily seen the building destroyed, along with the legal records it contained. In 1911, this came perilously close to happening when a fire started in the courthouse basement. The blaze was extinguished before much damage was done, to the disappointment of the Medicine Hat News, which thought that the fire might hurry a replacement.

## The First Attempt

Although not a first priority, Medicine Hat was not forgotten in the first flush of the boom. Initially prospects for a replacement looked promising. In 1909, the Architectural Branch prepared the first plans for a new courthouse in the city.[308] A.M. Jeffers, the Provincial Architect, based it on same design used for Wetaskiwin and Lethbridge, which he intended as a standard blueprint for a medium-sized courthouse. Early in the year, the Department of Public Works started looking for a location. By March it had picked out a site overlooking the river, well west of the railway tracks, along what would become 1st Avenue. The government bought lots 7 and 8, block B, from the town postmaster, W.J. Mclean, for $4,500 and lots 9 and 10 from Robert J. Rice for $6,500.[309] The local MLA, William T. Finlay, probably had a hand in facilitating this sale, and acted as a liaison between the two men and the government.

Hopes for a new building were fuelled by the fact that Medicine Hat had representation in the provincial cabinet in the person of Finlay, the Minister of Agriculture and also a former mayor. As the province headed toward an election in 1909, the honourable member was pleased to announce to the voters of Medicine Hat a $40,000 hall of justice.[310] It was one of several important new projects slated for the area, including a traffic bridge and a demonstration farm, which Finlay proclaimed to the public at a constituency meeting on March 4, 1909, held in the Territorial courthouse. The News lauded Finlay's hard work in obtaining these boons for the city; the opposition Conservatives and their standard bearers, the Medicine Hat Times, had a rather different interpretation.[311] The government's largesse was labelled as rampant electioneering, an act of pure bribery.

The announcement created a great deal of excitement in Medicine Hat. Finlay, not surprisingly, was easily re-elected. In June the *News* carried a description of the expected structure. Like the courthouses under construction at Wetaskiwin and Lethbridge, it would be two storeys high and brick with sandstone trim. The only complaint the paper had was the lack of architectural decoration: "Externally the building presents a substantial appearance though somewhat plain, as no attempt at an elaborate exterior has been made, outside of the carving at [the] main entrance, the front porch with its pediment and Provincial Seal and the cornice work."[312]

The year ended with no tenders for the new courthouse. In March 1910 a deputation from Medicine Hat went to Edmonton to discuss railways. In an interview with Premier Rutherford, Mayor Milne asked about the courthouse. Rutherford assured him that the facility would be started that year, and likely finished in 1911. But in the fall, the government was singing a different tune. By this time there had been a severe shakeup in the ruling Liberal Party. The Alberta and Great Waterways affair had brought down Rutherford and several of his cabinet. William Cushing, the Minister of Public Works, left after falling out with Rutherford over the government's plan for the railroad's financing. It delayed the budget by months, and no new capital projects could be started. Finlay departed as well, but due to poor health rather than any taint of corruption. The Honourable A.L. Sifton, Chief Justice of the Supreme Court, took over the premier's office. One of his first cabinet appointees was Charles R. Mitchell, a judge from the district court, as the Attorney General.[313] Mitchell had been a lawyer in Medicine Hat before his appointment to the bench in 1907. Not surprisingly, he stood in the by-election for Medicine Hat, the Liberal prodigal son, and was easily elected.

The new member, however, had the dubious pleasure of explaining to the electors why there had been no action on the courthouse. Mitchell used a novel approach. He told them the truth – but with a twist. Alluding to the recent troubles faced by the Rutherford administration as the cause of the delay, the new Attorney General informed one crowd of voters that they should be glad the building had fallen by the wayside.[314] The delay was "a blessing in disguise," which would ensure a bigger and better edifice for Medicine Hat. Pointing to the Lethbridge courthouse, completed only months before, he informed his audience it was already too small. Now there was the opportunity for Medicine Hat to lobby for a much more impressive building for their district, rather than making do with something less grand. By waiting until the town had grown larger, and perhaps the headquarters of a judicial district, Medicine Hat would be guaranteed a substantial courthouse.

Unknown to Mitchell's audience, the provincial government had decided almost a year before, even before the A & GW crisis, that there would be no courthouse for Medicine Hat, at least in the immediate future. In a memo dated December 28, 1909, to W.H. Cushing, Deputy Minister John Stocks advised that the department had too much work on hand to realistically begin more projects.[315] To wit, he felt the proposed courthouses in Calgary and Medicine Hat and the land titles building in Edmonton would have to be put off. Stocks felt the delay might be protracted. Accordingly, the province decided to buy outright the old Territorial courthouse in Medicine Hat, paying the Dominion government $9,717 for the building in 1910.[316] The department had agreed to purchase it in 1906 but had delayed making any payment. Now, needing the courthouse for a few more years, the provincial government decided to settle matters.[719] While Mitchell pleaded for patience from the electors, the department abandoned the courthouse plans for the city. The site for Medicine Hat's fine new hall of justice sat vacant. The following year, the local lawn bowling club was given permission to set up lanes and greens.[318]

### CHARLES R. MITCHELL

Courthouses were destined to play a large role in the political career of Charles Richmond Mitchell. As Minister of Public Works from 1912 to 1917, Mitchell was responsible of the erection of new public buildings in the province.

Mitchell was born in Newcastle, New Brunswick on November 20, 1872. His father was the inspector of lighthouses for the province, while an uncle, Peter Mitchell, was a leading Liberal, Father of Confederation and the first federal Minister of Marine and Fisheries. After graduating in 1894 from the University of New Brunswick, where he studied the liberal arts and civil engineering, Mitchell decided on the law as a career and took a degree at Kings College in Windsor, Nova Scotia. Like many Maritimers, he answered the call of the west and came to Medicine Hat in 1898, only a year after graduating from Kings. Opening his own law office, Mitchell was soon caught up in municipal politics and elected a town alderman. He also worked as the town solicitor, and in 1901 was made the crown prosecutor for the district. It was no great surprise that Mitchell was tapped to become a District Court judge in 1907 and assigned to Calgary.

He returned only three years later when he followed another respected jurist and Liberal, Arthur Sifton, into provincial politics. Sifton saved the Liberals from the scandals of the Rutherford administration, and the appointment of a fellow judge as Attorney General and Minister of Education sent a clear message. It also guaranteed the constituency of Medicine Hat for the government. The popular incumbent, William Finlay, had been a pioneer's son and cabinet minister, and the riding was solidly Liberal. Well known in the town and already earmarked for cabinet, Mitchell easily succeeded him in a by-election on June 29, 1910. The new Attorney General became Sifton's right-hand man.

Mitchell took over the portfolio of Public Works in 1913 and was later made Provincial Treasurer. By the time he left politics in 1925 he also had been Minister of Municipal Affairs and Minister of Health. His political career over, Mitchell returned to the bench in 1926, this time to the appellate division of the Supreme Court. After ten years, he became Chief Justice of the Trial Division. Ironically, he did not sit on any trials, acting as administrator of the division but spending much his time on the review board for the 1936 Farmer's Creditors' Arrangement Act. His health failed several years later, and Mitchell died on August 16, 1942.

## The Second Attempt

If the Liberals took some chaffing in 1909 about election promises, it was going to get much worse, as four years later the Medicine Hat courthouse turned into a major political embarrassment. On the eve of the provincial election in 1913, Medicine Hat was surprised – and pleased – when Mitchell, now Minister of Public Works, announced that a combined courthouse and land titles building would soon grace the city. The saga began with the budget debates in March. The Department of Public Works was up for an appropriation of close to three million dollars. Among the items to be approved was a new class of public building combining a large courthouse with a land titles office, which would be placed at the seat of new judicial and land registration districts.[319] The opposition smelled a rat – and an upcoming election. The large allocations for public works and the awarding of new district headquarters sounded like the right prerequisites. The Conservatives demanded that Mitchell declare where the department intended to build its roads, bridges, and courthouses before the budget was brought down.

The worst suspicions of the Conservatives were confirmed when Mitchell, in Medicine Hat on March 28 for the Liberal nomination meeting, announced that the government had decided to put a new courthouse in the city, pursuant to making it a judicial and a land registry district. The courthouse would cost at least $112,000 and there would also be a proper telephone exchange built. Mitchell had brought plans for the courthouse, including a lovely sketch by the Provincial Architect that showed up in the News shortly afterward. After proclaiming these gifts, Mitchell told his audience it was the fruition of his policy of patience. Now that Medicine Hat was a booming city of "thirteen thousand," a much better courthouse would be built than had been planned four years earlier.[320] Of course, the approval of the courthouse had nothing to do with the election but was a matter of government policy.

Mitchell's opponent, Nelson Spencer, the mayor of Medicine Hat, was not impressed with the rhetoric. Notwithstanding Mitchell's explanations at the meeting in 1910, Spencer reminded the voters that the last time a courthouse had been promised right before an election, it had never materialized. Spencer left no doubt in anyone's mind that he regarded Mitchell's new promises as nothing but election posturing. And he had a point. Shortly before the polls were due to open on April 17, the department registered a building permit with the city for the courthouse and the telephone exchange and crews from Public Works dumped gravel on the site for the new courthouse.[321] It might have been just too blatant for the electors. Despite the largesse promised Medicine Hat, despite the fact Mitchell was the incumbent and sat in cabinet, Spencer beat him when the voters went to the polls.

Mitchell himself was quite surprised. According to the Medicine Hat Call, "on the eve of polling Mr. Mitchell declared that he had not found the fight a severe one, but the figures the next day contradicted his words."[322] It had been an incredibly close contest, so close that Mitchell asked for a recount, due to the number of disputed ballots, some sixty-four in total. Accompanied by their lawyers, the candidates and chief returning officer William P. Dundon went through them on April 28, ironically enough at the old Territorial courthouse. Mitchell came away with a majority of eight votes. The News, as the local Liberal organ, crowed victory. Spencer and the Conservatives served notice that they would appeal the count and lay a complaint against Dundas, backed with affidavits concerning irregularities in the voting.[323] There had been delays in delivering the boxes of ballots from the polling station to the returning officer, and they had been stored in the Hull block at Dundas' office, but not under lock and key. Meanwhile Mitchell's supporters talked of vote-buying with liquor on the part of the Conservatives.[324] On May 8, Judge A.A. Carpenter dealt with Spencer's complaint in District Court by tossing it out; but at Spencer's insistence also ordered a judicial recount. Nine days later, the judge carried out his count, and on May 18, Mitchell conceded defeat as Spencer came away with a tiny majority.

A month later, nothing had materialized for either the courthouse or the telephone building, something the Times was quick to point out. "We were told before the election that these necessary works would be proceeded with at once. A team was put to work on the courthouse site and the News published pictures of stately buildings, which we were told would speedily be placed for the convenience of the people. But after the election was finally settled there was silence deep as death… Mr Mitchell is understood to have thrown out more than a hint that Medicine Hat would be punished for its lack of appreciation of him."[325] It was a replay of 1909 and 1910, but this time Mitchell was not coming to Medicine Hat to plea for patience.

The Minister of Public Works was forced to run in a by-election in the riding of Bow River in June. The incumbent Liberal, rancher George Lane, resigned his seat so the party's second-in-command could return to the house. The Conservatives, oddly enough, did not run a candidate against Mitchell, missing a second chance to embarrass him. However, humiliation was waiting for the Minister of Public Works several months later. On October 16, as the legislature debated the budget, Spencer rose and unleashed a powerful attack on the minister:

> Speaking of public buildings, in my home city we had a unique experience. During the election campaign we had the city posted with plans of the court house to be erected there, alongside of which were pictures of the minister of public works which bore the strange device 'the man of the hour' and said the minister of public works in his campaign speeches 'here is the courthouse that I am bringing to Medicine Hat. It is no election dodge. I am not handing it out to get your votes, for the simple reason that it has already been decided upon and the money voted for it. As soon as the government can let the contract work will be commenced and the building will be completed as soon as possible.'[326]

Not content with belabouring Mitchell with the minister's own speeches, Spencer returned to the attack several days later. As the debates turned to the appropriations for Public Works on October 18, Spencer pressed Mitchell again on his promises for the courthouse. Much to the astonishment of even his own party, the furious Mitchell retorted: "I am no longer the Member for Medicine Hat. No responsibility rests upon me now. It's up to you."[327] Mitchell further declared he saw no reason to push for the courthouse, as the voters had rejected him and his government. His remarks turned the house on its ear. The opposition accused Mitchell of reneging on his word and lying to the electors of Medicine Hat. Under the headline "Mr. Mitchell's Startling Frankness," the Edmonton Journal asked with fine rhetorical flourish, "Could flagrantly corrupt use of public office go further?"[328]

Mitchell backpedalled frantically. He pointed out that he had never said the courthouse would not be built – which was in fact true – but simply that the original appropriation had lapsed, and the executive council would have to examine the matter again.[329] The following day, he tried to qualify his remarks to Spencer about his responsibility to the electors. Mitchell claimed his comments were misinterpreted: he had only meant that he no longer would press for the courthouse as he would have as the member for Medicine Hat. As Minister for Public Works, his decision would be based on the dictates of finances, necessity, and the opinions of the executive council. The liberal press, including the *Medicine Hat News*, stood behind their man, but their faith was shaken. As Spencer assailed the honourable minister again the following day, Premier Sifton suddenly interrupted him. Coming to the defence of his beleaguered lieutenant, Sifton blandly announced the courthouse would be built as promised. He neglected to say that it would be six years late!

Ironically, the decision to postpone the Medicine Hat courthouse and land titles building had a sound economic basis. Over the course of the year, conditions in Alberta had noticeably worsened, and it was clear the boom was over. The government was already pinched financially even without the spectre of an economic recession; the Liberals had spent heavily on the assumption of bright times ahead. In the spring, shortly before the election, Mitchell had slammed the opposition for their fear mongering over the public debt. A few months later, the government was probably regretting his confident words.

When all was said and done, the question remained: Did Mitchell and Liberals intend to build the courthouse, or was it a hollow election promise? There is certainly evidence that the Department of Public Works had decided months before the election to proceed with the building. In December 1912, the department insisted the City of Medicine Hat cease flooding the courthouse site as a skating rink, as they had done the previous winter.[330] They explained that they intended to build in the spring and did not want any problems with ice or saturated ground. When Mitchell made his promise in April 1913, he had the plans in hand for the building. The drawings for the courthouse were relatively advanced, including details of the architectural decoration, although full floor plans had not been determined.[331] It is unlikely that Richard Blakey and his staff drafted them at the last moment. The government had planned over three million dollars of public works in their estimates for the year and given notice of its intentions to build more land titles offices and courthouses. It is interesting to note that neighbouring Saskatchewan actually built combined land titles office and courthouses at Swift Current and Humbolt in 1914 and 1915, so the idea was in the air.[332] Just as in 1909, the department may have decided to drop its plans due to fiscal concerns.

Once all the dust settled, Medicine Hat still did not have courthouse, and any hopes of obtaining one were soon dashed as a serious recession took hold in the province. Premier Sifton had said Medicine Hat would get a courthouse, but he hadn't said when. The provincial government curtailed its spending, and the planned land titles and courthouse project in Medicine Hat was one of the casualties. The outbreak of war in August 1914 made it clear it would not be revived for some time. With the conflict in Europe, the citizens of Medicine Hat had other things to occupy their time, and the courthouse was forgotten during four long years of conflict. The field along 1st Avenue gathered weeds, and the department eventually gave permission for the local horticulture society to plant it with potatoes.[333]

## A Third Attempt

The need for a better building at Medicine Hat, however, was not forgotten in the Attorney General's office or at Public Works. After the armistice, the government of new premier Charles Stewart wasted little time in reviving the project, and drawings were taken off the shelf, the dust blown off, and ground finally broken for a new courthouse. The 1913 building was found wanting: in his 1919 Annual Report, Blakey stated that "plans for this building as prepared some years ago were discussed and it was decided that the modifications required were such that a new design seemed advisable."[334]

Starting from scratch, Blakey planned a two-storey building on an unusual L-shaped plan, with a load-bearing steel frame, concrete foundation, and masonry walls of brick and hollow tile, 63 feet deep with a 114-foot facade. He followed the basic scheme for courthouses, placing the main courtroom on the upper floor in the short leg of the L, along with the judge's room and jury room, which entered directly into the courtroom. A substantial space for the chambers of the District Court sat at the other end of the floor with the judge's office. The library was situated overlooking the front entrance. On the main floor were the offices of the clerk and the sheriff of the courts, while in the basement there was a smaller secondary courtroom, the prisoners' holding area, and more office space. Blakey entirely eliminated such amenities as the suite for travelling judges and the caretaker's suite found in Jeffers' smaller courthouses. It was not as clever a floor plan as the earlier buildings. While Blakey did include a private service stairway to allow unobtrusive movement between the different floors, especially by the judge and prisoners, the witness rooms were simply down the main hall from the courtroom, a less secure arrangement.

Although no longer incorporating a land title office, the courthouse was still expected to serve double duty. In this respect, it represented a shift from previous provincial courthouses, and pointed toward future developments. The Medicine Hat building incorporated a brand recorder's office, taking up a considerable part of the main floor, as well as a public health clinic in the basement. As drawn in April 1919, there were also several small offices with no specified use, and other provincial bureaucrats would in time occupy these. By the time the courthouse

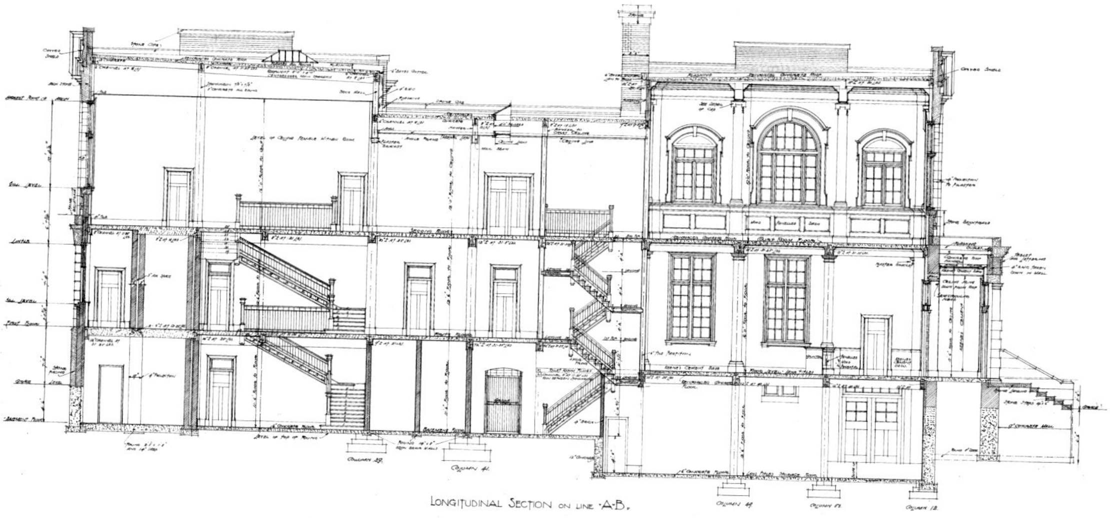


Section, proposed 1913 Courthouse. AI

Elevation, 1913 Courthouse. AI

was finished and ready to open in 1920, an official in charge of road building in the district had been added to the building's complement.

The incorporation of other government offices into courthouses at the design stage was an interesting shift in policy. Although almost all the provincial halls of justice ended up hosting other departments as time went on, they had not been intended for this duty and it was mostly a matter of a cash-strapped government trying to save money. A couple of edifices, like Wetaskiwin, took on a role in their districts much like the American county courthouse, with most of the local provincial offices to be found there. It was not Blakey's intention to make Medicine Hat's courthouse a provincial building; it was clearly a hall of justice. It was a cost-effective way, however, of providing room for expansion beyond the immediate needs of the court. If the administration of justice required more space, other

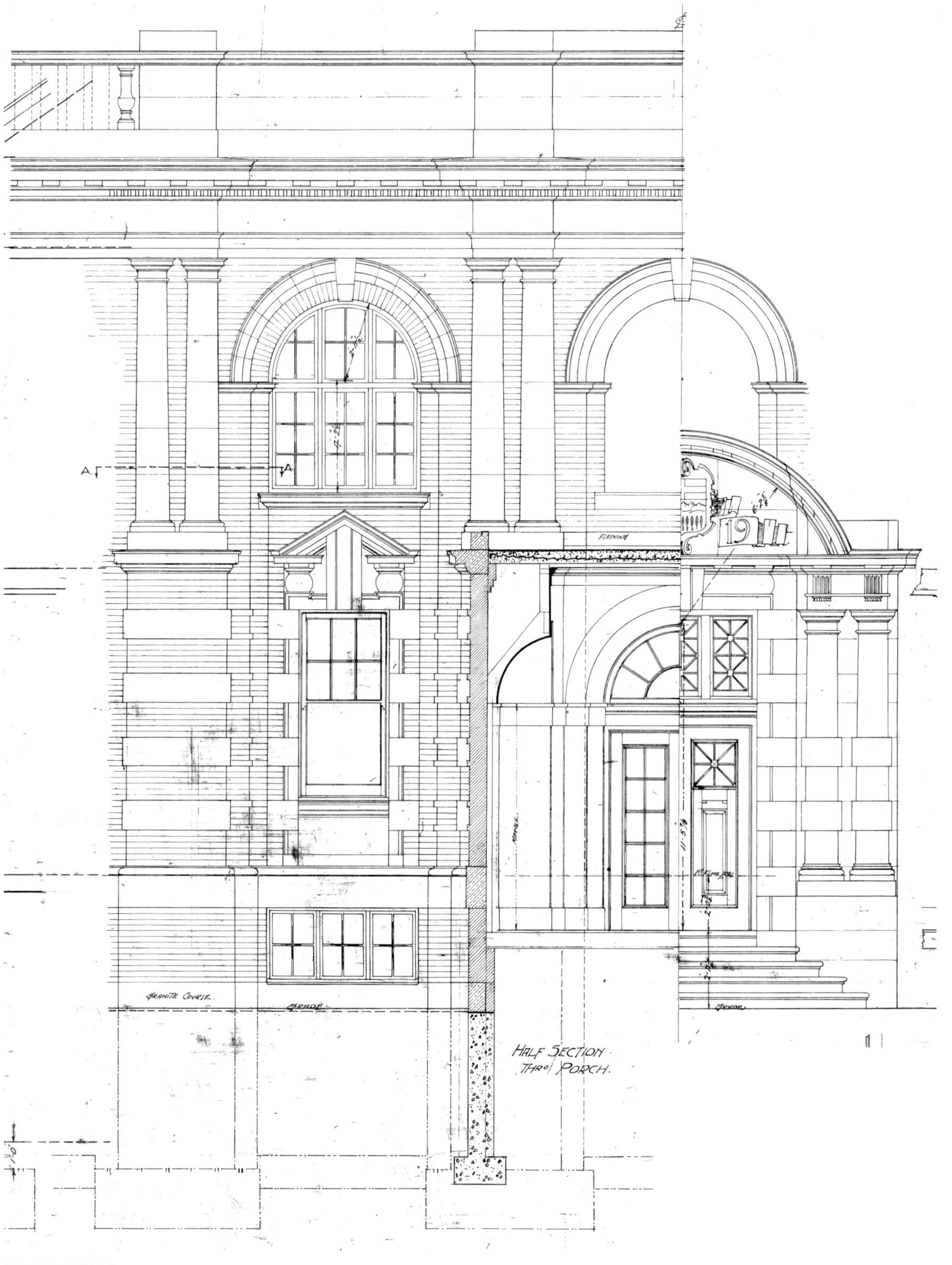


*Front Entrance Details, Medicine Hat Courthouse, 1919. AI.*

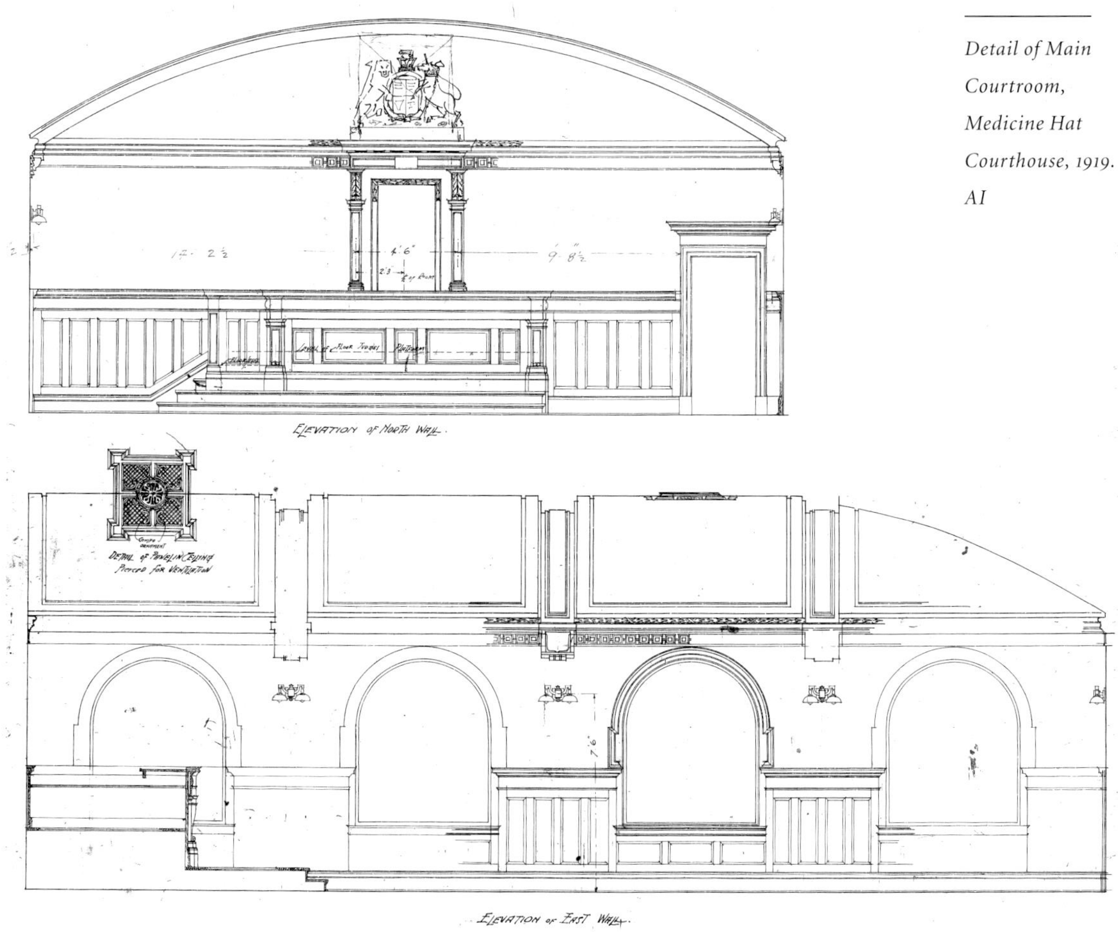


*Detail of Main Courtroom, Medicine Hat Courthouse, 1919. AI*

departments could be removed, but until then, the province could save rents or the expense of another building.

The real glory of the Medicine Hat courthouse was its magnificent facade. It stood in stark contrast to the Calgary courthouse, which had been austere to the extreme. No longer working under financial constraints, Blakey designed an elaborate building quite unlike any of the province's previous courthouses. The Medicine Hat courthouse was very much Beaux-Arts in its design, done in a style described as "Italian Renaissance" by local papers, who likely quoted Blakey himself. The facade was divided into nine bays by heavy brick piers. Within each bay were a main floor and second floor windows. The lower window had a sill and quoins of white limestone and was surmounted by an elaborate pediment, while the upper window was arched with a limestone voussoir. The piers defining the middle five bays were more elaborate, divided between brick and limestone up to the second storey, where each pier was topped by paired Doric columns, also in limestone, a motif used by Blakey in his redesign of the entrance of the Calgary courthouse. There was a simple cornice and stone balustrade along the roof edge above the middle five bays. A stone course separated the basement and first floor. The main entrance had a projecting porch, heavily detailed in stone with a segmental pediment containing a carved relief of the coat of arms to the province. The

*The palace of justice: postcard view of Medicine Hat's fine courthouse. PAA, 10.593*

*(right) An imposing façade. MHA, 0672-0029*

exterior decoration was carried around onto the east and west elevations. The rear was much simpler, with sandstone sills and lintels on the windows, with the exception of a wonderful nine-foot-high leaded glass window at the top of the main staircase, giving the visitor an excellent view of the river below the courthouse.

The symmetrical facade, with its receding and advancing planes, marked the courthouse as a Beaux-Arts building, but it was much more eclectic than the earlier buildings of Jeffers. The hip roof with its red tile was usually seen on Spanish Colonial Revival or Mission Revival buildings. These styles had been popularized in the western United States, especially California, and had certain vogue in North America by 1919. Blakey showed a certain affinity for these styles: his Blairmore police barracks, finished in 1924, would be a Mission Revival building. He was not alone in combining a formal Beaux-Arts building with Spanish elements: the Clarke County courthouse of 1914 in Las Vegas, Nevada, was quite similar.[335] The eclecticism of Blakey was not unusual among post-war architects.[336] The extensive use of white limestone with red brick was another demonstration of this. Reminiscent of the polychromy popular in Victorian and Richardson Romanesque architecture, it gave the Medicine Hat building a certain exuberance that offset the long, weighty facade. This decorative scheme also served as a nice reference to some of the town's more prominent civic and commercial architecture, which featured limestone or sandstone trim with red brick.

The interior finishing of the 1919 courthouse lived up to the building's striking facade. The entrance led through a vestibule into a large entry hall and the main staircase, lit by the high leaded window. Marble was used for the main staircase, on the floor of the vestibule and as wainscoting in the entry hall and the hallway on the upper floor. Ceramic mosaic floors were used in the halls, with linoleum in the offices. Railings and light fixtures were done in brass. Red birch trim was used throughout the main floors of the building, with doors in mahogany. The courtroom itself was another pièce de résistance. It was a lovely room, bright and airy with a high arched ceiling and many windows. Plaster pilasters supported the ceiling ribs and an elaborate crown moulding ran along the top of the walls. Above the judge's bench perched another provincial coat of arms. Red birch wainscoting complemented the trim around the windows and doors. The courtroom was supplied with permanent wood accoutrements: a judge's bench, prisoner's box, jury box, and seating for barristers and the public. In another departure, the fittings for the courtroom were manufactured by Public Works itself in its Edmonton shop.[337]

The Medicine Hat courthouse was not only one of the most impressive and attractive built by the province, but was very influential on the design of courthouses between the wars. It was the model for buildings in Red Deer and Vegreville ten years later. Long after Blakey left the service of Public Works, it remained his legacy to the province. If Edmonton had Alberta's temple of justice, thanks to Blakey Medicine Hat had the palace.

## Construction

Unlike the earlier provincial courthouses, the Medicine Hat building was completed quickly. Edmonton had taken almost four years, Wetaskiwin and Lethbridge over two. Medicine Hat took just over one year to finish from groundbreaking. And unlike the edifices in the capital and in Calgary, there were no tragedies during construction. Tenders were called for on May 8, 1919 by the Department of Public Works on three separate contracts for the general construction, the electricals and the plumbing and heating.[338] Bennett and White of Calgary, a large building firm, was awarded the general contract as lowest bidders, while the Hillas Electric Company of Edmonton was to provide the wiring, and Mr. J.H. Rieve of Medicine Hat got the plumbing and heating work.[339] The building was to cost over $130,000 and house all the court services for the town, a very welcome development

The awarding of the Medicine Hat contract marks a significant change in the policy of Public Works and in the building industry. Up to that point, local contractors had built nearly all of the Territorial and provincial courthouses. Every courthouse constructed after 1920 was done by a builder from outside the town or city where it was located. The post-war recession had driven many builders out of business, and of those that survived, the larger firms were likely able to submit bids on major projects impossible for smaller companies. The government, accepting lowest tenders, did not try to favour local builders. Courthouse construction would become more and more dominated by firms from Calgary and Edmonton. In way of compensation, much of the material used for the building in Medicine Hat was produced locally: both the roof tiles and the brick came from Alberta Clay Products, a company started by Harry Yuill, who had converted the Immigration Shed into the town's first courthouse.[340]

The limestone, however, came from Bedford, Indiana, cut by the Furst-Kerber Cut Stone Company of Chicago.[341] If the choice of contractors did not cause a stir, the choice of stone supplier did. Bennett and White was at least an Alberta company. Not surprisingly, the protests over the use of American stone came not from Medicine Hat, which did not have a large stone quarry industry, but from Calgary, which did. Calgarians had already shown themselves very sensitive to the matter of foreign stone during the construction of their own courthouse. The vice-president of the Great War Veterans Association asked the mayor of Calgary to write the government on behalf of the local stonecutters and protest the decision.[342] The request captures perfectly the insecurities of the time: veterans and local workers worried about jobs in a weak economy as well as the old booster insistence on using local products.

Charles Mitchell, familiar enough with Medicine Hat and the whole stone issue, replied on the part of the government. He informed the mayor that the decision to use Indiana stone was partly due to the "very ornamental style" of the building, which required more durable material, and partly due to the fact the contractors could not get any reliable quotations on price and supply for local sandstone.[343] The stonecutters of Calgary clearly did not understand that the age of sandstone was finished in the city, and that future controversy would be over the choice of Manitoba or American limestone.[344].

Both the contractors and Blakey were to arrive in Medicine Hat toward the end of June, with the work to get underway at once. Excavation actually began in early August, but proceeded smoothly. Blakey noted in his 1919 Annual Report that the contractors had managed to get the roof on and close off the building by the end of the year, allowing them to continue working during the winter.[345] The Provincial Architect had Bennett and White on a tight schedule, and had originally looked for the building to be finished by March the following year. They would not make this deadline, but as the fall assizes approached, the courthouse was nearing completion. As workers strove to finish the interior in early September, the staff of the courts moved the library from the old Territorial building to the new one.[346] The structure ultimately cost the government $147, 693, finished and furnished.[347]

On September 21, 1920 the courthouse was officially opened as Justice William L. Walsh entered the courtroom for the fall session of the Supreme Court.[348] He congratulated the people and bar of Medicine Hat and district on their new courthouse, pronouncing that "he could not begin to express the satisfaction that he felt in being allowed to preside at the opening."[349] W.A. Begg gave an address on behalf of the bar, reminiscing over the change in the city in his many years there, and the long wait of the good citizens for their courthouse. Once the speeches were over, the court proceeded to business. As usual for Medicine Hat, it was a small court list, consisting of five cases, four of theft, one for fraud. Somehow it was fitting, as the city's courthouse for the twentieth century opened, that one case dealt with horse rustling, while another with auto theft.

---

JUSTICE WILLIAM LEGH WALSH

William Legh "Daddy" Walsh was a rambling judge, one of the few Supreme Court justices who actually enjoyed going on circuit. A popular lawyer, he was also a popular judge. To Walsh often fell the task of opening new courthouses or inaugurating judicial districts. He held his first session of court in Medicine Hat in 1912, not long after ascending to the bench, and was quite familiar with all the shortcomings of the old Territorial hall of justice.

Walsh had a most adventurous career. From Simcoe, Ontario, he had left a prosperous law practice with prominent Conservative politician D'Alton McCarthy in Orangeville to go to the Yukon. There he was counsel in one of largest mining claims of the gold rush, pocketing a record fee in the settlement. After the rush petered out around 1904, Walsh came to Calgary, where he practised with the firm of Walsh, McCarthy and Carson and dabbled in politics with the Conservative Party until his appointment to the bench. He was a popular member of the judiciary, which was impressive, as he tended toward severity. A "hanging judge," Walsh reputedly sentenced eighteen offenders to death during his tenure, including the notorious rum runner "Emperor Pic" and his accomplice Florence Lassandro for the murder of an APP officer in Crowsnest Pass. The distinguished Walsh had an enormous white moustache and a whisky-lover's nose, and fooled many a young defence counsel with his quiet demeanour in the courtroom. More than one assumed he was napping or in his cups, only to be corrected quickly and firmly when they made a mistake.

Walsh left the bench in 1931 to become the third Lieutenant Governor of Alberta. He died in Victoria in 1938.

In one sense Medicine Hat was indeed fortunate that it received its courthouse so late. It was spared the difficulty with overcrowding that afflicted so many of the provincial courthouses within a short time of their opening. Unlike Lethbridge, which was almost immediately deemed too small, or Edmonton, which didn't have enough space for its compliment of judges within two years of opening, there were no complaints from Medicine Hat about overcrowding for many years. The extra space turned the courthouse into a provincial building, more so than even the designers intended. Right from its opening, it accommodated the Alberta Provincial Police detachment, a child welfare clinic, the brand recorder, and the local man of the Department of Highways. By 1949 there was a school inspector, a game inspector, and an office of the department of municipal affairs.[350] As happened to many other courthouses in the province, the government essentially used the courthouse as a de facto provincial building for many years.

## Epilogue

The magnificent Beaux-Arts courthouse overlooking the river came very close to the same end as the Territorial courthouse. By the early 1960s, the building was in some disrepair. Serving double duty as courthouse and provincial building, it was severely overcrowded. In 1964, the Department of Public Works carried out a comprehensive review of the entire building.[351] Numerous problems were evident. The plumbing was badly corroded and inadequate; the ventilation system outmoded and indeed no longer used; the boilers and heating system were inadequate, and the basement floor was severely damaged. The inspectors also thought the building might be settling. Their conclusion: "This building has a very pleasing appearance and is set on a beautiful site. It is however in poor condition and has probably out served its usefulness ... the cost of renovating the building would be quite high.... It was felt therefore, that the replacement of this structure with a modern structure would be in order...."[352]

It was not a foregone conclusion that the building would be destroyed. The Minister of Public Works, F.C Colborne, wanted to consider the possibility of an addition.[353] The City of Medicine Hat, in the middle of drafting an urban renewal scheme, was anxious to incorporate a new courthouse into their own plans for a city hall, and offered to take the old one off the government's hands in return for finding a location for a modern building. The city and the province were not able to find a parcel of land that suited them both. In November 1965, E.E. Wilson, the property administrator for Public Works, met with J.E. Hart, the Deputy Attorney General, and afterward advised Colborne he felt a new facility should be built. Colborne gave his assent. The property adjoining the courthouse was bought to accommodate a larger building, and the Medicine Hat architectural firm of Russell and Needham was hired by an Order-in-Council passed on September 27, 1966.[354] It appeared Blakey's masterpiece was doomed.

The building got a last-minute reprieve, thanks to the bar and citizens of Medicine Hat. Civic authorities tried again in October 1966 to interest the government in building the new courthouse as part of the proposed civic centre.[355] Public Works decided to send their building committee to Medicine Hat, to review the plan and proposed location, and take another look at the old courthouse. The committee arrived in the city on November 16. A week later the deputy Attorney General was informed the old courthouse would be renovated, not replaced.[356] It was quite unexpected, but the building committee had been convinced by their visit to save the picturesque pile. As Wilson put it to Hart, "This trend of thought has been based largely on local sentiment with respect to the building and the building's monumental character." Pressure had swiftly mounted to retain the old courthouse. The City of Medicine Hat wished to see it retained in some form, and

*The grand re-opening: bench and Bar celebrate the salvation of Blakey's Courthouse, 1969. MHA, 0131-0001*

the local bar, press, and public opinion quickly rallied in favour of preserving the majestic old lady. Financial expediency probably also helped save it. The planned renovations, budgeted around $300,000, were less than half what a new building was projected to cost.

The courthouse officially reopened on June 25, 1969 with appropriate pomp and ceremony. The $250,000 renovation made it "just like a new building to work in."[357] Along with the mechanical and electrical upgrades, "the cold and austere décor has been tempered through modernising the 1919 architecture."[358] The courtroom was given more acoustic protection, but the fine brass light fixtures throughout the building were removed and replaced, much of the old oak furniture replaced with modern desks, and carpet laid – unfortunately, in the style of the time!

However, much of the interior was left untouched except for restoration efforts, and the facade was cleaned and repaired but not altered. Among the more popular changes was the addition of a barristers' lounge in the basement.

Thirteen years later, the courthouse was once again an issue. In 1978, the province had made the courthouse a historic site, but a major expansion of court services in Medicine Hat necessitated a new building. An innovative solution incorporating the 1919 courthouse gave the city the best of all worlds. Ironically, Russell and Needham, commissioned previously to come up with a replacement for Blakey's courthouse, were now hired to restore it. The old courthouse would be home to the Court of Queen's Bench. A seamless two-storey addition increased the floor space, although it modified the building's original L shape into a more conventional rectangle. The architects determined local manufacturers I-XL could exactly match the original brick, and they tracked down the limestone quarries in Indiana where the white stone blocks had been cut. They also designed an entirely new provincial court building and joined it to the old building with an innovative basement level. Once it was landscaped, the illusion of two separate buildings was maintained, as was the setting around the Court of Queen's Bench. Under the grass, however, was a substantial structure with that greatest of modern conveniences: a parkade.

Today, Medicine Hat's palace of justice continues to house the Court of Queen's Bench and is the oldest continuously occupied courthouse in the province. The provincial court building sits unobtrusively nearby, the machinery of the legal system working efficiently behind its bland brick exterior, leaving the original courthouse to embody the majesty and drama of the law.

# CONCLUSION

The early provincial courthouses were built in an entirely different atmosphere than the Territorial buildings before them. Alberta was at the beginning of an incredible boom in 1905, and the new provincial government was as committed as any civic booster to providing suitable public buildings. No longer would small utilitarian facilities do; instead, impressive new halls of justice would grace the cities and towns of Alberta. The provincial liberals left a legacy of five major courthouses and three smaller buildings before leaving office in 1921. However, there were still many controversies concerning courthouses as the Liberals found their grand schemes difficult to sustain in the face of a faltering economy, and the party also succumbed to the temptation of using the buildings as political fodder.

The first administration of A.L. Rutherford quickly made courthouses a major part of its public building program. It did not have a systematic program for construction, but to some extent the need of all the province's major centres for a new hall of justice made this unnecessary. Simply building a facility in every city of the province was enough to keep the Department of Public Works busy for several years. Rutherford's government was quite free with promises of courthouses, however, both in the spirit of optimism and also to keep voters happy. A number of these edifices never materialized. His successor, A.L. Sifton, followed a more conservative course and a more explicit set of criteria for building courthouses, tying them to creation of new judicial districts. Ironically, his government would only build one courthouse, that in Calgary, despite establishing several new districts. The coming of recession and war limited the ambitions of Sifton's government and the administration ended up converting several existing buildings as a stopgap measure. The last liberal premier, Charles Stewart, continued the general policy of supplying courthouses to the electors. Also constrained by a poor post-war economy, his administration was only able to build one major courthouse before leaving office. Although some courthouses turned out to be very expensive buildings, for the most part the three liberal administrations were quite economical, to the extent of delaying desperately needed facilities for years.

The development of the office of Provincial Architect assured that the new courthouses would be much grander than their federally designed predecessors. One man, A. M. Jeffers, the second holder of the office, brought the architecture of provincial courthouses into contemporary fashion with his Beaux-Arts classicism. Although not particularly innovative, Jeffers' buildings had a stylistic coherence that focused on an austere and pleasing simplicity. His successor, R.P. Blakey, continued the Beaux-Arts tradition with his only major courthouse, Medicine Hat, but also introduced even newer influences, such as Mission and Mediterranean, to courthouse construction. Although Jeffers favoured a relatively plain style, his unadorned buildings could still satisfy the expectations of the public for courthouses that possessed presence. His buildings were less successful in filling their functional role, despite their clever internal design. Overcrowding was a constant problem at the Edmonton courthouse, while poor acoustics bedevilled the buildings in Lethbridge and Wetaskiwin. Blakey's courthouse fared better; it would later be the model for more buildings. Ironically, Jeffers' austere courthouses were expensive and time consuming to build, while Blakey's edifices were models in efficiency and cost-effectiveness.

Courthouses were still an issue for civic bodies, but less so than in the Territorial days. In major centres, new buildings were expected as a matter of course, although delays caused complaints and in the case of Medicine Hat, a major political storm. There was also a general expectation that the new courthouses promised by the provincial government would also be commodious and attractive buildings. Residents kept a sharp eye on the structures as they were built to make sure this was the case. The courthouses of Jeffers in some respects did not live up to expectations: there were complaints that they were too plain in appearance. This was especially the case in Calgary. The buildings still remained subjects of contentious debate. One of the major controversies with the early provincial buildings was their siting and placement. As Lethbridge demonstrated, local boosters had generally strong opinions on this subject. Suspicions were also easily aroused, as in Wetaskiwin, that friends of the government might be the ones benefiting from property purchases. And other new issues arose, such as the debate over the use of imported stone and other materials over locally available products.

While courthouses were not quite the hot button topic they had been, outside the major centres, there was still much the same spirit seen in the Territorial days. Almost every locale with any claim to importance, present or future, asked for a courthouse and some quite persistently. Centres like Hanna, Vermillion, Vegreville, Stettler, and Red Deer still lobbied hard to be made judicial districts and expected a proper courthouse to quickly follow. Either as part of a larger plan or as a sop to these ambitions, the Rutherford government bought a large number of sites in Alberta towns for courthouses. Only a few of them were ever utilized; in the cases of Vegreville and Red Deer, when courthouses were eventually built, new property was necessary.

The temptation was strong for the Liberals to use courthouses as a reward to local electors, and the balance of evidence suggests the party succumbed. Members of the legislature did not hesitate to remind their constituents that they had been instrumental in getting a courthouse built. The buildings in Cardston, Fort Saskatchewan, and later Taber, seem to have been built to please particular constituencies or because of persistent lobbying by a member of the legislature, rather than any pressing need – or at least, greater need than other places in the province. Medicine Hat presents an example where there was clearly political manoeuvring involved with courthouse promises. It was not alone. Red Deer, for instance, had an increasing need for a courthouse before World War I. As will be discussed in the next section, the city, despite its growth, elevation to the status of a judicial district, and loss of its Territorial courthouse, ended up using a converted warehouse until 1931. The fact that the local member for Red Deer was a conservative from 1909 onward seems like an unlikely coincidence. While the courthousedid not become the same issue as in Medicine Hat, it was a source of some bitterness in the city.

The early provincial courthouses were not as contentious as the Territorial buildings. Much larger and more elaborate, they provided Alberta with more than mere facilities. The courthouses built by the Liberals met the expectations of the voters of the province head-on, and while not entirely successful, they were for the most part the sort of edifice that people envisioned as courthouses. The new halls of justice were at the same time a significant drain on the treasury, and the lack of a coherent policy for courthouse construction as well as political opportunism meant the province was less effective than it might have been in providing facilities. The Liberals, despite the strong political incentive to build more courthouses, left a number of deserving towns without a proper facility. The early provincial courthouses were, however, very successful in one respect: most of them have survived, and now with legal protection as historic sites, are an architectural legacy of Alberta's first optimistic years.

# PART THREE
# **A NEW REGIME** THE UFA YEARS

The United Farmers of Alberta replaced the Liberals as Alberta's governing party in 1921. Premier Charles Stewart, although himself a former homesteader, could not harness the tide of agrarian discontent that swept the province. The UFA administration, among other things, pledged to eliminate patronage and run the province in a business-like fashion, keeping government expenditures down. The party did not have much choice. The neophyte government of Premier Herbert Greenfield was immediately saddled with the enormous debt run up by the Liberals as well as a weak economy and a drought crisis. The financial crisis naturally affected any plans to build courthouses.

Nevertheless, some new buildings were necessary. At the prompting of John Brownlee, the Attorney General, the government followed through on Liberal plans to build police barracks in a number of locations, and the building for Blairmore in the Crowsnest Pass area, erected in 1923, included quarters for the courts. As the economy strengthened in the late 1920s and government finances improved, the United Farmers felt able to undertake a significant amount of new construction. The Administration Building in Edmonton, meant to supply office space for government departments being squeezed out of the legislature, was an impressive Neo-classical building worthy of the Liberals. Also on the agenda were a number of courthouses. Grande Prairie, Hanna, Red Deer, and Vegreville were all to receive facilities, Calgary a large addition to its existing courthouse. Only four were built. Grande Prairie became the northernmost courthouse in the province, Hanna the easternmost, and both were in a sense "frontier" courthouses, built in more recently settled areas and very basic. The buildings in Red Deer and Vegreville were more substantial, and the hall of justice for Red Deer even received classical decoration as a sop to the city's greater importance.

## The Courts

Under the UFA, little significant change occurred in the province's justice system. Several new judicial districts and sub-districts were added, and by the time the Vegreville courthouse was finished in 1931, the judicial system had reached an apogee. There were eleven judicial districts and five sub-districts, eleven Supreme Court judges and ten for the District Court. In some respects, the administration of the courts shrank. Continuing a process that had started when the Liberals were still in power, District and Supreme Court staffs were amalgamated in many districts, and in new districts, right from the outset one man functioned as sheriff or clerk for both courts. This had the effect in some courthouses of drastically reducing the amount of office space needed by the court.

The Depression would affect the administration of justice just as it affected everything else. In 1933, a new statute amending the District Court Act was passed.[1] It ended the tradition of resident judges. The judicial districts remained, but the court itself was divided into separate benches for the north and south of the province, and judges visited the districts on circuit. Judges had to live within their assigned half of the province, which meant they mostly moved to the big cities. In the north, all the judges moved to Edmonton, but in the south it was a little more complex: Calgary and Lethbridge each had two judges, with Judge Greene remaining in Medicine Hat until his death in 1936.[2] His replacement, J.W. McDonald, chose to stay in Fort Macleod after his appointment in 1940.

The purpose of the amalgamation was efficiency: the rural districts saw a drastic drop in the amount of legal activity and did not need a full-time judge, who could be better put to use in the busier courts at Calgary and Edmonton. The change in the District Court was part of an overall reform of the judicial districts. The Brownlee government contemplated eliminating some of the districts and sub-districts, but held off due to political pressure. After Social Credit came into power, the dire state of the province's finances made the decision easier. Stettler, Taber, and Camrose were all disestablished at the end of 1935.

Growth of the justice system was not a huge factor in courthouse construction by the UFA. Rather, the administration was to a large extent trying to play catch-up with facilities for centres that had needed them for years. Only Vegreville gained judicial status under the UFA, as a sub-district. Grande Prairie, Hanna, and Red Deer had already been granted court officials; these towns just needed some place to put them.

## Courthouse Policy

Like the preceding Liberal administrations, the UFA government did not seem to follow an explicit and set policy toward courthouses, or at least, no record of such a policy survives. Once again, lobbying from civic groups was combined with an attempt to provide facilities at points where they were most needed, to determine where courthouses were built. All the courthouses were placed at the headquarters of judicial districts or sub-districts, however, and to a large extent the UFA finished the work of the Liberals in supplying court facilities at important points in the province.

For the first few years under the UFA, calls from the public for new courthouses were muted. Other concerns such as improved highways dominated the agenda for provincial public works. With the advent of the automobile, good roads had become much more important to residents of the province, and by the mid-1920s, were recognized as vital for economic well-being. But the courthouse was not forgotten. Although perhaps not as great a priority for the towns of Alberta as it had been, having a hall of justice was still desirable. Towns continued to campaign to be made judicial districts and competed with others for that honour. Hanna, made the headquarters for the District of Acadia by the Liberals, mobilized its civic leaders quickly to prevent Drumheller from usurping their position, while Drumheller was itself successful in becoming a new district. In the north, Grande Prairie vied with Peace River, the former getting a courthouse while the latter was made headquarters of the judicial district. A permanent hall of justice remained a way to cement the status of a town as a judicial centre.

Demands for a courthouse continued to be couched in pragmatic terms, but the buildings still fulfilled a symbolic role. Towns like Red Deer and Vegreville welcomed a hall of justice as an important addition to their civic architecture. In Red Deer, the classical detailing and imposing size of their brick and stone courthouse was greeted warmly by civic boosters, who threw an enormous banquet to celebrate its opening. Advocates of courthouses still worried about the dignity of the courts when they were held in inadequate buildings. A proper edifice for the courts of justice remained in their minds a way of instilling a proper respect for the institutions of justice. In Vegreville, an area with a large immigrant population made up largely of Russians and Ukrainians, the editor of the local paper voiced the same sentiments heard almost thirty years before in Red Deer: "In a community like this, the forms, the ceremonials, the environment of law administration should be duly impressive. The government cannot afford to cheapen law administration by placing it in unsuitable surroundings."[3]

It is less clear that courthouses were a political tool for the UFA as they had been in the hands of the Liberals. The UFA had come to power as reformers, and very much stressed their opposition to old-style party politics and patronage. They presented themselves as administrators working on "business principles," which presumably meant budget-conscious and driven by policy over political expediency. The party was determined there would be no pork-barrelling on their watch. For the most part, UFA courthouses were notably utilitarian. It is interesting to note that under the Liberals, the administration had always purchased courthouse sites, usually at market value. The Liberals were not too interested in economizing, and if the pattern of purchases is any indication, it allowed the local Liberal member a chance to exert some influence. But in the atmosphere of restraint in the UFA years, the government tended to drive a hard bargain. If property was not offered by a municipality, the province asked for it as a condition preceding a commitment to build.

However, the party was not immune to the desire to score political points through public works. The timing of the Red Deer courthouse was suspiciously close to the election of 1931, in a riding notorious for close races. The local UFA candidate, George W. Smith, did not hesitate to make political hay out of the impressive brick courthouse. And as had been the case under the Liberals, local party associations did not hesitate to demand consideration from the government. Certainly patronage did not die, and the opinion of the local MLA and riding association was still important for government jobs such as courthouse caretakers and even court officers like sheriffs.[4]

## Architecture and Design

Under the UFA, the Department of Public Works did not live up to the standards of Jeffers and Blakey. Although there were still draftsmen in the department under the direction of F.H. MacDonald, who increasingly referred to himself as an architect, they were temporary employees and their design work was not of the same calibre.[5] Not only were the buildings in Hanna and Grand Prairie simple and utilitarian, the plans themselves were crude compared to the drawings produced under Jeffers, works of art in their own right. Even the two larger courthouses at Red Deer and Vegreville did not show the fine drafting seen previously in the department. None of the courthouses built under the UFA showed innovation in style or design, but instead used earlier buildings as models. Only the Red Deer courthouse demonstrated some of the grandeur cultivated by the earlier provincial halls of justice.

The department lost its architect when Blakey left in 1924. When the UFA assumed power in 1921, cutting costs and unnecessary bureaucracy was part of its mandate. The particulars around Blakey's resignation are not clear, and it is not known if he decided to resign and precipitated the abolishing of the branch, or if he left because the branch had been cut. Before his departure, Blakey built the Blairmore courthouse and police headquarters, a project that had begun under the Liberals. It was a symbolic transition: although the Blairmore building was a pleasing design, it was a small and fairly utilitarian building. It was a preview of what would come later in courthouse building, and is arguably the last courthouse built before World War II that used a truly contemporary architectural style. At the end of the 1920s, neighbouring Saskatchewan was building court buildings with a contemporary Colonial Revival look, while Art Deco and Stripped or Modern Classicism, styles that would become popular in the Depression, were starting to appear elsewhere.

The designs the department turned out were entirely derivative. The Hanna and Grande Prairie buildings were small and almost without any external architectural decoration aside from stucco parapets, and had simple internal layouts, based on the Macleod Territorial courthouse built over twenty-five years earlier.[6]

The two major courthouses at Vegreville and Red Deer slavishly emulated Blakey, and may have been based on extant designs he had produced.[7] The two buildings used the same L-shaped layout as well as red brick facades, tile roofs, and Tyndall stone detailing found in Blakey's Medicine Hat building. Missing was the elaborate architectural decoration. A classically detailed porch was added to the Red Deer courthouse to provide a more monumental air to the building – and reflect the higher expectations of the residents of that city. But Vegreville's building was given just a few accents and only its brick construction and larger size elevated it above utilitarian buildings like Hanna.

The functions of the courthouse also expanded somewhat under the UFA into the non-judicial. This was partly a result of the shrinkage of court offices by the early 1920s in most districts, when it became clear that the legal business of the province did not require them. In Wetaskiwin, the Clerk of the Supreme Court took over the duties for the District Court as well, and the same amalgamation occurred throughout the province. In some courthouses, this created surplus space, and the government saved on rental expenses by moving other provincial offices to the courthouse. There was never a consistent policy toward the use of the courthouse outside the administration of justice – while Vegreville contained government offices from the beginning, in Red Deer they were kept out. It was still the preferred policy of the Attorney General's office to have courthouses for the courts. It did not, however, stop most courthouses from becoming de facto provincial buildings.

The department may have lacked a high calibre of architectural talent, but it still had Daniel E. McDonald. He had been hired in 1913 and worked with Blakey as the department's Superintendent of Buildings, looking after the construction and maintenance of its building stock. McDonald was born in Nova Scotia around 1875. He had come west in 1906, moving first to Calgary before joining the Department of Public Works in Edmonton. He held the position of Superintendent until resigning in 1935 – possibly due to the ascension of the Social Credit party. McDonald did not retire, but instead went to work for the federal government and was the acting district architect for the Department of National Defence until his death in Edmonton in 1947.[8] After the Architectural Branch was abolished, McDonald was in charge of all government buildings and supervised their design and construction.

McDonald was responsible for the construction program undertaken by the UFA. He was a strong personality who worked hard to make sure the projects under his supervision were carried out expeditiously and economically. He was not afraid to snub local interests, as happened in Grande Prairie over the contractor chosen for the building, or take his own superiors to task, as happened in Red Deer when controversy arose over the courthouse site. McDonald was also well suited to dealing with contractors and sub-contractors and took a hard line whenever the interests of the department seemed threatened. His hiring in 1913 was probably responsible for the sudden jump in the efficiency of the Architectural Branch – the 1914 Calgary courthouse took less than half the time to build than the comparably sized Edmonton building. It may have been thanks to a new hands-on style: Blakey, in his 1914 annual report, mentioned that "general supervision was further given by frequent visits of Mr. D.E. McDonald, General Building Superintendent."[9] Even the largest UFA courthouse, in Red Deer, was built very quickly under McDonald's direction. Ten months of construction was a stark contrast to the years spent commissioning the buildings in Wetaskiwin or Lethbridge.

To a large degree, the courthouses of the UFA represented a retrenchment. Driven by financial exigencies, the Department of Public Works returned, literally, to the precepts of the Territorial days and concentrated on building courthouses that were for the most part inexpensive. At the same time, the administration was sensitive to the continued aspirations of its constituents. Thus in a well-established and relatively important regional town like Vegreville, the courthouse was larger and more imposing, while in a city like Red Deer, extra funds were spent to elevate their courthouse beyond the purely functional. While the architectural legacy of the courthouses at Grande Prairie, Hanna, Red Deer, and Vegreville was not as rich as that found in the earlier provincial buildings, they represent a distinct period in courthouse construction.

# BLAIRMORE

Built in 1923 primarily to fill the needs of the local police detachment, the Blairmore building was a courthouse in name only. Most of the building was intended as a barracks for the Alberta Provincial Police, and the court facilities took up a relatively minor amount of space. The Blairmore edifice was a new type of courthouse, partially anticipated by the Taber courthouse built several years earlier. Whereas the earlier provincial courthouses had been built not only to house the machinery of justice but also to impress the public – the recently completed edifice at Medicine Hat was no exception – the barracks at Blairmore was a simple building that was intended to provide some needed facilities. The resulting building was attractive and blended well into the town, but sacrificed the element of grandeur usually seen in courthouses. Blakey's Blairmore design would influence courthouses built a few years later in Grande Prairie and Hanna.

The Blairmore courthouse also represents a transition between two different political regimes. First conceived under the Liberals, it was built by their successors, the United Farmers of Alberta. The courthouse was a structure designed and constructed in a new atmosphere of restraint. The Blairmore courthouse would be the new administration's first such building. It also was destined to be the swan song of Blakey; only a year after it was completed, the position of Provincial Architect was eliminated. Thus in many ways, the domicile of justice in the Crowsnest Pass straddled two eras and two different ideals for public buildings.

## Blairmore – The Early Days

Few events in the history of the Territories were more eagerly awaited than the railroad to the Crow's Nest Pass. The region was the doorway to the rich mineral resources and mining communities in the interior of British Columbia. In 1897, the CPR began construction of their line. With the building of the railroad, a number of mines opened in the area, and several hamlets sprang up, among them Bellevue, Blairmore, Coleman, and Frank. Blairmore started as a settlement known as the Springs at Siding Ten, and in 1898 was officially named after the Honourable A.G. Blair, Minister of Railways, and Mr. More, the Divisional Superintendent in the Crow's Nest. The nearby Frank Mine opened in 1901, creating a little boom in the area.[10] That same year, Blairmore became a village under the Territorial Ordinances.

The first two residents of the Springs were railway employees, H. E. Lyons, the agent and Felix Montalbetti, who built log homes at the siding. Lyons also opened a store. Soon others joined them and three hotels and other businesses sprung up. A bitter controversy arose when both Montalbetti and Lyons claimed squatter's rights to the village townsite. Montalbetti had sold it to Malcolm Mackenzie, a lawyer from Macleod, and he in turn had subdivided it into lots and put it on the market. Lyons immediately filed a caveat to prevent the sale, and the whole affair proceeded to the courts, where it became a major scandal.

The legal tussle over the townsite was nearly the end of Blairmore, freezing settlement and development. The village was saved from economic ruin by the Frank Slide and by Western Canadian Collieries. The nearby village of Frank had benefited immensely from Blairmore's legal troubles. When a substantial chunk of Turtle Mountain detached itself early one morning in 1903 and swept down on the sleeping town, the tables were turned. While the slide only destroyed a small part of Frank, it made people think twice about locating there. In 1911, the federal government ordered mining to cease under Turtle Mountain, fearing another slide.[11] Western Canadian Collieries, one of the largest of the mining companies active in the Pass, decided to make Blairmore its headquarters. Shortly afterward a huge seam of coal was discovered nearby and Western Canadian opened the Greenhill mine. The economic fortunes of the town were secured and other industries, including a cement plant, were attracted to the area.

Coal continued to dominate the economy of the Pass. Unfortunately, the industry was dependent on the same foreign capital that fuelled the boom on the prairies, and when the bust began in 1913, the mining towns of the Crow's Nest were badly affected. This would set the pattern for the Pass for the next fifty years, with cycles of prosperity and poverty depending on the demand for coal. Strikes were hardly unknown before World War I, but a new note of radicalism crept into the mining unions in the Crow's Nest. Mining was one of the few industries in Alberta where militant unionism had taken root. In the early years of the Depression, the radicalism of the miners reached new heights. Blairmore elected a worker's council and renamed its main street Tim Buck Boulevard in honour of the "martyred" – or at least imprisoned – leader of the Communist Party in Canada. Strikes led to strife, not only with the mine owners but also frequently within the unions themselves. And the frequent accidents in the mines, including disasters such as took 189 lives at Hillcrest in 1914, added a tragic note to life in the Crow's Nest.

## The Courts in Blairmore

The Crow's Nest area always remained beholden to the judicial headquarters at Macleod. Generally, both criminal and civil matters concerning residents of the district were tried in Macleod. After the District Courts were established in 1907, the judge resident at Macleod visited the area on circuit, and held an assize not only in Blairmore but also in nearby Coleman. As was usually the case, the courts were held in whatever locations were available for the assizes. In Blairmore, officials resorted to the Oddfellows Hall and later the Masonic Hall.[12] In Coleman, the town hall and council chambers were available for sittings.

While the District Court was a regular visitor to Blairmore, it was point of contention – as usual – that there was no scheduled Supreme Court session. Loring

H. Putnam, leader of the local bar, complained to the Attorney General's department about it late in 1921.[13] Although welcoming the addition of two more sittings of the District Court to the calendar, he pointed out the extra expenses involved in attending the Supreme Court in Macleod for both the Crown and the defence. As it was, many cases that should have heard by a superior court justice went before the District Judge by consent of the parties involved. Trenholme Dickson, Inspector of Legal Offices for the province and formerly the clerk of court at Macleod, was sympathetic and advised Putnam to write directly to Chief Justice Harvey. He was not as open to the request. There were simply not enough judges to accommodate more sittings, and Harvey was also leery of setting a precedent with sittings outside of judicial centres:

> You will see from a perusal of the list of assignments for the coming six months that even with six judges and sitting at only judicial centres there is very little free time available. I feel once started holding regular sittings at outside points there would be requests no doubt from very many places all of which probably have equal rights for consideration.[14]

Harvey did say that special sittings, however, were a possibility. In the end he did relent. The first Supreme Court assize was held on March 8, 1922 in Blairmore, but the presiding judge was A.M. McDonald, the District Court judge for the Macleod District.[15] Although the District Court visited regularly, the superior court rarely held assizes even after a courthouse was built, and most serious crimes were still tried in Macleod.

## The Courthouse

It might have been an easier task to get the assizes scheduled if Blairmore had had a proper place to hold them. However, a courthouse was not an obsession in Blairmore in the way it had been in frontier communities like Macleod and Lethbridge. It was the sort of amenity the town certainly would not turn down, but it was not a great priority.

The impetus behind a court facility came from a different but not surprising source: the Alberta Provincial Police. After its formation in 1917, one of the problems facing the APP was finding suitable buildings to use as barracks and lockups. The new commissioner of the force, Alfred Cuddy, who had done wonders as the police chief in Calgary, wanted proper detachment buildings as part of his efforts to get the organization up and running. Due to prohibition and the town's proximity to the international and provincial border, Blairmore was a particular hot spot for law enforcement that demanded a larger facility. The Department of Public Works had been made aware of the wants and needs of the police and had started to design detachment buildings in 1920, and actually built one in Peace River.[16] In the fall of 1921, the APP made a formal request for a number of new detachment buildings,

Blairmore among them.[17] Accordingly, Blakey's staff prepared new plans for facilities in Drumheller and Blairmore late that year.[18] No decision about construction was taken immediately, but by June 1922, the Department of Public Works was given the go-ahead from the Attorney General's office.[19] It had already begun looking for a site for the proposed building.

Like towns before and since, Blairmore was quite prepared to bribe the government with free land in order to get a public building. Rumours had been surfacing in town during the spring of 1922 that a new edifice for the police detachment was contemplated for the district. In March, Daniel McDonald, the Superintendent of Buildings for Public Works, came down to Blairmore with Inspectors Bavin and Nicholson of the APP to look over possible sites.[20] Apprised of the government plans, the town was quick to act, realizing that the court facilities proposed for the barracks would mean the District and Supreme Courts would hold their sittings in Blairmore. Thus on May 5, 1922, the council communicated with Commissioner Cuddy to say they had a lovely location right on the main business thoroughfare.[21] In June the council voted to grant four lots on Victoria Street, and with that the town fathers sat back to await construction.[22]

Although the offer of lots did not settle the location, at first it looked like construction on the barracks might still start in 1922. Provincial Architect Blakey already had plans prepared for a detachment building, and in July the Department of Public Works called for tenders on the edifice.[23] After the tender went out, however, it was decided to expand the buildings in both Blairmore and Drumheller to add court facilities. The older plans were scrapped, and new revised drafts prepared to incorporate the changes. These were substantial enough that a new tender had to be called for, and it was not advertised until December. In the interim, the department left the matter of the location to be decided at a later date. Meanwhile, the town was not apprised of the change in plans and left in suspense.

The earlier sketches of the Blairmore barracks no longer exist, so we do not know what changes Blakey made before he settled on a final version. The new design heralded the introduction of a new architectural style for courthouses, Mission Revival. First popularized in California, where it originated, and throughout the American West, it made a belated appearance in western Canada after World War I, in houses, commercial buildings and schools, but to a lesser degree for public buildings.[24] The style was characterized by stucco exterior finishes, stepped and rounded gables or parapets, balconies with wrought iron railings, and hip roofs covered in "Spanish Tile." The Provincial Architect was enamoured of buildings that showed Spanish or Mediterranean influences. His grand Medicine Hat courthouse had used an Italian Renaissance decorative scheme, except for the red tile hip roof, which was a Spanish Revival motif. The Drumheller police barracks design also used the tile roof.

At Blairmore, Blakey sought a straightforward Mission Revival look. Constructed of hollow tile and brick on a concrete foundation, the building used stucco and brick finishing on the exterior.[25] The symmetrical facade was divided into three parts, with two projecting bays on either side. On each of the bays and

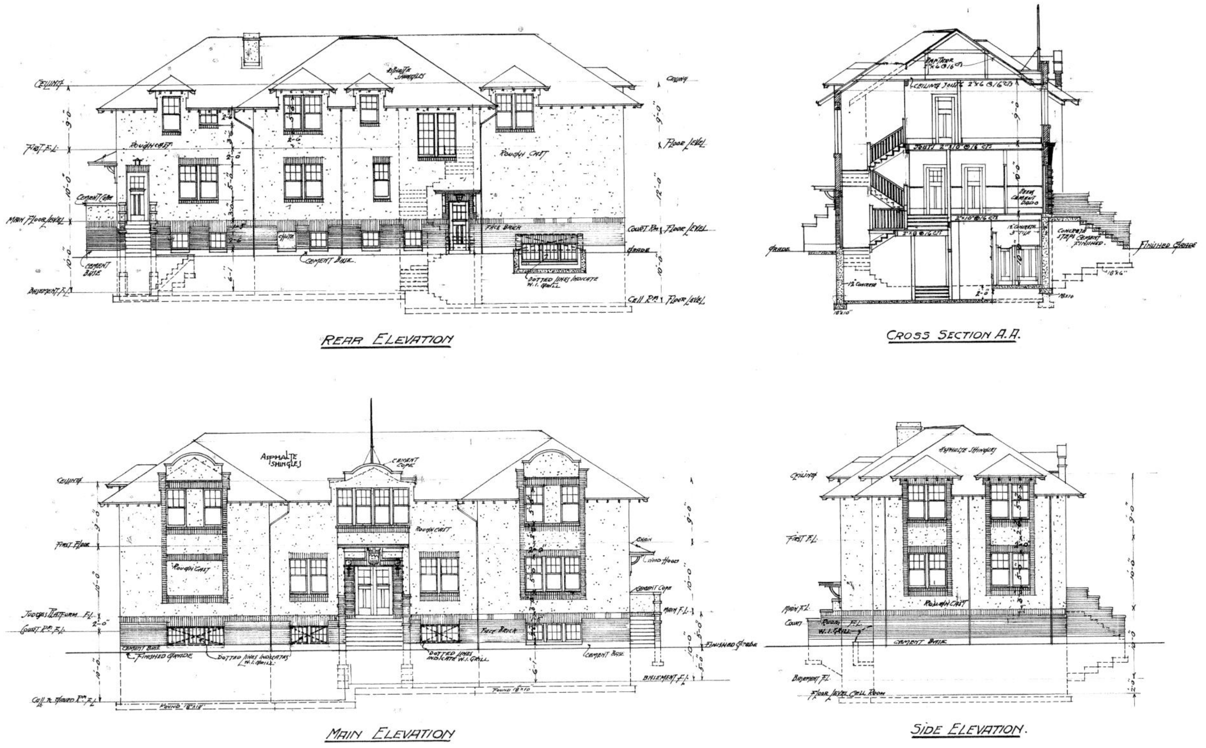


*New Styles: Elevations and Section, Blairmore Courthouse, 1922. PAA*

over the main entrance there was a stepped and rounded gable dormer, which, along with the stucco exterior, gave the building the distinctive Mission look. A simple but pleasing brick trim was used for the window treatments and also to face the foundations. The main entrance, a double-door, was given an uncomplicated, almost Art Deco brick trim with the provincial coat of arms on the lintel. There were two jarring notes. Blakey specified asphalt shingles on the roof instead of tile, which would have been far more congruent with the style. This may have simply been a cost-conscious decision, just as the decision to eliminate the ground floor windows on the left side of the facade was likely for better security in the courtroom. Like Blakey's courthouse at Taber, the Blairmore barracks was relatively utilitarian building, but the architect deftly gave it a simple but pleasing contemporary architectural decor that put it head and shoulders above later efforts at Grande Prairie and Hanna.

The interior layout was straightforward and dedicated largely to the police. It deviated from accepted layout for courthouses by placing the courtroom and offices on the main floor, reflecting the fact the courts were a secondary function in the building. The building had two wings and a central portion. On the main floor, the left or west wing was given over to the courtroom. This was intended primarily for the police court and the District Court, and there was no provision for a jury room or witness room. The office of the police magistrate adjoined the courtroom and had a door directly beside the judge's bench. The main part of the building had the magistrate's office, police superintendent's office and the general office of the police, and a stairwell at the back. The right, or east, wing was given over to a living room and a kitchen for the men of the detachment, who were indeed housed barracks-style on the second floor. There was one large dormitory room and several bedrooms, while the west wing had more office space. The basement had the cells directly under the courtroom, including a separate female cell with a police matron's office. These facilities were not just for holding prisoners for trial; the cells also served as the local jail and minor offenders served their sentences there.

The location of the new edifice became a matter of some controversy, hardly unheard of in the annals of courthouse construction. Although the council had offered a free site, it was found wanting by the police, who then picked a new location, which had the disadvantage of not actually being within the Blairmore townsite. West Canadian Collieries complicated matters with an offer of yet another piece of land. With several spots to choose from, the government apparently found itself frozen in indecision.

This indecision was destined to drag on into the new year. After seeing a long parade of officials from the police, the Attorney General's department, and the Public Works department, but still no decision on the site or announcement the project would commence, the town was getting restless. The editor of the *Blairmore Enterprise* suggested sardonically that "the government next take a vote of the kindergarten of the local school, any of whom seem quite as capable of deciding on the site for such a public building."[26] Finally, the town solicitor contacted the Department of Public Works:

> A great deal of controversy has taken place here as to this building, especially as to location, as well as to whether the building is to be proceeded with as soon as the weather will permit or not ... will you kindly advise me the settled location and when the building is expected to be started; also when it is expected to be finished.[27]

Blakey quickly responded to say that the contract had been let and that the department had decided on the site originally offered by the town. He requested a transfer of title for lots 5 to 10 in block 8 of Plan 3319-I.[28] The second call for bids had gone out the previous December, and on the basis of these tenders the contract was awarded to Calgary builders Watson and Abercrombie, on a bid of $29,740.[29] The heating and plumbing contract also went to a Calgary firm, Ross Snyder and Co. While no great fuss was made about this fact, the Enterprise did note coolly, "We understand that so far but one contract in connection with the new building has been awarded locally – that to Mr. S. Ennis for hauling materials to the site."[30]

Any hard feelings over the contracts were quickly forgotten when Abercrombie arrived in Blairmore at the beginning of April and immediately set to work on the edifice.[31] Within a week, the company was ready to start the foundation. Progress was impressive. By the end of May, the roof was almost done and the stucco crew was busy covering the brick superstructure.[32] Despite severe floods in June, the

An excellent background: Blairmore Fire Department in front of new courthouse, c. 1926. Glenbow Archives, NC-54-2267

building was fully enclosed in another month and the contractor was busy working on the interior. By August, the building was more or less done. Blakey came down from Edmonton for an inspection on August 13, and the local APP detachment commander prepared to move into his quarters with his family.[33] Shortly thereafter, the local police magistrate began to mete out justice in the new courtroom, in the form of fines and time in the lockup to Blairmore ne'er-do-wells, while Judge Macdonald and the District Court made an appearance, with no fanfare, at the beginning of October.[34]

The attractive little building quickly became a Blairmore landmark. Although originally built for the police and housing the APP, and then the RCMP, well into the 1960s, the edifice was known generally as "the courthouse." A 1937 profile on the town in the Calgary Herald titled "Blairmore Grew to Beautiful Town" singled it out: "Special mention deserves to be made of the Court House erected in 1923."[35] Anchoring the east end of Main Street, the building was one of the more substantial edifices in the town and the source of some civic pride.

---

CRIME AND PUNISHMENT IN THE CROW'S NEST PASS

After coal mining began in the Crow's Nest Past at the beginning of the century, the towns of Blairmore, Bellevue, Hillcrest, and Frank dominated the civil and criminal court docket for the Supreme Court at Macleod. Mine accidents were the source of many claims in the civil courts, but it was the violence and drunkenness that shocked the middle class Anglo-Canadian society of southern Alberta. The miners were by and large immigrants from eastern and southern Europe, usually Orthodox Catholics. They were also a large population of young single men, many recent immigrants who had left their families behind in Europe, engaged in dangerous, demanding and poorly paid labour. There was little for them in the mining settlements in the way of more wholesome entertainment, and little attempt by "respectable" society to integrate them. From court records, drinking, gambling, brawling, and whoring emerge as the main recreation of the miners.

Inevitably, people would end up in court charged with serious offences. Wasyl Mudri was put on trial on October 14, 1913 for the murder of Ignace Kalcek, found wounded in his shack in Police Flats in April 1913.[36] Kalcek died of septic poisoning from his injuries. Witnesses testified that a group of men, all Russians, had been drinking and a fight broke out. Mudri hit Kalcek with a beer mug, badly injuring him. Originally charged with assault, Mudri was tried for murder when the latter died. The jury clearly felt that under the circumstances that Kalcek's death was an unfortunate accident, and acquitted Mudri. The presence of alcohol influenced the verdicts brought down in these cases. Pietr Salvadore, an Italian, was arrested on a charge of attempted murder after allegedly shooting at Bill Mustica. The two had had an altercation earlier outside a bar after drinking; the verdict was guilty, but the sentence was one year for simple assault.[37] In a 1909 incident, John Kulcychi was charged with the murder of Angus Ruis. It was another case of a drunken brawl breaking out over a card game. Kulcychi initially got the worst of it, but in the scuffle Ruis was knifed and later died from his wounds. Kulcychi, however, was acquitted.[38]

If the court was inclined toward leniency in the many cases involving booze, it was much tougher when there was premeditation involved. Angelo Mont of Lille was tried for the murder of Antonio Castania in 1908.[39] A fight had broken out in the boarding house where both the accused and the victim lived. After the victim's brother Sam had broken it up, Angelo went up to his room and returned with a shotgun, shooting both the Castanias. Antonio was killed, Sam lightly wounded. Convicted, Mont received some leniency from the court when his charge was reduced to manslaughter, but he was given fifteen years. We do not know the judge's reasoning behind the sentence. Presumably a much longer sentence was called for because the accused had had the time to think of what he was doing, but the circumstances of the fight, including the threats uttered by the victim after it had broken up, were enough to ameliorate the punishment.

Conditions in the Pass continued much the same through the 1910s, and was only exacerbated by the declaration of Prohibition in 1916. By the time the Blairmore courthouse was built, however, much of the lawlessness of the

> Pass was already a thing of the past. Ironically, the courthouse was not the scene of sensational trials. Famous incidents like the Bellevue Café shootout and the Picariello and Lassandro affair had been the products of Prohibition, a policy that had just about run its course in Alberta. The mining communities themselves became much more peaceful as the industry matured and the miners put down roots. It was still a busy precinct, but most of the work was done in the police court and the District Court, and even with the new courthouse, more serious trials were heard by the Supreme Court in Macleod.

The courthouse was left in the care of the Alberta Provincial Police. When this force disbanded in 1932, the RCMP took over the Blairmore facility. Due to the nature of the building as a barracks and police court, there was more traffic and wear and tear in Blairmore than in other courthouses. Although it was only a bit more than a decade old, by 1937 the building was already showing some age. A report from the detachment sergeant detailed the damage.[40] The floors had all subsided, in some places "as much as an inch," and the plasterwork had begun to crack badly in many rooms. A troublesome furnace had coated the walls in soot, and efforts to clean them had only damaged the wallpaper and plaster. While the commanding sergeant at Blairmore blamed the Department of Public Works for the poor condition of the building, the real culprit was the Depression. Maintenance budgets were cut down to the bone and all the courthouses in the province suffered the consequences. In the larger centres, this helped fuel a round of demolitions and rebuilding after World War II, but in Blairmore the courthouse was adequate for the modest needs of the district, and the courts continued to use it for over fifty years.

## Epilogue

The Crowsnest settled into relative stability after World War II. In the years following the opening of the courthouse, parts of the police quarters were converted into offices as the detachment shrank. The RCMP finally left the barracks in 1955.[41] The family court was installed on the second floor, and other provincial offices got space on the main floor.[42] Thanks to pressure from the local MLA, the local recreation board was even allowed to move in, much to the chagrin of the Deputy Attorney General and despite official policy discouraging non-judicial and non-government use of courthouses.[43]

In 1980, a new provincial building for the Crowsnest, which would be placed in Blairmore, was announced.[44] Completed in 1983 at a cost of over four million dollars, it incorporated a courtroom and necessary office space. After nearly sixty years of service, the old police barracks was no longer needed. Two years before, the local historical association had urged the Municipality of Crowsnest to look into acquiring the courthouse from the government.[45] The municipality looked into having it designated a historic site, meeting with a representative of Alberta Culture in March 1983.[46]

For the next couple of years, the building hosted a kindergarten, municipality offices and served as headquarters of the 1984 Alberta Summer Games.[47] In 1986, the new Crowsnest Pass Ecomuseum Trust bought the building from the province to serve as its offices, a visitor's centre, and for interpretative displays. The Trust had been formed by the municipality to work toward preserving various aspects of the history of the Crowsnest Pass.[48] The old courthouse seemed like a perfect fit for the organization. The trust undertook extensive renovations and finally obtained historic site designation for the building in 1993.[809]

The Ecomuseum became rather overextended, and was forced to divest itself of a number of assets, including the courthouse.[50] Fortunately, a new owner, in the form of the Nippon Institute of Technology, appeared. Based in Japan, the institute offered an English immersion course. They turned the courthouse into a Canadian campus, but carefully preserved and restored the building's exterior and even retained all the original courtroom fixtures, using the chamber as a meeting room.[51] It is one of the more interesting – and viable – courthouse renovations done in Alberta. Classrooms and lectures are a long way from bar fights and rumrunners, but the courthouse in Blairmore serves on.

# GRANDE PRAIRIE

By 1928, the unofficial capital of the Peace River Country was still very much a frontier town, with only two thousand residents and many recent settlers, drawn to one of the last repositories of fertile homestead land in western Canada. Towns like Macleod, Wetaskiwin, and Medicine Hat had long before acquired such markings of civic stability as town halls, post offices, and courthouses. In Grande Prairie, they were still things to fight for. Thus, some twenty years after courthouses ceased to be an issue in most of the province, the people of the Peace River sought their just due.

Upon its completion in 1929, the Grande Prairie building was the northernmost courthouse in the province, and the only one past Edmonton until 1957. Under the United Farmers of Alberta, caution and parsimony were the watchwords of government. In some ways, it was a return to the Territorial days, when governments were reluctant to spend much money on the frontiers. When the UFA finally found it necessary to fund a program of courthouse construction in the late 1920s, they looked at Grande Prairie very much in that spirit. Under the new regime, the Department of Public Works produced a small utilitarian design, adequate for the administration of justice, but divorced from the majesty of the law.

## Grande Prairie – The Early Days

The first recorded settlement in the vicinity of the present city of Grande Prairie was a Hudson's Bay Company post built in 1880. Toward the end of the century, a few Métis families began farming in the area. By this time, rumours abounded in the rest of Alberta about the rich land along the Peace River. Getting there was problematic: the fertile plains of Grande Prairie were guarded by miles of dense bush, muskeg, and rough hill country with few trails. As long as land was plentiful elsewhere, few homesteaders cared to brave the difficult trek. Attempts to create an overland trail to the Yukon brought more people into the region in the late 1890s. It was not until the land boom took hold throughout the prairies that speculators began to look at the north in a new light. In 1909 Edmonton lawyer and real estate developer W.A. Rae incorporated the Argonaut Company after visiting the region.[52] Rae's company surveyed a townsite and began selling lots.

Thus Grande Prairie was born. Argonaut was joined by Grande Prairie Townsite Company, which purchased an adjacent parcel of land in 1910. Meanwhile, the government land surveyor had begun to mark off quarter sections in the area for homesteading. Businesses sprang up and the settlement acquired its name. The Department of Public Works cut a new trail to the hamlet from the Grand Trunk Pacific line at Edson in 1910. More importantly, after several years of intense lobbying and many stormy debates in the Legislative Assembly, a railroad was built to the Peace River area. The Edmonton, Dunvegan and British Columbia line finally reached Grande Prairie in 1916, after having gone bankrupt two years before and been taken over by the government.[53] The Peace River country was ready to boom, and as the terminus or the railroad, Grande Prairie's fortunes were guaranteed over the other settlements of the area, including arch-rivals Lake Saskatoon and Peace River Landing.[54] Formally incorporated as a village in 1914, Grande Prairie attained town status in 1919.

## Grande Prairie and the Courts

The administration of justice was an erratic affair along the Peace River until well into the twentieth century. The region was nominally part of the Judicial District of Northern Alberta under the Territorial Supreme Court. The population was extremely sparse, crime and litigation rare, and the nearest court was in Edmonton. The North West Mounted Police made its first appearance in the Peace River Country with a dog team patrol in the winter of 1897.[55] The first permanent police post was established at Peace River Crossing on April 13, 1898.[56] It remained the headquarters of the Mounties in the region for many years. As for Grande Prairie, the law did not have a presence there until 1908. A mounted police party under Constable Sidney G. Clay had passed through Grande Prairie in 1906 on the way to Fort St. John in British Columbia. Two years later Clay was back, manning an improvised post at nearby Flying Shot Lake. Historian J.G. MacGregor claims that the first sitting of the District Court took place at Clay's barracks in 1908, with Judge Noel of Edmonton presiding.[57] Noel subsequently became the District Court Judge for the Judicial District of Athabaska, formed in 1909 and encompassing all of northwest Alberta.[58] The district was headquartered in Edmonton, due to the primitive conditions in the north country. Noel and the court officers lived in the capital, a relief from the rigours of frontier life when they went on circuit.

Travel remained a great obstacle to the timely administration of justice in the Peace River valley. Going overland was slow and difficult, and without a rail connection, a journey of many weeks was necessary to hold circuit. The long intervals between courts predictably caused great irritation among residents. It was not until August 24, 1915, with the E.D. & B.C. line approaching Grande Prairie, that the Alberta Supreme Court visited the area.[59] The judicial party was forced to travel over fifty miles by democrat when their automobiles rapidly succumbed to the rough trails from the end of the steel to Grande Prairie.[60] It was the first official sitting of both the Supreme and District Courts in the village, presided over by Justice Nicholas Beck of Edmonton. Beck, a pioneer lawyer in the Northwest, complimented the people of Grande Prairie on their industry, and remarked how similar he found conditions to Edmonton when he had first arrived there – in 1883![61] Despite the long wait for a judge, the docket was small, consisting of an assault charge, a case of libel, and one civil matter. The court was held in the Club Hall, Grande Prairie's dance hall and general meeting place. The local board of trade,

*Frontier justice: judicial party on river ferry, PAA, 66.135/20*

that mainstay of civic improvement, held its first meeting in the same venue the following November.[62]

As had been the case with their Territorial forebears, the state of the court system became an increasing source of irritation among the residents of the Peace River. One concession to local feelings was the appointment of Sheriff Peter Gunn in 1916: he had been a Grande Prairie pioneer, coming as an employee of the Hudson's Bay Company in 1886.[63] But it didn't change the fact there were no permanent officials in the area, not even deputies. Gunn lived in Edmonton, the headquarters of the district remained there as well, and court officials were seldom seen in the Peace River. Thus in 1918, the local paper commented: "Sheriff Gunn of Edmonton paid Grande Prairie a flying visit.... This was the sheriff's first visit here for some months...."[64] More importantly, the assizes remained sporadic. Regular District Court dates were eventually set by the government so Noel visited more often, but sittings were often cancelled if there was not enough business to justify the expense of sending him north.

The real sticking point was Supreme Court sittings. There was not a great deal of traffic before the bench in the area, so as an economy measure, assizes were scheduled as necessary by the Attorney General's Department, and this was not often enough for the residents of the district.[65] Furthermore, the justices of the Supreme Court disliked going north and the Attorney General could not order them to do so.[66] It was a less than ideal situation, but with a war on, the citizens of Grande Prairie made do in the proper pioneer spirit.

When Camrose, a town close to Edmonton, became the seat of a judicial sub-district in 1918, the Peace River Country was outraged. The creation of a sub-district guaranteed a monthly sitting of the District Court, and more frequent sittings of the Supreme Court, as well as resident court officers. The Grande Prairie Herald had no doubts that the new district in Camrose was politically motivated:

> Camrose ... gets a sub-judicial district because a cabinet minister represents it.... If Camrose needs a sub-district so badly, what of the Peace River and Grande

> Prairie districts?... If as the Hon. Mr. Cross would have us believe, the judicial districts are being arranged [on merit], why not begin where it is needed and not merely as a reward for services rendered.[67]

This last point was particularly galling to the paper, for if rewards were being handed out, the district was equally deserving: "Peace River gave the government an enormous majority last June and we would suggest to the government that we expect at least a square deal. We have suffered patiently for long and our patience is becoming exhausted."

## Campaigning for a Courthouse

The situation demanded a response, and the lawyers of Grande Prairie provided one by forming a bar association on May 13, 1918. It wasted no time in addressing the problem. The Herald noted that "The organisation has already taken steps towards securing better facilities for the administration of justice and is being supported by other organisations in the district."[68]

Better facilities, of course, meant a courthouse as well as resident judge and officers of the court. The bar association did not stand alone. Along with the board of trade, the local Liberal Association also jumped into the fray. At the Peace River Association's annual meeting in 1920, Grande Prairie lawyer M.W. Eager put forth a motion that "the government be urged to forthwith build a Court House in the Town of Grande Prairie, for the use of the Clerk of the Courts, Deputy Sheriff and other officials, and that same be properly equipped to safely care for the documents filed therein."[69] The association duly passed the resolution.

The demands for a better judicial service were helped by the fact that the town was experiencing a settlement boom, with many new homesteaders, including veterans under the soldier resettlement scheme. Grande Prairie had been made a town in 1919 and its population had jumped to about fifteen hundred. Although the government took no immediate action on a courthouse, it did decide to reorganize the Athabasca Judicial District. Horace Harvey had written to A.G. Browning, the Deputy Attorney General, in the fall of 1919 about the visits of the Supreme Court, stating that, "It was thought that the time had come to give these sittings a more definite assignment than in the past."[70] Browning and J.R. Boyle, the Attorney General, were themselves re-evaluating the situation in the north after the untimely death of Judge Noel. They felt that the boundaries of the Athabaska District needed to be changed, and that the time had come for a resident judge. Accordingly, the new Judicial District of Peace River was formed in 1920, with Peace River Landing as headquarters. Grande Prairie was made a sub-district.

Boyle hastened to reassure the residents of Grande Prairie that it was in no way a slight: "There is no difference excepting in the name ... the reason why sub-judicial districts are established ... is to avoid unnecessary appointments of Judges."[71] As Boyle explained to the Grande Prairie Board of Trade, the area did not have enough work yet to merit more than one judge, but it was recognized that a clerk and sheriff's office was necessary at more than one point in the district. Furthermore, the judge, when appointed, could choose to live in Grande Prairie if it suited him. The new judge, Lucien Dubuc, had no interest in living anywhere in the north. The government had promised the new judge would reside in the new district, but Dubuc, like Noel, stayed in Edmonton when not on circuit. He did sympathize with the complaints of the residents of the region, and promised to do everything in his power to hold a monthly court, short of actually living there.[72] A deputy clerk and sheriff were duly appointed in Grande Prairie and court offices opened in Peace River Landing, although like Dubuc, Sheriff Gunn declined to leave Edmonton for the north.[73]

Despite the fact both judge and sheriff were not going to live among them, the residents of the Peace River Country were pleased at the changes – the local Liberals made sure to send "our thanks to the Attorney General" – and had some hope that perhaps the lack of proper court facilities would be addressed. Premier Charles Stewart visited the town on October 12, 1920, accompanied by A.J. Maclean, the Minister of Public Works.[74] A domicile for the courts was clearly on their agenda. Although there was no public announcement made, it became known shortly after the visit that the government intended to buy the Club Hall, which the court had been renting for the assizes, and convert it into a courthouse and telephone exchange. This was a strategy the government had started using back just before the war: in Red Deer a factory had been modified, in Camrose a meeting hall, and in Stettler an old schoolhouse. It was a temporary measure until a proper courthouse could be afforded – although "temporary" turned out to be a relative term – the Stettler courthouse served until 1975.

Far from being pleased with the suggestion, the citizens of Grande Prairie were horrified. The town council called a special meeting for October 16 and passed a motion condemning the government's plan:

> And whereas in the opinion of this council the said building is entirely unsuited for the purpose mentioned ... it is therefore resolved: That this Council go on record as being strongly opposed to the purchase of the said building by the Provincial Government and that the Hon. the Minister of Public Works be so advised.[75]

The bar association was also quick to react and fired off a letter with a resolution protesting against the plan. The bar objected to the Club Hall because it was a fire-trap and because it was small and unprepossessing. As the resolution put it:

> ... said building is of the cheapest frame construction, non-habitable in the winter, without any inherent fire resisting qualities, and not situate on a street where hydrants are installed for fire protection.[76]

While concern for the safety of the court records was paramount, the bar and council clearly wanted something better for the town. Appearances were important in a small growing centre: a converted frame building just wasn't going to be enough, and Grande Prairie was not going to let the government off that easy. The bar's resolution called on the province "to erect a suitable building" The province's response was to say it was out of the question – there was no money and construction costs were too high, although this had not prevented the recent erection of the Medicine Hat hall of justice.[77] The government did drop the proposed conversion after an inspector for the Department of Public Works decided it was unsuitable and reported as much to the Superintendent of Buildings, but instead simply rented offices for the court deputies and continued to use halls for the sittings of the court.[78] The court itself stopped using the Club Hall and moved over to the Oddfellows Hall.[79] It would later use the Herald Hall, headquarters of the *Grande Prairie Herald*. No one was happy with the arrangement, not even the government, which also fretted over the fire danger.[80]

---

JUDICIAL TRAVEL – AND RELUCTANT JUDGES

In the earliest years of the courts in Alberta, travel on circuit was by any means possible. As both Stipendiary Magistrate and Supreme Court Justice, Colonel Macleod traveled thousands of miles on horseback, by sleigh, by dog team and by carriage to visit the far-flung settlements in his jurisdiction. The Colonel's letters are replete with the hardships of travel, including frostbite and blizzards in winter and heat stroke, bugs, and sudden thunderstorms in the summer.[81] Railroads and hotels reduced the burden, and over the last years of the nineteenth and early years of the twentieth century, most major towns were either on a spur line or close to one. But it was still frequently necessary for judges to travel by stage or carriage. Accommodations were often lacking in small towns. Judges who came to the bench after the turn of the century did not have to sleep under the stars like Macleod, but in more remote areas, the judge on circuit might still rely on friendly locals for a bed, or sleep on a cot in a makeshift courtroom.

By the end of World War I, the introduction of the automobile and a growing network of good roads had vastly improved travel. In more settled areas of the province, judges could drive to towns in a fraction of the time it had taken previously. And accommodations had improved – a hotel was available in most small towns and villages, and most of courthouses built by the province incorporated a judge's quarters. But in the Peace River Country, travel remained difficult until after World War II. Across the border in British Columbia, a judicial party was dumped into the Parsnip River when their motorboat was swamped.[82] Their entire luggage was lost, and they were left with a little coffee and bread and didn't get a decent meal for a day and a half. At his next stop, Judge Robertson "dispensed justice in Mackinaw breeches and a flannel shirt." Jurists going to Grande Prairie did not have to brave a wild northern river, but the railroad was slow and inefficient, with a poor track that often had to be closed for repairs. The condition of the line interfered with judicial travel; on November 29, 1920, the *Grande Prairie Herald* reported that "it is possible a special car may be provided over the E.D. & B.C. to avoid discomforts experienced by Supreme Court judges in previous trips to the north." This announcement came at the end of weeks of uncertainty about when the court would sit in the Peace River area. To get from Grande Prairie to Fort Vermilion, the court had to travel for several days by riverboat. And even with cars available, the state of the roads in the Peace meant it was not the most reliable means of travel. Members of the court, judge included, might have to assist in giving the car a push out of a mud hole!

The poor travelling conditions, along with makeshift court facilities and accommodations that left something to be desired, meant that judges did not enjoy the northern circuits and avoided them. In 1920, the barristers of Peace River begged for a Supreme Court sitting. Chief Justice Harvey told the crown prosecutor for the area that "all the Judges were adverse to going into that country and he did not know as he would be able to induce any of them to go." In response to complaints from the bar associations and boards of trade in the Peace River district, the Attorney General had to admit that they had no direct authority over the judges, as a matter of constitutional arrangements.[83] Lawyer and MP Ged Baldwin remembered that "it was a fact of life that some jurists did not take kindly to being sent north. They were often impatient to rush through the docket and get back to Edmonton or Calgary. To accomplish this, they would push and manipulate a lawyer to hurry cases.... A favorite gambit in civil actions was to hint that if there were not a settlement and the case were tried to the bitter end, costs might be limited or not awarded at all."

Baldwin also saw many incidents when lack of familiarity with the north could throw a wrench into the machinery of the courts. In one case where a bar brawl ended in a death, the Crown refused to take a guilty plea for manslaughter and pursued a murder conviction. The jury was infuriated at being kept in court for several days during harvest season. Angry at a patronizing trial judge, who more or less ordered a conviction, the jurors acquitted the accused! At the same time, Baldwin also singled out judges such as William L. Walsh for their interest in the north and willingness to go wherever justice required. An old Yukon hand, Walsh enjoyed visiting some of his old cronies when on circuit in the Peace Country.

Having rejected the plan to convert the Club Hall, Grande Prairie's immediate hopes for a new courthouse were dashed with the defeat of the Liberals in the 1921 provincial election. The United Farmers of Alberta followed the Liberals into power and immediately had to wrestle with huge deficits, thus guaranteeing that there would be no courthouse immediately forthcoming for Grande Prairie.

Thus, despite pressure from the bar association and board of trade, nothing was done about a hall of justice in Grande Prairie for almost a decade. The constituency of Peace River had elected the UFA candidate in 1921. The new Premier, Herbert Greenfield of Westlock, who had not run in the election but was chosen to form a government when the UFA won its surprise victory, took the seat in a hastily arranged by-election. Even with this representation in government, no courthouse was immediately forthcoming. The UFA, advocates of radical ideas such as group government, frowned on the old style of politics where a member of the legislature's main duty, it seemed, was to get as much as possible for his district from the public purse. If representations were ever made to Greenfield about getting a courthouse built in the town, he did not respond.[84]

Lobbying efforts for a courthouse were also muted by the railroad and highway issues of the day. Although Grande Prairie had a rail connection with the E.D. & B.C, it was less than satisfactory: the locals claimed the initials stood for Extremely Dangerous and Badly Constructed.[85] Throughout the 1920s, the entire Peace River Country obsessively schemed and lobbied for a rail line that would give them direct access to the Pacific. A perusal of local papers such as the Grande Prairie Herald and Peace River Record reveals how pervasive were railway concerns. Almost every visiting government dignitary was buttonholed about a new rail connection, and politicians on tour knew that supporting railroad construction played well in the district. The constituents of the area understood that their agricultural economy depended on transportation and immigration. And with the arrival of the automobile, roads began taking on more importance. After the Pacific outlet, better road connections topped the agenda of the boards of trade in Grande Prairie, Peace River and other towns of the region. For the moment, courthouses were far down on the list.

---

### UNSOLVED MYSTERIES

One of the most dramatic trials held in Grande Prairie did not result in a conviction and solemn declaration of sentence. Instead, Daniel Lough walked out of the Club Hall, doubling as a hall of justice, a free man. A good thing for him, as six murders had hung over his head.

On June 15, 1920, an editorial in the *Grande Prairie Herald* reminded its readers that "Two years have practically passed, since one of the foulest murders in the annals of Canadian crime took place in our midst, and what has been done to bring the murderer or murderers to justice – apparently nothing." The north country had been gripped in fear for months. On June 20, 1918, Lough, a homesteader, had reported his neighbor's house on fire. Police, upon investigating, found two bodies in the charred ruin of the farmstead of Joseph and Stanley Snyder, father and son. Lough had been awakened by cries for help at about midnight only to find the Snyder's cabin ablaze. The coroner's inquest established death by foul means. Scarcely had news of the double murder been made public when four more bodies were found two miles from the Snyders in a shack belonging to a trapper named Paton. He and three other men had been murdered and the cabin set alight. The four men had been preparing to settle at Fort Vermilion. Having sold their land in the area, they had had large sums of money on their persons. Investigators determined that the Snyders had been shot with a pistol belonging to Paton.

The new Alberta Provincial Police force had not covered itself with glory pursuing the case. Despite intensive investigation, no one was brought to trial. Two drifters of questionable character, "Shorty" Salisbury and Norman Keeler, were arrested after a spectacular gunfight, but no case could be made against them.[86] Even Inspector John D. Nicholson, chief detective of the APP, could not turn up a suspect – except for Dan Lough. The farmer lived nearby and had bought land off one of the quartet found at Paton's. His story about discovering the Snyders seemed too pat; Nicholson, for one, wondered why Lough had ridden straight to the police rather than stopping for help at any number of farms on the way. When interviewed by Nicholson, Lough allowed that he never locked his house or kept a gun, which seemed strange just after six gruesome murders no more than two miles away. The farmer had also left for Edmonton and tried to send his family back to the United States not long after the killings. Later, the APP was criticized for arresting Lough simply through lack of a better suspect. Lough was brought into custody on June 22, 1920, a week after the *Herald-Tribune's* editorial. The local police magistrate, Percy Belcher, decided that there was enough evidence to commit the farmer to trial.[87]

Lough faced Justice Simmons of the Supreme Court and a jury on December 8, 1920. The Crown's case was weak, amounting to little more than the suspicions of Nicholson and a burning desire to convict someone. The one person who may have been able to shed light on Lough's alleged involvement was his wife, but she had died of the Spanish Flu in 1918. Lough's lawyer, M.W. Eager, did not call his client to the stand. In his address to the jury, he summed up his defense: "there is no evidence against the accused, and therefore [I] have no hesitation of leaving the accused's fate in your hands"[88] The jury deliberated an hour before pronouncing Lough a free man. The six murders remain unsolved.

## The 1929 Courthouse

After almost a decade of waiting, Grande Prairie finally got a hall of justice. Toward the end of the 1920s, a vastly improved economy and a couple of years of budget surpluses loosened the government's purse strings. The residents of the area developed a new determination to get a building and a resident District Court judge.[89]

The details of the town's lobbying efforts are a bit vague. The local paper did not join in wholeheartedly, and it was apparently a campaign carried out mostly behind the scenes. The board of trade and the local bar association had once again joined forces. In 1928, the president of the board, W.C. Pratt, thanked "the members of the Bar for the splendid assistance they have given us in this behalf," referring to the recent announcement that the government was to build a courthouse later that year.[90] Years later, the local superintendent for the Department of Public Works, A.H. McQuarrie, reminisced about the crusade:

> I think it was in or about 1925 that demands for a Court House became very insistent and the government decided to take some definite action. Perhaps it was unfortunate that it should have been in that particular year, for the late Dan Macdonald, superintendent of buildings, wished to construct a brick building. That year, however, his branch had an over-expenditure of more than $100,000, a serious state of affairs at that time. He therefore had plans made for the more moderate present building and tenders were called for. But the bids were so much over what he was given permission to spend that he was about to make further changes in the plans when Mr. Arnett, a contractor, offered to build it for a price which these days would be the cost of a five or six room bungalow.[91]

McQuarrie's description of the new hall of justice was quite accurate. Of wood frame construction on a concrete foundation, the courthouse was a simple two-storey building with a moderately pitched hip roof, measuring thirty-four by forty-eight feet.[92] There was very little in the way of architectural elaboration or direct stylistic references. The entire building was finished with stucco, with no stone or even brick trim work. The sole decorative elements were a pair of small parapet gables, one on the roof above the entrance, a second gracing the porch that projected from the facade, which also featured a plain stilted arch around the doorway. The vaguely castelate gables announced the official nature of the structure to passers-by. The interior conformed to the usual courthouse design, with the offices of the sheriff and clerk on the main floor along with a library and district judge's office. One thing missing was holding cells for prisoners awaiting trial, although there was a side entrance where defendants could be brought in and a rear stairs. The basement was given over to storage and several offices. The main courtroom was upstairs along with the judge's chamber, which doubled as a sleeping area, and antechambers for the jury, witnesses, and barristers. As had become standard, the judge was able to enter his quarters by the rear stairwell and the courtroom by a door behind his bench. The interior decor was quite basic with wood trim setting off white plaster walls.[93] The projected cost was about $19,500 including furniture.[94]

It was a very utilitarian structure, which was to serve as a model for the hall of justice in Hanna built the following year. Designed under the supervision of D.E. Macdonald, Superintendent of Buildings, it was a far cry from the architectural glories of an earlier era. Although the office of Provincial Architect was no more,

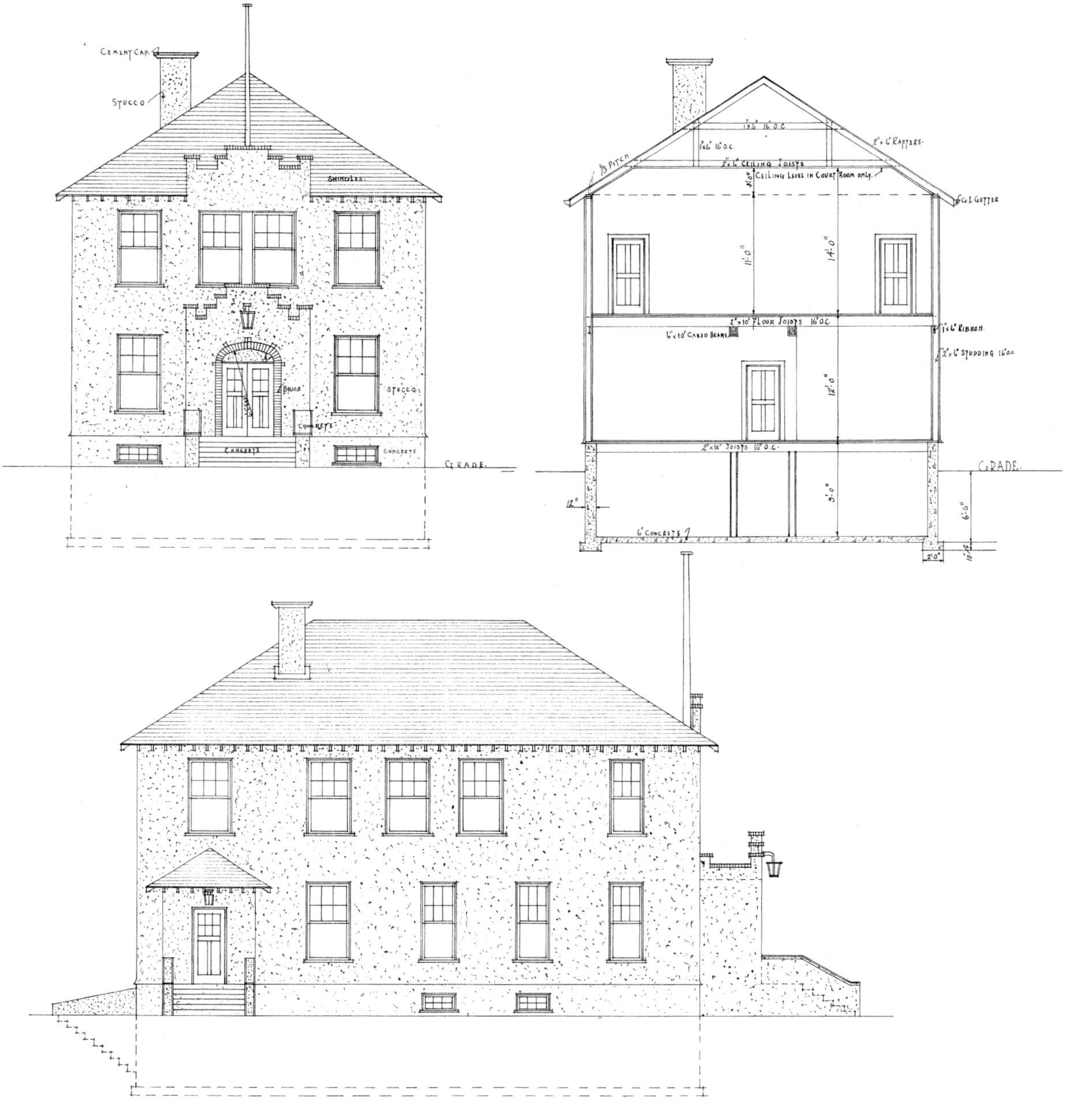


the department still maintained a staff of draftsmen, and could produce in-house designs of some sophistication, if called upon. In the case of Grande Prairie, they weren't and didn't. The new court building was very much a throwback to the frontier courthouses of the Territorial days, such as had been built in Medicine Hat, and in fact the floor plan was based directly on the old Macleod courthouse. It was intended to be inexpensive, easily built from local materials, with no pretensions to architectural distinction.

*More frontier justice: elevations and section, Grande Prairie Courthouse, 1928. PAA*

The announcement of the new courthouse was greeted with approval in Grande Prairie. It was not, however, very popular in other parts of the region. The Peace River Board of Trade wrote the Attorney General immediately: "We trust that the newspaper article referred to is premature and that your department will undertake to place this public building at some more accessible point as the maps clearly show that very little of the Peace River Judicial District lies either south or west of Grande Prairie."[95] The arguments put forward by the businessmen of Peace River were much like those heard years before in other parts of the province when towns competed for judicial facilities. Grande Prairie – of course – was inconveniently placed to serve the district, while Peace River – of course – was right in the centre of the region, and much more equitable to the district as a whole. "We believe that a public building such as this should be centrally located in justice to all, and no partiality shown."[96] It was convenient that Peace River was obviously the best placed to fulfill this goal. The burghers of Peace River were destined for disappointment, but their board of trade was galvanized to campaign for their own courthouse.[97]

There must have been fear in Peace River that the courthouse in Grande Prairie would automatically make its rival the headquarters for the judicial district and also home for the resident judge. The whole matter of the judge was even more of a sore point in the area than the courthouse. Although a Peace River Judicial District had been created in 1920, the district court judge still lived in Edmonton. As far as the Record was concerned, "we have practically none of the advantages to which such a district entitles us through having no resident judge." The citizens of Grande Prairie agreed wholeheartedly. But as to where to locate him – the Record felt that a judge in the south part of the Peace River country was almost as inaccessible as if he were in Edmonton.[98] As matters went, the district never received a resident judge: the Attorney General reorganized the district courts in 1933 into two jurisdictions, Northern and Southern Alberta, and removed all the resident judges, basing them in Calgary, Edmonton, and Lethbridge. This ended once and for all the bickering over judges.

Once the government decided to build a courthouse in Grande Prairie, a site had to be chosen. This was a tricky proposition: it was usually a very contentious decision within a growing town. With the announcement of the project, property owners quickly came forward, eager to supply the necessary lots. Finding a suitable site became the responsibility of A.H. McQuarrie:

> The next thing to come up in an effort to cut costs was a suggestion from Premier Brownlee that the town be asked to donate a site and the request was passed on to me for action. I selected the two lots on which the building stands and to which the town had title and with reluctance I took the matter up with the Mayor, pointing out that the Public Works Department had given its reservation to the School Board for the public school … and that under the circumstances it would appear that the Town Council should donate the lots. This was agreed to and arrangements were made accordingly. For reasons which I thought necessary to forestall an agitation for a change, I suggested that no publicity be given the matter.
>
> Most people wanted the Court House built down town [sic]. Some wanted it built on the lot on which the (Forbes) Presbyterian Church was built later. It,

> however, was a noisy part of the town and that would have been objected to by the Attorney General's Department. The ground was low there and it would have been hard to have kept the basement dry without sewage.[99]

McQuarrie did not make the decision entirely on his own: the Attorney General and the Minister of Public Works had passed his suggestions on to Hugh Allen, the MLA for Peace River, for his approval.[100] Presumably Allen had the final say. The donated lots were across from Grande Prairie's first permanent school, the Montrose Public School, on the northwest corner of 99th Street and 101st Avenue. The residents considered it an odd location – the Herald would later make light of its proximity to the school – and inconvenient.[101] McQuarrie remembered being on site with the contractors when "one of the town's businessmen who was going by, stopped to enquire what was going on and when he was informed that the Court House was being started he proceeded to 'blow his top' about putting the Court House so far out of town and ended his tirade by saying 'It is about what we can expect from a Homesteader(UFA) Government.'"[102]

Courthouses were inevitably political buildings, and Grande Prairie's edifice was no exception. In constructing it, the department violated one of the most important rules of public works: hire locally, whenever possible. Although courthouse contracts were always awarded on tender, both the Dominion and provincial governments had managed to give the majority of the earlier courthouses to local builders. This was no longer the case after World War I. For Grande Prairie's hall of justice, an Edmonton builder, J.L. Arnett, was given the contract on July 28, 1928, on a tender of $14,410, the lowest of four submitted.[103] The contractors in Grande Prairie only discovered this on July 31, when Superintendent Macdonald and Arnett stepped off the train onto the station platform and proceeded to stake out the site the following day.[104] Reaction was swift. Within days, a letter arrived in Macdonald's office from Spencer and Campbell, contractors, expressing the "strong feeling of surprise and resentment by every Builder and Contractor in this district that they were not allowed the oppertunity[sic] of tendering for the erection of the courthouse."[105] The local building fraternity felt they had been slighted, and were surprised given the government's usual policy:

> It has invariable[sic] been the rule to allow the local men at least the same treatment as those outside of the district in the tendering but on this occasion we were ignored and the first thing we were to know was the outside contractor arriving from Edmonton with the contract in his pocket. None of us consider this a square deal and would like to know the opinion of the Department concerning this departure from the long established precedent.[106]

The Department of Public Works was forced to account for itself. The deputy minister replied to Spencer and Campbell in September, stating that before awarding the contract the superintendent had made inquiries in Grande Prairie about contractors and forwarded plans to one of the lumber companies.[107] Spencer was not mollified: he immediately checked with the only lumberyard in town, the Frontier, which disclaimed any knowledge of plans or tenders.[108] Finally McDonald himself wrote to Spencer and Campbell, to say that he had indeed wired Frontier Lumber to get recommendations for local contractors. The company had forwarded the name of Frank Spinney, and plans and specifications had been sent to him so that he could prepare a tender, which the department had never received despite several telegrams.[109] At this point, it chose from the tenders on hand. McDonald had found the parcel at Frontier when he came in July, unopened. The Building Superintendent was tough-minded and not easily cowed, and as far as McDonald was concerned that closed the matter: "As the contract has been awarded and work commenced I do not think there is any need for further controversy in this matter."[110]

Departmental records do bear McDonald's story out, but it was very odd that Public Works had neglected to advertise the contract in any of the local papers. The reason for this oversight lay in one crucial item the superintendent neglected to mention to Spencer and Campbell. Before contacting Frontier, McDonald had wired the department's local inspector, A.H. McQuarrie, to ask him about local contractors. McQuarrie sent a terse reply: "Do not care to recommend any Grand Prairie contractor for that class of work and if contract given to local man strictest supervision will be necessary."[111] McDonald, perhaps to his credit, tried to get a second opinion on the matter, but obviously he decided against throwing open the tender, thus limiting the participation of local contractors. The sole telegram on file from Frontier also recommended Harry Shaver, not Frank Spinney, a name unfamiliar in the area – could there have been some subterfuge on McDonald's part? Some local residents certainly thought so! In any case, the whole affair left some bad feelings behind in Grande Prairie. The UFA representative for Peace River, Hugh Allen, received a scathing letter from one C.S. Kezer, who remarked:

> My idea of voting the Farmer's ticket was because I want to see everybody have an equal chance and an honest deal and I believed you were the man that would do your best to see that we had a square deal. I believe you will look into this for it was certainly a raw deal.[112]

As McDonald had said, though, the contract had been let and the building started. The department had not been able to design a building within the $15,000 allocated in the estimates for 1928, for although Arnett's tender was within the amount, McDonald estimated another $3,500 would be necessary for the plumbing, heating, and electrical systems. When he approved acceptance of Arnett's tender, the Minister of Public Works also gave permission for the department to apply for a warrant to cover the extra expense, which was put before the legislature in the fall and approved. Work proceeded swiftly on the new building, perhaps too swiftly: complaints were laid when the plasterers were seen working on Sunday. This was in contravention of the Lord's Day Act, and hard as it is to believe today, the Attorney General's department proceeded to charge the contractor after the Minister of Public Works disavowed his department from Arnett's actions.

The new courthouse opened to general acclaim in late spring. It had been finished at a cost of over $24,000, significantly more than the original budget.[113] There were plans for a grand opening with a number of dignitaries. Despite the sentiments of the press, the building was a disappointment to local boosters, small, plain and not located in the central business district. As with court buildings before it and after it, the Grand Prairie edifice did not live up to the expectations and ambitions of the locale it was to serve. However, the boom of the late 1920s ended soon after the courthouse was finished. For the next twenty years, the Peace River Country stagnated. It was spared the horrible droughts of the south and saw a little growth as displaced homesteaders moved north to start over, but remained a quiet corner of the province until the 1950s. The courthouse was left as it was, with the only modification being the addition of sewage and water service when it became available in the 1930s.[114] The parsimony of Brownlee and the UFA looked eminently reasonable in hindsight.

## Epilogue

The Grande Prairie courthouse remained the sole edifice for the courts north of Edmonton for over two decades. Although it was not much larger than a big house, the town was lucky to have it. Other settlements made do with rented quarters or space in other provincial buildings. In Peace River, the headquarters of the district, the court used the local police barracks, then the United Church and the Boyd Theatre depending on availability.[115]

By the early 1950s, Grande Prairie was growing fast. Pending as well was a re-organization that would see two new judicial districts formed, Grande Prairie and Peace River. In a moment of foresight, the government decided to construct new courthouses in both towns, using the same design and realizing some economies of scale. Under the direction of Chief Architect H.A. Henderson, the Department of Public Works planned a pair of two-storey steel and concrete structures, laid out in an L-shape. Although the building was a relatively uninspired example of modernist institutional architecture, it had considerably more presence than the little courthouse, and a marble stairway and lobby and polished oak woodwork guaranteed the new building would be "in keeping with the dignity of Canadian law."[116] The new courthouse was well equipped and even included sleeping suites, for both judge and justice came to Grande Prairie on circuit and needed overnight accommodation.

The contract was given to Poole Construction on October 18, 1955 on a bid of $247,228, with the courthouse projected to cost $320,000 altogether when finished.[117] Work began immediately and the building was officially opened September 27, 1957. A mob of dignitaries, including the Minister of Public Works, John Hartley, the local MLA, Ira Mclaughlin, the Deputy Attorney General, H.J. Wilson, Chief Judge Nelles V. Buchanan of the District Court, and Supreme Court Justice E.B. Wilson gathered at the new courthouse with a scarlet-clad honour guard of the

*A step back to the past: Grand Prairie's Courthouse, c. 1929 GPRM, 74.74.28*

*A step into the future: new Grand Prairie Courthouse, c. 1957 GPRM, 05.03.30*

RCMP.[118] Courthouses in Alberta, however, seemed to have a useful life of about twenty-five years. In 1980, with Grande Prairie now a major city, a third structure for the law courts designed by Field, Field and Field of Grande Prairie was begun and the second court building turned into an arts centre.

As for Grande Prairie's original courthouse, it survived until 1972. Public Works and City of Grande Prairie had negotiated a land and building swap to provide a site for its replacement. The city gladly donated four lots directly north of the original courthouse in exchange for the old stucco building, which they also agreed to move, and council ratified the arrangement on July 20, 1954.[119] The new courthouse was built beside the old, and when the former was ready, the 1929 building was moved across the street and turned into a library.

The first courthouse was placed on skids and moved across the road in June 1957. The contractor commented: "Not a rotten board in that building. The building is in sound shape."[120] After serving as the town's library, the courthouse became a drop-in centre. The wheels of progress, however, eventually rolled right over the old stucco building. It was demolished in May 1972 to make way for the Nordic Court, Grande Prairie's first high-rise commercial development. Six storeys high, the glass and concrete symbolized the beginning of a new boom for the province. Few were interested in looking backward and preserving a forgotten piece of their city's heritage.

# HANNA

Although it was on the opposite side of the province, Hanna shared the frontier atmosphere of Grande Prairie. The dry country around the small hamlet, known as the Hand Hills, was slow to fill up with settlers. Like Grande Prairie, Hanna benefited from the spurt of courthouse design and construction by the United Farmers of Alberta during their second term in office. It is perhaps not entirely coincidence that all four UFA courthouses were built in jurisdictions under party control, and in towns that had strong ties to the rural agricultural hinterlands around them. Yet as the Liberals had done before them, the UFA also tried to predict where facilities would be needed and provide them in an economical fashion. In the case of Hanna, the edifice built by the government was more than just a courthouse, housing other departments and services. Thus, while the courts in Hanna were not so busy as to desperately require a purpose-built facility – in fact, rather the opposite was true – a domicile for the courts was an opportunity for the UFA to create space for other government offices, build for the future needs of the judiciary, and provide some largesse for their faithful supporters.

## Hanna – The Early Days

The first homesteads in the Hand Hills were registered in 1909, mostly by Americans who flooded into Alberta in the latter part of the immigration boom.[121] Many were experienced farmers who had sold their operations down in the United States to take advantage of the generous terms offered by the Dominion government for homesteaders. Around 1912, squatters appeared on the spot that would become Hanna. J.C. Trenaman, who would become one of the town's leading citizens, was the first recorded resident.[122] By the end of the year, Trenaman had enough neighbours that Hanna could graduate from hamlet to village. A board of trade had preceded the village council, but in early January 1913 the first civic government was constituted.[123] Situated as it was on the right-of-way for the Canadian Northern Railway, the villagers astutely named their home after D.B. Hanna, then president of the company.[124] How could the railroad possibly ignore a settlement that was the namesake of its chief?

The coming of the railroad filled the new village with great hopes. The residents hoped that at the very least Hanna might be made a divisional point and perhaps maybe a major junction for branch lines. In 1914, the townsite was officially registered, and shortly thereafter the village incorporated with a claimed population of nine hundred.[125] Whether or not naming itself Hanna helped, the town was indeed made a divisional headquarters when the railroad came through in 1914, with a freight yard and a roundhouse, much to the delight of local boosters. Although the flood of settlers dried up the same year and the dreams of the towns-

*Law office soon to be judicial office: Trenaman Block, Hanna, 1912. HDM, PH-402*

folk of overtaking Medicine Hat as a regional centre never materialized, Hanna was on a sound footing before the recession after World War I. Nearby Drumheller became a competitor for new businesses and government largesse, but the community held its own, a typical prairie town serving the local farmers.

## The Courts in Hanna

Not long after Hanna's incorporation the District Court of Calgary began to visit the hamlet. Judge A.A. Carpenter held the first recorded assize on October 21, 1914.[126] Court was held in Fleming's Hall for the first few years.[127] It was a small commercial building on Main Street, with a hall on the second floor above stores. Later the court switched to Shacker's Theatre, the main source of entertainment for the small town.[128] There the court shared billing with country dances, lectures, recitals, and movies. In some respects it was fitting: in a small prairie town, court day was yet another source of entertainment and often attracted large crowds.

Hanna may have been a town of recent vintage, but that did not prevent its citizenry from pursuing the services that were felt proper for a growing regional centre. The placing of Hanna in the Judicial District of Calgary almost guaranteed that the administration of justice would become contentious. It was the same problem of convenience and expense that had beset the justice system since the Territorial days. Despite the fact Hanna was on a rail line to Calgary, the city was

still some 140 miles distant and there were no officers of the court in the town. The litigators of Hanna therefore had to wait until a judge came to town to present applications to the court, a difficult task when the District Court might only be in town for a couple of days. Otherwise lawyers had to go into Calgary or enlist the services of a city lawyer. For Supreme Court, everyone as a matter of course had to go to the city, as the court did not sit in Hanna. Aside from filing the relevant paperwork, in both civil and criminal matters plaintiffs, defendants, complainants, and witnesses had to go to the Calgary courthouse.

*(left) Corner Drug Store, previously Fleming Hall, used by the court. HDM, PH-88*

*(left) Another court venue: Shacker's Theatre. HDM, PH-420*

Once the war was over, civic leaders lost little time in bringing their demands to the attention of the provincial government in classic booster fashion. A number of other issues, such as telephone service, required the government's attention, and thus a delegation was duly formed by the board of trade and packed off to Edmonton early in 1919. It got results. The local paper expressed some surprise when the delegates reported that Hanna would be the headquarters for an entirely new judicial district: the delegates had only been asking for simple sub-district status.[129] Part of it was simply good timing: the Attorney-General, J.R. Boyle, had started a sizable overhaul of the judicial system which would include adding new districts. The quick and positive response the delegates from Hanna received, however, is quite surprising.

After considering the matter for several months, the government came to a final decision in August, and announced that a new judicial and registration district would be created on September 15 with Hanna as the centre. Initially called Acadia, after the village where the local member of the legislature lived, the district was renamed to reflect its headquarters after several years of court papers going to the wrong town.

Given the amount of business in the court, the creation of a district looked very much like a tactic to placate the voters of the area. It was a relatively peaceable area – District Court usually only required a single day to dispose of its docket, and it was a matter of note if proceedings ran longer.[130] Accordingly, one man was appointed as Sheriff and Clerk of Court in Hanna, looking after both the District and Supreme Court. A.R. Dickson had been the Sheriff in Wetaskiwin (as well as a former mayor there) and was an experienced official.[131] It was a portent of things to come throughout the province, as the Attorney General's department realized that many of the judicial districts did not require more than one official to handle the workload. Dickson arrived promptly, only a week after the new district was officially announced, and rented the former offices of lawyer C.A. Coughlin.[132] He hired masons to build a vault and renovated the building to suit his needs. A judge for the new district was appointed in November, John Douglas Reginald Stewart, a Calgary lawyer just recently discharged from the military. It was four months, however, before the new judge made his first appearance in Hanna.

The citizens of Hanna were jubilant over the new judicial district. The Hanna Herald summed up local feeling, commenting that "No little importance can be attached to the setting up of this new district. A judge, sheriff, clerk of court and assistants will be located here, and Hanna will incidentally be put on the map as a result of the new district."[133] The advantages and prestige of being a judicial headquarters was still very much a prize for civic boosters. The opening of the District Court on February 25 was a major event.[134] Most of the local bar attended, and a dinner was given for the judge at the National Hotel attended by the notables of Hanna and area. Much satisfaction was expressed, naturally, at the fact Hanna was now a full-fledged district.

It would, however, be some months before the Supreme Court came to town. For all its elevation in status, Hanna remained a judicial backwater. Chief Justice Harvey found it difficult to persuade a judge to go to the Hand Hills, and was sympathetic to his colleagues: "We could hardly expect to hold sittings of the Supreme Court there unless the accomodation [sic] is suitable and there is enough work to justify the additional expense."[135] The following November, with even greater fanfare, the higher court made its first visit to the town.[136] The indomitable Justice Walsh, who enjoyed circuit more than most of his colleagues, presided. At the end of the assizes, all repaired to the National for another banquet, this time attended by other notables such as James Muir, President of the Law Society, and Leonard Brockington, city solicitor for Calgary. A sad note was interjected into the affair when a toast was made to Sheriff Dickson, who had died that summer after less than a year in office.

## The Courthouse

The main concern of the citizens of Hanna had been with improving the judiciary in their parts, not with a courthouse per se. Once they had obtained a judicial district, however, the townsfolk fully expected a hall of justice would follow in short order. When nothing had been heard about a government building by the spring of 1921, a delegation was sent to Edmonton. Their first priority was getting money for waterworks and sewers, but the courthouse was a close second.

In short order, the delegates talked to Attorney General Boyle, Public Works Minister Archie Maclean, and Provincial Treasurer and acting Premier Charles R. Mitchell. All were effusive with promises that a building would be shortly forthcoming. The delegates were told the government was contemplating a provincial building, including a telephone exchange and police barracks. The ministers promised a site would be purchased that year and a building erected no later than the following year, and Mitchell "gave our committee just such assurances as they sought."[137] If any of the delegates had remembered the debacle over the Medicine Hat courthouse eight years before, they might not have been so confident about Mitchell's assurances – and no one seemed to realize an election was forthcoming.

It is tempting to view the promises of the Stewart government as merely election year ploys, but as was usually the case with the Liberals, it was also a matter of policy. As the headquarters of a judicial district, Hanna certainly "rated" a courthouse, and this had been the policy under Sifton, Stewart's predecessor. However, the enthusiasm of the Liberals for new public buildings faltered with a worsening economy.

Despite this, and the obliteration of the Liberals in the 1921 election, optimism remained high in Hanna. Hand Hills had gone UFA, as had the Hanna Herald. When the new Minister of Public Works came to Hanna that September, the paper could hardly contain itself. Under a headline reading "Does Minister's Visit Mean Early Decision Regarding Erection of Court House," the Herald commented:

> When Alex Ross, Minister of Public Works in the new U.F.A. Government, calls around on a tour of inspection one naturally pinches himself, sits up and takes notice, for is not this the new minister's first tour since the election?
>
> No less a person, however, than the minister himself paid a visit to Hanna yesterday. Moreover he was accompanied by Mr. Blakey, Provincial Architect. An inspection was made of the present site of the Sheriff's Office, also a general survey of the townsite [sic] with a view of reporting on the new site and proposed courthouse.
>
> The wheels of action may have already started. Here's hoping that they have. And it will be a mighty good stroke of business on the part of the Farmer's Government, too.[138]

The Herald and the town would be sadly disappointed. Although the courthouse at Blairmore was built, other promised edifices, including Hanna, were dropped. It was a simple matter of economy. Hope for a courthouse remained alive, and in 1923 the Herald tried to interest the town in donating a site out of the property it had seized for tax arrears to the government as an incentive.[139] The appearance of Daniel E. McDonald in Hanna in the fall, however, was the death knell for any immediate action on a provincial building. He was there to finalize a lease on the Trenaman block on Main Street and 2nd Avenue for the sheriff's office and supervise some renovations.[140] As for the court, it continued renting I.F. Shaker's theatre for sittings, as it had done for several years. While not the sort of setting thought suitable for a court of justice, at least everyone could be assured a seat at Shacker's.

---

### THE HILSABECK TRIAL

Every seat was needed in Shacker's Theatre for the June 1924 murder trial of William A. Hilsabeck. It was a case that seized the imaginations of the people of Hanna, involving the brutal beating of his young son by the accused. Despite the horror in the community at the crime, it still exerted a twisted fascination and there was no shortage of spectators over the several days the trial lasted.

It was the sort of thing that happened all too frequently in isolated farm holds on the prairies. The Hilsabeck family lived in abject poverty in the Clivale District, two adults and four children in a tiny one-room shack. During the winter of 1923, the family often went without food. Arthur L. Smith, one of the great defence counsels of the time, related to the jury that Hilsabeck himself had a hard upbringing and suffered from severe mental problems.

On January 3, 1924, his two oldest children, Irene and Archer, had been playing with his violin and got grease on it and the case. The children, who were not supposed to touch it, had somehow got a key to the case. Enraged, Hilsabeck proceeded to beat them, first with a riding whip, then a board, and finally burnt them with matches when they could not produce the key. It was not the first time they had been whipped, but the ferocity of the attack was beyond anything the children had ever experienced. Archer, aged seven, died that evening in the presence of another farmer, Henry Van Kirckvorde. Another neighbour alerted the local APP Constable, who arrested Hilsabeck the next day.

As far as the facts of the case went, it was simple. Although only Hilsabeck's wife Nellie and daughter were eyewitnesses, the accused himself had admitted to the whipping to his neighbours and, overcome with grief, voluntarily provided a confession to Constable Vernon. Smith's line of defence was insanity. The testimony of Nellie and Irene showed the violent temper of Hilsabeck and a history of beatings that had been getting more severe. The defence produced other witnesses to show Hilsabeck was prone to sudden unprovoked rages. The age of the psychologist in the courtroom had already dawned. Smith had expert witnesses testify as to Hilsabeck's mental condition, while the Crown prosecutor, A.A. McGillivray, did the same in rebuttal. The issue for the jury to decide was not whether Hilsabeck had been unable not only to control himself on that winter night but whether he even could understand what he had done was wrong.

Justice Tweedie, the former partner in law of prosecutor McGillivary, gave instructions to the jury described by the local paper as "one of the fairest charges ever made."[141] After only a half-hour, the verdict was returned at 8:30 p.m. – guilty of murder. Tweedie had no choice but to pass sentence of death in front of the packed theatre. Hilsabeck was led away to be taken to Fort Saskatchewan. In the end, his sentence was commuted to life imprisonment due to the lack of premeditation in the crime. Just as McGillivray himself had argued in his summation, the conviction of the unfortunate farmer was hailed in the *Edmonton Bulletin* as a step toward the proper legal protection of children.

For the moment, the matter was allowed to rest where it was. The stagnation brought on by the post-war recession lasted until the middle of the decade. Part of the problem was drought. In the agricultural economy that still characterized Alberta, when the farmers faced difficult years everyone felt it. After bumper crops and high prices during the war, low prices and miserable growing conditions were quite a shock. The area around Hanna was particularly prone to drought, and for several years people had other things on their minds than courthouses. The local board of trade was one casualty. The government also suffered. Although handily re-elected in 1926 under the leadership of John Brownlee, the United Farmers still struggled with deficits. That began to change as economic prospects suddenly improved. Magically, the UFA was able to post a surplus in their second mandate. They also began to spend more money on public works.

In Hanna, a threat to the town's status as a judicial headquarters reminded the residents of the need for a courthouse. Early in 1926, rumours began circulating that the Attorney General's office was planning to make Drumheller the centre of the judicial district. The board lost no time in sending a strongly worded protest to the Attorney General and the local member of the legislature, Gordon Forster.[142] The citizens of Hanna were not being excessively paranoid. At the end of the summer, the registration district of Hanna, coterminous with the judicial district, was abolished and moved to Drumheller. This innovation did not last long – a deputation from Hanna that included Forster and representatives of the UFA local sped to Edmonton and buttonholed acting Premier George Hoadley.[143] The result was two Orders-in-Council that established judicial and registration districts at both Drumheller and Hanna. The possession of a courthouse would serve to make the arrangements of the court in Hanna more permanent, and thus the town began to agitate for a hall of justice once again.

Accordingly, at the beginning of 1928, the town council offered a free site for a provincial building on the condition that it would be built within a year.[144] Hanna was not alone in lobbying for a courthouse. There was a clear need for more court facilities, especially on the edges of the province, areas that had still been frontiers before the war but now had become settled. Grande Prairie had kept up intermittent demands for a building and was rewarded in 1928, which must have been heartening to the citizens of Hanna.

On March 20, 1929 the government telegraphed Gordon Foster, the Hand Hills MLA, to announce that a public building would be constructed that summer to the tune of $30,000.[145] It was a banner headline in the Herald. Frederick H. MacDonald, the senior draftsman in the building department of Public Works, began working on a design to go with the announcement.[146] It was a relatively simple task, as the Grande Prairie building provided a handy template. By April a set of plans had been produced, showing a two-storey, L-shaped building that included space for the Alberta Provincial Police as well as local government offices. Interestingly, after the plans were publicly unveiled a month later, the Hanna Herald claimed the new edifice would be "built of brick and stone."[147] The extant plans showed plainly that it would be stucco. Wishful thinking on the part of the paper and other local boosters? Or did the government tell the locals one thing while fully intending something different? There is no sign of a second set of drawings showing a different brick structure, but the newspaper article invites speculation. Was the Hanna building to be a smaller version of the more substantial brick courthouses at Red Deer and Vegreville, built shortly thereafter? Or was it, as built, a twin to the modest structure in Grande Prairie?

The courthouse in Hanna was larger than the building erected in Grande Prairie, but was essentially two separate structures, the main courthouse and the annex. It had a concrete foundation, and a wood frame was reinforced with several steel posts and beams. There was no internal communication between the two parts of the building. The annex was intended for the APP detachment in the town and to house other government offices. The entire building was quite small. Shaped in an "L," it was fifty-eight feet wide and fifty-four feet deep, with the main facade about thirty-five feet wide. Two storeys, with a finished basement and a shingled hip roof, it had a decidedly residential appearance. On the facade, a stepped and rounded Mission-style parapet with an imitation stone cap above the main entrance was one of the sole bits of decoration. The main entrance had a small projecting porch. Unlike the northern courthouse, the porch had a gable roof with an enclosed end, with two engaged columns and an attractive fanlight transom window above the double doors. The annex had a separate entrance facing the street, while a sunken stairwell provided an outside door for the annex basement and the police cells. It was not an imposing building, and the minor decorative elements only just saved it from total anonymity.

The internal layout was somewhat cramped, reminiscent of the small Territorial courthouses at Macleod and Medicine Hat, and more or less identical to Grande Prairie. Immediately inside the main entrance of the courthouse was the office of the clerk on the left, and the stairs up to the courtroom on the right. Next came the general office, behind that the library, and at the back of the building the district judge's office, bathrooms, and stairs to the second floor. The courtroom took up most of the second storey. At the front of the building was a witness room with a door into the courtroom. At the other end of the court there were entrances to the barristers' chamber and the jury room. These also had doors out into a private hallway connecting to the stairs. The judge's room was back here as well, allowing him to enter directly to the bench by means of another small door. This room also served as the visiting judge's quarters, and was quite Spartan.

From the outset, the courthouse in Hanna was intended to function as a general-purpose government building. In the annex the basement was given over to cells and an office, while the main floor was the quarters for the duty constable in Hanna. The second floor was divided into four offices for other government departments. The division of the structure into courthouse and annex allowed the province to locate its offices in one place while keeping non-judicial traffic out of the court facility. The Hanna courthouse shows the increasing temptation to make these buildings into multi-purpose facilities, hearkening back to the older county courthouses of eastern Canada and the United States. It was an economic solution in many respects to the problem of providing office space for government departments. In this regard, the design of the Hanna building was a neat solution, whatever its shortcomings as a courthouse.

Now that they had a building to build, the government needed a place to put it. The town of Hanna had already offered a site, and the Department of Public Works was happy to take them up on it. The town council had at least two locations in mind for the hoped-for courthouse. The ever-canny Daniel McDonald, the Superintendent of Buildings, knew very well the way local politics could intrude in choice of a site. He decided to have an agent look things over before he went out to Hanna. It was well that McDonald took the action he did, as the Hanna Chamber of Commerce lost no time in making its preference clear. Writing directly to the Minister of Public Works, O.L. McPherson, the chamber suggested lots 1 to 9 of block 10, which would put the building on Main Street and 2nd Avenue.[148] The minister obligingly approved the site.

McDonald had other ideas. There was certain amount of friction between the Superintendent and his minister over choosing sites for buildings. When he came down to Hanna to view the location, McDonald immediately decided he didn't like it. After talking to the council and some of the residents, he made his own choice: four lots in block 29, with two more available if the town seized them for tax recovery. This had been the site originally chosen by the town council.[149] McDonald had good reasons for rejecting the other site: it would require grading that would add considerably to the cost of the building, and he also thought it was too restricted. The new site was open and would have ample space for a landscaped lawn, an important consideration. But one also suspects that McDonald was not pleased that a site had been chosen without consulting him, and took a certain pleasure in stirring things up by deciding on a new location. McDonald did not like decisions to be made on matters in his jurisdiction without being duly consulted, as the subsequent to-do over the site for Red Deer's courthouse makes clear. The Hanna courthouse would stand facing Main Street between 4th and 5th Avenue.

When McDonald came down to Hanna that May, he arrived knowing that the contract, on his recommendation to Premier Brownlee, had gone to B.P. Scanlan of Medicine Hat for $17,800, the lowest bid received.[150] McDonald visited the Hanna Herald office himself to break the news, perhaps to head off the sort of grumbling that had been heard in Grande Prairie about the contract going to an outsider.[151] In this case, the tender had been well advertised and two local builders had put in bids. One, A.W. Stubbs, had recently been given the contract for the telephone exchange, so McDonald could, if necessary, claim to be fairly treating the good folk of Hanna. In any case, with the new site staked out, it was not long before the contractor started work. Under McDonald's regime, the department ran very efficiently, and generally no time was wasted getting projects up and running. While Scanlan excavated a foundation, the department let the contracts for the plumbing to Ideal Heating and Plumbing of Edmonton and the wiring to William Frakes of Hanna.

One advantage of simple buildings for the courts was that they could be erected with great speed. The Hanna courthouse was ready for its first court by November 1929. There were no major problems during construction, aside from some delays in obtaining millwork for the interior from Calgary, probably due to the construction boom the province was experiencing. Rumours surfaced around Hanna after the building was finished that workers and subtrades did not get paid, but the local inspector for Public Works could not find grounds for any complaints.[152] Except one. A plasterer from Cardston made himself a nuisance for several months, claiming he had not been fully paid by Scanlan. McDonald duly corresponded with the contractor, who claimed that he had settled the account in what he thought was a reasonable fashion. When the plasterer, J.C. Shaw, had his lawyer

*Hanna's pride: the newly completed courthouse, 1929. HDM, PH-555*

return Scanlan's cheque to McDonald with the threat of a lien against the courthouse, the superintendent did not mince words. He replied: "Our buildings, as you should know as a Solicitor, are not subject to lien so that part of it does not worry us to any extent, and would advise Shaw to take this matter up with Scanlan ... as I have no further interest in the matter and Scanlan has been completely paid up for the job."[153] As usual, McDonald did not allow anyone to browbeat him. Ironically, almost fifteen years later, Shaw's lien would resurface when it was discovered that the government did not have clear title to the grounds of the courthouse.

The new edifice was not quite complete when the District Court sat in it on November 7, 1929.[154] A civil case involving a stray stallion was heard to open the new courthouse. Two weeks later, the Supreme Court, with Justice Ives presiding, visited for the fall assizes and the official opening of the courthouse. As was traditional, he complimented the town on the new building. One remark throws considerable light on the difficulties that faced the judges on circuit, and why proper courthouses with amenities like sleeping quarters were so important:

> It was not, he stated, so much a question of comfort as of suitability and convenience, that in staying in a hotel to which also came some of the jurymen, parties and witnesses, a judge could not avoid at times overhearing remarks concerning some case being dealt with at the moment, not intended for his ears, and which in spite of himself and being human might almost unconsciously have some prejudicial effect.[155]

It might be noted that judicial impartiality was not the only concern of judges while on circuit. More than one could recount stories of being accosted in hotels by members of the public and harangued about one trial or another, encounters that could be annoying and sometimes a little frightening.

The docket before Ives was small. He discharged one William Sutherland, on charges of unlawfully assisting Joe Kelly by providing a getaway car for a robbery, on grounds of insufficient evidence of intent. Ives took the opportunity to warn Sutherland that he fully believed him guilty even if he couldn't convict him, telling the youngster "You are known by the company you keep." In a sign of the times, one of the cases Ives handled was a divorce proceeding. Up to 1922, divorces in Canada had to be obtained by a private Act in Parliament, but this had been changed by the adoption of the 1857 English Matrimonial Causes Act. This gave authority for divorce actions to the courts, and it was soon modified by the Marriage and Divorce Act. Separations and divorces, which hereto had been rare and the source of much social disapproval, would soon become ubiquitous, even in rural Hanna.

As for the new courthouse, it was not entirely perfect. It was somewhat small, even cramped. The sheriff soon found that it was very difficult to find a good spot for the jury in the courtroom. Either they couldn't see the witnesses, or the judge couldn't see them, or the judge could see them but couldn't see the witness.[156] Apparently the courthouse did not include a great deal in the way of furniture and fixing – the sheriff wanted a proper jury box he could place permanently. Jury trials in Hanna were rare, however, and they were stuck with a simple row of chairs.

The courthouse in Hanna was received for what it was: a utilitarian building, built along economical lines to serve a set purpose. Although it was not entirely unadorned and was very nicely positioned in the town, with its decidedly residential appearance it did not live up to the expectations most contemporaries had of the county courthouse. It paled in comparison to the Red Deer and even to the Vegreville courthouses that were built shortly afterward. They were substantial brick buildings, and although Vegreville did not receive the amount of architectural decoration lavished on Red Deer, they were both more along the lines of what people thought a courthouse should be.

There is a strange postscript to the story of the Hanna courthouse. The land underneath the courthouse was actually not the property of the provincial government until 1944. Somewhat surprisingly, given the usually efficient character of the Department of Public Works under Deputy Minister J.D. Robertson and Dan McDonald, the site was never properly transferred from the town of Hanna to the government. It was an omission finally caught fifteen years after the edifice was built, when the survey wing of the department was in the midst of a routine update of their books and realized they had no title on record for the Hanna courthouse.[157] And indeed, not only the town but a certain Cyrus F. Chamberlain of Minneapolis owned a lot used for the courthouse site, and to add insult to injury, the mechanic's lien filed by J.C. Shaw was still on the title to the lots. The head of surveys hesitated to appropriate the lots under the Public Works Act, which would involve too much paperwork, and it was not necessary as the town of Hanna was glad to co-operate.[158] The one lot held by Chamberlain already had a caveat filed against it by the town for taxes, and the secretary promised to start proceedings to seize it immediately. He did his best, however, to get the government to give a promise that the land would only be used for courthouse purposes. The department refused to be tied down to anything definite, but assured the town they did not anticipate any other use for the site: not exactly set in stone. The town acquiesced, and in May the government got the title to its land.

The concern of Hanna about the future use of the site was not unfounded. By the 1940s, only fifteen years after it had been built, there were persistent rumours the province might shut the courthouse and the town would lose its status as a judicial district. A delegation was sent to see Premier Manning in 1944, to impress upon him the importance of the facility to the local populace.[159] The following year the board of trade wrote Manning again to stress the amount of judicial work done in the courthouse. The premier's reply was a model of non-committal reassurance, saying almost nothing: "With respect to the Court House at Hanna, it is not the intention of the Government to make any change in the present arrangement during the coming year. In other words the service will be continued at Hanna as it is at present."[160]

Despite the Premier's blandishments, the town had good reason to be worried. Early in 1945, the Deputy Attorney General instructed the Department of Public Works to prepare the court building in Drumheller to receive the court records and library from Hanna. The local sheriff was quite alarmed by this idea and tried to dissuade his superior, informing him that there was insufficient room for his own district's records, much less Hanna's. George Monkman, the Deputy Minister at Public Works, duly sent down W.D. Stacey, the Superintendent of Buildings, to see about making the requested modifications. Stacey was mystified by the decision:

> ... from a building standpoint, whoever made this arrangement did not consider the building proposition, for this reason; the Court House in Drumheller was never built for a court house, but was intended originally for a Police Barracks ... no provision was made for the following: Vault, Witness Rooms, Jury Room, Law Library, etc. so that at Drumheller there are none of the above accommodations while at Hanna all these are in the Court House there, as this building was properly constructed for court facilities.[161]

Clearly there were communication problems between the two departments, as well as a certain amount of ignorance in the Attorney General's office about its own facilities. The ill-advised plan to amalgamate the two judicial districts was soon put to rest by the protests that immediately came from Hanna, and the courthouse remained in service for years to come.

FALL SESSIONS IN HANNA

Generally, the Supreme Court trial justices were not very enthusiastic about going on circuit. Stories abound about judges rushing through court calendars, insisting all cases be organized before they arrived, and adjourning anything where there might be a delay so that they wouldn't have to stay in Drumheller, or Lethbridge, or Vegreville any longer than necessary. There were some exceptions, however. The district around Hanna was famous for its bird hunting, and in the fall the judges who liked to hunt were glad to go to Hanna and hear cases. But not too many. Tom Malcolm, a court reporter for many years, remembered that when Justice Jimmy Cairns arranged to go on the "Autumn Assize" he made sure to schedule as few cases as possible, so as to leave as much time as possible for duck hunting.[162] Normally the most fastidious man imaginable, Cairns took great delight in hunting. Nor was he the only judge who did so. Chief Justice Campbell McLaurin was another great hunter, as was Val Milvain, Chief Justice in turn. McLaurin was allegedly not above adjourning a trial to free up time for some shooting.[163] A trip to Hanna usually featured the whole judicial party, including the local clerk of court, heading out to hunt – and drink – and then repairing back to the Hanna Hotel to drink some more. In the 1950s and 1960s, most of the judges drove out for assizes rather than take the train, greatly facilitating their shooting. Malcolm remembers that some of the judges were a terror as drivers. McLaurin and Harold Riley, in particular, had notorious reputations for speeding, but it was a rare cop who would try to write the Chief Justice of Alberta a ticket.

## Epilogue

Hanna's modest courthouse continued in use for almost forty years. Unlike Grande Prairie, Hanna never lived up to its promise as a regional centre. In 1951 the population stood at 2,027, and by 1971 it had only increased to around three thousand.[164] There was no huge demand to replace the old stucco building, and it soldiered on until 1982, when a new provincial building incorporating a courtroom and offices was finished.[165]

Some changes were made in the intervening period. After the RCMP left the building for modern quarters in 1968, the annex was turned over entirely to provincial offices.[166] In 1969, with the decision to empanel twelve-man juries instead of the old six, something had to be done to provide space for their deliberations without removing them from the courthouse. The solution was to pierce the wall into the annex, setting up a larger room with a separate washroom.[167] Ironically, the last jury trial had been in 1958. Along with this modification, however, a thorough and much-needed renovation was carried out.

Once new court facilities were available, the government followed a by-then established precedent and after some tough bargaining sold the building to the town for a nominal price.[168] The town of Hanna also petitioned the provincial government to turn it into a historic site, although this was never done.[169] The province did throw in a $35,000 renovation of the building before turning it over to the town, which installed the Hanna and District Allied Arts Association as a tenant. [170] The group had lobbied the town to acquire the courthouse for use as a fine arts centre.[171] The building was turned over to the association in July 1987.[172] Unfortunately, as is sadly too often the case with arts centres, long-term viability was a problem. After seven years, the association disbanded after running into financial difficulties.[173]

In 1999, unwilling to look after the mostly vacant building any longer, the town council jumped at an offer by a businessman in Calgary to purchase the courthouse.[174] The Hanna council and many citizens were happy that someone had come forward with an idea for the building that would ensure its survival, in this case a teahouse, antique store, and family residence.[175] However, the deal ignited the greatest controversy in the building's history. Former mayor and local lawyer Eugene Kush charged that the edifice had been turned over to the city specifically for use as a cultural centre, which the town had enshrined in its own bylaws. Organizing a new arts and culture association, he slapped a caveat on the property.[176] After arduous and sometimes acrimonious negotiations, the obstructions to the sale were removed and the courthouse was turned over to its new owners, who vowed to preserve it and with it an important part of Alberta's legal heritage.

---

## DRUMHELLER

When is a courthouse truly a courthouse? Drumheller had court facilities as early as 1921, housed in a building that became known to one and all as the courthouse. But in actuality, the town did not really have a proper courthouse until 1955. The original edifice was intended as a police barracks, with the courtroom was added as an after-thought, and not surprising the building was never very adequate for the job. However, it was enough to cause great apprehension in nearby Hanna, where the residents feared losing their judicial offices to their neighbour.

The Drumheller courthouse had much the same origins as Blairmore's. In 1920, the newly formed Alberta Provincial Police decided it needed better accommodation for several of its detachments. Drumheller was a rough-and-tumble mining community that had already been the scene of several nasty strikes, and the police gave it high priority:

> This is a very important point and at the present time we occupy a very small building there with four rooms. The cell is in the office and the three men there occupy the one spare room as a bedroom. We should have accommodation for at least eight men and stabling for three horses and one

car. As this is in the centre of a large mining district, we may have to send extra men there at any time.[177]

Some plans had been drawn up in 1920 by the Provincial Architect, but shelved for lack of funds.[178] The following year the Attorney General, John Brownlee, decided the police buildings were important enough to request the Department of Public Works to dip into its emergency funds for the proposed barracks. Drawings prepared in 1921 were revised the following year "to meet the demand for other public offices," referring to court facilities. [179] A courtroom and office for the police magistrate was added, which could also be used for sittings of the District Court. Surprisingly, the town of Drumheller showed little enthusiasm over the new structure. The property already owned as Public Works reserve in the town had been turned into a playground, and protests forced the government to buy a new site well outside the business district and almost half a kilometre from the nearest sewer line.[180] Most towns of the era couldn't be helpful enough to when a government building was proposed for their town. There may have been some hostility toward the police.

The contract in Drumheller was given to Foote & Allyn of Edmonton.[181] It is unclear exactly what the police barracks looked like. Plans for Drumheller and Blairmore had been prepared in 1921 but revised before construction took place. The one surviving plan of the original design shows details for the main entrance, which R.P. Blakey, the Provincial Architect, borrowed from his grand Medicine Hat courthouse finished two years before.[182] It had a segmented pediment, keystone and quoins of stone, while the roof was to use Spanish tile. Most of the building was faced with stucco, with brick trims around windows and the main entrance. It was to be two storeys in height. Aside from offices, a dormitory and cells for the police, it had a courtroom for the police magistrate. A new set of plans was created in 1926 by F.H. MacDonald of Public Works for a simple one-storey stucco courthouse, but it was never built.[183]

MacDonald had drawn up the design because the province had decided that Drumheller should be a separate judicial district. However, it was more expedient to simply modify the existing police barracks for offices, vaults and a larger courtroom, and the building now became a courthouse as well.[184] It saved the government the trouble of building a new, proper courthouse. On the other hand, it was also a small and cramped building. When the government contemplated amalgamating the Districts of Hanna and Drumheller in the latter city, the sheriff quickly informed his superiors that this was not practical. H.J. Wilson, the deputy Attorney General, wrote to Public Works:

> I am advised by Sheriff Needs that he has not even now sufficient accommodation for his own documents and files and it will be impossible for

*(following page) Elevations, Drumheller courthouse, PAA*

*(following page) Front entrance detail, Drumheller courthouse, PAA*

*(following page) Sketch of the new Drumheller courthouse. PAA, PA-2663-2*

*(following page) Photo of new Drumheller courthouse. PAA, PA-193-14.*

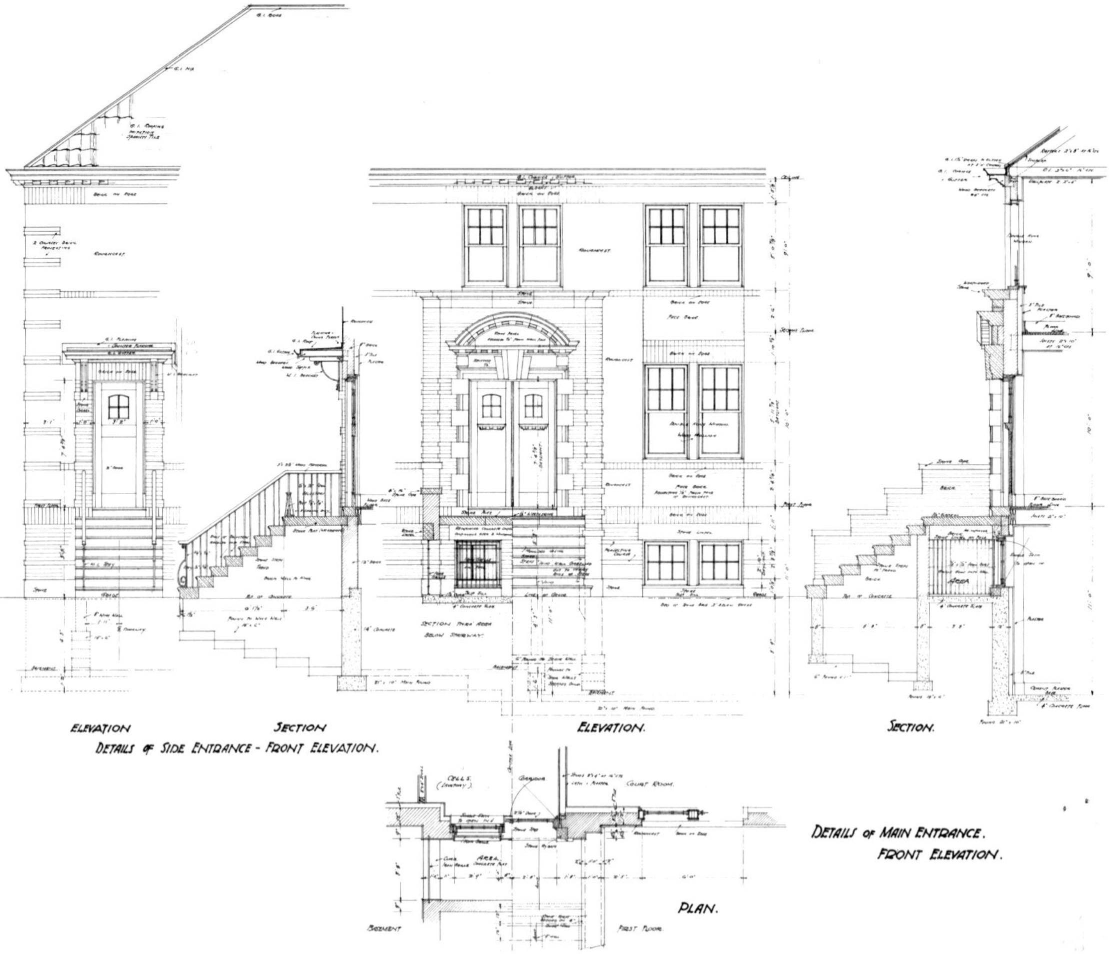
ELEVATION
SECTION
ELEVATION.
SECTION.
DETAILS OF SIDE ENTRANCE - FRONT ELEVATION.
DETAILS OF MAIN ENTRANCE.
FRONT ELEVATION.
PLAN.

½ Front Elevation.
Scale ½ = 1'0"

COURT HOUSE

COURT HOUSE

> him to keep the Hanna records properly unless some changes are made in his offices.[185]

The matter rested there for several years, but it was clear that Drumheller would require a new building and soon. The present building was starting to fall apart.[186] In 1953, a modern courthouse was designed by the staff of Public Works and the contract given to Buchanan Construction of Edmonton on a bid of $242,038. It was the province's second post-war courthouse, preceded by the Lethbridge law courts. It was finished in 1955, and while a vast improvement on the old building, it was not an unqualified success. The judges from Calgary who would use the courthouse were not happy with the layout, and were especially disappointed by the lack of overnight accommodation.[187] Echoing sentiments voiced by Justice W.C. Ives in Hanna years before, Judge Luke Stack of the District Court wrote:

> Of all the places in the province, Drumheller is the one place where sleeping quarters should be provided, not because there are not hotels there, but because the hotel atmosphere is most unsuitable for a Judge, who necessarily has to mingle too publicly with litigants, witnesses, and interested or inquisitive busybodies.[188]

As for the old police barracks, it still housed the RCMP detachment. The province offered it to the federal government and negotiations ensued.[189] The police had no interest in the old building and intended to demolish it and build again on the site.

## RED DEER

Excitement had been building for weeks. The new provincial courthouse on Ross Street was due to be finished in March 1931. The city of Red Deer had waited almost twenty years for the building, and as it neared completion, plans were laid for an elaborate opening ceremony. The banquet was attended by every notable citizen of Red Deer, and dignitaries came from around the province, including the Premier, the Attorney General, the Chief Justice of Alberta and the mayors of Edmonton and Calgary. The festivities did not just mark another milestone for the city. Put on jointly by the Red Deer City Council and the Red Deer Board of Trade, the affair tried resolutely to spark some optimism in a town sinking deeper and deeper into the mire of the Great Depression. With unemployment skyrocketing and businesses closing, it was no surprise that the invited guests seized the opportunity to celebrate something positive. The jovial dinner adjourned to the new law courts afterward for a tour of inspection. Chief Justice Harvey opened the first court in full regalia. Not a man usually noted for his sense of fun, Harvey cited Mayor Douglas of Edmonton for contempt for some remarks made earlier in scorn of courthouses, and gave him a suspended sentence, conditional on his good behaviour! It was easily the most elaborate – and good-humoured – opening any courthouse had ever received in Alberta.

Everyone had good reason for celebration. The citizens of Red Deer had finally obtained an edifice worthy of their little city, and the judges and officers of the court a proper facility for their work. For the United Farmers government of Premier John E. Brownlee, it was an important symbol of his administration's accomplishments in the face of a deepening crisis. The Red Deer courthouse was one of the most significant public buildings erected during fourteen years of UFA rule, and marked the high point of a substantial program of construction undertaken in the twilight of the Roaring Twenties. It was not a building free of controversy. For some, the courthouse was only belated recognition of the city after years of near total neglect by the government. The timing of the courthouse, announced shortly before a provincial election, gave the appearance of a bribe, an appearance that UFA advertisements did little to contradict. For Daniel E. McDonald, Superintendent of Buildings, and the Department of Public Works, however, Red Deer's courthouse was an unqualified success, reminiscent in design and stature of the courthouses built in the province's youth, constructed expeditiously and almost flawlessly to the department's own design.

### The Promised Courthouse

The Territorial courthouse had scarcely been finished and the citizens of Red Deer were hopeful it would soon be replaced. The Dominion was loath to part with the courthouse because it housed the land office and customs office. In the 1906 negotiations over public buildings, the province agreed to rent the court quarters but leave the building in the hands of the federal government. Instead, the province would pick up the expense of a new building.

Word must have got round Red Deer that a new courthouse might soon be in the offing. The local boosters were quick to act: a delegation was sent to Edmonton, shepherded by John T. Moore, the local MLA.[190] The delegation was promised that a building would be soon erected, and the Department of Public Works began scouting around for property early in 1907.[191] Lawyer J. Carlyle Moore brokered a deal with the government on behalf of H.H. Gaetz, scion of the city's founding family, for block J in Plan 6901-R. The property was not ideal, being removed from the commercial district to the east. The ever-competent John Stocks, Deputy Minister of Public Works raised this point – prophetically, as it turned out.[192] Stocks did allow that it was likely the best affordable site. John Moore applied a great deal of pressure to the government to buy the land, making dire predictions of rising prices and rampant speculation.[193] The government paid $5,000 for the property.[194] It was not the first or last time the family was involved with the town's courthouses. J.J. Gaetz had, of course, been one of the local Liberals active in pursuing the first courthouse, and H.H. Gaetz would later rent out an old factory as an abode for the courts.

Buying property did not necessarily mean the government would break the sod any time soon. Red Deer was not the centre of a judicial district, and when additional jurisdictions were formed in 1906, Red Deer found itself placed in the district of Wetaskiwin. When it came time to establish new districts, Wetaskiwin, through its resident member of the provincial assembly, A.S. de Rosenroll, had beat Red Deer to the punch. It was a matter of more effective lobbying. Rosenroll was a relatively strong supporter of Premier Rutherford; the member for Red Deer, John T. Moore, also a Liberal, was lukewarm. It would cost Red Deer the headquarters of the judicial district, which in turn would cost Moore his seat. In the 1909 election, Moore went down in defeat before Mayor Edward E. Michener, running as an Independent Conservative, and the debacle over the district was one of the issues that hurt Moore with the electorate. Red Deer was finally made a judicial district in 1913.

Michener inadvertently plunged the town into a crisis in judicial facilities. Although a provincial politician, he was well connected with the federal Conservatives and persuaded the Borden government to grant a customs office for Red Deer early in 1912.[195] The Dominion also promised the city a new public building, but as an interim measure, the customs office would be placed in the courthouse immediately. The only place for it was the second floor. As had happened in Lethbridge several years before, suddenly the province had no facilities for the courts. The Oddfellows Hall was rented for District and Supreme Court sessions and the court offices were scattered about the downtown: a room in the Michener Block was fitted up as a courtroom, the law library and judge's chambers were in the main Smith and Gaetz block on Ross Street, and the clerk and sheriff's offices

*Courts and commerce: Smith and Gaetz Block, used for court offices, c. 1912. RDDA, P-362-4*

were in the Smith and Gaetz building on Gaetz Avenue, while prisoners were still kept for trial in the basement cells of the old courthouse.[196]

The following year, George Greene, in his departing address as president of the board of trade, urged that Red Deer lobby hard for a law courts building and also consider making it part of a grand civic square.[197] The town had been promised a post office and an armoury from the Dominion government and a block of land had been reserved for civic purposes in the centre of Red Deer. The idea caught on, and when Red Deer became a city in 1913, the civic council commissioned local architect C.A.J. Sharman to develop a plan for the square.[198] However, a major recession was lurking in the wings, and the grand schemes of Sharman and city council were doomed to be unfulfilled.

## The Jeans Factory

The ridiculous arrangement of rented offices and halls served the town until March 22, 1916, when the province opened a temporary courthouse in a mothballed overall factory, which would serve until 1931. The government leased the two-storey brick building on 49th Avenue and 51st Street from H.H. Gaetz at the beginning of 1916.[199] Built in 1910, it had been designed by C.A.J. Sharman. It was an unprepossessing building, constructed on a slightly sloping lot, with large windows on both floors, and some pleasing decorative touches, including brick arches over the

*Jeans or justice? The Gaetz Co. Building, manufacturers of denim work clothes, would be Red Deer's courthouse for 15 years. RDDA, P-125-b-3-5*

windows, stone sills and courses, and a small cornice above which the legend "The Gaetz Co. Ltd" was emblazoned. A courtroom was put on the second floor, along with the judge's office, a jury room, and a place for the barristers. The first floor had the sheriff's office, a general office for the public, a space for the District Court judge as well as Chambers, which shared space with the library.[200] The basement was given over to six holding cells and storage space. There was none too much room in the building: there was no witness room, which had become a normal feature of courthouse designs, and no central corridor to facilitate movement between offices.

### WOMEN IN JURIES

The converted garment factory in Red Deer was the site of a victory for feminism when the first women jurors in Alberta were empanelled to hear a case on November 14, 1922. Even after women got the vote, there was still a great deal of prejudice against the idea of female jurors. There was a widespread belief that the sordid and unpleasant circumstances involved in criminal cases were inappropriate for the tender ears of respectable women. Attitudes had begun to change however, and women had already been working in court offices for a number of years. The new Jury Act of 1921 allowed for women to be jurors in a limited way, although they could refuse the duty if they wished.[201] In civil cases where a woman was involved as a plaintiff or a defendant, she could insist that half the jurors should be women, and if both plaintiff and defendant were women, the jury could be all-female.[202]

The trial before Justice Maitland McCarthy between Gladys Straub and David Hardie Larking was for breach of promise and seduction. Straub alleged that in 1921, while caring for the defendant's sick mother, Larking made persistent advances and seduced her under the promise of marriage. Zelma Isabelle Smith, Jessie B. Huestis, and Maude Horn were the three women on the six-person jury. Whether or not a feminine perspective made a difference, the court held for the plaintiff and awarded her a very stiff $4,000 and costs.

All in all, the work cost the department about $2,400, a fraction of the cost of a new courthouse.[203] It was ready for business by March 1916, and His Honour Justice James Hyndman opened it officially with an assize of the Supreme Court on March 22.[204]

Red Deer's new courthouse didn't quite fit in with fantasies of an elegant civic square. There is evidence the Liberals had plans to build a courthouse after the war, but the severe post-war recession killed it. The courthouse site purchased in 1907 was leased to the local tennis club. The new UFA government, elected in 1921, struggled with a weak economy and a massive provincial debt, and Red Deer would not receive its due for nearly another decade.

---

STETTLER'S SCHOOLHOUSE

Red Deer was not the only place promised a courthouse that had to make due with a converted building. In 1913, the Attorney General's department decided to cut up the somewhat large and unwieldy Judicial District of Wetaskiwin into three, with the two new districts centred around Red Deer and Stettler. It was not a popular move in Wetaskiwin, but was greeted in the other two towns as proper and just. The new districts were necessary for the proper administration of justice, but also allowed the government to please the constituents of two other ridings, an advantage not lost on them. The local Stettler member up until 1913, Robert L. Shaw, had been lobbying for the previous five years to get a judicial district and courthouse.[205] The Stettler board of trade decided to give Shaw a special banquet to honour his hard work.[206] For not only would Stettler be on the map as a judicial headquarters, it had been promised a $40,000 courthouse, a promise that had every booster in the town very pleased.

The townsfolk of Stettler, indeed, Shaw himself, would have been outraged if they had realized the duplicity of the provincial government. In December 1913, the Inspector of Legal Offices telegrammed the Stettler School Board to offer $9,000 for the town's old school property, recently replaced by a new brick facility.[207] The town was told – or assumed – it would be the site of the new courthouse. In the meantime, the province intended to convert the school into a temporary courthouse, a plan the local *Stettler Independent* applauded: "The use of the old building will enable the department to organise the Judicial Centre immediately and will save a year in that way."[208] The fact that the school board's outstanding debt was settled by the sale pleased Stettlerites even more.

If the government had ever intended to immediately build a swank new courthouse, however, it soon changed its mind. In February 1914, not much more than a month after the banquet for Shaw, the Deputy Attorney General wrote to John Stocks, the Deputy Minister at Public Works, about the "temporary" Stettler courthouse: "I also note the cost of alterations at $3,000. I think this amount should make the building suitable for purpose intended for next ten years."[209] This was a far cry from what the town had been expecting. In fairness to the provincial government, they may well have originally intended constructing an imposing edifice. The Sifton administration had not made any public promises about the courthouse during the elections the preceding April, so the courthouse had not been a bribe. It was more or less policy to build a proper courthouse for each judicial headquarters, but economic conditions in Alberta had become noticeably worse by 1914, and the word "depression" was on everyone's lips. Clearly the government felt they had to renege on their promise. Stettler was not the only centre that did not get their courthouse

No one in Stettler seemed to notice that there was no sign of a new courthouse, although progress on the school conversion was followed carefully. Work started in March under the direction of C.E. McGowan of the Public Works Department, and the local paper noted approvingly that he had hired men from the district and that all the subcontracts were to go to area firms.[210] The building was gutted and rebuilt along traditional courthouse lines. On the first floor, the offices of the court officers and the judge were placed along with two holding cells, and on the second floor the main courtroom, as well as a lawyers' chamber and retiring rooms for jury and witnesses, were fitted. A new modern furnace was installed, although it was tight squeeze. The old Territorial courthouse in Calgary, in the process of being converted to a headquarters building for the North West Mounted Police, provided the courtroom fixtures.[211] The conversion would cost the government $6,292.[212] By September the building was ready for occupation, and soon Sheriff Grigg and Clerk Harding were hard at work undergoing training from the deputy sheriff at Red Deer and the District Court clerk of Edmonton.[213] It was somewhat ironic, considering how often the Territorial assizes had to resort to schoolhouses, that a whole school would be given over to the courts.

Stettler was destined to never see its promised courthouse. The war quashed any plans to erect a grander structure, and even when the province resumed courthouse construction Stettler did not rate a new building.

The population of the town hovered around twelve hundred residents for decades, and at the end of 1935 the province actually disestablished the Stettler Judicial District – there just was not enough traffic in the courts to merit court offices and officials in the town. The converted schoolhouse continued in use until 1975, when a new provincial building was opened with a courtroom.[214] The old building survives today. Turned over to the town, it was moved and now houses the Stettler and District Museum.

## The Depression Courthouse

Anticipation built in Red Deer when the lease on the old Gaetz building approached renewal at the end of the 1920s. A new home for the courts was long overdue. By the mid-1920s the converted factory was not a prepossessing sight, desperately in need of a renovation and a coat of paint, a tattered flag flying over the building.[215] The roof had begun leaking badly, and the sheriff and caretaker anticipated with dread each new thunderstorm.[216] And it was too small: at the October 1929 assize, the Advocate reported that "The courtroom was probably as crowded as it has ever been, the overflow filling the stairs and downstairs hall and entrance, right into the street."[217]

The state of the courthouse had not escaped the notice of local boosters, and when economic conditions improved, they started lobbying in 1928 for a new edifice. The board of trade led the campaign, which met with swift success. The government had committed itself to a major program of courthouse construction, and in the fall of 1929, Attorney General Lymburn asked the cabinet for funds to build a new courthouse for the city. The government already had a spot for it: the land bought back in 1907 sat empty except for weekend tennis players plying their rackets in a rather different court.

---

### GEORGE W. SMITH

Of all Red Deer's worthies, only E.E. Michener had a richer political career than George Wilbert Smith. It encompassed several decades and two political parties as well municipal politics. More importantly, he was deeply involved in getting not just one, but two courthouses built in the city of Red Deer.

Smith was from Nova Scotia, born on April 24, 1855 in Selma. Reverend Leonard Gaetz was his uncle. He became a schoolteacher and in 1886 came west to join Gaetz and teach in the first Red Deer district school. With only seven pupils, Smith had time to homestead and eventually gave up teaching to farm and raise cattle. His connection with the Gaetz family was strengthened further when he married his cousin Carrie Addison Gaetz in 1888.

Smith proved a canny businessman, opening the first butcher shop in the new townsite in 1891 and diversifying into cattle trading, farm implements, flour and feed, hardware, and, inevitably, real estate.

He was as prolific in politics as in business. At first Smith was a convinced Liberal. He was a member of the Liberal Association and became President in 1901 and again in 1907. As leader of the local liberals, Smith led the charge to get a courthouse from the Dominion government. He also lobbied hard to have the Rutherford government make Red Deer the provincial capital. After selling many of his business interests in the early teens, Smith entered the municipal arena as a city councillor. After four terms he was elected mayor in 1917 and 1918. Returning to provincial politics, he moved his sympathies from the ruling provincial Liberals to the United Farmers of Alberta and won the Red Deer seat as the UFA candidate in the rout of 1921. Never in cabinet, Smith nonetheless was an influential voice and was instrumental in getting a new courthouse built in 1930, a fact he trumpeted loudly in subsequent campaign advertisements. Ironically, despite the excitement over the new building, Smith almost lost his seat in 1931 in a close election.

Smith also served as the chairman of the Red Deer Hospital Board, the School Board and Agricultural Society. When the board of trade formed in 1894, Smith was a charter member. Not surprisingly, he was active in the local Methodist congregation. On his death in 1931, the Premier, two cabinet ministers and his old rival Senator Edward E. Michener attended the funeral. His seat in the provincial house almost immediately went to the Conservatives in the by-election, a harbinger of future trouble for the UFA. Red Deer's imposing brick courthouse, finished within Smith's lifetime, is a legacy of his contribution to the city.

The site immediately became a matter of contention. Red Deer had changed in the twenty-odd years since the government had purchased land. The Canadian National Railway had run a spur line through the city that separated the courthouse property from the business district. The proposed courthouse was quite literally on the wrong side of the tracks. The property was close to the line, raising the possibility that noise from the trains would disturb the deliberations of judge and counsel. Mayor Snell went to Edmonton in early June 1929 to interview Premier Brownlee in person about the site.[218] He suggested that the government should consider four lots held by the city in block 28, on the corner of Ross and 49th Avenue, kitty-corner to the first courthouse and facing the civic square and beside the Alberta Government Telephone building. Brownlee himself was in favour of the offer. The city was willing to work out some sort of exchange.

What seemed like a straightforward deal rapidly became more complex. A lengthy and contentious wrangle ensued concerning the merits of first one, then two, and finally three possible alternate sites, involving the town council, the Minister of Public Works, Superintendent D.E. McDonald, and finally Premier Brownlee himself. McDonald, who had approved the property on Ross and 49th,

*Hardly grand enough: early version of Red Deer Courthouse, lacking classical entrance. AI.*

was particularly infuriated when Public Works Minister McPherson ignored his recommendations and chose the third site, favoured by some members of the city council, just east of the present-day city hall.[219] The superintendent carried the day when the premier personally inspected the three properties and decided in favour of the first choice. After some further debate on the orientation of the building, it was finally settled. The courthouse would face Ross Street and the civic square and would occupy lots 1 to 4 of block 28, on the corner of 49th Avenue and Ross. Ironically, this was more or less the same spot where Sharman had hoped to have the courthouse as part of his civic square plan, and the courthouse became one of the first elements that was actually built.

During the dickering over the site, McDonald's department had not been idle. The department had already produced two courthouse designs and would eventually create plans for six buildings, four of which were built. The buildings produced by McDonald and his staff were for the most part very utilitarian and took their cues from R.P. Blakey and his Spanish Revival influenced buildings. The drafting staff, under the direction of Frederick H. McDonald, did not attempt to follow more contemporary architectural styles such as Art Deco, already popular for public buildings in other parts of North America. For the Red Deer courthouse, the department used Blakey's Medicine Hat building as their model, but without the originality and assurance of the former Provincial Architect.

Although much fuss was made at the time – and since – about the classical architecture used for the courthouse, it was quite subdued. It was a two-storey hip-roofed building, with a red tapestry brick exterior and detailing in Manitoba Tyndall limestone. In style, it continued the conservative, Beaux-Arts-inspired designs characteristic of earlier provincial courthouses. Although the imposing entryway, which received almost all the architectural decoration, was reminiscent

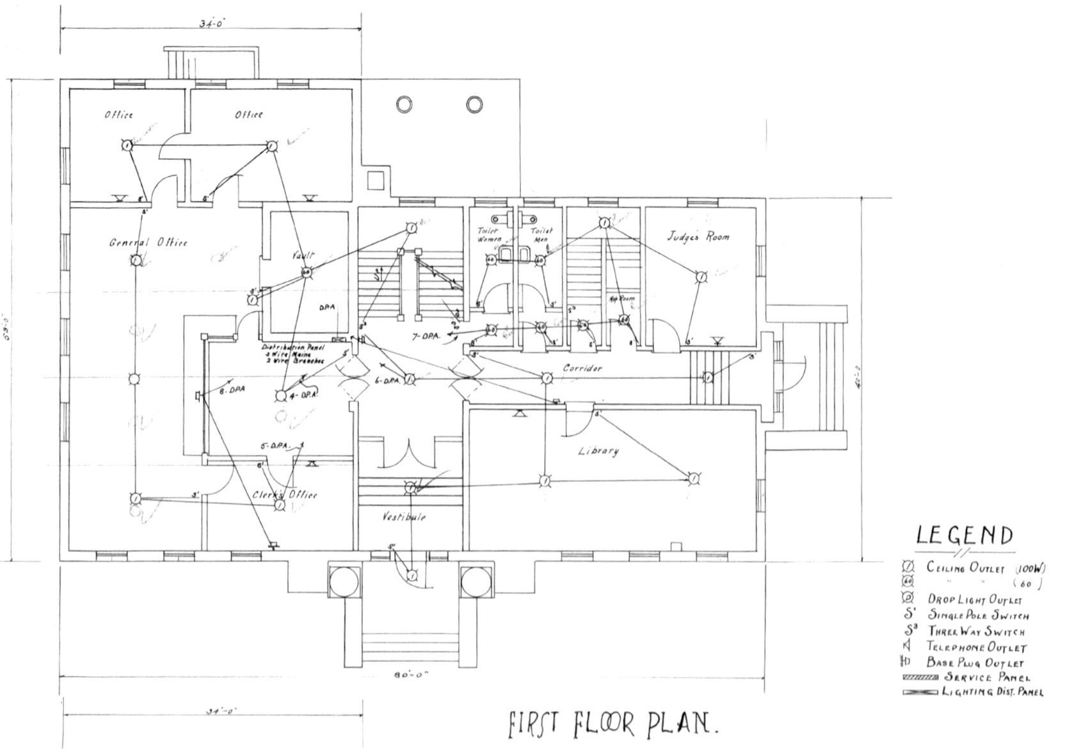


*Floor plans, Red Deer courthouse, 1930. AI*

of A.M. Jeffers' courthouses, the Red Deer building was clearly inspired largely by Blakey's Medicine Hat courthouse. The Spanish-tiled hip roof made this clear, as did the Italian-Renaissance-inspired decoration of the entrance. A porch formed by two massive brick piers were surmounted by a stone entablature bearing the legend "Court House," on top of which was a stone balustrade and parapet containing the provincial coat of arms. Two Doric columns placed *in antis* flanked the doorway, while the windows above the door had a cast iron railing supported by decorative brackets, reinforcing the Mediterranean look of the building. A big fan window over the double doors was surrounded by stone trim. A side entrance had a small projecting porch and the same fan window and double doors as the main entrance. The double-hung main floor windows had stone sills and lintels and a plain stone panel underneath, while the upper windows merely had stone surrounds. A stone course delineated the two floors. Unlike those of many earlier courthouses, the foundation wall was faced with brick, with only a small amount of stone showing above ground floor.

Interestingly, the Red Deer courthouse was originally quite plain. The classical detailing that so impressed contemporaries was an afterthought. In the first drawings for the courthouse, dated February 1930, the grand entryway was a simple porch around the doorway, the decoration consisting of a brick architrave with a Tyndall keystone.[220] It continued the government's policy of designing relatively unadorned and utilitarian courthouses, such as had been built in Grande Prairie and Hanna. The greater importance of Red Deer earned it a much bigger brick building, but the government initially had no interest in fripperies like Greek columns. No correspondence survives to show why the department added the grand portico. Was it merely the draftsman's dissatisfaction with a plain building? Did George Smith protest? Or did the Minister of Public Works, McPherson, and the executive council decide that with an election coming up, something a little more impressive was required? The answer may never be known, but it is clear that someone felt Red Deer deserved better. Within a month revised drawings had been prepared with a much grander entryway.

In layout, the Red Deer courthouse followed the L-shaped plan pioneered in Medicine Hat. The internal arrangement was quite different. The basement was initially little utilized, containing the mechanicals for the building and the vaults, as well as space for more offices. The building lacked the impressive foyer seen in earlier courthouses. The main floor, as usual, housed the sheriff and clerk, with a general office and three private offices in one wing to the west of the entry and grand staircase. In the east wing a visitor could find the library as well as the District Court judge's room and a second private staircase. The west wing had the courtroom. It did not have the elaborate plaster decoration found in some earlier courthouses, but was still an impressive space, with a lovely curved ceiling supported by steel trusses. The courtroom itself was finished in birch with imitation stone on the walls, and a prominent plaster cornice.

It was more awkward than the Medicine Hat courtroom. The entrance was in the middle of the east wall, meaning spectators had to file in quite close to the bench and judge's entrance. The witness rooms were on the other side of the floor, so that they had to walk down a long corridor and past the main stairs to enter the courtroom. The second floor also had the Supreme Court justice's chambers and sleeping quarters. For decoration, the building was tasteful but fairly restrained. The entry vestibule had marble stairs and frosted glass partitions. The offices all had maple floors, but the courtroom used the same rubber tiles as was put down in the public corridors. A few cost-cutting measures were used as well: while real marble was used for thresholds throughout the building, the wainscoting in the stairwells was "asbestos marble dado."[221]

Once the site had been settled, McDonald and his men lost little time. On April 28, advertisement for tenders went out to all the major provincial newspapers.[222] An Edmonton builder, J.P. Desrochers, was awarded the main contract on a bid of $70,508 for a building done with Tyndall limestone trim. The other contracts also went to Edmonton firms. Indeed, it was not a Red Deer building: the steel was supplied by Dominion Bridge, the brick by Redcliffe Coke and Clay Products, the stone by the Tyndall Stone Company of Winnipeg, and the tile and marble by Empire Marble and Tile Works of Edmonton.

Work proceeded swiftly and the building was ready for opening at the beginning of March 1931, barely ten months after the excavation for the foundation. Excitement began to build in Red Deer as the building progressed from a steel framework to a solid mass of brick and stone. And unlike the older provincial courthouses, which opened their doors with almost no fanfare, the civic fathers

*Faster than most: the Red Deer Courthouse under construction, 1930. RDDA, mg-193-1-18-5*

*(top right) A bit ungainly: Red Deer Courthouse, 1933. RDDA, 90-81-1*

*(bottom right) The majesty of the law: an imposing view of the Red Deer Courthouse, 1930s. PAA, A946b*

would guarantee everyone in the province knew of the city's new prize. In the face of the deepening Depression, the building of the courthouse was a ray of light in the darkness, and well worth celebrating. The board of trade and the city council got to work and organized a massive banquet. It was a testament to the efficiency of the building branch under Daniel McDonald. No three- and four-year delays for a modest public building: things were done swiftly and well under his direction.

The Gaetz building, which had given yeoman service as a courthouse for fifteen years, was not abandoned. The announcement of a new courthouse brought a slew of requests from various departments requesting office space. The APP, the road inspector, and school inspector, and the police magistrate were already lined up, hat in hand. The Attorney General's department strongly preferred keeping the courthouse reserved for the superior courts alone, and with minimal alterations, McDonald felt the old courthouse could fill the gap. The estate of H.H. Gaetz sold the building to the government for $8,000, shortly before the new courthouse was opened. By June 1, it was renovated and ready for occupation.[223]

Using the old courthouse helped the Attorney General and the Public Works departments keep other provincial offices out of the new edifice. As usual, the Attorney General's department rather jealously guarded their building, and although ample precedent existed by this time for other uses of courthouses, the department took a stern line in Red Deer. Even the district court judge soon learned this. Upon hearing that Judge Mahaffy planned on moving into the judge's quarters in the building as if they were his private apartments, the two departments quickly took steps to prevent it. Sheriff Hogg, was notified that "the suite of rooms in the second floor of the new Court House at Red Deer is to be reserved for the use of the visiting judges when holding court.... Neither shall there be any cooking done or meals served in building."[224] In the 1940s and early 1950s, the quarters in the courthouse became quite a prize, due to the housing shortage in Red Deer.

Other requests, including one from a newly transferred RCMP corporal, were received sympathetically, but as H.J. Wilson, the Deputy Attorney General, wrote to W.D. Stacey, the Building Superintendent, in 1946: "... I am quite sure this would raise a storm of protest from the judges."[225] Though one wonders why: most of the visiting Supreme Court justices complained of the poor heating and leaking roof in their suite, and often stayed in a hotel instead.[226]

## AN ORDINARY KIND OF HERO – SHERIFFS & CARETAKERS PART TWO

Heroism comes in many forms. To Malcolm Millard, the sheriff in Red Deer in the 1940s, his courthouse caretaker Thomas Cosgrove was definitely a hero. In an era when employees worked long and hard hours, Cosgrove went above and beyond the call of duty.

It was during the winter of 1943. Normally there were two men on the caretaker staff of Public Works in Red Deer, one who looked after the old courthouse, and Cosgrove, who had care of the new building. Millard had always found Cosgrove's work to be totally satisfactory. The two caretakers covered for each other during holidays. In January temperatures plummeted, and the heating systems in both buildings needed round-the-clock attention. Even in the new courthouse, the coal-fired steam heating apparatus needed an experienced hand to keep it running, and in an age of imperfectly insulated buildings, it was vital to have them heated lest the plumbing and heating systems freeze up and be damaged. Just as temperatures reached forty degrees below zero, the other caretaker became seriously ill. There was no replacement available for him, and after gamely coming to work for a day or two, he went into the hospital. Without complaint, for the next twenty-two days Cosgrove kept the heat up in both buildings and made sure they were kept clean and properly maintained.

Millard thought the caretaker deserved not only overtime but also a bonus for this virtuoso performance. W.D. Stacey, the Superintendent of Buildings, was sympathetic, but hard as it is to believe, there was no mechanism for awarding extra pay for the rank and file of Public Works. Stacey and Deputy Minister Monkman also felt that the procedure to get relief help from the department should have been followed. The sheriff would not back down. He had no faith in the help available from the department. But first and foremost, he thought it ridiculous the department couldn't reward their employees properly:

> It is rather difficult for employees to understand rules and regulations which prevent them receiving recognition for service rendered in emergencies. Mr. Cosgrove has been a good and faithful servant for many years. There has never been a visitor to this building who did not remark on the condition in which it is kept. He has never had assistance and I know from personal knowledge he works harder than employees working for your Department in Calgary and Edmonton do.[227]

Strong words. Millard's support of Cosgrove was light years away from the constant fights between sheriffs and caretakers in the Territorial days. And he carried the day. The department arranged an Order-in-Council to provide a special payment to Cosgrove.

There was more than a little difficulty with leaks. Roof problems seemed a constant with most of the province's courthouses, and whenever one sprang a leak, it always seemed to involve the judge's quarters. There was one particularly bad incident in 1944 which damaged the plaster to the extent that the caretaker was worried some might pull away – and it wouldn't do for an august justice to be smacked on the head by falling ceiling bits. The barristers' room also suffered, and the ceiling and walls were in various places stained by water. The drains were the culprit, allowing water to back up under the roof tiles. Even with cleaning and repairs, leaks continued to plague the staff in the courthouse until the end of the 1950s.

The damaged roof and plaster work were not the only problems with the building. By the early 1950s, it had become dingy, some even said dirty. There had been no renovations, not even simple painting, to the courthouse since it had opened more than twenty years previously. The blame for the state of the building could be laid on the Depression and the war, which had made proper maintenance impossible. Lack of money, materials, and then manpower over the course of fifteen years had an effect, even on a relatively new building. And as brand new, modern buildings appeared in the province, it was inevitable that older edifices suffered by comparison. But as usual, when the judges started to complain, action was (relatively) swift. Cosmetic renovations – cleaning, painting and the like – were started later in the fall of 1950.

## Epilogue

In 1941, Red Deer's population had grown by only a few hundred over the previous twenty years, and in 1946 it was still just over four thousand. Five years later, it had almost doubled; within ten years, it had tripled! Like other cities in Alberta, court facilities were not adequate for handling this sudden increase. Although Red Deer's courthouse had only been built in 1931, the building was showing some wear and tear due to poor maintenance budgets during the Depression and the war. But it was lack of space that was the main difficulty. Matters came to a crisis in 1955, when it was necessary to accommodate an additional court reporter and no space could be found. As Harold Brettelle, Supervisor of Maintenance, succinctly put it: "the only possible way of getting additional space would be either to build an addition … or a new Court House."[228] Brettelle thought a four-room addition could be easily handled, and the idea was duly approved.[229] In August 1957 plans were started for the addition.

The layout of the courthouse made it easy to put an unobtrusive extension at the rear, nestled in the crook of the existing building. With brick exterior in the same style of the old courthouse, and a low flat roof, it did not detract from the original edifice. The addition was designed in the revived Chief Architect's Office of Public Works, and construction was supervised directly by the department, although a contractor was hired by tender to do the brick and masonry work and the interior decorating.[230] Louis Victor Bricklaying of Red Deer got the exterior contract, while an Edmonton firm, Bob Candido's Tile & Terrazzo, did the interior appointments. A simple box, the addition provided more offices, a place for the library, and courtrooms for the District Court and the Magistrate's Court.[231] Within five years even the addition was not enough: by the fall of 1963, "working conditions for the Court House staff, the Magistrates Court staff and the family Court staff in the Court House, Red Deer, are very crowded and in some instances quite unsuitable."[232] The department still had not adequately taken account of the phenomenal growth in the city and surrounding region.

After spending a year attempting unsuccessfully to convert the old AGT building beside the existing courthouse as an annex, the government decided it would build a "high rise type" of new courthouse that would "provide for two additional floors for future expansion."[233] It was to be designed by Bittorf-Wensley Architects of Edmonton.[234] The site for the new building at 49th Street and 49th Avenue was never used, however: in the spring of 1968 the province dropped the project due to cutbacks.[235] Instead, the old courthouse was given another renovation. [996] It would continue in service until late 1983, when a multi-million-dollar building designed by Ken Hutchinson Architect of Calgary was finished, ironically, on the property east of city hall rejected in 1930.

When a new facility was proposed, Red Deer's city council became concerned as to the fate of the UFA courthouse. The idea of simply destroying the building, even in the interests of progress, had become repugnant. Alderman T.J. Parkinson led the charge to save the building in 1966:

> Now that the A.G.T. Building has been removed from Ross Street it is possible to obtain a much better view than previously of the present Court House. It is revealed as a very handsome building indeed, possibly the most handsome building in Red Deer. Yet I believe that when the new Court House is constructed it is the intention that the present Court House shall be demolished. Is there any good reason why this building should be destroyed? Could it not be preserved with the present open space around, for some worthwhile community project?[237]

Parkinson planted the seed of an idea that would take almost twenty years to come to fruition, but that would save the Red Deer courthouse. City council retained Calgary architect J. Stevenson and Associates to look at the feasibility of converting the building into a library. When the building was finally vacated in 1983, several different groups interested in the space came forward, including Red Deer College and the Allied Arts Council, an umbrella group of local arts groups. The City of Red Deer approved the idea of a community arts centre. After tedious negotiations, the province agreed to renovate the building and lease it to the city for five years with the promise that it would be sold for one dollar at the expiration of the lease.

One condition the City of Red Deer pressed for was the designation of the courthouse as a historic site. The province showed some reluctance, wanting to retain some flexibility in deciding on how to dispose of the structure. But with a great deal of community support for preservation, including an editorial campaign

by the Red Deer Advocate, the hoped-for designation was arranged and took effect on July 29, 1986.[238] The new arts centre opened in November 1986. Five years later, the province transferred the title to the city after carrying out more renovations, including removal of asbestos. And in 1994, it was once again the site of a trial – this time an imagined one, part of an American movie entitled For the Love of My Daughter. Alas, while museums, art centres, and libraries are favourite ideas for rehabilitating old courthouses, the long-term survival of such institutions is often not assured. The Allied Arts Council was not able to keep the centre afloat. In 2000, the building passed to a private owner, who intends to restore it and keep the building a monument to the rich and fascinating legal history of Red Deer.

*Well hidden: Red Deer Courthouse in the 1960s, showing out of character addition. PAA, A948b*

## VEGREVILLE

Finished in 1931, the Vegreville courthouse would be significant simply for the fact it was the last provincial hall of justice built before World War II, and one of the most substantial constructed under the UFA government in its belated building program. Far more significant, however, was the function of this courthouse in the community as a symbol of law and order. In no other location was the courthouse more pronounced as an agent of assimilation as it was in Vegreville. The district had a large number of immigrants from Russia and the Ukraine, and some residents found this unsettling. Local opinion, in the form of Vegreville's newspaper, made explicit that the courthouse was not just about the dignity of the court, but about instilling a proper respect for the law for those citizens who came from lands not under the British flag:

> The forms, the ceremonies, of law are most impressive within their proper setting. The Observer submits that there is no chance to make the law impressive when the police magistrate, the district court judges, or the Supreme Court judges, have to take pot luck on whatever premises may be available for cases that come before them. In this district it is particularly necessary that justice shall be meted out with meticulous care. Our heterogeneous population can sooner be brought to a realization of the application of Canadian Law, with all its formalities, if trials, civil and criminal, are carried out with due observance of comparatively small, yet singularly important details. There is no room in Canada, still less room in this district, for any free and easy application of the law.[239]

It was not a new sentiment, but one that was not usually so boldly expressed. It was also an argument that was used to convince provincial officials that a hall of justice was absolutely necessary. The courthouse in Vegreville was not just about convenience or civic pride, it was about establishing the rule of law.

### Vegreville – The Early Days

The town's namesake, Father Valentine Vegreville, was a priest of the famed Oblate Missionary Order of the Roman Catholic Church, but had nothing to do with the founding of the settlement.[240] The first homesteaders in the area were Quebecois who immigrated back to Canada from Kansas around 1894.[241] By the turn of the century, there were enough settlers in the district to establish a hamlet called Vegreville, in honour of the missionary from St. Albert, north of Edmonton. The Oblates had strong presence in the district and the first church was Roman Catholic, built in 1903, so the villagers decided to honour the order and their work in northern Alberta. By this time, however, the original homesteaders had been joined by

*Vegreville street scene, c. 1913, PAA 10,455*

settlers from the United States, Ontario, and Britain, who were in turn followed by waves of immigrants from the Ukraine and other parts of southeastern Europe, known colloquially and inaccurately as Ruthenians.

When the Canadian Northern Railway surveyed their line through area in the autumn of 1905, it bypassed the hamlet several kilometres to the northeast, following the Vermilion River.[242] The business community, which included two banks in log shacks and a hotel, quickly moved their buildings to a new townsite, trading a well-drained spot on higher ground for a swampy patch prone to spring flooding. But the railroad, the lifeline for pioneer communities, made up for the deficiencies. Incorporated as a village on April 15, 1906 and as a town exactly four months later, by 1911 Vegreville had a population of perhaps a thousand, but more importantly was already the centre of a rich agricultural hinterland. The town had a rich cultural diversity with its large eastern European population, which also created a degree of ethnic tension. It was the most important centre on the CNR line between Edmonton and the Saskatchewan border, lying a hundred kilometres east of the capital. The town also had an active board of trade, first established in 1906, which would play a large role in establishing Vegreville as a judicial centre.

## The Law Comes to Vegreville

The RNWMP had established a barracks in Old Vegreville and continued to have a presence in the new town. The first civilian justice of the peace was appointed to the area in 1906.[243] The higher courts soon visited Vegreville. A sitting of the Supreme Court of the Northwest Territories was scheduled for March 18, 1907, although there is no record confirming if a justice and his court visited on that occasion. When a new provincial judiciary took the place of the old Territorial court shortly thereafter, Vegreville was placed in the Judicial District of Edmonton, which extended east right to the Saskatchewan border. The District Court made its first visit in the summer of 1908, Judge H. C. Taylor presiding.[244] It was a short sitting, lasting only a day, with the majority of cases "appeals from the decisions of magistrates," according to the Vegreville Observer. It was no easy task to get out to the town: years later, Judge Lucien Dubuc reminisced about the three-day journey to Vegreville from Edmonton before the railroad was finished.[245] In some respects, however, the court was better off in Vegreville than in most other towns. The town had built itself a substantial hall and was happy to rent the council chamber to the judge when he was in town.[246]

It was not long before the citizens of Vegreville decided that a town of such stature had to be the centre of its own judicial district. And in their local member in the Legislative Assembly, James B. Holden, they had exactly the man to put on the job. Holden was a Vegreville businessman, and was one of two legislators who aggressively pursued a judicial district and courthouse for the town. He lost little time in lobbying for the district, and attracted the support of the town council and the board of trade, if a little belatedly. The Observer felt it necessary to berate the board for its lack of support for Holden's work, after which it formed a committee to help with the campaign. Holden himself kept pushing for the district whenever possible. In early 1913, as the government contemplated a reorganization of the land titles office, rumours abounded that Vegreville would receive a local office, which the Observer welcomed as a "step toward the establishment of a Judicial District here, a matter which has been urged time and again on the government."[247]

Holden had made some headway. The government had grandiose plans as far as courthouses went, and Vegreville was put on the "B" list: no immediate promise of a building, but the province purchased a site as a token of its intentions. It was also a matter of prudence, a hedge against rapidly rising real estate prices that carried the inestimable bonus of action without commitment for a relatively small price, and sites had been bought in a number of other towns aside from Vegreville. Public Works Minister W.H. Cushing and J.B. Holden personally arranged the purchase with M.A. Worth, the agent for Davidson and McRae of Winnipeg, acting for the Canadian Northern Railway. The department spent $1,750 for block 51 in the townsite. After some confusion as to the dimensions of the land – which turned out to be a mistake on the part of the brokers – the government received their transfer in March 1910.[248]

Thus heartened, Holden continued to press for a judicial district and court building. He was able to get the new premier and Minister of Public Works, A.L. Sifton, to promise that Vegreville would be the headquarters of a new judicial and registration district and would receive a courthouse. In later years, the Vegreville businessman recounted that he and the premier, who represented nearby Vermilion, hammered out an exchange whereby the latter got the provincial agricultural school and the former would get the courts.[249] Vegreville, however, did not see its half of the bargain for many years. Mounting government debt, a major recession and then the beginning of World War I ended any plans for more courthouses. When the province once again took up construction of public buildings, Vegreville remained without its promised law courts. The Provincial Architect apparently started planning buildings for Vegreville and Red Deer in 1919, but they never left the drafting table, doomed by the post-war recession and a change of government in Edmonton.[250]

To some degree, the fact that Vegreville was not yet even a judicial sub-district weakened any claim the town had for a courthouse. Fortunately, the judicial district was an issue that would not die. A revitalized board of trade formed another committee in the summer of 1925 to take the district's concerns to Edmonton and stuck with it through the next year. Holden had resigned his seat long before the Liberal rout of 1921, but the United Farmers of Alberta member, A.M. Matheson, was just as enthusiastic a courthouse booster as his predecessor. He pestered the Attorney General for years, tirelessly promoting Vegreville as "the logical choice" for a judicial headquarters. His persistence eventually paid off. In 1928, as part of a general reorganization of the judicial districts, the government decided to make Vegreville a sub-district within the district of Edmonton, as well as a land registration district.[251]

Although not as much of a victory as being raised to full district status, it was a vindication of sorts. It did mean court offices and a deputy sheriff and clerk of court, but no resident judge. It also gave renewed hope that a courthouse would soon grace the town, although the local paper was somewhat cynical about the prospects. "Babies born when the judicial district was proposed will be eligible to vote by the time the courthouse is erected," it noted sourly. Still, the boosters of the town were pleased and the *Observer* did note that the district would "give Vegreville considerably increased prestige and adds to the confidence that citizens of the town has always felt as to its assured future."[252]

---

VERMILION

Of course Vegreville was not alone in vying for a judicial district for eastern Alberta. The burghers of Vermilion also had their eye on this prize. When rumours spread in 1926 that more judicial districts would be formed, the town immediately saw it as Vermilion's rightful inheritance: "... there is little doubt but that the town of Vermilion will be selected as the judicial centre, being the most central location. The new district would entail the building of a courthouse and the appointment of a resident judge,"[253] commented the *Vermilion Standard*. Just as in other towns, the board of trade and town council organized a delegation to be sent to Edmonton and petitions were circulated. And when the Attorney General agreed to meet them, the town was confident that "the building of a courthouse will add another splendid structure to the fine brick buildings which have gone up in this block within the past few years."[254]

Vegreville was also not the only town in the district where the government had bought land for a courthouse site. Property had been purchased even earlier in Vermilion, in 1908. Then, allegedly, when Premier Sifton was member for Vermilion, the town got an agricultural college but gave up hope for a courthouse in favour of Vegreville. Not that it was such a bad deal; a year before the Vegreville building was finally announced, Vermilion received a $150,000 dormitory addition to the college, a project that would dwarf the modest $50,000 courthouse. Still, the fact that Vermilion had actually got the college, whereas Vegreville was waiting for a courthouse, did not stop the former from pursuing the judicial district. The town clearly felt unconstrained by a decades-old deal between two politicians since retired from office.

The Deputy Attorney General, G.B. Henwood, came out to Vegreville himself and arranged the rental of offices in the Rice Block for J.W. Dodds, the new deputy sheriff and clerk. Dodds had formerly been in the Edmonton Judicial District office. The sub-district became official on September 1, 1928. With the town's new status, there were renewed calls for a proper courthouse and the board of trade sent off yet another delegation in the new year. The demands became more urgent when the town hall nearly burned down in March 1929, forcing the courts to find alternative venues for sittings, included the local Elks hall.[255]

This did not sit well with the *Observer*, as we have seen, and it editorialized on the subject of the importance of presenting the right demeanour for the courts. The paper was not alone in seeing the courthouse as an important buttress to the rule of law. The perception existed among the business and political elite of northeastern Alberta, mostly of Canadian or British descent, that the eastern European immigrants who flooded into the area after the turn of the century had to be assimilated. There was a strong and ill-founded belief that the Ukrainians and Russians of the district had a tendency toward crime and violence as well as a great mistrust and contempt of the authorities.[256] The manager of the local Bank of Commerce likely spoke for many when he stated in a letter to the Minister of Public Works:

> It seems to me that in a district where the population is so largely of a foreign element ... it would be the height of wisdom to have everything pertaining to the administration of justice on as impressive a basis as possible. A proper Court House here would go a long way in this connection....[257]

It was a point that A.M. Matheson would make two years later when celebrating the opening of the Vegreville courthouse.[258]

The calls for a building were so insistent that finally J.F. Lymburn, the Attorney General, told Vegreville to stop sending delegations; he agreed that a courthouse was important and promised to get one underway as soon as possible.[259] He was true to his word, although by 1929, the UFA government had taken on a great deal of construction, including three courthouses and a new administration building in Edmonton. The need in Vegreville had been duly acknowledged, but there was no rush to erect the building. One matter that could be settled immediately was the site. The original property that W.H. Cushing had purchased was no longer thought suitable for a courthouse. It had been bought in anticipation of Vegreville's continued and vigorous growth, and now was well outside the business district and completely without sewer or water connections.[260] The town had already assured the government that it was quite happy to do a property swap to situate the courthouse in a better spot. The secretary treasurer brought the idea to the attention of Public Works again in 1929 and offered lots six to nine of block 17, plan LXVI, right on main street and across from the new post office. Daniel McDonald, the Superintendent of Buildings, gave it his approval the following spring and the transfer was subsequently carried out.[261]

The announcement in May 1930 that the courthouse was going to be built that year was greeted with a certain degree of relief. Economic conditions were worsening in the district and the construction of a major public building would be a boost to the local economy. The board of trade sent its thanks to the government and Minister of Public Works; the mayor of Vegreville, former MLA J.B. Holden, wrote the department to ask that the contract go to Vegreville firms[262]

The town continued to press for the immediate construction of the courthouse as a way to alleviate the deepening employment crisis.[263] A certain apprehension started to rise as the summer came and there was no sign of any activity. There quickly came charges of electioneering, as the UFA had gone to polls in April 1930 but now no courthouse had been produced.[264]

In fact, the call for tenders had gone out on May 17, 1930, and the contracts awarded by the end of May – R.H. Trouth of Edmonton for the general contract, Hillas Electric and R.P. Speis of Vegreville for the plumbing – but nothing more was heard.[265] Ironically, the town itself was the cause of the delay. After the first design was finished early in the year, plans had been forwarded to Vegreville and found wanting. A deputation duly went off to Edmonton and interviewed the Deputy Minister of Public Works, complaining the courthouse was too small.[266] J.D. Robertson, a veteran official who understood the political ramifications of trying to build a public building in an election year, immediately put the courthouse on hold until after the election, promising that the plans would be reviewed by the minister. The matter went back to cabinet, where in July it was decided to increase the size of the courthouse.

Poor Trouth! Having successfully bid on the first contract, the firm, now Nesbitt, Trouth and Company, had to go through another tender and lost to the $37,988 bid of Foote and Allyn, also of Edmonton.[267] Hillas Electric was replaced by J. McGregor.[268] Speis managed to hang on to his contract for the heating and plumbing, but it was a near thing. The company had been underbid substantially by another Edmonton firm, but it transpired that the latter had not included the cost of a boiler in their tender. The board of trade and city council, desperate to land some of the work to a local contractor, threw their support behind Speis, who for his own part was quick to point out that he would be well placed to provide immediate service in case of an emergency.[269] Although McDonald was not generally swayed by such arguments, in this case he recommended that "the contract be awarded to the Local Man" even though the Fitzgerald bid was still slightly lower.[270] It was a popular move in Vegreville, which welcomed the $7,000 contract.

The town was pleased when the new tender was announced on August 18. When the ground was broken within days of the awarding of the general contract, the Observer ran the headline "Court House Now An Actual Assurance."[271] Construction was swift. As with the buildings in Grande Prairie, Hanna, and Red Deer, there were none of the long delays that characterized most of the older provincial courthouses. This is not to say that construction was trouble-free. In November, McDonald visited the work site in Vegreville and was shocked by the quality of stone that the contractor had procured. In his opinion, "it does not measure up, in any way, to the specifications." The superintendent chastised Foote & Allyn:

> I think it is very poor advertisement for any Firm to ship this quality of stuff, and I would advise you to protect yourself with a substantial hold back, on the Firm's contract, as I consider it will be necessary in the Early Spring, to spend quite a little money, cleaning the Stone work, and possibly replacing some of it.[272]

## Design

Like the other UFA courthouses, the Vegreville building was produced by the drafting staff of the Department of Public Works, under the supervision of Frederick H. MacDonald. No drawings remain of the first design, rejected by the burghers of Vegreville, but the subsequent version, like the other courthouses MacDonald had charge of, was essentially derivative. The department turned to the Medicine Hat courthouse again for a model, using the same L-shaped plan of two wings. Designed more or less at the same time as the Red Deer courthouse, it was very similar to the other building, but smaller and less ostentatious. It measured sixty-eight feet by sixty-two feet, with the two wings twenty-eight feet wide.[273] Like all the early provincial courthouses it was two storeys high, and used the same hip roof seen in Medicine Hat but abandoned the red tile that gave the latter courthouse and Red Deer their Mediterranean flair. Asbestos shingles were substituted. The smaller Vegreville courthouse did not use a full internal steel frame, utilizing load-bearing brick and hollow tile walls with steel columns and beams in strategic areas.

The building was faced with tapestry brick. Tyndall limestone from Manitoba was used for the trim work. There was a minimum of architectural decoration. The Vegreville courthouse stuck close to the original conception of the Red Deer courthouse. Window treatments consisted of simple lintels and sills using Tyndall stone, which also appeared in a belt course and the architrave under the eaves. The projecting porch was attractively executed, also in Tyndall stone. Two engaged Doric columns flanked the double doors ending in a fully classical cornice. Above the doors was a transom window with a stone voussoir, with two carved provincial coats of arms under the cornice. There was a double window on the second floor, with engaged brick columns on either side. A small gabled dormer on the roof had an oculus (a round window) which acted as the attic vent, trimmed in stone. This feature was a reference to the Italianate style post office built a year earlier just up the block, which featured the same brick, Tyndall stone, and prominent oculus. Clearly, Macdonald or another staff member had visited the town, and was familiar with the streetscape. The Vegreville building was simple but well conceived, and might even be considered more attractive than the Red Deer courthouse with its much more pretentious facade.

The interior layout was much like that of other courthouses. After entering the building and alighting a short flight of stairs, one could proceed straight up the main stairwell, turn left into the main office, or right down a hall with more offices. In the left wing of the building, through the clerk and sheriff's office, and beside the room designated for the library, there was a small private stairwell up to the rear of the courtroom on the second floor where the judge's quarters and jury room was located. The design staff at Public Works had learned some lessons from Red Deer, and the second stairs were much more private than in the earlier building, and had an exit to the outside where defendants could be brought in and up to the courtroom. The witness rooms, however, were down the hall from the courtroom and had no separate entry. The police court and magistrate got space in the basement in the courthouse from the outset, so all court activities were centred in the building. As in Red Deer, holding cells were no longer incorporated into the building.

Less money was spent on the internal fixtures than in Red Deer. The same rubber tiling was used in halls and courtroom and maple flooring in the offices, but the faux marble wainscoting and real marble trims were not present. Gone, too, were the extensive plasterwork and elaborate wood trim from courthouses of years past. A picture moulding could be found in the offices, and the courtroom still had wood panelling and maple fixtures, but the interior decor, like the exterior, was kept simple if nonetheless attractive. The final cost of the courthouse, everything included, was $54,454.33.[274]

From the outset, the building at Vegreville was intended to house more than just the courts. Of all the UFA courthouses, Vegreville was one of the closest to being a provincial building, and expanded on the precedent set a decade before in Medicine Hat. More office space for other provincial departments was one of the objects of the reworking of the original plans. The UFA, like the Liberals, were inconsistent in how they approached alternative uses of courthouses. In Red Deer, the government had gone out of its way to keep other offices out of the local hall of justice. At Vegreville, however, allowing other government officials into the building not only saved on rents, it also allowed a larger courthouse to be built. The extra

*Front and side elevations, Vegreville Courthouse, 1930. AI.*

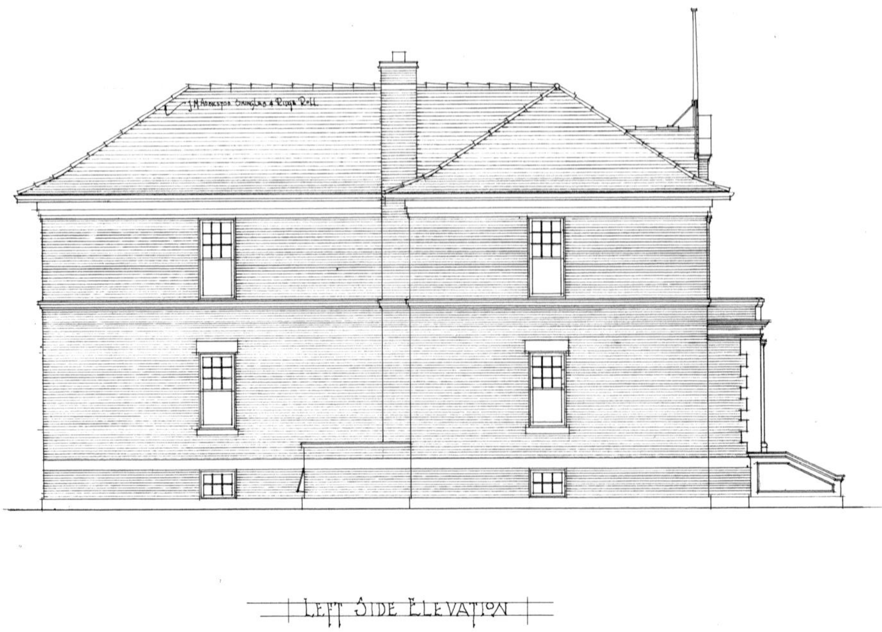

REAR ELEVATION

RIGHT SIDE ELEVATION

*Rear and side elevations, Vegreville Courthouse, 1930. AI.*

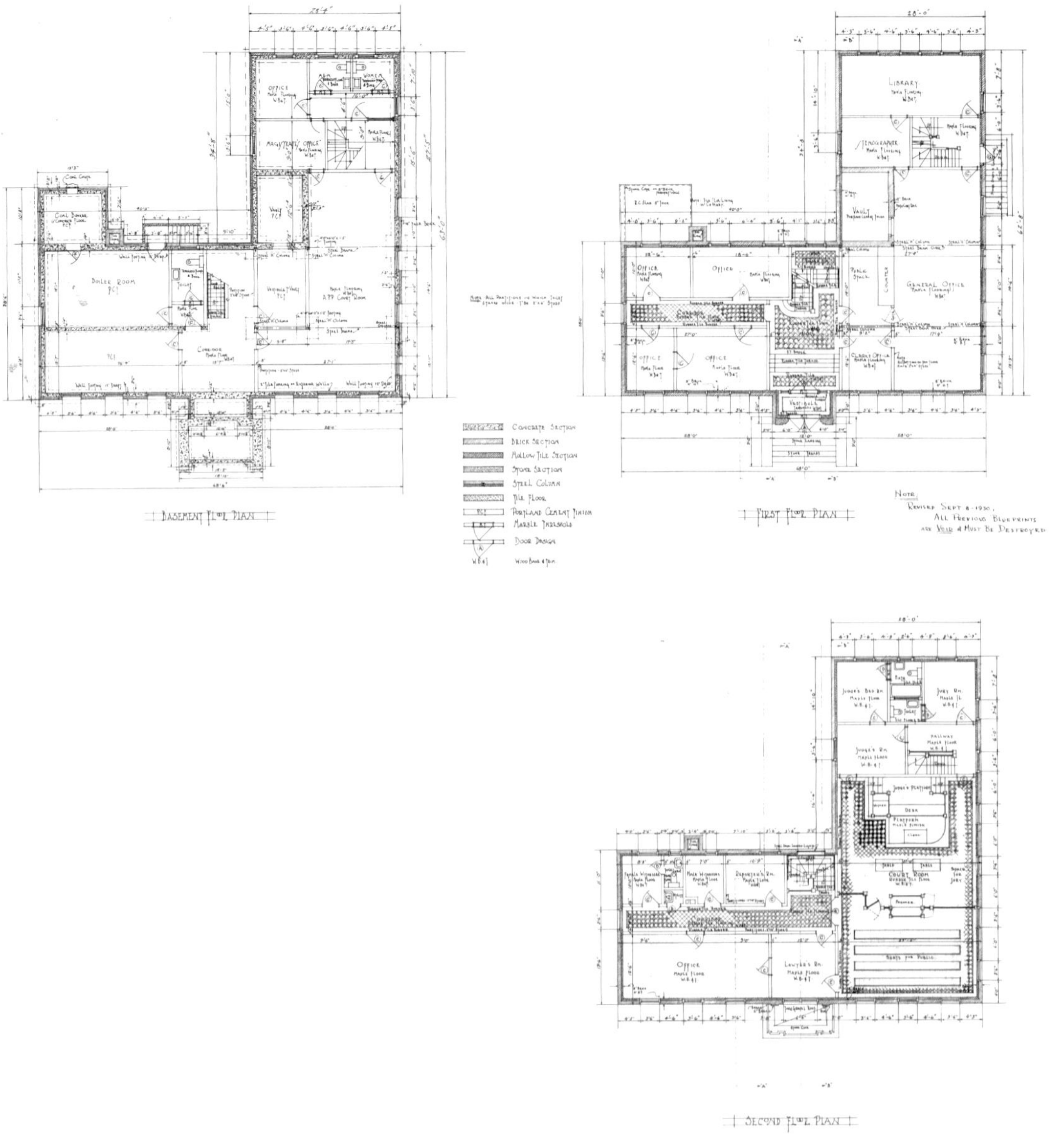


*Basement and main plans, second floor and roof plans, Vegreville Courthouse, 1930. AI*

space was put to good use, and when the courts needed the room, these tenants could presumably be moved out.

Vegreville started with a full complement of guests. The police magistrate had both an office and a courtroom in the basement, and the local Alberta Provincial Police detachment was also given office space, which later served the RCMP. The district agriculturist, the public school inspector, the public health nurse and even the officer of the Alberta Farm Women's Bureau was allowed space in the courthouse.[1035] The complement was further rounded out with the local school division offices. The presence of the nurse meant all sorts of people, including infants, might be found in the courthouse during the day. The local bar was not pleased about the other tenants of the courthouse, feeling the building was too crowded.[276] They were especially annoyed by attempts to take over the law library. The RCMP wanted it

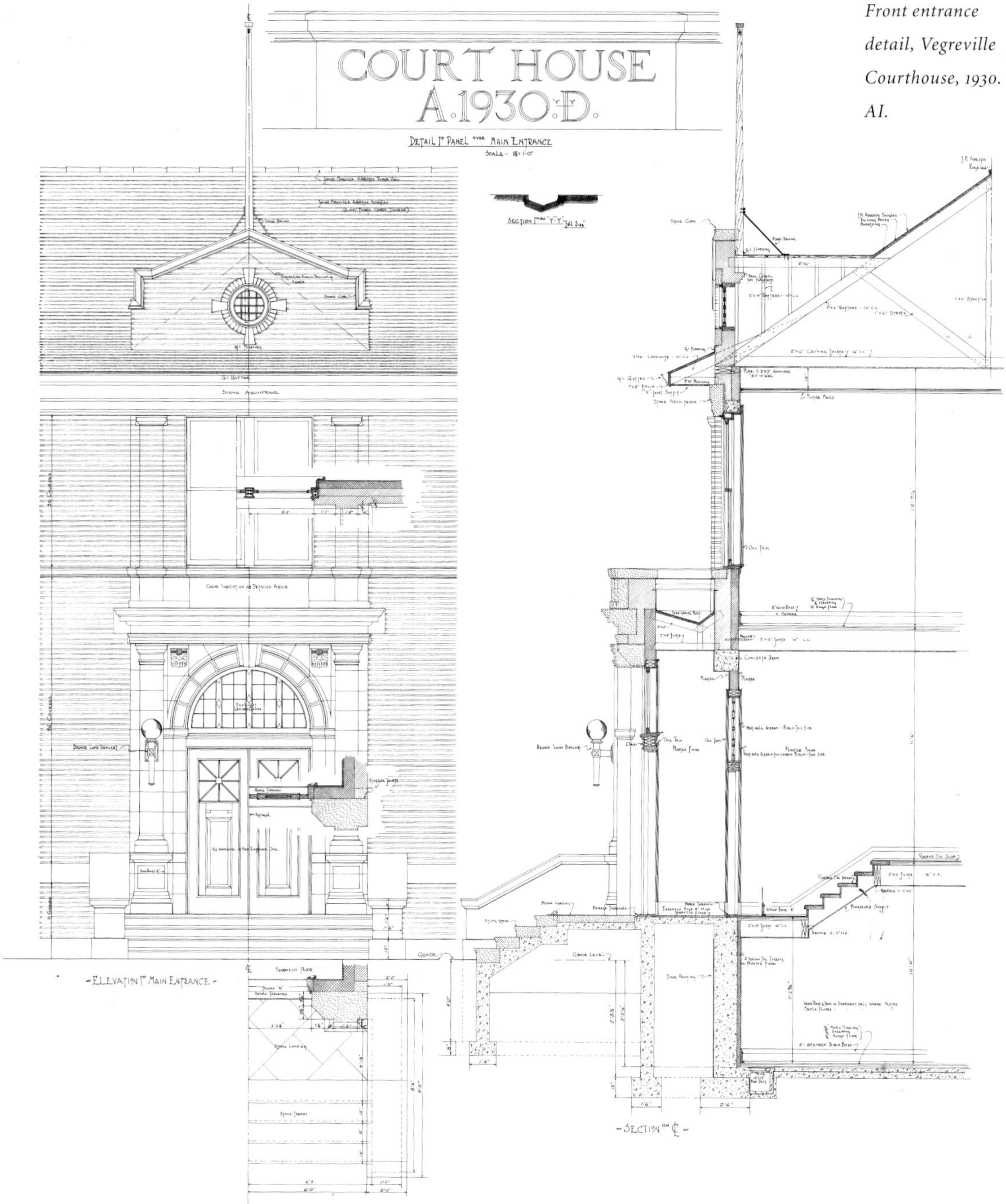


*Front entrance detail, Vegreville Courthouse, 1930. AI.*

for office space, and even the local public library coveted it, to use as – a library.[277] The government did recognize it could go too far in its generosity. Discussing the police request with McDonald, the Deputy Attorney General said: "… we would be in hot water with the Local Bar at Vegreville if we took away the room provided for a library, even though at present it is not used as such."[278]

*A pleasing simplicity: Vegreville's new Courthouse*
*PAA, A7869*

## Opening Day

With great excitement the Vegreville Chamber of Commerce organized a special committee to take charge of the opening ceremonies for the courthouse. The deputy sheriff, the clerk, and their staffs had moved into the new building in February, but finishing work was still underway and the recent death of Judge Taylor of the District Court delayed the next assize. The official opening was set for April 8, and as in Red Deer, the local chamber went all-out to make sure it was a lavish event. Supreme Court justices and cabinet members were invited as well as prominent members of the Edmonton Bar. Matheson, Mayor Holden (the former MLA), and most of the Vegreville elite were there as a matter of course. Vegreville did not get quite the same glitterati as Red Deer. Chief Justice Simmons of the Supreme Court's trial division and Justice Walsh of the Appeal Court came, with Judge Dubuc representing the District Court, but R.G. Reid, Provincial Treasurer, came on behalf of the cabinet while McDonald was the representative of Public Works and Deputy Attorney General Henwood stood in for his boss. After a ceremonial opening of the court, the distinguished guests repaired to the King Edward Hotel for a banquet. Simmons reminisced about competing with Mayor Holden for public works when the two were rookie legislators. A great deal of praise was directed toward the chamber of commerce, but especially to A.M. Matheson for his strenuous efforts on behalf of Vegreville. His constant lobbying was thought to be instrumental in securing the town's judicial status and fine new courthouse.

While in town, Judge Dubuc and Justice Simmons held their respective courts and inaugurated the new edifice. Dubuc would be back in a month for the regular District sitting, while the Supreme Court would return in the summer with

*A new landmark: Vegreville's courthouse 1932. Vegreville Museum Society.*

Justice Ives. The Vegreville courthouse had commenced a career that would last until 1989. With its assemblage of provincial offices, the Vegreville building had a central role in the day-to-day life of the town. As was increasingly the case, however, it was for the most part taken for granted. It was the start of a change of attitude toward courthouses, wherein they no longer aroused the same passions seen in earlier years. Before the courthouse had officially opened and curiosity was at its height, the Observer had this advice for its readers:

> The building is not quite ready for complete inspection yet, so with the exception of those who have business in the Clerk's offices, perhaps it would be well for the public to refrain their natural curiosity.... Anyway, now courts and courthouse are generally first class things to avoid.[279]

## Epilogue

The Vegreville courthouse still stands, remarkably unaltered. An important centre in the agricultural economy of the 1930s, Vegreville was less so in the new oil and gas economy of the post-war years and grew slowly. The courthouse remained adequate for the needs of the area for years. Vegreville became centre of an eponymous

*Vegreville bonspiel, 1935. Vegreville Museum Society.*

judicial district in 1955, but this did not necessitate any major changes to the building. The Department of Public Works hedged by buying adjacent property in case an expansion became necessary. This had a side benefit of eliminating concern for the government over what might be built beside the courthouse – Arthur Arnold, the official involved, rather liked the way the building looked on its property and did not want it crowded.

In the mid-1980s, the government began planning a new courthouse, but there was no talk of demolishing the original edifice in favour of the new: times had changed, and throughout the province old court buildings were receiving protection as historic sites instead of facing the wrecker's ball. The new courthouse never materialized. Feeling the pinch of an economic downturn, the government provided court facilities in the local provincial building, an alternative that had already been used in other low-traffic areas like Cardston and Hanna. And far from resurrecting the courthouse project, after a review of judicial services, the government cancelled Court of Queen's bench sittings in the town. The citizens of Vegreville are now once again forced to trek into Edmonton if they have business with the province's high court.

As for the original brick courthouse, it became the offices of the County of Minburn. After a complete refurbishment, the building was reopened in 1991 and has served the county administration ever since. The courtroom is now a council chamber with the offices easily reconfigured for county officials. Given the long tradition of courthouses in North America as the seat of county government, the building's fate is most fitting.

# CONCLUSION

The UFA and its program of courthouse construction very much represent a period of retrenchment. After the grander gestures of the spendthrift Liberals, the United Farmers government turned to the precepts of Dominion government in the Territorial days, aiming to build utilitarian structures where they were absolutely necessary. The results were very much the same. In two centres, Red Deer and Vegreville, where larger facilities were necessary and politically expedient, the government was willing to spend some extra money. In others, where frontier conditions still existed, the UFA took a page from the book of the federal government and tried to minimize its commitment. But even with the Red Deer courthouse, far and away the largest and most imposing courthouse built by the UFA, the architectural decoration that elevated the edifice beyond the strictly functional was an afterthought. This was a government that clearly had little time for architectural symbolism.

Consequently, the provincial Department of Public Works was not asked to produce grand courthouses, and it may no longer have been capable of doing so. For all of its courthouses, with the exception of the Blairmore building, the department turned to existing models, even if they were obsolete. For Grande Prairie and Hanna, the architectural staff reached back to the Territorial courthouse at Macleod for their floor plan, which seems hardly a coincidence. Blakey's Medicine Hat courthouse provided the template for Vegreville and Red Deer, and there may already have even been some plans in existence for these buildings. The general policy of restraint did not encourage innovative design, and the abolition of the Provincial Architect's office had lowered the standard of design. There is evidence that the government also tried to produce cheaper buildings for both Vegreville and Red Deer, but in these cases decided to go a bit further to please local opinion.

The courthouse remained an important building in the public consciousness. A small city like Red Deer still felt strongly about possessing a decent hall of justice, for pragmatic but also symbolic reasons. In Vegreville, elite opinion saw an impressive courthouse as an important bulwark of the justice system. Though perhaps a little more erratic than in previous decades, lobbying campaigns were still organized that had the full participation of civic and political bodies, such as the chamber of commerce, the local bar association, and the leading newspaper. Grande Prairie, Red Deer, and Vegreville all presented united fronts on the subject of a courthouse. Disapproval of substandard buildings was also quickly expressed. The burghers of Grande Prairie were horrified when the government wanted to use the Club Hall for a courthouse and protested in the strongest terms. Vegreville was apparently able to obtain a better class of building by complaining vociferously. At the same time, in Grande Prairie and Hanna, comment was limited to perceived inequities in the tendering process. If residents in these two towns were disappointed in their buildings, they kept it to themselves.

The United Farmers government in Alberta added another dimension to courthouse architecture to the province, and their legacy is well represented. Only Grande Prairie's little court building has been lost in the subsequent years. It is admittedly, not a legacy of architectural innovation and aesthetic achievement. However, during the years of UFA rule, the courthouse remained a fundamentally important and universal public building to Albertans, its symbolic role and its importance to civic prestige and economics only somewhat diminished. In some regions of the province, frontier conditions still existed, and towns emulated their predecessors in more settled areas by lobbying for public works. Courthouses were not, however, as sensitive an issue for the United Farmers party as they had been for previous governments. Ironically, a courthouse played a significant role in the end of the UFA as a force in Alberta politics. Both O.L. Macpherson, the minister of Public Works who oversaw the UFA's construction program, and the popular John Brownlee, the party's second premier, had their political careers destroyed in an Edmonton courtroom. Two separate sex scandals ended in highly publicized civil trials, and contributed to the demolition of the UFA at the hands of the Social Credit party in 1935.

# EPILOGUE
## THE ALBERTA COURTHOUSE SINCE WORLD WAR II

Alberta is a young and dynamic province. Except for a thirty-year period that ended with World War II, the story of the region has been generally one of growth, and with growth there has always been a need for new infrastructure, especially public buildings like courthouses. After World War II, a profound shift took place in the public consciousness toward architecture, led by the discipline itself. The historically inspired styles of yesteryear were suddenly swept away by the rising tide of modernity, architects and planners stressed functionality over form, and the rich symbolism of classical architecture was replaced by the universality of the International Style. Perhaps as a consequence, the public at large, even the dedicated civic boosters, lost interest in courthouse planning and procurement, at least in comparison to the frenetic lobbying of previous years. Courthouses were left increasingly to the bureaucrats and architects. Something of the time-honoured relationship between people and their hall of justice survived, however, in the mounting concern over the fate of the province's original courthouses.

After the completion of the Vegreville courthouse, it would be over twenty years before a new hall of justice would be built in Alberta. The Great Depression ended courthouse construction in Alberta until well after World War II. The province's existing buildings, whether holdovers from the Territorial days, the halls of justice of the first decade of provincial rule, jury-rigged conversions, or the pragmatic brick and stucco of the UFA, soldiered on. Municipalities realized the futility of asking for a large public building from the provincial government. Indeed, for several communities like Taber and Stettler, keeping their status as a judicial headquarters was an issue, and they were disestablished as sub-districts in 1935. Alberta's third political dynasty, the Social Credit party, had to wait until the beginning of the 1950s to try their hand at courthouse design. But after the war, the booming oil economy rapidly put the provincial government in a position to address the pressing need for public works of all sorts.

New court buildings were certainly much needed. The spending cutbacks of the Depression and war years meant that all the existing buildings were in need of repairs. Budgets for maintenance had been cut to the bone during the 1930s.[1] All the courthouses had suffered accordingly, and even relatively new buildings like Red Deer's were prematurely worn. The business of the courts would grow exponentially in the 1950s and 1960s and so would staff. Many old courthouses ran out of space. In Edmonton, for example, the courthouse opened in 1912 with a staff of ten, not including the judges; by the late 1960s, the staff numbered over a hundred. Designs that were state of the art before World War I had been inadequate for years, with poor security, inadequate ventilation, and simply not enough space.

Consequently, courthouses were given relatively high priority by the administration of Premier Ernest Manning. Over a ten-year period, four new courthouses were built and additions for two others. At the end of the decade, plans were underway for an entirely new building in Calgary, and by the mid-1960s, the government was planning to replace the halls of justice in Red Deer, Medicine Hat, Fort Macleod, and Edmonton. In a familiar pattern, however, economic difficulties led to delays and cancellations of new projects, which had the benefit of saving the provincial courthouses in Medicine Hat and Red Deer. At the end of the 1970s, in the aftermath of the Kirby Commission on the provincial justice system, another round of courthouse construction began. All the original courthouses, with one exception, were replaced with new buildings, or else new facilities were provided in all-purpose provincial buildings. Even the post-war courthouses in Lethbridge and Grande Prairie, built in the 1950s, were replaced, already outgrown and inadequate.

The need to replace older buildings with improved courthouses became a direct threat to the continued existence of older halls of justice. In many cases, now enumerated, the destruction of obsolete facilities was felt to be necessary to expedite their replacements. To some extent, this has reflected the obsession with the new and the devaluation of the old that was characteristic of the immediate post-war period, and which doomed many buildings that in retrospect had great historic or aesthetic value. The process was not unique to Alberta; it has occurred in many jurisdictions in North America where growth made old halls of justice simply inadequate to modern needs, and economics as well as notions of progress dictated demolition over preservation.

The post-war period saw a major shift in the way courthouses were designed. Initially, the government turned to private architects, no doubt because after such a long period of inactivity, the Department of Public Works no longer had adequate architectural staff. By 1954, this had changed again, and design moved back within the department. Within another decade, the government had once again started commissioning private architects for their courthouses. Problems with the 1962 Calgary courthouse may have prompted the government to turn to outside expertise – this building took a long time and had many difficulties. The department's architectural office remained an important part of the planning process, but did not engage in building design. By the 1960s, courthouse planning had reached a new height of sophistication. Building committees representing the judiciary, the Attorney General's Office, Public Works, and the commissioned architects set the criteria for new buildings, engaged in comprehensive consultations with courthouse occupants, and even travelled extensively to look at new facilities in other jurisdictions.

Both the department's commissioned and in-house designs participated in the prevailing post-war architectural trends. The courthouses that were built after the war represented the progressive spirit of the age. Gone were historical styles in courthouse architecture. While there remained a vestigial consciousness that courthouses should somehow be more impressive and dignified than other buildings, function was more and more crucial. To a large extent this was forced upon designers by the sheer expansion of the judicial system and its bureaucracy. After World War II, courthouses became office buildings instead of ceremonial spaces dedicated to physically embodying the law. The International Style, which swept North America as the architecture of choice for business, government, and institutions, also became the standard for courthouses. Classical porticoes, stone and brick were replaced with strip windows and plain wall surfaces. Only the extensive use of expensive and exotic finishes in public spaces and courtrooms, one small concession to the symbolic role of the buildings, singled out courthouses from other types of public structures. It was a change that did not please everyone. Justice Harold Riley, clearly disenchanted with the aggressively modern Calgary courthouse, made this comment in 1967:

> The new Edmonton Court house should look like a Court House, and not an office building. In the past, Court Houses have been surrounded with majesty and dignity secondary to the provincial Parliament buildings.[2]

The change in architecture from the monumental to the institutional may also have contributed to a noticeable shift in public attitudes toward courthouses. No longer were the buildings the focus of civic pride. As buildings blended in more with commercial and other institutional architecture, their hold on the public consciousness diminished. The idea that a courthouse had to symbolize justice in an obvious and universal way was almost entirely lost, or simply became irrelevant. The procurement of new courthouses became a matter of bureaucratic planning and decision making rather than local lobbying. Courthouse planning was important to civic governments in the context of urban renewal: in almost every Alberta city, civic squares were proposed for government buildings. City planners in Edmonton, Lethbridge, or Medicine Hat wanted a new courthouse placed there if one was forthcoming. Civic boosters still took interest in new courthouse projects, and generally welcomed any such initiative, but the days of petitions, delegations, and demands were over. Generally, the strongest and most vocal lobbyists for new courthouses were judges, building staff, and local bar associations. Their concern was for a proper workspace.

Paradoxically, these same people also led the way in trying to save old courthouses, sometimes even giving up a promised new building to do so. Although they were, relatively speaking, small and undistinguished, Alberta's old courthouses still found a place in people's hearts. The symbolism and also the history that they embodied managed to live on in the public consciousness, even as new courthouses eschewed such associations. The well-publicized fight to save the Territorial courthouse in Calgary was a landmark struggle in Alberta. By the middle 1960s, an appreciation for historic buildings was growing, and at least in the smaller cities like Red Deer and Medicine Hat, both citizens and municipal governments showed a concern for their old halls of justice, wanting them preserved if at all possible. Civic involvement shifted to efforts to preserve older courthouses. But the local bar and bench, those who would most inconvenienced by staying in an old building, also sometimes demonstrated a stubborn attachment to the courthouses. At the reopening of the refurbished Medicine Hat courthouse, Judge Louis Turcotte noted pointedly:

> It is not often that the occasion arises in Western Canada when a building built 50 years ago is renovated so that it may be used for another 50 years.... I think it is the finest court room in the province. The thanks of all of us are due to those who mounted the campaign to preserve this building and we thank the Government of Alberta for preserving it.[3]

As the remaining of the province's early halls of justice were decommissioned in the 1970s and early 1980s, a much greater sensitivity and appreciation for historic architecture saved them from demolition, though sometimes not without a fight. Most of the surviving old courthouses of the province have been declared historic sites and given permanent protection. The continued viability of these old buildings has remained more of a challenge. With a somewhat specialized design, courthouses do not lend themselves to other uses.[4] Some became art centres, others museums, others galleries, and one a teahouse, and one, the 1914 structure in Calgary, became a courthouse once again for the provincial Court of Appeals. Many of these adaptations, however, have not proved financially successful. The upkeep and renovation expenses can be very high, and there are many difficulties in adapting these edifices to other uses. The story of Alberta's historic courthouses is far from over.

Architecture has often been used for ideological ends, and certain types of building take on a cultural resonance beyond their simple form. The courthouse in Alberta has been much more than just a functional public building. As elsewhere in North America, these buildings represented fundamental values within society: law and order, justice, and good governance. There was a strong emotional response to this symbolism. A population of immigrants brought with them notions about the courthouse developed over the course of two centuries, a belief that the courthouse embodied the law. These values, at least for the political and civic elites within Alberta, remained strongly expressed until the eve of World War II. Without embarrassment, civic leaders and provincial politicians could call for a courthouse in a centre like Vegreville as a civilizing influence and a bulwark for the rule of law, a physical manifestation that would create respect and even trust. It was a sophisticated understanding of symbolism but also a naïve belief in the power of architecture.

Albertans also looked to their courthouse as a manifestation of civic pride. This was especially true of that species common in the early years of settlement known as boosters. In many places in North America, courthouses were the responsibility of local authorities and reflected the aspirations of civic elites. A monumental courthouse demonstrated that a centre was well established and prosperous. A building for the courts was expected to have a pleasing appearance, generally in the architectural style popular for public buildings of the time, and to be of solid construction, meaning brick or stone masonry. These preconceptions were very strong. What Albertans wanted in their courthouses was an imposing piece of public architecture, one that would speak volumes about prosperity and permanence. Above and beyond the immediate pragmatic benefits involved, such as being a judicial headquarters and a legal centre, having a courthouse was also a way of making prophecies of growth and prosperity come true.

This tradition came to Alberta, but as courthouses were a responsibility of higher government, local boosters had to lobby the federal and then provincial government for buildings. This created a great deal of tension between the aspirations of residents and the aims of government, especially in the Territorial period. The value put on courthouses, however, is clear from the amount of energy that was spent on lobbying by civic bodies. Lethbridge, Macleod, and Red Deer all mounted sustained campaigns to the federal government; later, it was places like Vegreville or Grande Prairie doing the same with the provincial government. In all cases, the plea was the same: permanent court facilities are desperately needed, and such facilities should be objects worthy of pride and appropriate to the gravity of the law. Even in cities large enough to be ensured new courthouses, a close eye was kept on design and appearance and complaints came quickly if the building did not live up to promises. And as the long saga of the provincial courthouse in Medicine Hat amply demonstrates, if a hall of justice was delayed too long, it could swiftly become a major political liability.

Local pressure had an important impact on courthouse construction, as did confronting growth. Both the federal and provincial governments found it difficult to decide on where to best place courthouses and also to design buildings that would be adequate but not too expensive. A major concern for government was wasting money on an elaborate building in a town that never became a major centre. On the opposite end of the scale, in cases like Lethbridge's and Edmonton's provincial courthouses, cities could grow so fast that large and expensive halls of justice were already too small by the time they were commissioned. The federal government responded to this challenge by only building courthouses reluctantly, and with the exception of Calgary's sandstone hall, cheaply – even though government bureaucrats themselves sometimes bridled against the utilitarian designs that were produced. The province of Alberta responded to the first flush of optimism with relatively grand if austere courthouses, but quickly scaled back its plans in the face of recession and the rather large price tags. The later administration of the United Farmers, with its tight-reined fiscal policy, looked back to the Territorial halls for inspiration for their courthouse construction.

The prevailing climate within government determined more than any other factor the kind of courthouses that were built. The edifices constructed as halls of justice in Alberta were for the most part modest structures. Designed within government bureaucracies far from the places they would be built, and removed from local pressures, the majority of the early courthouses of Alberta did not aspire to architectural distinction. Instead, responding to less than ideal economic conditions or weak commitment, they were simple structures. For one golden period, under the provincial Liberals, Albertans could expect buildings that went beyond the purely utilitarian and fulfilled long-standing notions about what courthouses should be like. Jeffers and Blakey designed several buildings of merit, and for a brief time brought Alberta's early public buildings into the architectural mainstream.

The endless debates and emotionally charged demands for courthouses seem remote now. To the people of Alberta in decades past, however, the courthouse was a fundamental part of the civic fabric, a necessity and not a luxury, a necessary symbol of what they considered civilized society. Courthouses were caught up, as they have been throughout North America, in civic aspirations as well as the needs of judges, advocates, and accused.

Courthouses continue to be erected, some of them impressive, but they do not arouse the same passions that the smallest of Alberta's historic halls of justice created. For generations of Albertans, these buildings truly were the foundations of justice.

# NOTES

## Notes To Introduction

1 Sir Nikolaus Pevsner, *A History of Building Types* (Princeton: Princeton University Press, 1976), 34.

2 *Ordinances of the North-West Territories*, 1898, no. 21, s. 36. The ordinance creating the law society mandated it create law libraries "at such points in the Territories as they deem proper." In practice this meant the local courthouse when it was built.

3 Richard Pare, *Courthouse: A Photographic Document* (New York: Horizon Press, 1978), 20–25; Marion MacRae, *Cornerstones of Order: Courthouses and Town Halls of Ontario, 1784–1914* (Toronto: Osgoode Society, 1983), 70; John O. and Margaret T. Peters, *Virginia's Historic Courthouses* (Charlottesville: University Press of Virginia, 1995), 5–6 , Margaret Carter, ed., *Early Canadian Court Houses* (Ottawa : Canadian Parks Service. National Historic Parks and Sites, 1983), 38.

4 Pare, *Courthouse*, 27.

5 Ronald M. James*Temples of Justice* (University of Nevada Press, 1994); Willard Robinson, *The People's Architecture: Texas Courthouses, Jails and Municipal Buildings* (Texas State Historical Association, 1983), 80.

6 Alan F.J. Artibise, "Boosterism and the Development of Canadian Cities," in *Town and City, Aspects of Western Canadian Urban Development* (Regina: Canadian Plains Research Center, 1981), 209–36.

7 Terry Chapman, "The controversy over Courts and Courthouses," *Alberta History* 37, no. 4 (Autumn 1989): 2–3. This article discusses early examples of this in Fort Macleod, Lethbridge, and Medicine Hat, Alberta.

8 *Stettler Independent*, January 1, 1914.

9 Pare, *Courthouse*, 8; Robinson, 17, 47; Alan Gowans, *Styles and Types of North American Architecture* (New York: Icon Editions, 1992), 227.

10 National Archives of Canada (hereafter NAC), RG 11, B-2, a-i, vol. 1337, file 214533. These comments were made by Lethbridge lawyer C.F.P. Conybeare about the Territorial courthouse there.

11 NAC, RG 11, *Estimates of Canada, Public Works*, vol. 3102, 87.

## Notes To Part One

1 *Statutes of Canada*, 1873, c. 35, s. 15.

2 R.C. Macleod, *The North-West Mounted Police and Law Enforcement* (Toronto: University of Toronto Press, 1976), 4–5.

3 Lewis H. Thomas, *The Struggle for Responsible Government in the North-West Territories, 1870–1897* (Toronto: University of Toronto Press, 1956), 135.

4 *Ordinances of the North-West Territories*, 1897, no. 14, 357, "An Ordinance Respecting The Department of the Attorney General"; no. 17, 382, "An Ordinance Respecting the Department of Public Works."

5 Wilbur Bowker, "Stipendiary Magistrates and the Supreme Court of the Northwest Territories, 1876–1907," in *A Consolidation of Fifty Years of Legal Writings of Wilbur F. Bowker* (Edmonton: University of Alberta Faculty of Law, 1989), 697.

6 Ibid., 697.

7 Horace Harvey, "Some Notes on the Early Administration of Justice in Canada's Northwest" *Alberta Historical Review* 1, no. 3 (1953): 8–10.

8 *Ordinances of the North-West Territories*, 1877, no. 10, "An Ordinance respecting the Administration of Justice."

9 *Census of the Three Provisional Districts of the North-West Territories* (Ottawa: Maclean Roger & Co, 1886), 10.

10 Glenbow Archives, M776, "My Darling Mary," various letters.

11 Carter, *Early Canadian Court Houses*, 133. This claim should be investigated further. There is some mention in locales such as Lethbridge and Fort Saskatchewan of the magistrates using the barracks, but this claim seems to me conjecture at this point.

12 *Statutes of Canada*, 1886, c. 25, s. 3, 124.

13 Bowker, "Stipendiary Magistrates," 722.

14 *Statutes of Canada*, 1886, c. 25, s. 10, 125.

15 Ibid., s. 17, 126.

16 PAA, Acc. 66.166 box 2, file 16. This was certainly the case with Justice Macleod in the Southern Alberta Judicial District, and likely true of the other justices, though some more study may be warranted.

17 Bowker, "Stipendiary Magistrates," 729.

18 Ibid., 728.

19 NAC, RG 13, A-3, vol. 680, 621.

20 Bowker, "Stipendiary Magistrates," 729.

21 NAC, RG 13, A-3, vol. 677, 303; A-2, vol. 114, file 1900-99. These are just two letters of many to and from the justices in regard to courthouse requirements, respectively to Rouleau and Scott about the five new buildings to be built by the Liberals and to Scott about the Medicine Hat courthouse. While similar correspondence was not found for the earlier Calgary and Lethbridge courthouses, it likely exists or existed as well.

22 Janet Wright, *Crown Assets: The Architecture of the Department of Public Works 1867–1967* (Toronto: University of Toronto Press, 1997), 47.

23 Douglas Owram, *Building for Canadians: A History of the Department of Public Works 1840–1960* (Ottawa: Public Works Canada, 1979), 158–60.

24 Wright, *Crown Assets*, 73.

25 *Edmonton Bulletin*, June 9, 1899.

26 Wright, *Crown Assets*, 37.

27 Margaret Archibald *By Federal Design: The Chief Architects Branch of the Department of Public Works 1881–1914* (Ottawa : National Historic Parks and Sites, Canadian Parks Service, 1983), 15.

28 Wright, *Crown Assets*, 22–23.

29 Ibid., 75.

30 Ibid., 74.

31 Carter, *Early Canadian Court Houses*, 134.

32 This will be seen in the accounts of the individual courthouses, where Justices Rouleau, Scott, and also Sifton were involved with the design process. There does not seem to have been the same consultation with the earlier Calgary and Lethbridge buildings, although Macleod did complain about some aspects of Lethbridge's layout.

33 Owram, *Building for Canadians*, 158.

34 NAC, RG 11, D-2, vol. 3868, 260 to 657.

35 Glenbow Archives, M776, file 7, Correspondence, March 4, 1885 to Colonel James F. Macleod. Petitions attached.

36 Ibid.

37 *Annual Report of the Minister of Public Works* (hereafter *Public Works, Annual Report*) 1884–85, cx. The Estimates were essentially the government's budget document.

38 Ibid.

39 NAC, RG 13, A2, vol. 63, file 1885-948.

40 *Public Works, Annual Report*, 1885–86, cvi.

41 NAC, RG 13, A2, vol. 63, file 1885-948.

42 *Calgary Weekly Herald*, May 21, 1885, 2.

43 This account is largely derived from Max Foran's "The Travis Affair," *Alberta History* 19, no. 4 (Autumn 1971).

44 *Calgary Weekly Herald*, April 10, 1889, 4.

45 NAC, RG17, vol. 664, file 75701.

46 NAC, RG 17, vol. 553, file 61951–61980.

47 Ibid.

48 *Calgary Tribune*, July 17, 1889

49 *Calgary Herald*, March 1, 1888.

50 NAC, RG 11, D-2, vol. 3866, 24.

51 City of Calgary Archives, copy of *Estimates of Canada*, 1889–1890, 200.

52 NAC, RG 11, D-2, vol. 3866, 103.

53 *Calgary Weekly Herald*, November 14, 1888, 4.

54 *Calgary Herald*, December 14, 1985.

55 *Calgary Tribune*, November 14, 1888, 3.

56 NAC, RG 11, D-2, vol. 3867, 429.

57 *Edmonton Bulletin*, April 23, 1892.

58 NAC, RG 11, D-2, vol. 3867, 690.

59 Ibid., vol. 3868, 690.

60 NAC, RG 11, B-6, vol. 3046, 186.

61 Richard Cunniffe, *Calgary in Sandstone* (Calgary: Historical Society of Alberta, 1969), 7–9.

62 Wright, *Crown Assets*,14, 32. The mansard roof was a feature of the Second Empire style, used extensively by the Department of Public Works in the 1870s.

63 NAC, RG 11, D-2, vol. 3869, 176.

64 Ibid., vol. 3867, 690.

65 NAC, RG 11, B-6, vol. 3046, 187.

66 Robinson, *The People's Architecture*, fig. 49, 62. The Ward County courthouse (1892) and Dickens County courthouse (1892) both used a similar arcaded porch between two projecting pavillions with a mansard roof, a composite of Second Empire and Romanesque done in quarry faced stone.

67 Wright, *Crown Assets*, 37, 44–45.

68 *Calgary Tribune*, October 9, 1889, 4.

69 *Calgary Daily Herald*, July 14, 1890, 1.

70 *Calgary Daily Herald*, July 7, 1890.

71 *Calgary Weekly Herald*, August 13, 1890.

72 NAC, RG 13, A-2, vol. 137, file 1900-465.

73 Ibid.

74 NAC, RG 11, B-2, a-i, vol. 1356, file 281506.

75 NAC, RG 11, B-2, a-i, vol. 1348, file 216649.

76 *Calgary Daily Herald*, March 17, 1904.

77 Provincial Archives of Alberta (hereafter PAA), acc. 79.387, box 12, ledger; *Calgary Herald*, March 31, 1914. A yard was added for the prisoners that was also to be used "for the execution of murderers." This alarming prospect never occurred: the last hanging in Calgary took place in 1914 at the police barracks.

78 PAA, acc. 72.370, box 1, file 1, Annual Report of C Division, 39.

79 *Henderson's Calgary Directory*, various years.

80 City of Calgary Archives, City Council Minutes, January 21, 1957, 61.

81 Ibid.

82 *Calgary Herald*, n.d. Calgary Public Library clipping file, "Courthouses – Calgary."

83 NAC, RG 84, A-2-a, vol. 1424, file HS10-167.

84 Ibid.

85 Ibid., minutes of meeting, May 1959.

86 *Albertan*, March 13, 1958.

87 Georgia Green Fooks, *Lethbridge Portraits of the Past* (Burlington Windsor Publications, 1988), 17.

88 Alex Johnston and Andy den Otter, *Lethbridge: A Centennial History* (Lethbridge: Lethbridge Historical Society, City of Lethbridge, 1991).

89 Fooks, *Portraits of the Past*, 35; Johnston, *A Centennial History*, 40.

90 Glenbow Archives, M776(14a), letter to Mary Macleod, July 20, 1887, first mention of court in Lethbridge. No cases to try.

91 Ibid., October 28, 1891, 2.

92 *Lethbridge News*, December 22, 1905, 1.

93 Johnston, *A Centennial History*, 40.

94 *Lethbridge News*, July 27, 1887, 2; September 7, 1887, 3; October 5, 1887, 2.

95 *Lethbridge News*, June 7, 1888, 2; January 23, 1889.

96 Ibid.

97 *Lethbridge News*, February 12, 1890.

98 NAC, RG 13, A-2, vol. 70, file 1888-630.

99 *Lethbridge News*, January 6, 1891, 2.

100 Ibid., January 20, 1891, 2.

101 Ibid., September 16, 1891, 2.

102 Ibid., September 23, 1891.

103 NAC, RG 11, vol. 3056, 155.

104 NAC, RG 11, vol. 3056, 155.

105 *Lethbridge News*, April 20, 1892, 2.

106 Ibid., April 13, 1892, 3.

107 Ibid., June 8, 1892, 2.

108 Ibid., November 2, 1892, 2.

109 Archibald, *By Federal Design*, 14-15

110 NAC, RG 11, B-6, vol. 3913, 132–36.

111 *Public Works, Annual Report*, 1893, 41.

112 NAC, RG 11, B-6, vol. 3913, 139.

113 *Lethbridge News*, June 1, 1893, 2–3; *Public Works, Annual Report*, 1893, 41.

114 *Lethbridge News*, July 6, 1893, 3.

115 *Lethbridge Herald*, April 21, 1939.

116 Wright, *Crown Assets*, 13.

117 *Lethbridge News*, January 11, 1894, 2.

118 NAC, RG 11, D-2, vol. 3883, 766.

119 NAC, RG 11, D-2, vol. 3884, 302; vol. 3885 12.

120 NAC, RG 13, A-2, vol. 104, file 1897-331.

121 *Lethbridge News*, June 29, 1898; December 15, 1898.

122 NAC, RG 11, B-2, a-i, vol. 1337, file 214533.

123 David C. Jones, L.J. Roy Wilson, Donny White, *The Weather Factory, A Pictorial History of Medicine Hat* (Saskatoon: Western Producer Prairie Books, 1988), 2.
124 Ed Gould, *All Hell for a Basement* (Medicine Hat, AB: City of Medicine Hat, 1981, 15.
125 Jones, *The Weather Factory*, 2.
126 *Medicine Hat Times*, April 30, 1887.
127 Glenbow Archives, James. F. Macleod Family Papers, M776/14a, 1883/24.
128 *Medicine Hat Times*, July 30, 1887.
129 *Medicine Hat Times*, November 9, 1893.
130 *Ordinances of the North-West Territories*, 1891–92, no. 10, 18.
131 *Public Works, Annual Report*, 1884–1885, cx.
132 *Medicine Hat Times*, May 11, 1889; PAA, Acc. 92.361, box 4, file SO575-1, vol. 1.
133 PAA, , Acc. 92.361, box 4, file SO575-1, vol. 1.
134 *Medicine Hat Times*, June 5, 1891.
135 NAC, RG 11, B-6, vol. 3041, *Estimates of Canada, Public Works*, 204.
136 NAC, RG 11, B-6, vol. 3046, *Estimates of Canada, Public Works*, 196.
137 NAC, RG 13 A-2, vol. 86, file 1892–450.
138 *Medicine Hat Times*, March 30, 1893.
139 *Medicine Hat Times*, April 30, 1887.
140 *Public Works, Annual Report*, 1893–94, 7.
141 L.J. Roy Wilson, "Everlasting Squabble: Medicine Hat in Crisis, 1891–98," *Alberta History* 35, no. 1, 19871–12.
142 *Medicine Hat News*, August 30, 1894.
143 *Medicine Hat Times*, August 10, 1893
144 *Medicine Hat News*, August 6, 1896, 4.
145 Ibid.
146 Ibid., November 12, 1896.
147 Ibid., June 3, 1897.
148 Ibid., June 10, 1897.
149 NAC, RG 13 A-2, vol. 114, file 1900-99.
150 Ibid.
151 *Medicine Hat News*, June 9, 1898.
152 *Edmonton Bulletin*, June 9, 1899.
153 NAC, RG 11, B-6, vol. 3080, *Estimates of Canada*, 1900.
154 *Medicine Hat News*, April 6, 1899
155 Ibid.
156 Ibid., May 11, 1899.
157 Ibid., January 12, 1899.
158 NAC, RG 11, B-6, vol. 3080, 66.
159 NAC, RG 11, B-6, vol. 3894, 620.
160 *Public Works, Annual Report*, 1900, 25; *Medicine Hat News*, September 14, 1899.
161 *Medicine Hat News*, December 14, 1899.
162 Ibid., February 15, 1900.
163 Ibid., March 15, 1900.
164 Ibid., February 22, 1900.
165 Ibid.
166 Ibid., June 21, 1900.
167 PAA, Acc. 92.362, box 4, file SO575-1, vol. 1.
168 Ibid.
169 Ibid.
170 *Medicine Hat News*, October 18, 1969.
171 Ibid.
172 Ibid.
173 Sherill McLaren, *Braehead: Three Founding Families in Nineteenth Century Canada* (Toronto: McLelland & Stewart, 1986), 198.
174 *Macleod Gazette*, January 12, 1886.
175 Ibid., December 1, 1885.
176 Ibid., December 1, 1885; January 19, 1886.
177 Ibid., February 23, 1886.
178 Ibid., April 27, 1886.
179 Ibid.
180 Ibid., June 23, 1883.
181 Chapman, "The controversy over Courts and Courthouses," 3.
182 *Macleod Gazette*, February 22, 1888.
183 NAC, RG 13, A-2, Volume 104, file 1897-331.
184 *Macleod Gazette*, February 22, 1888.
185 *Macleod Gazette*, January 31, 1889.
186 *Lethbridge News*, February 6, 1889.
187 *Macleod Gazette*, February 14, 1889.
188 *Macleod Gazette*, March 27, 1890; *Lethbridge News*, March 18, 1890.
189 Chapman, "The controversy over Courts and Courthouses," 4–5.
190 PAA, acc 66.166, box 2, file 16.
191 NAC, RG 13, A-2, vol. 135, file 1905-117.
192 *Macleod Gazette*, November 3, 1893.
193 Macleod Town Council Minutes, Minute Book 1, 107.
194 *Macleod Gazette*, November 13, 1903.
195 NAC, RG 13, A-2, vol. 135, file 1905-117.
196 NAC, RG 13, A-2, vol. 104, file 1897-331.
197 Macleod Town Council Minutes, Minute Book 1, 104.
198 Ibid., 229.
199 Macleod Town Council Letter Book, February 1899–December 1900, 19–21.
200 Macleod Town Council Minutes, Minute Book 1, 262–63.
201 PAA, acc 66.166, box 2, file 16.
202 Chapman, "The controversy over Courts and Courthouses," 11.
203 Macleod Town Council Minutes, Minute Book 3, 65–66, 98; *Macleod Gazette*, January 6, 1899.
204 *Macleod Gazette*, February 10, 1899.
205 Archibald, *By Federal Design* (Ottawa : National Historic Parks and Sites, Canadian Parks Service, 1983), 5, 36.
206 Macleod Town Council Letter Book, February 1899–December 1900, 16.
207 NAC, RG 13, A-2, vol. 107, file 1898-55.
208 Macleod Town Council Letter Book, 1899, 1.
209 *Macleod Gazette*, October 13, 1899.
210 NAC, RG 13, A-2, vol. 107, file 1898-55.
211 NAC, RG 11, B-6, vol. 3102, 85.
212 *Macleod Gazette*, June 29, 1900.
213 Ibid.
214 NAC, RG 13, A-2, vol. 135, file 1905-117
215 Macleod Town Council Letter Book, February 1899–December 1900, 206.
216 *Macleod Gazette*, January 11, 1901.
217 Ibid., March 25, 1901.

218 Ibid., April 5, 1901.
219 Ibid., December 6, 1901.
220 Ibid.
221 NAC, RG 11, B-2 a-i, vol. 1358, file 219395.
222 NAC, RG 11, B-2 a-i, vol. 1397, file 227262.
223 Ibid.
224 NAC, RG 11, B-2,c-i, vol. 2400, file 127999, 435.
225 *Macleod Gazette*, February 21, 1902.
226 Ibid.
227 Ibid., August 22, 1902.
228 *Public Works, Annual Report*, 1904, section 3, 23; *Macleod Gazette*, October 10, 1902.
229 *Public Works, Annual Report*, 1906, section 3, 33.
230 *Macleod Gazette*, June 5, 1903.
231 Mills, *The Early Court Houses of Alberta*, Manuscript report no. 310 ([Ottawa] : Parks Canada, 1977), 86.
232 *Public Works, Annual Report*, 1904, sections 3, 23.
233 Carter, *Early Canadian Court Houses*, , 78–122.
234 The assigning of an architectural style to a building is a subjective exercise. My analysis of this building is based on Harold Kalman, *A History of Canadian Architecture, vol. 2* (Toronto: Oxford University Press, 1994), chapters 10 and 11; Leslie Maitland, Jacqueline Huncker and Shannon Ricketts, *A Guide to Canadian Architectural Styles* (Peterborough: Broadview Press, 1992), 84–105; Leslie Maitland, *The Queen Anne Revival Style in Canadian Architecture* (Ottawa : National Historic Parks and Sites, Parks Service, 1990), 77–82 and Wright, *Crown Assets*, 57–58, 73–84. The cross gable roof arrangement is apparently exceptionally rare in courthouses. According to Henry-Russell Hitchcock and William Seale in *Courthouse*–get publishing info (208, plate 72), only two examples of this survive in the United States; one in Florida built in 1894 is "wooden vernacular," and the authors also comment on its domesticity: "Domestic in scale, public in dimensions."
235 Maitland, *Queen Anne Revival*, 77–78.
236 NAC, RG 11, B-2, a-i, vol. 1511, file 259069.
237 NAC, RG 13, A-3, vol. 680, 711.
238 Carter, *Early Canadian Court Houses*, 134.
239 *Macleod Gazette*, February 6, 1903.
240 NAC, RG 11, D-2, vol. 3902, 516.
241 *Macleod Gazette*, May 4, 1904.
242 NAC, RG 11, B-2, a-i, vol. 1502, file 256652.
243 NAC, RG 11, B-2, a-i, vol. 1511, file 259069.
244 *Public Works, Annual Report*, 1902–3, vol. 38, no. 7, pt. 2, 7; 1903–4, vol. 39, no. 8, pt. 2, 12; 1904–5, vol. 40, no. 8, pt. 2, 12.
245 Ibid.
246 *Calgary Herald*, November 14, 1904.
247 NAC, RG 13, A-3, vol. 677, 305.
248 NAC, RG 11, B-2, a-i, vol. 1351, file 217275.
249 NAC, RG 13, A-2, vol. 135, file 1905-117.
250 NAC, RG 11, D-2, vol. 3906, 451.
251 Ibid., 609.
252 NAC, RG 11, B-2, a-i, vol. 1590, file 282633.
253 PAA, acc. 73.322, file 43a.
254 PAA, acc. 70.414, file 127, Public Accounts tabled in legislature, 8.
255 Ibid.
256 *Public Works, Annual Report*, 1924, 35; PAA, acc. 83.83, box 28, no. 10.
257 Ibid.
258 *Fort Macleod Gazette*, September 24, 1970.
259 *Fort Macleod Gazette*, September 30, 1971; unknown clipping, likely *Lethbridge Herald*, Glenbow Museum Library, clipping file "Fort Macleod–Buildings."
260 J.G. Macgregor, *Edmonton: A History* (Edmonton: Hurtig, 1967), 69.
261 Ibid., 82.
262 Dominion of Canada Census, 1901.
263 Bowker, "Stipendiary Magistrates," 713.
264 Ibid., 714.
265 NAC, RG 13, A2, vol. 60, file 1884-583; Glenbow Archives, M776, "My Darling Mary" – letters, 1883–84, correspondence dated August 9, 1883; and *Edmonton Bulletin*, April 17, 1886.
266 *Edmonton Bulletin*, December 12, 1881.
267 Ibid., June 17, 1882.
268 Ibid., November 13, 1886.
269 Ibid., May 14, 1887.
270 Ibid., May 20, 1887, and October 12, 1889.
271 Ibid., August 23, 1890.
272 Ibid., August 14, 1893.
273 Ibid., February 13, 1892.
274 Ibid., and November 23, 1892.
275 *Edmonton Bulletin*, February 9, 1893.
276 Ibid., September 19, 1892.
277 Ibid., May 11, 1893.
278 PAA, acc. 66.166, box 1, file 17.
279 *Edmonton Bulletin*, May 15, 1893.
280 Ibid.
281 NAC, RG 13, A2, vol.136, file 1905-256.
282 Alex Mair, "Now that was a courthouse," *RealEstate Weekly*, July 18, 1996.
283 Ibid.
284 Ibid.
285 PAA, acc. 66.166, box 1, file 17.
286 NAC, RG 13, A2, vol. 136, file 1905-256.
287 *Edmonton Bulletin*, March 23, 1893.
288 Ibid., May 3, 1894.
289 Ibid.
290 Ibid.
291 *Edmonton Bulletin*, May 17, 1894.
292 Ibid., May 31, 1894.
293 NAC, RG 13, A-2, vol.136, file 1905-256.
294 *Edmonton Bulletin*, June 19, 1899.
295 Ibid., October 16, 1899.
296 Ibid., November 6, 1899.
297 Ibid., December 18, 1899.
298 Ibid., December 22, 1899.
299 NAC, RG 13, A-2, vol.136, file 1905-256; *Edmonton Bulletin*, February 2, 1900.
300 *Edmonton Bulletin*, June 9, 1899.
301 Ibid., June 9, 1899.
302 NAC, RG 11, vol. 3096, *Estimates of Canada*, 1903, 83.
303 NAC, RG 13, A-2, vol.136, file 1905-256.

304 NAC, RG 13, A-3, vol. 677, 255.

305 NAC, RG 11, D-4, vol. 3899, 692.

306 NAC, RG 13, A-2, vol.136, file 1905-256.

307 City of Edmonton Archives (hereafter CEA), Town of Edmonton Council Minutes, Minute Book 5, 1898 to 1901, 337 and 352.

308 NAC, RG 13, A-2, vol.136, file 1905-256.

309 NAC, RG 13, A-2, vol.136, file 1905-256 and CEA, Council Minutes, Minute Book 5, 1898 to 1891, 368.

310 CEA, Council Minutes, Minute Book 5, 1898 to 1891, 368.

311 NAC, RG 11, B-2, a-i, vol. 1382, file 224421.

312 NAC, RG 11, B-2, a-i, vol. 1350, file 2126948.

313 NAC, RG 11, D-4, vol. 3900, 144.

314 NAC, RG 11, B-2 a-i, vol. 1397, file 227261.

315 NAC, RG 11, B-2, a-i, vol. 1382, file 224364.

316 NAC, RG 11, B-2 a-i, vol. 1397, file 227261.

317 *Edmonton Bulletin*, April 5, 1901.

318 NAC, RG 11, B-2, a-i, vol. 1397, file 227261.

319 *Edmonton Bulletin*, April 19, 1901.

320 NAC, RG 11, B-2, a-i, vol. 1397, file 227261.

321 NAC, RG 11, B-2, a-i, vol. 1391, 226017.

322 NAC, RG 11, B-2, c-I, vol. 2398, file 127028.

323 NAC, RG 11, B2, a-i, vol. 1382, file 224423.

324 NAC, RG 11, B2, a-i, vol. 1382, files 224364, 224423.

325 NAC, RG 13, A-2, vol. 136, file 1905-256.

326 NAC, RG 18, vol. 209, files 1901-241–250.

327 NAC, RG 11, B2, a-i, vol. 1382, file 224423.

328 *Edmonton Bulletin*, July 29, 1903.

329 *Edmonton Bulletin*, March 7, 1902; Council Minutes, Minute Book 6, 1902–3, 478.

330 CEA, RG 8, class 5, file 33.

331 Ibid.

332 Ibid.; *Edmonton Bulletin*, March 26, 1903.

333 CEA, Council Minutes, Minute Book 7, 1903–4, 159.

334 CEA, RG 8, class 5, file 33.

335 *Edmonton Bulletin*, January 13, 1902.

336 CEA, Council Minutes, Minute Book 6, 1902–3, 478.

337 NAC, RG 13, A-3, vol. 681, 85, 109.

338 Louis Knafla and Richard Klumpenhouwer (eds.), *Lords of the Western Bench: A Biographical History of the Supreme and District Courts of Alberta, 1876-1990* (Calgary: Legal Archives Society of Alberta, 1997), 123, 153; *Edmonton Bulletin*, March 10, 1902.

339 *Edmonton Bulletin*, March 10, 1902.

340 Ibid., May 16, 1902.

341 NAC, RG 13, A-2, vol.136, file 1905-256.

342 Ibid.

343 Ibid.

344 *Henderson's Edmonton Directory* for 1913 clearly lists the Supreme Court at the Sandison Block, 268 Jasper, beside the J.H. Morris store at 270. The *Edmonton Bulletin*, March 3, 1903, states that Sandison is to start building a new block between the Morris store and the Union bank. On January 13, 1903, the secretary of public works writes the deputy minister of justice, Newcombe, about renting the Sandison Block at $50 a month, indicating the move is about to take place. See NAC, RG 13, A2, vol. 136, file 1905-256.

345 *Edmonton Bulletin*, March 23, 1903.

346 Northwest Territories Gazette, vol. 2, no. 4, 1885, 70.

347 PAA, acc. 66.166, box 1, file 17.

348 Ibid.

349 Northwest Territories Gazette, vol. 12, no. 3, February 1, 1895, 36.

350 Red Deer Archives (hereafter RDA), Red Deer School District Minutes, Book 1, 50.

351 *Calgary Weekly Herald*, February 26, 1895.

352 NAC, RG 11, *Estimates of Canada, Public Works*, vol. 3102, 87.

353 NAC, RG 13, A-2, vol. 137, file 1900-498.

354 Census of Canada, 1911, vol. 1, p. 535

355 NAC, RG 11, D-2, vol. 3898, 135.

356 RDA, 62.4.1-2, Liberal Association Letter Book, August 13, 1900.

357 F.C. Jamieson, "Edmonton Courts and Lawyers in Territorial Times," *Alberta Historical Review* 4, no. 1, –1956, 9

358 NAC, RG 11, B-2, a-i, vol. 1348, file 216679.

359 NAC, RG 11, D-2, vol. 3898, 135.

360 NAC, RG 13, A-3, vol. 677, 259.

361 NAC, RG 11, B-2, a-i, vol. 1397, file 227264.

362 RDA, 62.4.1-2 Liberal Association Minute Book, December 23, 1901.

363 NAC, RG 11, vol. 3102, *Estimates of Canada, Public Works*, 1903–4, 86. The money was sent to a firm by the name of Nauton and Munson – probably realtors.

364 NAC, RG 11, B-6, vol. 3102, *Estimates of Canada, Public Works*, 1903-4, 86

365 NAC, RG 11, B-2, a-i, docket 238814.

366 NAC, RG 11, D-2, vol. 3902, 519.

367 NAC, RG 11, M79003/36, Plans of Red Deer Court House.

368 RDA, 62.4.1-2, Liberal Association Minute Book, April 7, 1902, June 18, 1902.

369 NAC, RG 13, A-2, vol. 137, file 1900-498.

370 NAC, RG 11, B-2, a-i, vol. 1496, file 254977.

371 NAC, RG 11, D-2, vol. 3904, 97

372 NAC, RG 11, D-2, vol. 3903, 211.

373 NAC, RG 11, B-2, a-i, vol. 1512, file 259317.

374 *Public Works, Annual Report*, 1903–4, 21. *Edmonton Bulletin*, September 1, 1903, makes reference to Paradis as the supervising engineer. NAC, RG 11, D-2, vol. 94, Hugh Clarke appointed the clerk.

375 RDA, 62.4.1-2, Liberal Association Minute Book, March 4, 1904.

376 Ibid., April 2, 1904.

377 *Calgary Herald*, October 1903.

378 *Calgary Herald*, October 1903, June 1904.

379 NAC, RG 11, B-2, a-i, vol. 1559, file 272798.

380 Ibid.

381 NAC, RG 11, D-2, vol. 3906, 355.

382 NAC, RG 11, D-2, vol. 3907, 401.

383 NAC, RG 13, A-2, vol. 137, file 1900-498.

384 Ibid.

385 *Red Deer News*, February 6, 1906, 1

386 NAC, RG 11, B-2, c-i, vol. 2464, 89

387 NAC, RG 13, A-2, vol. 2339, file 1908-128; RG 11, B-2, c-I, vol. 2475, letter 159474.

388 NAC, RG 11, B-2, a-i, vol. 1496, file 254977.

389 NAC, RG 11, *Estimates of Canada, Public Works*, vol. 3102, 87.

390 Red Deer City Records office, City Council Minutes, June1946–December 1948, 99; January 1949–April 1951, 225.

391 Ibid., May 1951–December, 1952, 5, 9.

## Notes To Part Two

1 *Alberta Gazette*, vol. 2, Extra, September 17, 1906.

2 *Morning Albertan*, October 10, 1907.

3 *Statutes of Alberta*, 1907, c. 4, 5.

4 *Edmonton Bulletin*, February 5, 1907.

5 To wit, of the Supreme Court of Alberta appointments up to 1921, Beck and Simmons, appointed before Laurier's defeat in 1911, were liberals, while Hyndman, Ives, McCarthy, and Walsh were all conservative. The political inclinations of the District Court are not as well known, but even so, Crawford, Noel, Mitchell, Taylor, and Winter were definitely Liberals, while Mahaffy, Morrison, and McNeill were all Conservatives. See Knafla and Klumpenhouwer, *Lords of the Western Bench*.

6 PAA, acc. 73.322, file 43d. In the letter, the minister continued: "It is necessary to have a District Court Judge for every judicial district, but our territory is so large in this province and the settlement so scattered that it is not convenient for the public in transacting business to only have on court centre in a territory containing a population and with legal business sufficient to keep one judge occupied. There was an understanding last year between the Dominion Government and the Governments of the various provinces that the Dominion which pays the salaries of all judges would add a thousand dollars to the salary of each District Court Judge (which formerly was very inadequate) provided that the provincial governments would not form any more judicial districts than is absolutely necessary, and therefore not put the Dominion Government to the expense of appointing any more judges that necessary for the trial of cases and the other duties which a District Judge performs. We have therefore adopted the policy of establishing judicial districts and then establishing from that territory sub-judicial districts. The sub-judicial district has exactly the same status as a judicial district excepting that the Clerk and Sheriff is described as Deputy Clerk and Deputy Sheriff, but has the same powers as Clerk and Sheriff of the judicial district."

7 *Statutes of Alberta* , 1913, 1st Sess., c. 9, s. 38, 24.

8 *Statutes of Alberta* , 1919, c. 3, ss. 5–9, 16–17.

9 *Edmonton Bulletin*, March 13, 1920; *Edmonton Journal*, April 7, 1921.

10 Knafla & Klumpenhouer, *Lords of the Western Bench*, 166.

11 Ibid., 68.

12 Ibid., 163.

13 [1922] 2 W.W.R. 317.

14 [1923] 3 W.W.R. 936–37.

15 *Public Works, Annual Report*, 1910, 105. See also PAA, acc. 76.213, box 39, file 167a.

16 PAA, acc. 92.361, box 4, file SO 626-1 P#1. In response to petitions from Pincher Creek, W.H. Cushing stated that decisions on courthouses were taken by the Executive Council.

17 Rostecki, *The Early Courthouses of Saskatchewan*, Manuscript Report no. 306, (Ottawa: Parks Canada, 1977), 16–17.

18 Ibid.

19 *Scrapbook Hansard*, Third Legislature, 1913, 157; *Edmonton Bulletin*, October 20, 1913.

20 See Lewis G. Thomas, *The Liberal Party in Alberta: A History of Politics in the Province of Alberta, 1905–1921* (Toronto: University of Toronto Press, 1959).

21 *Vegreville Observer*, April 8, 1931.

22 *Vegreville Observer*, October 13, 1926.

23 Mills, *Early Court Houses of Alberta*, 27, note 23 – this quote is from correspondence at PAA, acc. 76.213, but the citation is incomplete.

24 *Edmonton Bulletin*, February 10, 1917.

25 *Grande Prairie Herald Tribune*, May 5, 1972.

26 PAA, acc. 76.213, box 50, file 208b.

27 *Public Works, Annual Report*, 1907, 100.

28 *Public Works, Annual Report*, 1908, 51.

29 Michael Payne, "Allan Merrick Jeffers: One of Alberta's First Architects," *Alberta Past* (Winter 1994).

30 Kalman, *Canadian Architecture*, 556.

31 Payne, "Allan Merrick Jeffers".

32 Kalman, *Canadian Architecture*, 556.

33 *Construction* (October 1910): 79.

34 Kalman, *Canadian Architecture*, 556.

35 Medicine Hat News, June 10, 1909

36 Diane Bodnar, *Prairie Legislative Buildings of Canada*, MA Thesis, University of British Columbia, 1979, 27.

37 Hirsten, *Events Leading to the Settlement of the Community of Cardston, Magrath, Stirling and Raymond Alberta*, Dissertation, Utah State University, 196868.

38 *Cardston Record*, November 30, 1898.

39 Keith Shaw, ed., *Chief Mountain Country*, (Cardston: Cardston and District Historical Society, 1978-1987), 94.

40 Hirsten, 31.

41 PAA, acc. 66.166, box 10, file 190.

42 Macleod, *The North-West Mounted Police*, 155.

43 Colin Poole, "Identification of Mounted Police Outposts in Southern Alberta," in Hugh A. Dempsey, ed., *Men in Scarlet* (Calgary: McLelland and Stewart West, 1974), 210.

44 *Cardston Record*, November 16, 1898. Poole, "Identification," 204, gives a date of 1899, which seems in error.

45 *Cardston Record*, November 16, 1898.

46 Northwest Territories Gazette, vol. 20, no. 1.

47 NAC, RG 11, B-2 a-i, vol. 1382, file 224431.

48 *Alberta Star*, April 4, 1908.

49 *Lethbridge Herald*, June 1962; see Woolf, John W., clipping file, GAI Library.

50 PAA, acc. 81.186, OC #316, 1906; Kalman, *Canadian Architecture*, 555.

51 *Public Works, Annual Report*, 1908, 67.

52 PAA, acc. 83.86, Plan 0006.

53 *Public Works, Annual Report*, 1908, 68.

54 Edward Mills, *Early Court Houses of Alberta*, 34. This was also an opinion that was expressed by Alberta Culture officials during the site designation process.

55 NAC, RG 18, vol. 355, file 1908/172-182.

56 *Lethbridge Herald*, August 16, 1906.

57 PAA, acc. 79.387, box 12, ledger. The land the government bought was lot 2, block 21, plan 1793E.

58 *Lethbridge News*, April 19, 1906; *Alberta Star*, March 14, 1911.

59 *Public Works, Annual Report*, 1907, 100.

60 Ibid., 1908, 67.

61 *Cardston Record*, April 1, 1954.

62 PAA, acc. 76.213, box 49, file 203a.

63 Shaw, ed., *Chief Mountain Country*, vol. 1, 418.

64 *Alberta Star*, June 20, 1908, 5.

65 PAA, acc. 70.414, box 4, file 127.

66 NAC, RG 18, vol. 355, file 1908/172-182.

67 *Alberta Star*, January 28, 1910.

68 PAA, acc. 73.322, box 40, file 24c.

69 PAA, acc 73.322, box 40, file 24d.

70 Town of Cardston, Council Minutes, Minute Book 1914–1918, 365; *Cardston Globe*, February 28, 1918.

71 Town of Cardston, Council Minutes, Minute Book 1914–1918, 403.

72 *Cardston News*, December 3, 1925; December 10, 1925; February 4, 1926.

73 PAA, acc. 76.213, box 49, file 203a.

74 *Cardston News*, April 8, 1926.

75 PAA, acc 76.213, box 49, file 203g.

76 Ibid

77 PAA, acc 76.213, box 49, file 203i.

78 *Westwind News*, March 2 and 16, 1977.

79 *Lethbridge Herald*, October 27, 1978; *Chief Mountain Country*, vol. 2, 83.

80 *Westwind News*, November 21 and 28, 1979; *Chief Mountain Country*, vol. 2, 80.

81 A. Bert Reynolds, *Siding 16: An Early History of Wetaskiwin to 1930* (Wetaskiwin: RCMP Centennial Committee, 1975), 3–6.

82 Ibid.

83 Ibid., 9.

84 Ibid., 41, 46.

85 Ibid., 26.

86 Ibid., 84.

87 Ibid., 52.

88 Ibid., 59.

89 Ibid., 64.

90 NAC, RG 13 A-2, vol. 128, file 1903-742.

91 Ibid.

92 Ibid.

93 *Wetaskiwin Times*, November 13, 1902.

94 PAA, acc. 66.166, box 9, file 161.

95 Ibid.

96 Ibid., 30.

97 *Wetaskiwin Times*, September 6, 1906.

98 PAA, acc. 66.166, box 36, file 563.

99 *Scrapbook Hansard*, 1st Legislature, 1st Session, *Edmonton Bulletin*, May 8, 1906, no page no.

100 *Wetaskiwin Times*, August 23, 1906.

101 PAA, acc. 92.361, file SO836-1, vol. 1.

102 Ibid..

103 *Wetaskiwin Times*, August 30, 1906.

104 Ibid, September 6, 1906.

105 Ibid, August 30, 1906.

106 *Public Works, Annual Report*, 1908, 74.

107 Ibid., 74; *Wetaskiwin Post*, October 24, 1907.

108 *Wetaskiwin Post*, March 19, 1908.

109 *Wetaskiwin Post*, December 27, 1908.

110 PAA, acc. 68.308, box 9, file 1921-32; acc. 70.414, box 4, file 127.

111 PAA, acc. 76.213, box 52, file 216e.

112 PAA, acc. 76.213, box 52, file 216h.

113 PAA, acc. 73.322, file 107.

114 *Camrose Canadian*, March 14, 1918.

115 Ibid., February 7, 1918.

116 Ibid., January 7, 1909.

117 PAA, acc. 79.387, box 12, ledger; acc. 83.86, plan 193-31.

118 PAA, acc. 73.322, file 107.

119 PAA, acc. 76.213, box 53, file 216t.

120 PAA, acc. 76.213, box 52, file 216j.

121 PAA, acc. 76.213, box 52, files 215I, 215q, 215t.

122 PAA, acc. 92.361, box 13, file SO836-1.

123 PAA, acc. 76.213, box 52, file 216c.

124 PAA, acc. 76.213, box 53, files 216u, 216w.

125 Ibid., file 216x.

126 Ibid., file 216y.

127 Ibid., file 216z.

128 Ibid.

129 Ibid., file 216bb.

130 Wetaskiwin City Archives, 95.19/3, City Council Minutes, June 19, 1920.

131 Ibid., November 16, 1920; November 30, 1920.

132 PAA, acc. 73.322, file 43d.

133 *Edmonton Daily Capitol*, July 26, 1912; PAA, acc. 83.86, box 2, no. 16, Edmonton Courthouse Architectural Drawings, dated May 1908.

134 Ibid.

135 *Edmonton Bulletin*, Christmas 1907 special edition.

136 PAA, acc. 70.414, box 1, file 4; acc. 92.361, file SO325-1, vol. 1.

137 Ibid.

138 *Edmonton Bulletin*, January 24, 1908.

139 *Red Deer News*, February 17, 1909.

140 *Edmonton Bulletin*, March 13, 1907.

141 *Public Works, Annual Report*, 1907, 100.

142 Ibid., 8.

143 *Edmonton Bulletin*, January 10, 1908.

144 *Edmonton Bulletin*, February 27, 1908, 3; *Estimates*, 1908, 9.

145 *Fort Saskatchewan Reporter*, February 25, 1909.

146 PAA, acc. 83.86, plan 0024.

147 *Public Works, Annual Report*, 1909, 37, 59.

148 Ibid., 37; *Fort Saskatchewan Reporter*, July 8, 1909.

149 *Public Accounts*, 1909, 37.

150 *Public Works, Annual Report*, 1909, p. 37.

151 Peter T. Reach, *The Fort on the Saskatchewan* (Fort Saskatchewan Historical Society, 1974), 349.

152 PAA, acc. 76.213, file 265b.

153 Ibid., 350.

154 *Public Works, Annual Report*, 1908, 53.

155 PAA, acc. 83.86, box 2, no. 16, Edmonton Courthouse Architectural Drawings, dated May 1908. The personnel involved in each drawing are listed by initial on the drawing. Most of the Edmonton drawings were checked by Jeffers, while Blakey was frequently one of the draftsman or tracers.

156 *Public Works, Annual Report*, 54.

157 PAA, acc. 70.414, box 4, file 147.

158 *Edmonton Bulletin*, May 8, 1908.

159 Ibid., June 16, 1908.

160 Ibid., July 18, 1908.

161 Ibid., July 27, 1903.

162 Public Accounts, 1909, 79; *Edmonton Bulletin*, July 18, 1908.

163 There is no mention of a clerk of works or supervising architect; the *Bulletin* reported in a September 5, 1908 Special Supplement that the Architect's office was directly superintending the Parliament buildings. It is a reasonable supposition this was true of the courthouse.

164 *Edmonton Bulletin*, May 13, 1908. According to this article, the foundation work was to begin in the fall. The September 8, 1908 edition says construction had begun.

165 *Edmonton Bulletin*, June 5, 1908.

166 *Public Works, Annual Report*, 1909, 59.

167 *Public Works, Annual Report*, 1910, 39.

168 *Edmonton Bulletin*, November 5, 1910.

169 *Edmonton Bulletin*, July 20, 1911.

170 *Edmonton Daily Capitol*, August 22, 1911.

171 PAA, acc. 76.213, files 204a, 206c, 206f.

172 *Edmonton Daily Capitol*, March 7, 1912.

173 *Edmonton Journal*, January 30, 1912.

174 *Edmonton Journal*, June 19, 1912; *Edmonton Bulletin*, June 22, 1912.

175 *Edmonton Journal*, June 20, 1912.

176 *Edmonton Daily Capitol*, July 26, 1912.

177 PAA, acc. 76.213, box 49, file 204a.

178 Ibid.

179 Ibid.

180 Ibid,138.

181 PAA, acc. 76.213, box 49, file 204a.

182 Ibid.

183 Ibid.

184 Ibid.

185 PAA, acc. 69.287, box 7, file R1a.

186 PAA, acc. 68.308. box and file number not available. Copy of original in author's possession.

187 See James Gray, *Talk to My Lawyer* (Edmonton: Hurtig Publishers, 1987), 106–12. This account is essentially based on this chapter.

188 *Edmonton Journal*, June 24, 1972

189 *Public Works, Annual Report*, 1955–56, 18.

190 PAA, acc. 81.298 (unprocessed), file Courthouse, Edmonton 1952–53.

191 *Public Works, Annual Report*, 1955–56, 18.

192 PAA, acc. 81.298 (unprocessed), file Courthouse, Edmonton 1952–53; *Public Works, Annual Report*, 1955–56, 18.

193 *Edmonton Journal*, June 24, 1972.

194 Ibid., September 8, 1962.

195 PAA, acc. 92.361, file SO235-1, vol. 2.

196 PAA, acc. 92.361, file SO235-2, vol. 1.

197 Ibid.

198 PAA, acc. 81.298, file Courthouse, Edmonton, 1965–67; Acc. 92.361, file SO235-1, vol. 3.

199 *Lethbridge Daily News*, April 26, 1911, 4.

200 *Lethbridge News*, July 14, 1904, 2.

201 Ibid., October 20, 1905, 2.

202 *Lethbridge Herald*, May 25, 1906, 1.

203 PAA, acc. 66.166, box 37, file 565c.

204 PAA, acc. 92.361, box 3, file SO542-1, vol. 2.

205 *Lethbridge Herald*, May 25, 1906, 1.

206 *Lethbridge News*, June 8, 1906.

207 *Lethbridge Herald*, May 25, 1906; also May 31, 1906.

208 PAA, acc. 76.213, box 39, file 167q.

209 Ibid.

210 *Lethbridge Herald*, January 15, 1908, 1.

211 Ibid.; also PAA, acc. 92.361, box 3, file SO542-1, vol. 1.

212 *Lethbridge News*, February 5, 1908, 7.

213 Ibid., February 10, 1908, 2.

214 PAA, acc. 92.361, box 3, file SO542-1, vol. 1.

215 Ibid.

216 PAA, acc. 83.86, plan 18, sheet Q8.

217 The author's opinion was shared by the sheriff of the Wetaskiwin District, writing to the inspector of legal offices when renovations to the Wetaskiwin courthouse were done in the 1950s: "The construction of this building as you know does not lend itself to making additions as the walls can't be moved," implying this was the commonly held opinion. PAA, acc. 76.213, box 53, file 216z.

218 Knafla and Klumpenhouer, *Lords of the Western Bench*, 183.

219 One contemporary reportedly told Tweedie, who lived in Calgary, not "to go holding court in the shit house" next time he went to Edmonton.

220 *Lethbridge Herald*, October 5, 1944, 1.

221 *Lethbridge Herald*, March 19, 1909, 1.

222 *Lethbridge Herald*, March 1, 1906, 4.

223 *Lethbridge Herald*, June 26, 1909, 8.

224 *Public Works, Annual Report*, 1909, 61.

225 *Lethbridge Herald*, April 2, 1910.

226 *Scrapbook Hansard*, 2nd Legislature, *Bulletin*, March 21, 1910, 145.

227 *Public Accounts*, 1910, 48. Only $4,546.10 is charged against construction, but accounts brought down in 1914 in the legislature show $40, 546.48 was spent in 1910: see PAA, acc. 70.414, box 4, file 127.

228 *Public Works, Annual Report*, 1910, 39.

229 *Lethbridge News*, January 11, 1911, 8.

230 *Lethbridge Herald*, February 24, 1917.

231 PAA, acc. 72.370, box 1, file 1, Report of D Division, 1918, 26; box 2, file 6A, Report of D Division, 1923, 4.

232 City of Lethbridge City Clerk's Office, City Council Minutes, 1949, 168.

233 PAA, acc 92.361, box 11, file SO542-1, vol. 2, letter, November 14, 1949, G.H.N. Monkman to D.B. MacMillan.

234 Ibid.
235 Ibid., file 1642.
236 *Lethbridge Herald*, September 16, 1952.
237 Ibid., September 16, 1952.
238 Ibid., September 17, 1952.
239 Ibid., June 2, 1983.
240 City of Lethbridge Archives, Economic Development, Administration Files, box 1603, file 900-B3.
241 Mills, *Early Courthouses of Alberta*, 156.
242 *Taber Times*, April 24, 1913.
243 Ibid.
244 Ibid., September 3, 1914.
245 *Lethbridge Herald*, February 21, 1917; PAA, acc. 73.322, file 107.
246 *Public Works, Annual Report*, 1917, 203–4. Blakey does not say as much, but it is strongly implied.
247 *Taber Times*, June 6, 1918; Mills, *Early Courthouses of Alberta*, 158.
248 PAA, acc. 68.308, box 9, file: dept. 1921-32.
249 *Taber Times*, August 19, 1918.
250 *Taber Times*, February 20, 1919.
251 PAA, acc. 73.322, file 107.
252 *Taber Times*, October 30, 1919; *Lethbridge Herald*, September 30, 1982.
253 PAA, acc. 73.322, file 107.
254 Ibid.
255 *Taber Times*, December 5, 1935.
256 PAA, acc. 79.387, box 12, ledger; *Lethbridge Herald*, June 16, 1951.
257 *Lethbridge Herald*, July 10, 1995.
258 Dorothy Field, ed., *Calgary: Stephen Avenue and Area Historical Walking Tour* (Edmonton: Alberta Community Development, 1995), 44.
259 PAA, acc. 73.322, file 43a.
260 PAA, acc. 76. 213, box 39, file 167q.
261 *Albertan*, June 22, 1908.
262 *Calgary Herald*, May 12, 1909.
263 PAA, acc. 76.213, box 39, file 167q.
264 *Estimates*, 1911, 11.
265 *Public Works, Annual Report*, 1911, 36.
266 Edward Mills, in his excellent survey of the early courthouses for Parks Canada, feels Blakey's changes were to lessen the expense. I think the modifications to the entrance were for style not economy, as the changes were not that extensive and introduce a motif used by Blakey in the future, as is mentioned further on.
267 *Public Works, Annual Report*, 1913, 34.
268 City of Calgary Archives, City Clerks Papers, box 46, file 373.
269 Ibid.
270 *Calgary News-Telegram*, Saturday, August 10, 1912, 13.
271 *Albertan*, November 11, 1912.
272 Ibid., September 30, 1912.
273 *Public Accounts*, 1912, 137, and 1913, 145. Under "Courthouse, Calgary," contractors and suppliers are listed, as are pay lists of $38,000 in 1912 and over $37,000 in 1913. Other courthouses with a general contractor had very small pay lists, so presumably the department was hiring its own labour.
274 *Calgary News-Telegram*, March 5, 1912.
275 City of Calgary Archives, Building Permit Registers, 1912.
276 *Public Accounts*, 1912, 137; 1913, 145.
277 Ibid.
278 Ibid.
279 *Public Works, Annual Report*, 1912, 39.
280 *Calgary Herald*, August 17, 1912, 1, *Calgary News-Telegram*, August 19, 1912, 10.
281 *Calgary News-Telegram*, August 23, 1912.
282 Ibid., September 21, 1912.
283 Ibid., September 30, 1912.
284 *Albertan*, November 9, 1912.
285 *Calgary News-Telegram*, November 12, 1912.
286 *Albertan*, November 19, 1912.
287 *Calgary News-Telegram*, November 29, 1912.
288 *Scrapbook Hansard*, 2nd Legislature, February 10, 1910–March 23, 1913, 50.
289 *Calgary Daily Herald*, September 24, 1913, 14.
290 Ibid., October 16, 1913.
291 Ibid., January 12, 1914.
292 Ibid.
293 *Calgary News-Telegram*, January 13, 1914.
294 *Calgary Daily Herald*, March 17, 1904.
295 *Calgary News-Telegram*, January 19, 1914.
296 PAA, acc. 79.387, box 12, ledger; *Calgary Herald*, March 31, 1914.
297 *Public Works, Annual Report*, 1924, 36
298 PAA, acc 83.86, box 38, plan 189.
299 Gray, *Talk to My Lawyer*, pgs. 62-66. My account is largely derived from Gray's.
300 *Blairmore Enterprise*, October 5, 1922
301 Gray, *Talk to My Lawyer*, pg. 67
302 PAA, acc. 91.36, file, Calgary Courthouse, letter, June 14, 1956.
303 *Calgary Herald*, December 4, 1958, "Design of Courthouse Blasted By Liberals."
304 *Albertan*, February 7, 1962.
305 PAA, acc. 81.298, box 33.
306 *Calgary Herald*, November 24, 1964.
307 *Calgary Herald*, January 8, 1980.
308 *Public Works, Annual Report*, 1909, 36.
309 PAA, acc. 93.361, box 4, file SO575-1, vol. 1.
310 *Medicine Hat Weekly News*, March 4, 1909, 1.
311 Ibid., March 11, 1909, 1; March 18, 1909, 1.
312 *Medicine Hat Weekly News*, June 10, 1909.
313 *Medicine Hat News*, June 2, 1910.
314 Ibid., June 23, 1910, 1.
315 PAA, acc. 76.213, box 39, file 167q.
316 Ibid.
317 Ibid.
318 PAA, acc. 93.361, box 4, file SO575-1, vol. 1.
319 *Medicine Hat News*, March 20, 1913.
320 *Medicine Hat Call*, March 29, 1913
321 *Ibid*, April 19, 1913; *Medicine Hat Times*, June 2, 1913, 4; Medicine Hat Museum and Art Gallery, M86.
322 *Medicine Hat Call*, April 19, 1913.
323 *Medicine Hat Daily News*, May 1, 1913.
324 Ibid.

325 *Medicine Hat Times*, June 2, 1913.
326 Ibid.
327 Ibid., October 20, 1913.
328 *Edmonton Journal*, October, 21, 1913, 4.
329 *Medicine Hat News*, October 21, 1913.
330 PAA, acc. 92.361, box 4, file SO575-1, vol. 1.
331 PAA, acc. 83.86, plan 86, still held at Alberta Infrastructure.
332 Rostecki, *The Early Courthouses of Saskatchewan*, 88 and 106.
333 Ibid.
334 Public Works, Annual Report, 1919, pg. 68
335 Ronald M. James, *Temples of Justice* (University of Nevada Press, 1994), 46.
336 Kalman, *Canadian Architecture*, 741.
337 *Public Works, Annual Report*, 1920, 56.
338 *Medicine Hat Daily News*, May 12, 9.
339 Ibid., June 19, 1919.
340 Ibid., September 21, 1920, 1.
341 Ibid.; also see Alberta Infrastructure, Records Office, plan 86.
342 *Calgary Herald*, June 26, 1919.
343 Ibid.
344 The issue arose again in the late 1920s as the UFA started a public building program. The government of Manitoba put a great deal of pressure on the Brownlee government to use Tyndall stone, which Brownlee agreed to do in return for Manitoba buying coal from Alberta. PAA, acc. 69.251, file 310.
345 *Public Works, Annual Report*, 1919, 63.
346 *Medicine Hat Daily News*, September 20, 1920, 1.
347 PAA, acc. 68.308, box 9, file: dept. 1921–32.
348 *Medicine Hat Daily News*, September 21, 1920, 1.
349 Ibid.
350 PAA, acc 92.361, box 11, file SO575-1, vol. 2.
351 Ibid.
352 Ibid.
353 Ibid.
354 Ibid.
355 Ibid.
356 Ibid.
357 *Medicine Hat Daily News*, June 27, 1969, 23.
358 Ibid.

## Notes To Part Three

1 *Statutes of Alberta* , 1933, c. 15, 51.
2 *Canada Law List* (Aurora, Ont.: Canada Law Book, 1935), 12.
3 *Vegreville Observer*, March 6, 1929, 2.
4 Examples of this can be found throughout the individual courthouse chapters. It is also quite easy to find correspondence dealing with this in government files, especially for the Attorney General's office.
5 PAA, acc. 84.210, box 2, file: Staff, Departmental General. No drafting staff, not even Macdonald, are listed as permanent employees.
6 PAA, acc. 73.322, file 107.
7 Alberta Infrastructure, Records Office, plan 86, sheet Q50, Medicine Hat Courthouse. This plan of interior details, for "Courthouse Vegreville and Red Deer" is dated December 1919, and approved by R.P. Blakey. "Med. Hat" has been pencilled onto the title. It seems to clearly imply that Blakey was drawing up plans for a standard courthouse for these two centres and decided to use it, or aspects of it, for Medicine Hat. There is, however, no other documentation I could find, nor any mention of courthouses for these two centres in the annual reports for Public Works.
8 *Edmonton Bulletin*, December 9, 1947.
9 *Public Works, Annual Report*, 1914, 39.
10 Ibid., 43.
11 Ibid., 48.
12 *Public Accounts*, 1915, 75; *Blairmore Enterprise*, December 21, 1922.
13 PAA, acc. 73.332, box 1, file 3b.
14 Ibid.
15 *Blairmore Enterprise*, March 30, 1922.
16 *Public Works, Annual Report*, 1920, 56.
17 PAA, acc. 69.287, box 7, file R1C.
18 *Public Works, Annual Report*, 1922, 59.
19 Ibid.
20 *Blairmore Enterprise*, March 9, 1922.
21 PAA, acc. 69.287, box 7, file R1C.
22 *Blairmore Enterprise*, June 15,1922.
23 Ibid.
24 Maitland, *Canadian Architectural Styles*, 158; Whiffen, *American Architecture Since 1780: A Guide to Styles* (Cambridge, Mass: MIT Press, 1992), 213–16.
25 PAA, acc. 83.86, plan 00110. The following description is taken from these plans.
26 *Blairmore Enterprise*, January 11, 1923.
27 *A Guide to Canadian Architectural Styles*, March 1, 1922.
28 Ibid.
29 Ibid., January 4, 1922.
30 *Blairmore Enterprise*, March 1, 1922.
31 *Blairmore Enterprise*, April 5, 1923.
32 Ibid., May 24, 1923.
33 Ibid., August 16, 1923.
34 *Blairmore Enterprise* October 4, 1923
35 *Calgary Herald*, September 7, 1935.
36 PAA, acc. 78.235, Supreme Court Criminal Case Files, 1882–1971, file 1281.
37 Ibid., file 1283.
38 Ibid., file 1056.
39 Ibid., file 1003.
40 PAA, acc. 73.322, file 107.
41 Ambrosi, *The Courthouse: Recollections from the Past: A History of the Blairmore Courthouse* (Lethbridge: Joey Ambrosi [1998]), 14
42 PAA, acc. 92.361, box 16, file SO047-1, pocket 1.
43 PAA, acc. 92.361, box 16, file SO047-1, vol. 1.
44 Ambrosi, *The Courthouse*, 16.
45 Municipality of Crow's Nest, Council Minutes, 1981, 5.
46 Ibid., March 22, 1983 meeting.
47 Ambrosi, 17.
48 Crowsnest Pass and Its People, 1900-1950: A Photo Companion, (Coleman, AB: Crowsnest Pass Historical Society, c1990), 353.

49 *Lethbridge Herald*, October 29, 1993.
50 Ibid., April 25, 1994.
51 Ambrosi, *The Courthouse*, 69–71.
52 David W. Leonard, "The Origins of Grande Prairie," *Alberta History* (Autumn 1997): 14.
53 James G. MacGregor, *Grande Prairie* (Grande Prairie: City of Grande Prairie, 1983), 18.
54 Leonard, "Origins of Grande Prairie," 15.
55 Irving Kurz, *Policing the Central Peace* (Spirit River: I.A. Kurz Publications, 1987), 2.
56 Ibid., 3.
57 MacGregor, "Origins of Grande Prairie," 16. Unfortunately, no source is provided by the author. An Order-in-council did set sittings of the court for September 1908 at the nearby settlement of Peace River Landing. So Noel may well have visited Clay's post.
58 *Alberta Gazette,* vol. 5, no. 10, May 1909, pg. 9.
59 *Lethbridge Daily Herald*, August 31, 1915.
60 *Grande Prairie Herald-Tribune*, June 27, 1940. This was a personal account of W. F. Ellis, court reporter on the 1915 expedition.
61 *Grande Prairie Herald*, August 31, 1915.
62 Ibid., November 9, 1915.
63 Ibid., July 4, 1916.
64 Ibid., January 10, 1918.
65 PAA, acc. 73.322, box 1, file 3a; also *Grande Prairie Herald*, April 2, 1918.
66 PAA, acc. 73.322, file 43d.
67 *Grande Prairie Herald*, April 2, 1918.
68 Ibid., May 21, 1918.
69 Ibid., March 16, 1920.
70 PAA, acc. 73.322, box 1, file 3a.
71 PAA, acc. 73.322, box 55, file 43d.
72 *Grande Prairie Herald, November 23, 1920*
73 PAA, acc. 73.322, box 56, file 43e.
74 *Grande Prairie Herald*, October 19, 1920.
75 Ibid., October 26, 1920.
76 PAA, acc. 73.322, file 43d.
77 Ibid.
78 Isabel Campbell, *Grande Prairie, Capitol of the Peace* (Grande Prairie: n.p., 1968), 60; PAA, acc. 68.308, box 9, file: dept. 1921–32.
79 *Grande Prairie Herald* June 22, 1920.
80 PAA, acc. 73.322, file 43d.
81 Glenbow Archives, M776, Correspondence.
82 *Grande Prairie Herald*, October 4, 1926.
83 PAA, acc. 73.322, file 43d.
84 No correspondence dealing with the courthouse can be found in Greenfield's papers at the Provincial Archives of Alberta, nor in correspondence generated by the premier's office. This does not rule out the possibility that it might have existed and been lost.
85 MacGregor, "Origins of Grande Prairie," 18.
86 Campbell, *Capitol of the Peace*, 59.
87 *Grande Prairie Herald*, June 29, 1920.
88 Ibid., December 14, 1920.
89 Ibid., December 27, 1929, article about local bar association passing resolution for a resident judge, which makes reference to previous efforts "some time ago" on the part of the board of trade. This is also referred to in a letter to Hugh Allan, MLA on January 27, 1928 in PAA, acc. 75.188, box 1, file 62.
90 *Grande Prairie Herald*, March 28, 1928.
91 Campbell, *Capitol of the Peace*, 59.
92 PAA, acc. 83.86, plan 151.
93 *Grande Prairie Herald*, Novemberl6, 1928.
94 PAA, acc. 76.213, box 1, file 7A.
95 PAA, acc. 75.188, box 1, file 62.
96 Ibid.
97 *Peace River Record*, October 26, 1928.
98 Ibid., April 13, 1928.
99 Campbell, *Capitol of the Peace*, 60.
100 PAA acc. 75.188, box 1, file 62.
101 *Grande Prairie Herald*, October 26, 1928.
102 Campbell, *Capitol of the Peace*, 60.
103 PAA, acc. 76.213, box 1, file 7A.
104 *Grande Prairie Herald*, August 3, 1928.
105 PAA, acc. 76.213, box 1, file 7A.
106 Ibid.
107 Ibid.
108 Ibid.
109 Ibid.
110 Ibid.
111 Ibid.
112 PAA, acc. 75.188, box 1, file 63.
113 *Public Accounts*, 1929, 170.
114 *Public Works, Annual Report*, 1938–39, 21.
115 PAA, acc. 73.322, file 107.
116 *Grande Prairie Herald-Tribune*, March 1, 1957, 12.
117 PAA, acc. 76.213, box 1, file 7G; *Grande Prairie Herald-Tribune*, October 18, 1955.
118 *Grande Prairie Herald-Tribune*, September 27, 1957.
119 PAA, acc. 76.213, box 1, file 7C.
120 *Grande Prairie Herald-Tribune*, June 28, 1957.
121 John T. Gorman, *Historic Hanna* (Hanna: Gorman and Gorman, 1987), 14.
122 Ibid., 14; *Hanna Herald*, June 21, 1917.
123 *Hanna Herald*, January 30, 1913; September 4, 1913.
124 Gorman, *Historic Hanna* , 2.
125 Ibid., 8.
126 *Hanna Herald*, October 22, 1914.
127 Ibid., October 14, 1915; May 10, 1917.
128 Ibid., November 3, 1921.
129 Ibid., January 16, 1919.
130 Ibid., February 27, 1919.
131 PAA, acc. 73.322, box 19, file 14a; also *Hanna Herald*, September 25, 1919.
132 *Hanna Herald*, September 25, 1919.
133 Ibid., August 28, 1919.
134 Ibid., March 4, 1920.
135 PAA, acc. 73.322, box 1, file 3b.
136 *Hanna Herald*, November 18, 1920.
137 Ibid., March 3, 1921.
138 Ibid., September 8, 1921.
139 Ibid., January 25, 1923.
140 Ibid., October 11, 1923.
141 Ibid, June 19, 1924
142 Ibid. October 11, 1923.

143 Ibid., September 2, 1926.
144 Hanna Town Minutes, January 20, 1928.
145 *Hanna Herald*, March 21, 1929.
146 PAA, acc. 83.86, plan 162A-C. The design is signed as drawn by F.H. Macdonald.
147 *Hanna Herald*, May 9, 1929.
148 Ibid.
149 Ibid.
150 Ibid.
151 *Hanna Herald*, May 30, 1929.
152 PAA, acc. 76.213, box 2, file 14d.
153 Ibid.
154 *Hanna Herald*, November 7, 1929.
155 Ibid., November 28, 1929.
156 PAA, acc. 76.213, box 2, file 14c.
157 PAA, acc. 92.361, box 3, file SO424-1, vol. 1
158 Ibid.
159 PAA, acc. 69.251, file 1571.
160 Ibid.
161 PAA, acc. 76.213 , file 260b.
162 LASA, Fond 09-00-00, vol. 12, file 60, Barnett and Malcolm Interview, 28.
163 Ibid., 29.
164 Census of Canada, 1951, 1971.
165 *Hanna Herald*, March 24, 1982.
166 PAA, acc. 92.361, box 9, file SO0424-1, vol. 2.
167 Ibid.
168 Town of Hanna Archives, file 4194, Discovery of Documents. From Town Council Minutes, April 8, 1984, 33.
169 Ibid., letter, Mayor Dookie to Alberta, Culture, May 9, 1985.
170 Ibid., letter, March 18, 1986, Culture Minister M. LeMessurier to town; letter, November 27, 1986, Minister of Public Works to Mayor; letter, December 18, 1986; letter, Municpal administrator to Public Works Minister; also file 250-3 Courthouse.
171 Ibid., Minutes, June 13, 1985, 93.
172 *Calgary Herald*, July 30, 1987, D-2.
173 Town of Hanna Archives, file 4194, letter, 1994, Chair Hanna District Allied Art Association.
174 Town of Hanna Archives, file 4194, letter, January 27, 1999, Town Manager to Victor and Beverly Fortinski.
175 *Calgary Herald*, April 10, 1999.
176 Town of Hanna Archives, file 4194.
177 PAA, acc. 76.213, file 103b.
178 *Public Works, Annual Report*, 1920, 56.
179 Ibid., 1922, 59.
180 PAA, acc. 69.287, box 7, file R1a.
181 *Public Works, Annual Report*, 1923, 59.
182 PAA, acc. 83.86, plan 00150, 1921.
183 Ibid., plans 00150 and 00110. For some reason, a detail of the entrance for this building is included in the plans for the Blairmore police barracks.
184 *Public Works, Annual Report*, 1926, 32.
185 PAA, acc. 76.213, file 260b.
186 Ibid., file 260c.
187 Ibid., file 260e, 260f.
188 Ibid., file 260e.
189 Ibid., file 260g.
190 University of Alberta Archives, Rutherford Papers, box 8, 2/3/7/2-20.
191 *Red Deer Advocate*, February 1, 1907.
192 PAA , acc. 92.361, box 5, file SO 662-1, vol. 1.
193 Ibid.
194 Ibid.
195 *Red Deer News*, January 24, 1912.
196 *Red Deer News*, December 11, 1912; *Red Deer Advocate*, December 31, 1915.
197 *Red Deer News*, January 20, 1913.
198 City of Red Deer, Council minutes, Book 5, September 1913–May 1917, 3.
199 *Public Works, Annual Report*, 1916; *Red Deer News*, January 5, 1916.
200 PAA, acc. 92.361, box 5, file SO662-1, vol. 1, plans 192-193.
201 *Statutes of Alberta*, 1921, c. 8, s. 22.
202 Ibid., s. 32.
203 *Public Works, Annual Report*, 1916; *Red Deer News*, January 5, 1916.
204 *Red Deer News*, March 22, 1916.
205 *Stettler Independent*, January 15, 1914.
206 Ibid., January 8, 1914.
207 Ibid., December 25, 1914.
208 Ibid.
209 PAA, acc. 66.166, file 132k.
210 *Stettler Independent*, March 19, 1914.
211 Ibid., June 14, 1914.
212 *Public Accounts*, 1914, 190.
213 *Stettler Independent*, September 24, 1914.
214 Mills, *Early Court Houses of Alberta*, 143.
215 PAA, acc. 76.213, box 51, files 215h, 215i.
216 Ibid., file 215i.
217 *Red Deer Advocate*, October 9, 1929.
218 PAA, acc. 92.361, box 5, file SO66-1, vol. 1.
219 PAA, acc. 76.213, box 51, file 213a.
220 PAA, acc. 83.86, plan 178.
221 Ibid.
222 PAA, acc. 76.213, box 51, file 213a.
223 *Red Deer Advocate*, June 3, 1931.
224 PAA, acc. 76.213, box 51, file 213e.
225 PAA, acc. 76,213, box 52, file 213ff.
226 Ibid., file 215dd.
227 Ibid., file 215cc.
228 Ibid., file 215jj.
229 Ibid.
230 *Calgary Herald*, March 24, 1958; PAA, acc. 76.213, box 51, 213f.
231 Ibid.
232 PAA, acc. 92.361, box 12, file SO662-1, vol. 2, memo, October 30, 1963.
233 PAA, acc. 81.298, box 36, file 1670.
234 Ibid., letter, September 6, 1966.
235 PAA, acc. 81.298, box 36, file 1670.
236 Ibid.
237 City of Red Deer, Council Minutes January 10, 1966–September 12, 1966, 179.

238 RDDA, Heritage Planning Preservation Committee Minutes.

239 *Vegreville Observer*, December 25, 1929.

240 *Vegreville in Review: History of Vegreville and Surrounding Area, 1880–1980* (Vegreville: Vegreville and District Historical Society, 1980), 2.

241 Ibid., 1.

242 Ibid., 6.

243 *Alberta Gazette*, vol. 2, no. 15, August 15, 1906, 1.

244 *Vegreville Observer*, June 10, 1908.

245 Ibid., April 8, 1931.

246 Ibid., June 10, 1908; March 6, 1929.

247 Ibid., February 19, 1913.

248 PAA, acc. 92.361, box 5, file SO786-1, vol. 1.

249 *Vegreville Observer*, October 13, 1926.

250 Alberta Infrastructure, Records Office, plan 86, sheet Q50, Medicine Hat Courthouse.

251 *Vegreville Observer*, October 13, 1926.

252 Ibid., July 25, 1928.

253 *Vermillion Standard*, October 7, 1926.

254 Ibid.

255 *Vegreville Observer*, March 6, 1929.

256 Greg Thomas Robinson, *British-Canadian justice in the Ukrainian colony: crime and law enforcement in east central Alberta, 1915–1929*, MA Thesis, University of Alberta, 1992, 39–40, 58 and 74.

257 PAA, acc. 76.213, box 15, file 47a.

258 *Vegreville Observer*, April 8, 1931.

259 Ibid., December 25, 1929.

260 PAA, acc. 92.361, file SO 786-1, vol. 1.

261 Ibid.

262 PAA, acc. 76.213, box 15, file 47a.

263 Ibid.

264 *Vegreville Observer*, August 27, 1930.

265 PAA, acc. 76.213, box 15, file 47a.

266 Ibid.

267 Ibid.

268 Ibid., file 47b.

269 Ibid.

270 Ibid.

271 *Vegreville Observer*, August 27, 1930.

272 PAA, acc. 76.213, box 15, file 47c.

273 PAA, acc. 83.86, plan 00181.

274 PAA, acc. 70.414, file 1111; *Public Accounts*, 1931, 194.

275 *Vegreville Observer*, March 18, 1931.

276 PAA, acc. 73.322, file 107.

277 Ibid.

278 Ibid.

279 *Vegreville Observer*, February 25, 1931.

## Notes To Epilogue

1 PAA, acc. 76.213, file 35d. The correspondence in this file is only one example of some of the problems faced by the government. At one point, it was having difficulty paying for utilities.

2 PAA, acc. 81.298, file: Courthouse, Edmonton, 1966–67.

3 PAA, acc. 70.217, box B, file 7a/b.

4 Herbert Allan Johnson, *Historic Courthouses of New York State* (New York: Columbia University Press, 1977), 15.

# BIBLIOGRAPHY


## Primary Sources

City of Calgary Archives
- City Clerks Department Fonds
- City Council Minutes

City of Edmonton Archives
- Town Council Minutes
- RG 8, Class 5, City Clerk's Fonds, 1892–1974
- RG 11, Class 28

City of Lethbridge, Record Administration
- City Council Minutes
- City Clerks Records

Economic Development, Administration Files

Crow's Nest Municipal Office
- Blairmore Town Minutes
- Coleman Town Minutes, 1905–11
- Municipality of Crow's Nest Council Minutes

Glenbow Museum Archives
- M776, Colonel James Farquarson Macleod Papers

Hanna Town Office
- Hanna Town Minutes
- File 250-3 Courthouse

Legal Archives Society of Alberta
- Fond 09-00-00, Calgary Bar Association Oral History Project

Fort Macleod Town Office
- Macleod Town Council Minutes
- Macleod Town Council Letter Books

Medicine Hat Museum and Art Gallery Archives
- M96.6 Town council minute books
- M86.9 Board of Trade Minute Books

National Archives of Canada
- RG 11, Department of Public Works
  - Series B2, a-i, Central Registry Files
  - Series B-2, c-I, Letterbooks, outgoing correspondence
  - Series D-2, Letterbooks of the Chief Architect
  - Series D-4, Letterbooks of D.A. Hewitt
  - Estimates of Canada
- RG 13, Department of Justice, Series A2 Central Registry Files
  - Series A-3, Letterbooks, Outgoing correspondence
- RG 18, Royal Canadian Mounted Police
  - Series A-2
- RG 17, Department of Agriculture
  - Series I-1
- RG 84, Canadian Parks Service
  - Series A-2-a, Central Registry Files

Provincial Archives of Alberta
- 66.166 Attorney General, General Administrative Files,
- 68.302, Charles Borromee Rouleau and Horace Harvey, Notebooks and other Papers
- 68.308, Public Works, Minister's Files, 1921–40
- 69.251, Premier's Office, Executive Council, 1921–59
- 69.287, Attorney General, J.E. Brownlee Office Files
- 70.414, Sessional Papers of the Legislative Assembly, 1908–60
- 72.370, Alberta Provincial Police
- 73.322, Attorney General, Inspector of Legal Offices
- 75.188, Hugh W. Allen, MLA, Peace River, Papers, 1926–35
- 76.213, Public Works, Government Services, 1906–69
- 78.235, Supreme Court Criminal Case Files, Macleod District, 1882–1971
- 79.285, Supreme Court Criminal Case Files, Calgary District, 1910–74
- 79.387, Housing and Public Works, Miscellaneous Records
- 81.186, Orders in Council
- 81.298, Housing and Public Works, Public Buildings, Operational Files, 1944–73
- 83.192, Attorney General, General Administrative Records,
- 83.83 Department of Labour, Collective Agreements
- 83.86, Public Works, Supply and Services, Contract Administration, Plans and Specification for Government Buildings, Demolished or Sold, 1906–80
- 83.210, C.W. Cross, Attorney General, Papers.
- 84.210, Public Works, J.D. Robertson, Deputy Minister, Working Records, 1913–38
- 87.94, Attorney General, Fort Macleod Courthouse File
- 90.592, Public Works, Supply and Services, Construction, 1977–84
- 91.36, Public Works, Supply and Services, Case Files, Public Buildings
- 92.361, Dept. of Public Works, Supply and Services, Accommodations

Red Deer and District Archives
- MG 254, Red Deer Chamber of Commerce Fonds, Red Deer Board of Trade Minutes
- RG 6, City of Red Deer, Office of the City Clerk Fonds
- RG 39, City of Red Deer, Heritage Preservation Committee Fonds
- MG 227, Red Deer Public School District No. 104 Fonds, Red Deer School District
- Minutes
- 62.4.1-2, Liberal Association Letter Book

Red Deer City Records Office
- Town Council Minutes
- City Council Minutes

Town of Cardston
- Council Minutes

University of Alberta Archives
- Rutherford Papers

Vegreville Town Office
- Town Minutes

Wetaskiwin City Archives
- Accession 95.19, Town and City Council Minutes

# Secondary Sources

## Government Publications


Alberta *Alberta Gazette*, Edmonton: 1905–45

——— *Annual Report of the Department of Public Works*, Edmonton: 1905–80

——— *Estimates of the Province of Alberta*, Edmonton: 1905–18

——— *Public Accounts of the Province of Alberta*, Edmonton: 1905–18

——— Sessional Papers and Legislative Journals. Edmonton: 1907–31.

Alberta Attorney General *Court of Appeal of Alberta – Calgary* [pamphlet]

Canada *Annual Report of the Department of Public Works*, Ottawa: Sessional Papers of

Parliament of Canada, 1882–1918

——— *Dominion of Canada Census* Ottawa: 1901–1971

——— *Census of the Three Provisional Districts of the North-West Territories*, Ottawa:

Maclean Roger & Co, 1886

Northwest Territories Gazette

Ordinances of the North-West Territories

Statutes of Alberta

Statutes of Canada


## Newspapers


*Alberta Star*
*Blairmore Enterprise*
*The Brickbuilder*
*Calgary Albertan*
*Calgary Herald*
*Calgary News-Telegram*
*Calgary Tribune*
*Camrose Canadian*
*Cardston Record*
*Construction*
*Edmonton Bulletin*
*Edmonton Daily Capitol*
*Edmonton Journal*
*Fort Macleod Gazette*
*Fort Saskatchewan Reporter*
*Grande Prairie Herald*
*Grande Prairie Herald-Tribune*
*Hanna Herald*
*Lethbridge Herald*
*Lethbridge News*
*Macleod Gazette*
*Macleod Times and Weekly News*
*Medicine Hat News*
*Medicine Hat Times*
*Peace River Record*
*Red Deer Advocate*
*Red Deer News*
*Southern Alberta News*
*Stettler Independent*
*Taber Times*
*Vegreville Observer*
*Vermilion Standard*
*Western Weekly Reports*
*Westwind News*
*Wetaskiwin Post*
*Wetaskiwin Times*


## Glenbow Museum Library, clipping files


"Calgary – Courthouse"

"Fort Macleod-Buildings"

"Woolf, John W"


## Books and Articles


*Administration of Justice in the Provincial Courts of Alberta.* Edmonton: Alberta Board of Review Provincial Courts of Alberta, 1974.

Ambrosi, Joey. *The Courthouse: Recollections from the Past: A History of the Blairmore Courthouse.* Lethbridge, Alta.: Joey Ambrosi. [1998?].

Anderson, Frank W. *A Dance With Death: Canadian Women on the Gallows, 1754 –1954.* Saskatoon: Fifth House Publishers, 1996.

Archibald, Margaret. *By Federal Design: The Chief Architects Branch of the Department of Public Works 1881–1914.* [Ottawa], Hull, Quebec: Canada: National Historic Parks and Sites Branch, Parks Canada, Environment Canada; Canadian Government Publishing Centre, 1983.

Artibise, Alan F.J. *Western Canada Since 1870: A Select Bibliography and Guide.* Vancouver: University of British Columbia Press, 1978.

———. "Boosterism and the Development of Canadian Cities." In *Town and City, Aspects of Western Canadian Urban Development.* Regina: Canadian Plains Research Center, 1981.

Attebery, Jennifer Eastman. "Courthouse Architecture in Idaho 1864–1940." *Idaho Yesterdays* (Fall 1987).

Babcock, Douglas R. *Alexander Cameron Rutherford: A Gentleman of Strathcona.* Calgary: Friends of Rutherford House and University of Calgary Press, 1989.

Baker, H. Robert. "Creating Order in the Wilderness: Transplanting the English Law to Rupert's Land 1835–51." *Law & History Review* 17, no. 2 (1999).

Baker, William M. *Pioneer Policing in Southern Alberta: Deane of the Mounties, 1888–1914.* Calgary: Historical Society of Alberta, 1993.

Bakken, Larry A. *Justice in the Wilderness: A Study of Frontier Courts in Canada and the United States 1670–1870.* Littleton, Co.: Fred B. Rothman, 1986.

Baldwin, Ged. *Frontier Justice: The Reminiscences of Ged Baldwin.* Edmonton: University of Alberta Press, 1987.

Ball, Norman. *Building Canada: A History of Public Works.* Toronto: University of Toronto Press, 1988.

Beahen, William, and Stan Horrall. *Red Coats on the Prairies: The North West Mounted, 1886 –1900.* Regina: Centax/ Printwest, 1998.

Bercuson, David J., and Louis A. Knafla, eds. *Law and Society in Canada in Historical Perspective.* [Calgary]: University of Calgary, 1974.

Bindon, K.M. "Hudson's Bay Company Law: Adam Thom and the Institution of Order in Rupert's Land, 1839–54." In *Essays in the History of Canadian Law Vol. 1*. Edited by David J. Flaherty. Toronto: Published for the Osgoode Society by the University of Toronto Press, 1981.

Binnie, Susan W., and Knafla, Louis A. eds. *Law Society and the State: Essays in Modern Legal History.* Toronto: University of Toronto Press, 1995.

Bird, H.I. "Some Early Personalities of Bench and Bar." *Advocate* 22 (1964): 177–81.

Bodnar, Diane. "Prairie Legislative Buildings of Canada." Master's thesis, University of British Columbia, 1979.

Bowker, Marjorie M., ed. *A Consolidation of fifty Years of Legal Writings 1938–1988 by Wilbur F. Bowker.* Edmonton: University of Alberta Faculty of Law, 1989.

———. "Juvenile Court in Retrospect: Seven Decades of History in Alberta 1913–1984." *Alberta Law Review* 24, no. 2 (1986).

Bowker, Wilbur F. "Which is the Chief Justice – David Lynch Scott or Horace Harvey." *Alberta Law Review* 30, no. 4 (1992).

———. "The Honourable Horace Harvey, Chief Justice of Alberta." *Canadian Bar Review* 32 (1954): 933–81, 1118–39.

———. "The Stipendiary Magistrates and Supreme Court Justices in the North West Territories 1876–1907." Papers of the Canadian Law in History Conference, vol.1. Carleton University. Ottawa, 1987.

Brown, D.H. "Unpredictable and Uncertain: Criminal Law in the Canadian Northwest Before 1886." *Alberta Law Review* 17 (1979).

Cable, Carole. *The Courthouse and the Law Court: Their Design and Construction.* Monticello, Ill.: Vance Bibliographies, 1978.

Campbell, Isabell. *Grande Prairie, Capitol of the Peace.* Grande Prairie: n.p., 1968.

Carpenter, James H. *The Badge and the Blotter: A History of the Lethbridge Police.* Lethbridge: Whoop-up Country Chapter, Historical Society of Alberta, 1976.

Carter, Margaret, ed. *Early Canadian Court Houses.* Comp. [Ottawa]: National Historic Parks and Sites Branch, Parks Canada, Environment Canada, c1983.

Chapman, Terry. "The Controversy over Courts and Courthouses." *Alberta History* 37, no. 4 (Autumn 1989).

*Chief Mountain Country: A History of Cardston and District, Cardston and District Historical Society.* Cardston, 1978.

Cote, J.E. "The Introduction of English Law Into Alberta." *Alberta Law Review* 3 (1964): 262–92.

Cousins, William James. *A History of the Crow's Nest Pass.* Historic Trails Society of Alberta, 1981.

Craufurd-Lewis, Michael. *Macleod of the Mounties: The North American Saga as seen through the life of a Scottish-Canadian Hero.* Ottawa: Golden Dog Press, 1999.

Cunniffe, Richard. *Calgary in Sandstone.* [Calgary]: Historical Society of Alberta, Calgary Branch, 1969.

Dawson, Brian J. *Crow's Nest An Illustrated History and Guide to the Crow's Nest Pass.* Vancouver: Altitude Publishing, 1995.

Deane, R. Burton. *Mounted Police Life in Canada: A Record of Thirty-One Years' Service.* London: Cassell, 1916.

Decore, J.N. "The District Court of Alberta." *Alberta Law Review 25th Anniversary Issue* (1980): 23–24.

Dempsey, Hugh. *Charcoal's World.* Saskatoon: Western Producer Prairie Books, 1978.

Denny, Cecil E. *The Law Marches West.* Edited by W.B. Cameron. Toronto: J.M. Dent & Sons, 1939.

Field, Dorothy, ed. *Calgary: Stephen Avenue and Area Historical Walking Tour.* Edmonton: Alberta Community Development, 1995.

Flaherty, David H., ed. *Essays in the History of Canadian Law.* 7 vols. Toronto: Published for the Osgoode Society by the University of Toronto Press, 1981.

Francis, Daniel, and Michael Payne. *A Narrative History of Fort Dunvegan.* Watson & Dwyer, 1993.

Fooks, Georgia Green. *Lethbridge Portraits of the Past.* Burlington Windsor Publications, 1988.

Foran, Max L. "The Calgary Town Council 1884–1895: A Study of Local Government in a Frontier Environment." Master's thesis, University of Calgary, 1970.

———. "The Civic Corporation and Urban Growth: Calgary 1884–1930." Ph.D. diss., University of Calgary, 1981.

*Fort Macleod: Our Colourful Past.* Fort Macleod: Fort Macleod History Book Committee, 1977.

Foster, Hamar. "Long Distance Justice: The Criminal Jurisdiction of the Canadian Courts West of the Canadas 1763–1859."*American Journal of Legal History* 34, no. 1.

———. "Sins Against the Great Spirit: The Law the Hudson's Bay Company and the Mackenzie River Murders 1835–1839." *Criminal Justice History*10 (1989): 23.

Fox, Jason. "The Last Hanging at Calgary Barracks." *Alberta History* 41, no. 4 (1993): 10–15.

Getty, Ian. "The Role of the Mounted Police Outposts in Southern Alberta." In *Men in Scarlet.* Edited by Hugh Dempsey. Calgary: Historical Society of Alberta McClelland and Stewart West, 1974.

Gorman, John T. *Historic Hanna.* Hanna: Gorman and Gorman Publishing, 1987.

Gould, Ed. *All Hell for a Basement: Medicine Hat 1883–1983.* Medicine Hat: City of Medicine Hat, 1981.

Gowans, Alan. *Building Canada.* Toronto: Oxford University Press, 1966.

———. *Styles and Types of North American Architecture.* New York: Icon Editions, 1992.

Gray, James H. *Talk to My Lawyer.* Hurtig Publishers, Edmonton, 1987.

Hainsworth, Melody M., ed. *A List of Federally Approved Judges 1887 to May 31,1987.* Calgary: Law Society Library, 1987.

Harvey, Horace. "Some Notes on the Early Administration of Justice in Canada's Northwest." *The Alberta Historical Review* 1, no. 3 (1953): 5–20.

*Henderson's Edmonton Directory.* Winnipeg: Henderson's Publishing Company, 1906–.

*Henderson's Northwest Directory.* Winnipeg: Henderson's Publishing Company, 1882–.

Hirsten, John R. "Events Leading to the Settlement of the Community of Cardston, Magrath, Stirling and Raymond Alberta." Ph.D. diss., Utah State University, 1968.

———. *The Pictorial History of the Royal Canadian Mounted Police.* Toronto:McGraw-Hill Ryerson, 1973.

———. "Sir John A. Macdonald and the Mounted Police Force for the Northwest Territories." *Canadian Historical Review* 53 (1972): 201–25.

Hubner, Brian. "Horse Stealing and the Borderline: The NWMP and the Control of the Indian Movement, 1874–1900." *Prairie Forum* 20, no.2 (1985): 281–300.

Hyndman, L.D. "The Early Years of the Edmonton Bar. *Alberta Law Review 25th Anniversary Issue* (1980).

———. "The Legal Profession in Alberta." Unpublished Paper (n.d.), Provincial Archives of Alberta.

James, Ronald M. *Temples of Justice*. University of Nevada Press, 1994.

Jamieson, F.C. "Edmonton Courts and Lawyers in Territorial Times." *Alberta History* 4, no. 1 (1956): 3–9.

Jennings, John. "The Plains Indians and the Law." In *Men in Scarlet*. Edited by Hugh Dempsey. Calgary: Historical Society of Alberta and McClelland and Stewart West, 1974.

Johnson, Herbert Allan. *Historic Courthouses of New York State*. New York: Columbia University Press, 1977.

Johnston, Alex, and Andy Den Otter. *Lethbridge A Centennial History*. Lethbridge: Lethbridge Historical Society, City of Lethbridge, 1991.

Jones, David C., L.J. Roy Wilson, and Donny White. *The Weather Factory, A Pictorial History of Medicine Hat*. Saskatoon: Western Producer Prairie Books, 1988.

Jordon, Robert H., and J. Gregg Puster. *Courthouses in Georgia*. Norcross, Ga: Harrison Co., 1984.

Kalman, Harold D. *History of Canadian Architecture*. 2 vols. Toronto: Oxford University Press, 1994.

Kellogg, Thomas. "Courthouse Planning." *The Brickbuilder* 17, no. 11 (November 1908).

Knafla, Louis A. "Be it Remembered: Court Records and Research in the Canadian Provinces." *Archivaria* 18 (1984).

———. "Crime, Criminal Law and Justice in Canadian History: A Select Bibliography, Origins to 1940." In *Law and Society in Canadian Historical Perspective*. Edited by David J. Bercuson and Louis A. Knafla.[Calgary]: University of Calgary, 1979.

———, ed. *Law and Justice in a New Land: Essays in Western Canadian Legal History*. Calgary: Carswell, 1986.

Knafla, Louis A., and Richard Klumpenhouwer. *Lords of the Western Bench: A Biographical History of the Supreme and District Courts of Alberta, 1876–1990*. Calgary: Legal Archives Society of Alberta, 1997.

Kurz, Irving. *Policing the Central Peace*. Spirit River: I.A. Kurz Publications, 1987.

Langton, H.H., ed. "The Commission of 1885 to the North-West Territories." *Canadian Historical Review* 25 (1944): 38–53.

Leonard, David W. "The Origins of Grande Prairie." *Alberta History* (Autumn 1997).

Lewis, Herbert Thomas. *The Struggle For Responsible Government in the North-West Territories 1870–1897.* Toronto: University of Toronto Press, 1956.

Leyten-Brown, Kenneth Bryan. "The Origins and Evolution of a System for the Administration of Justice in the North-West Territories, 1870–1905." Ph.D. diss., Queen's University, 1988.

Linden, Rick, and Russell Smandych. "Administering Justice Without the State: A Study of the Private Justice System of the Hudson's Bay Company to 1800." *Canadian Journal of Law and Society* 2, no. 1: 21.

MacGregor, James G. *A History of Alberta*. Edmonton: Hurtig Publishers, 1972.

———. *Grande Prairie*. Grande Prairie: City of Grande Prairie, 1983.

*Macleod, Alberta, Where Nature is Making a Big City*. Macleod: Spectator Presses, 1912.

MacLeod, R.C. "Law & Order on the Western-Canadian Frontier." In *Law for the Elephant, Law for the Beaver: Essays in the Legal History of the North American West*. Edited by John McLaren, Hamar Foster, and Chet Orloff, 90–105. Regina: Canadian Plains Research Center, 1992.

———. "Canadianizing the West: The North West Mounted Police as Agents of the National Policy, 1873–1905." In *Essays on Western History: In Honour of Lewis Gwynne Thomas*. Edmonton: University of Alberta Press, c1976.

———. *The Northwest Mounted Police and Law Enforcement, 1873–1905*. Toronto: University of Toronto Press, 1975.

MacRae, Marion. *Cornerstones of Order: Courthouses and Town Halls of Ontario, 1784–1914*. Toronto: Osgoode Society, 1983.

Maitland, Leslie, et al., *A Guide to Canadian Architectural Styles*. Peterborough, Ont: Broadview Press, 1992.

Maitland, Leslie. *Architecture of the Queen Anne Revival in Canada*.

Malcolm, M.J. *The Pursuit of Ernest Cashell*. Saskatoon: Western Producer Prairie Books, 1984.

Malliah, H.C. "A Socio-Historical Study of the Legislators of Alberta 1905–1967." Ph.D. diss., University of Alberta, 1970.

Martin, Roderick. "The Common Law and the Justices of the Supreme Court of the North West Territories 1870–1907." Master's thesis, University of Calgary, 1992.

McCaul, C.C. "Precursors of the Bench and Bar in the Western Provinces." *Canadian Bar Review* 3 (1925): 25–40.

McConnell, John C. "The Houses of the Law." *Courthouses of the Commonwealth*, Amherst: University of Massachusetts Press, 1984.

McConnell, W.H. *Prairie Justice*. Calgary: Burroughs and Co., 1980.

McDonald, Dan. *Stipendiary Magistrates, Police Magistrates, Magistrates, Provincial Judges and Family and Juvenile Court Judges for Alberta 1893–1978*. Calgary: Provincial Law & Library.

McGinnis, Janice Dickin. "Bibliography of the Legal History of Western Canada." In *Law and Justice in a New Land: Essays in Western Canadian Legal History*. Edited by Louis A. Knafla, 333–354. Calgary: Carswell, 1986.

McLaren, John, Hamar Foster, and Chet Orloff, eds. *Law for the Elephant, Law for the Beaver: Essays in the Legal History of the North American West*. Regina, Sask.: Pasadena, California: Canadian Plains Research Centre, 1992.

McLaren, Sherill. *Braehead: Three Founding Families in Nineteenth Century Canada*. Toronto: McLelland & Stewart, 1986.

Mills, G. Edward. *The Early Court House of British Columbia*. Manuscript Report Series No. 288. Ottawa, Parks Canada, 1977.

———. *The Early Court House of Alberta*. Manuscript Report Series No. 310. Ottawa: Parks Canada, 1977.

———. *Former Territorial Court house, Fort Macleod, Alberta*. Ottawa: Minister of Supply and Services Canada, 1988.

Mills, G.E., et al. "Early Court Houses of the Old Territorial North West and the Prairie Provinces." *Early Canadian Court Houses.* [Ottawa]: National Historic Parks and Sites Branch, Parks Canada, Environment Canada, 1983.

Morrow, W.G. "An Historical Examination of Alberta's Legal System: The First Seventy-Five Years." *Alberta Law Review* 19 (1981): 148–70.

———. *Northern Justice: The Memoirs of Mr. Justice William G. Morrow.* Edited by W.H.Morrow. Toronto: Joint Publication of the Osgoode Society for Canadian Legal History and the Legal Archives Society of Alberta, 1995.

Owram, Douglas. *Building for Canadians: A History of the Department of Public Works 1840–1960.* Department of Public Works, Ottawa 1979.

Owram Douglas, ed. *The Formation of Alberta: A Documentary History.* Calgary: Alberta Records Publication Board: Historical Society of Alberta, 1979.

*Palliser's Court Houses, City Halls, Jails Etc.* New York: J.S. Ogilivie, 1889.

Pare, Richard, ed. *Courthouse: A Photographic Document.* New York: Horizon Press, 1978.

Pare, Richard. "Court Houses: County Symbols." *Historic Preservation* 29, no. 4 (October–December 1977).

Parker, Graham. "Oral History Project: The Bench and Bar of Alberta." *Now and Then* 2 (1981): 3.

Patterson, H.S. "The District Court of Southern Alberta." *Alberta Law Review 25th Anniversary Issue* (1980): 25–29.

Payne, Michael. "Allan Merrick Jeffers: One of Alberta's First Architects." *Alberta Past* (Winter 1994).

Pecover, J. [Jack Ferris]. *The Work of Justice: The Trials of Robert Raymond Cook, the story of the Last Man Hanged in Alberta.* Edmonton: Wolf Willow Press, 1996.

Peters, John O., and Margaret T. *Virginia's Historic Courthouses.* Charlottesville: University Press of Virginia, 1995.

Pevsner, Sir Nikolaus. *A History of Building Types.* Princeton: Princeton University Press, 1976.

Poole, Colin. "Identification of Mounted Police Outposts in Southern Alberta." In *Men in Scarlet.* Edited by Hugh Dempsey, 198–212. Calgary: McClelland and Stewart West, 1974.

Randall, G.P. *A Handbook of Designs, containing Plans in Perspective of Courthouses, Universities, Academies, School Houses, Churches, Dwellings Etc.* Chicago: Church Goodman and Donnelly's.

Reach, Peter T. *The Fort on the Saskatchewan.* Fort Saskatchewan, Alta.: Fort Saskatchewan Historical Society, 1974.

Reynolds, A. Bert. *Siding 16, An Early History of Wetaskiwin to 1930.* Wetaskiwin: RCMP Centennial Committee.

Reynolds, T.M. "Justices of the Peace in the North West Territories 1870–1905." Master's thesis, University of Regina, 1978.

Ridge, Alan D. "C.C. McCaul, Pioneer Lawyer." *Alberta History* 21, no. 1 (1973): 21–25.

Robinson, Greg Thomas. "British-Canadian Justice in the Ukrainian Colony: Crime and Law Enforcement in East Central Alberta 1915–1929." Master's thesis, University of Alberta, 1992.

Robinson, Willard. *The People's Architecture: Texas Courthouses, Jails and Municipal Buildings.* Texas State Historical Association, 1983.

Rostecki, R.R. *Early Court Houses of Manitoba.* Manuscript Report no. 285. Ottawa: Parks Canada, 1977.

———. *Early Court Houses of Saskatchewan.* Manuscript Report no. 306. Ottawa: Parks Canada, 1977.

Sibenik, Peter M. 'Doorkeepers: Legal Education in the Territories and Alberta 1885–1928." *Dalhousie Law Journal* 13, no. 1 (1990): 419.

Sissons, Jack. *Judge of the Far North: The Memoirs of Jack Sissons.* Toronto: McClelland and Stewart, 1969.

Smandych, Russell C., Catherine J. Matthews and Sandra J. Cox. *Canadian Criminal Justice History: An Annotated Bibliography.* Toronto: University of Toronto Press, 1987.

Smith, Barbara. *Deadly Encounters: True Crime Stories of Alberta.* Toronto: Hounslow Press, 1993.

Smith, S.B. "The Superior Courts of Alberta." *Alberta Law Review 25th Anniversary Issue* (1980): 8–14.

Swainger, Jonathan S. "Law in the Parkland: A History of The Red Deer Judicial District 1907–1922." Master's thesis, University of Calgary, 1987.

Thomas, Lewis G. *The Alberta Liberal Party, a History of Politics in the Province of Alberta, 1905–1921.* Toronto: University of Toronto Press, 1959.

Thomas, Lewis H., ed. *Essays on Western History:In Honour of Lewis Gwynne Thomas.* Edmonton: University of Alberta Press, 1976.

———. *The Struggle for Responsible Government in the North-West Territories, 1870–1897.* Toronto: University of Toronto Press, 1956.

Thorner, Thomas. "The Incidence of Crime in Southern Alberta." In *Law and Society in Canada in Historical Perspective.* Edited by David J. Bercuson and Louis A. Knafla. Calgary: University of Calgary, 1979.

———. "The Not-so-Peaceful Kingdom – Crime and Criminal Justice in Frontier Calgary." *Frontier Calgary: Town, City and Region 1875–1914.* Calgary: University of Calgary and McClelland and Stewart West, 1975.

———. "Sources for Legal History in the Archives of Saskatchewan and Alberta." *Canadian Society for Legal History Proceedings 1977.* Edited by Louis A. Knafla. Toronto: The Society, [1977?].

Thorner, Thomas, and G.N. Reddekopp. "A Question of Seduction: The Case of MacMillan v. Brownlee." *Alberta Law Review* 20 (1982): 447–74.

Turcotte, L.S. "Some Notes on the Legal History of Southern Alberta." Paper presented at Lethbridge Bar.

Turner, John P. *The North-West Mounted Police, 1873–1893.* 2 vols. Ottawa: King's Printer, 1950.

*Vegreville in Review: History of Vegreville and Surrounding Area, 1880–1980.* Vegreville: Vegreville and District Historical Society, 1980.

Ward, W. Peter. "The Administration of Justice in the Northwest Territories, 1870–1887." Master's thesis, University of Alberta, 1968.

Whiffen, Marcus. *American Architecture since 1780: A Guide to Styles.* Cambridge: MIT Press, 1992.

Whisenhunt, Donald W. *New Mexico Courthouses.* El Paso, Texas: Texas Western Press, Southwestern Studies Series, 1979.

Wilson, L.J. Roy. "'Everlasting Squabble' Medicine Hat in Crisis, 1891–98." *Alberta History* 35, no. 1.

Wright, Janet. *Crown Assets: The Architecture of the Department of Public Works 1867–1967.* Toronto: University of Toronto Press, 1997.

Wyatt, J.B. Noel. "The Designing of a Courthouse." *The Brickbuilder* 16, no. 10 (October 1907).

# INDEX

Skylight
4"x8" Ridge
Scuttle
Rafter
10"x10"
2x6
7/8" Shiplap
Bone Bridging
W.I. Strap 1/2"x3"
8x8"
2"x6"
2"x4" Studs
2"x6" Studs
Plaster
Plaster
Continuous studs
7/8" boards
3" Concrete
1" Tile
Bone Bridging
2"x12" Joist 16" C to C.
1"x6" Ribbon
Wood
Plaster bead
Gl.
11'-10"
2"x12" Joist
7/8" Maple Flooring
Plaster Bracket
Plaster Cornice
Plaster Bracket
Plaster Bracket
Gl.
13'-6"